A DICTIONARY OF THE MARTIAL ARTS

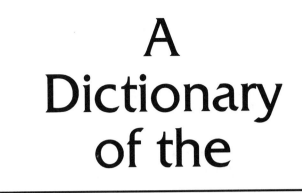

A
Dictionary
of the
MARTIAL
ARTS

Louis Frederic

Translator and editor
Paul Crompton

Charles E. Tuttle Company
Rutland, Vermont • Boston • Tokyo

First published in France 1988
by Éditions du Félin, Paris
as *Dictionnaire des Arts Martiaux*
© 1988 Éditions du Félin, Paris
Translation © 1991 The Athlone Press
First United States publication 1991

Published by Charles E. Tuttle Company, Inc.
28 South Main Street
Rutland, Vermont 05701
with editorial offices in
Boston, Massachusetts and Tokyo, Japan

Library of Congress Catalog Card No. 91-061445
ISBN 0-8048-1753-7
ISBN 0-8048-1750-2 (paperback ed.)

A
Dictionary
of the
Martial
Arts

A
bdomen see *Hara, Tanden.*

Abe-ryu *Kendo.* The oldest traditional *Kendo* school, adapted from *Ken-jutsu* and dating from the seventeenth century. It belonged to the Abe family, who were of imperial descent. They were *Daimyo*, or heads of a province. Also *Abe Tate-ryu.*

Abe Tadashi *Aikido.* A Japanese weapons master (1920–84) who introduced *Aikido* into Europe and lived in France from 1952 to 1960. He was one of the most faithful disciples of *Ueshiba Morihei.*

Abe Tate-ryu see *Abe-ryu, Kendo.*

Abise-taoshi *Sumo.* A technique of pushing against an opponent's chest, when *Tori's* arms encircle *Uke's* shoulders. See *Kimarite.*

Abise-taoshi

Age. 'To lift or raise from a low to a high position.'
— **Age-oshi** see *Ju no Kata.*
— **Age-tsuki** *Karate.* A rising blow with the fist, similar to an 'uppercut'.
— **Age-uke** *Karate.* A rising defensive block carried out with the arm or leg.
— **Age-uke Gyaku-tsuki** *Karate.* A rising block using the rear foot.

Ai 'Love, harmony'. The fundamental concept of all the martial arts. From a philosophical point of view, it is the basic identity of all human beings and of nature itself. It is the vital force which governs the universe and keeps it in harmony. It always acts in a circle, never in a straight line; very similar

Age-tsuki

Age-uke

to the Chinese theory of the Dao (Tao). In this context, *Ai* cannot be separated from the idea of *Ki* or 'universal breath'. In a wider sense it means sympathy, mutual understanding which unites individuals, enabling them to understand one another, even without words, by virtue of the *Yomi* or 'reading the thoughts of another'. This mutual understanding allows each person to accept the other, just as he or she is; to be open to him or her. Broadly speaking, it is the love between all living beings.
— 'Union, reunion'. When one or more individuals are confronting a situation of conflict, opposition or agreement, they find themselves in harmony.
— See *Aikido, Aiki, Ki, Kiai, Aiki-ho.*

Symbol of the union of opposing energies.

Ai-gamae (Ai-kamae) *Aikido.* Normal posture facing an opponent, one foot ahead of, not in front of, the other (right, *Migi*; left, *Hidari*), both in same posture, before carrying out a movement. It is the 'confrontation posture'. See *Gyaku-gamae.*
— **Ai-hanmi** *Aikido.* Refers to a situation at the moment of combat when two partners find themselves in identical postures, right foot (or left) in front. If they have different

feet in front, one the right foot, one the left, they are said to be in *Gyaku-hanmi*.

Aiki (Meeting of the *Ki*). The impassive state of mind of the combatant, in which all his or her force is collected in the *Hara*. Thus his or her mind must be completely free from all intention of injuring anyone and remain alert. This is the static mode of the *Kiai* of *Aiki*. The dynamic *Kiai* may be expressed aloud or not; it is this which gives one the power of overcoming an opponent, morally or spiritually, without the use of weapons. It is that psychological condition which demands 'win without striking a blow'. Finally, Aiki 'is that form of conduct, of being, resulting from a coming together in an individual of all that constitutes his life force'. [André Protin, *Aikidô, un art martial, une autre manière d'être* (Aikidô, a martial art, another mode of existence) (1970), p. 269]

Mitsu-tomoe, the union of the three energies of man, earth and sky in universal rotation.

Aikido. *Ai*: union, harmony; *Ki*: vital breath, energy; *Do*: way. (The way of harmony [or union] with the universal energy.) A martial art (*Budo*) developed from 1931 onwards by *Ueshiba Morihei* (1881–1969) with the creation of his first *Dojo*, the *Kobukai*, where he taught his techniques and philosophy. The foundation of the Aikido Association, the *Aikikai*, dates from 9 February 1948. It is therefore a modern form of Budo, adapted to our times. Besides his techniques of personal self-defence, he put forward a 'way of life' based on *Aiki*. From early youth, and with great dedication, Ueshiba Morihei studied the techniques of *Ju-jutsu*, *Ken-jutsu*, the use of the *Naginata*, and the stick fighting of the *Daito-ryu* tradition. Finding that these techniques were overly coloured by the warrior philosophy, he conceived a uniquely 'defensive' system. This combined a decisive attitude, a knowledge of anatomy and swift reflexes in the execution of defensive movements against one or more attackers. Contrary to the methods of *Ju-jutsu*, he did not accept 'hand-to-hand' combat in his system, in order to avoid close contact with a potential assailant. From the old *Jutsu* techniques he preserved only the swift and precise movement and the decisive mind (*Kime*) – the only techniques, in his judgement, suitable for defending oneself (*Nage*) effectively against an armed or unarmed attack.

These techniques enabled one to nullify the force of an attack, not with strength but by a subtle use of evasive movements, body shifting (*Tai-sabaki*) and counter-measures which aimed to turn the force of an adversary (*Uke*) back on him- or herself. Equally, he wanted to create an art of self-defence which was unique and typically Japanese (this was at a time when Japanese nationalism was at its height, and rebuffed foreign influences), free from 'Chinese techniques' (*Kempo*). He was inspired too by the old techniques of sword-fighting without, however, resorting to the weapon itself. Aikido thus became an art of unarmed combat, to be used even against an armed opponent. Ueshiba was deeply religious and wished his techniques to be inspired by a feeling of harmony towards all men; he himself defined his art as 'the way of the love of mankind'. He made his own an ancient Japanese saying from sword-fighting: *Kuatsu-jin-ken*, which roughly means 'to bring men back to life through the sword' or 'to make one understand the essence of man's true nature by cutting through everything which is bad in him'. 'Bad' for him meant everything contrary to the concept of *Ai*: hate, desire to harm, failure to appreciate oneself and others, vanity. The sword, not being necessary in peace-time, was to be replaced by the 'sword of the mind'; in his judgement just as effective and less murderous.

In his Aikido he emphasized the importance of reaching a harmony between the breath (*Ki*) and the body (*Tai*) combined with nature; but he emphasized equally a harmony between the mind (*Shin*) and the moral outlook (*Ri*), symbolized by the *Do* or the way to be followed to reach self-perfection.

According to Ueshiba, only those who had fully materialized in themselves that intuitive perception of the harmony of everything in the universe, and were stamped with a pure love towards all creatures, could enter that higher state which put them beyond fear, cowardice, laziness and pride, and made them truly 'free'. He wished that this Aikido should become a school of self-perfection, a new religion based on knowledge of the body and the mind, with religious rites being replaced by the 'softening' of the first and the purification of the second.

For only a mind freed from material demands, possessed of perfect calm, was capable of anticipating the movements of an eventual adversary and reaching a permanent state of intuition and alertness (*Sen-no-sen*).

All the movements of Aikido are aimed at teaching students to free themselves from psychological and muscular barriers, to help them to breathe in tune with their movements, and to enable them to feel alive and in total harmony with everything which surrounds them. If one breathes well, if one's posture is natural, completely without tension, then the body will be better supplied with blood and a perfect physical balance will be obtained, centred on the focus of gravity of one's entire being, the *Hara* (or *Tanden*). One will then be able to anticipate the attacking movements of an opponent, block or parry them, without making use of one's own force, and throw him or her with great speed in a circle whose centre is one's own *Hara*.

Aikido is therefore 'essentially the preparation of a state from which the relationship between oneself and the cosmic world allows one a movement of self-expression, not with aggression, but above all through a state of union and harmony between two partners' (M. Random).

It follows from this that the movements must be carried out smoothly, describing a continuous circle, without breaks, like a force which moves continuously in the same direction. When an opponent pushes, the parry will take the form of a turn (*Taisabaki*) and against a pull, an 'entry' is the counter-attack. Also, the techniques of Aikido call above all upon two categories of movement: those of 'control' (*Katame-waza*) and those of throwing an opponent (*Nage-waza*).

There are over seven hundred movements in Aikido belonging to these two *Waza*, all more or less derived from the basic *Kata* (forms), consisting of freeing oneself from grips (*Te-hodoki*), throwing an opponent to the ground by pressure on the limbs (*Rofuse*), and finally immobilizing him or her by pressure on the joints (*Kansetsu-gaeshi*). In Aikido, these three series of movements are the foundation of all the self-defence movements.

According to some martial arts historians, Aikido originated from the teachings given to *Samurai* during the Kamakura period (1185–1333). The fundamental techniques were codified by *Minamoto no Yoshimitsu* (1045–1127), a famous warrior of this epoch. The *Takeda* family, from the Aizu clan, were the ones who perfected this method of combat (then called *Aiki-jutsu*) and defined the vital or weak points of the human body (*kyusho*) which must be struck (*Atemi*) to place an enemy at one's mercy. The range of Aikido techniques is completed with these methods of attacking the weak points on the body of an enemy, *Atemi-waza*, and the use of *Te-gatana* or *Shuto* (sword-hand). Added to these fundamental techniques are the principles of upsetting an opponent's balance using the techniques of *Kansetsu-waza*, based on twisting the joints of the limbs. These techniques have been supplemented by methods of immobilization (*Osae-waza*) and, should the need arise, strangulation (*Shime-waza*).

Complete Aikido training sometimes includes the use of the short staff (*Jo*), medium staff (*Tambo*) or long staff (*Bo*).

The principle 'schools' of Aikido are the *Aikikai So Hombu* (techniques of Ueshiba and his disciples), the *Yoshinkai* (techniques of master *Shioda*), the *Yoseikan* of master *Mochizuki*, the *Korindo*, the *Daito* and the *Takeda-ryu*. The *Kodokan* of Tokyo also has an Aikido section.

— **Aikidogi.** Training uniform worn in Aikido *Dojo*, consisting of a *Keikogi* for the first six grades (*Kyu*). Those who have black belt grade wear a black *Hakama* and white

Master Ueshiba Morihei demonstrating boar-spear technique.

jacket. Teachers have a black Hakama and black jacket. 'Masters' have a white Hakama and a white jacket. See *Kyudan*.
— **Aikido-ka.** A practitioner of Aikido.

Aiki-ha. The doctrine developed by the *Yagyu Shinkage-ryu*, amongst others, which put the accent on not resisting the push, weight or pull of an opponent, just like 'the willow branch which bends beneath the weight of snow and allows it to fall off'. Adopted by numerous other *Ryu* of martial arts.

Aiki In-yo Ho. The doctrine of 'Harmony of mind based on the concept of *Yin* and *Yang*', elaborated by the learned Takeda Takumi no Kami Soemon (1758–1853) of the Aizu clan (today the prefecture of Fukushima in the north of the island of Honshu) and used in the teaching of martial arts. See *Yin-Yang*.

Aiki-jo see *Aiki-ken*.

Aiki-jutsu see *Aikido*.

Aikikai see Aikido.

Aiki-ken *Aikido*. Art of unarmed fighting against opponents using a sword or staff (*Aiki-jo*).

Aiki-taiso *Aikido*. Exercises done alone, without a partner. A kind of gymnastic exercise emphasizing breath control (*Kyoku*) and mental concentration in order to harmonize the physical functions and the spiritual energies. Also called *Aiki-undo*.

Aiki-undo see *Aiki-taiso*.

Aikuchi see *Swords*.

Ai-nuke. Situation in which two potential opponents have arrived at a union of their respective *Ki*, either before a confrontation or during it, and are not able to fight; there can be neither a winner nor a loser. The two opponents have thus reached a mutual understanding which goes beyond the mere physical combat, and reunite in a mental state which surpasses it, in perfect harmony. See *Ai*, *Aiki*.

Aio-ryu. Old martial arts tradition using the techniques of handling a lance (*Yari*) combined with those of *Jujutsu*.

Aite *Kendo*. When two opponents find themselves face to face in the same posture. Similar to the *Ai-gamae* of *Aikido*.
— **Aite no Tsukuri** *Judo*. Action of preparing for a movement on the part of Uke. See *Jibun no Tsukuri*.

Ai-Uchi. Simultaneous actions of two opponents making the same movements at the same time. See *Ai*.

Aizu Iko see *Kage-ryu*.

Aizu Kage-ryu see *Kage-ryu*.

Aka. 'Red'.

Akiresuken (Achilles tendon) see *Feet*.

Akiyama Shinobu see *Yoshin-ryu*.

Ako-Gishi. 'Tale of the doughty men of Ako'; Japanese name given to the epic of the 'Forty-seven *Ronin*' (*Samurai* serving no master) staged in theatres under the title *Chushingura* (Treasure of the faithful retainers) in the eighteenth century. This exemplary tale demonstrates how a Samurai should behave and recounts the exploits of forty-seven warriors in the service of Asano, lord of Ako. In 1701 Asano was outraged by the behaviour of a lord at the court of the *Shogun* at *Edo* (Tokyo). This lord, Kira, was wounded by the incensed Asano in the very palace of the Shogun. This lapse in etiquette was condemned by the Shogun *Tokugawa Tsunayoshi*, and Asano was obliged to commit *Seppuku*. But forty-seven of his faithful vassals, now without a master, resolved to take revenge on Kira and wash the honour of their lord in his blood. For two years they waited while they prepared in secret. At last, on 14 December 1702, they all reunited and attacked Kira's home, killed him and handed themselves over to the authorities. The Shogun ordered them to commit Seppuku, which they did, in front of Asano's tomb, on 4 February, 1703. The people acclaimed them as heroes and they rapidly became symbols of loyalty, courage and honour. Every year their tombs, placed in the garden of the Sengaku-ji temple in Tokyo, are decorated with flowers by the Japanese who still admire their deed. The theatre, literature and cinema have all popularized this exemplary warrior figure, so characteristic of the spirit of *Bushido*.

Am see *Yin* (*Yin-Yang*).

Am-duong see *Yin-Yang*.
— **Am-duong Tan** see *Bo Phap*.

Ami-uchi *Sumo*. A movement of wrapping one's arms around the inside of an opponent's arms, in order to lift and throw him forwards. See *Kimarite*.

Anzawa-ryu. A traditional school of fighting using the *Naginata*, which was invented

Ami-uchi

in the seventeenth century as a weapon for women to protect the family honour and to assure their safety in the event of an attack on the home.

An Long see *Phuong Duc*.
— **An Long Son** see *Thu Phap*.

Antachi-waza *Karate*. Position at the beginning of a movement from the floor when one of the opponents is standing (*Tachi*) and the other is on his knees (*Suwari*).

Anzawa Heijiro (1887–1970). A master of *Kyudo*, disciple of Master *Awa Kenzo*. He studied Kyudo and wrote a small work called *Dai-sha-do* (The Great Doctrine of Archery Including the Thoughts of Master Awa Kenzo). He was the first Kyudo master to come out of Japan and give demonstrations, particularly in France, where he inspired people to follow his art. In Japan he had a considerable influence on the development of Kyudo, which he helped to revitalize. He is regarded as one of the last great masters of Kyudo.

Ap-cha-gi *Tae-kwon-do*. Direct frontal kick.

Ap-ku-bi *Tae-kwon-do*. A forward-moving position with the front leg bent.

Ap-seu-gi *Tae-kwon-do*. Normal walking position or stance.

Araki (Mujinsai) Mataemon Minamoto Hidetsuna see *Araki-ryu*.

Araki-ryu. School of martial arts founded by *Araki (Mujinsai) Mataemon Minamoto Hidetsuna* (*c.* 1584–1638) of the Matsudaira family from Echizen province (now Fukui-ken), using round wooden swords covered with white fabric and called *Shirobo* or 'white sticks'. It was one of the last schools (*Ryu*) to use this weapon for training and followed the methods of classical *Kendo*. Araki Mataemon had studied the techniques of *Yagyu Shinkage-ryu* and *Muso Jikiden-ryu* before founding his own school. At first he called it *Torite-kogusoku*, then *Moro Budo Araki-ryu-kempo*; here he taught various other martial arts, including unarmed combat (*Ju-jutsu*).

Ariake *Kyudo*. Technique of taking aim when firing an arrow, in such a way that the whole target can be seen (*Monomi*) on the left of the bow, so that the aim (*Mikomi*) can be perfected before the arrow is released (*Hanare*). See *Yami*.

Armlocks see *Rofuse, Katame, Kansetsu-waza*.

Armour. In every period of their history the Japanese have used armour to protect themselves in combat. The oldest examples were made of iron and covered the torso. They were found in megalithic tombs (*Kofun*) dating from the fifth to seventh centuries. Other suits of armour from the eighth century have been preserved in the Shoso-in museum at Nara. After the twelfth century most warriors wore armour which was to a greater or lesser extent highly ornate and richly decorated. The style continued to become more and more complicated, making the *Samurai* look like magnificent steel beetles. Two types of armour continued in use. These were the *O-yoroi*, sometimes called *Kachu* or simply *Yoroi*, which covered the whole body, and the *Haramaki*, which almost from the outset did not include a helmet and covered only the torso. It was the custom that *Yoroi* were reserved for the chief Samurai, while the Haramaki were mainly used by ordinary Samurai and foot soldiers (*Zusa*).

The complete armour (*Yoroi*) consisted of a helmet (*Kabuto*) with its accessories, a corselet of lacquered iron, usually made up of several pieces laced together (*Do*), shoulder guards (*Sode*) made of articulated plates, arm and hand protectors (*Kote*), metal leg guards (*Sune-ate*) and a type of skirt made up of several overlapping pieces to protect the thighs and abdominal region (*Hae-date*). Sometimes a large linen cloth resembling a flowing cape (*Horo*) was attached to the back of the armour to intercept the flight of arrows coming from the rear. The helmet was a very important element which served not only to protect the head but also as a distinctive sign of rank and of the wearer's function. It was often decorated at the front with hornlike ornaments made of metal or other insignia of quite

An example of O-yoroi or complete suit of armour (eighteenth century).

large dimensions (*Kuwagata*) and by two 'wings' or *Fuki-gaeshi* to stop blows from a sword. The visor (*Mae-bashi*) was fixed. A neck protector was fixed at the base of the helmet, and was called (*Shikoro*). Finally a face mask (*Men*) made of lacquered iron (sometimes with a movable nose-piece to allow the wearer to blow his nose) covered either the entire face (*So-men*) or a part of it (*Menpo*). A jaw-piece (*Ho-ate*) protected the throat in the same fashion as the throat-piece (*Nodo-wa*). Helmets could take on a multitude of forms, according to the period or rank of their owner. The whole set of armour was often completed by a pair of bearskin shoes (*Ko-gake*, *Ke-gutsu*) and, in certain cases, a fixture to take the shaft of a banner (*Sashimono*), attached to the back of the *Do*.

Each suit of armour had a name which varied widely according to the period or the name of the man who had incorporated improvements into the design. In times of peace or when simply not in use they were kept in a wooden chest carried by servants. Before 923 they were called *Kawara*, as they were most often made of thick leather. See *Do*, *Yoroi*, *Kogusoku*, *Kumiuchi*.

Arms. Arm movements play a very important part in martial arts, and the specific terms applied to different parts of the arms should be known, as they are included in numerous Japanese expressions applied to particular techniques:

Arms: *Wan*
Shoulder: *Kata*
Elbow: *Empi* (*Hiji* is an older term)
Forearm: *Kote*, *Ude*
Wrist: *Tekubi*
Articulation, joint: *Kansetsu*
Inside of the arm: *Nei-wan*
Outside of the arm: *Gai-wan*

See *Body*, *Hands*.

Arrows see *Ya*, *Hanare*, *Hikime*, *Kabura-ya*, *Kyudo*.

Asa-geiko. 'Morning training', a type of training principally observed in Japan which took place at the height of summer. This type of training complemented the one which took place in winter (*Kan-geiko*) and

was widely practised by the *Budoka*. In English the word for 'training' is sometimes written with an initial 'K' to give *Keiko* or with a 'G' to give *Geiko*. This variation is frequently found in martial arts terms which come from Japan, and depends on the position of the word in an expression or phrase. Usually a 'K' is used if the word is the first word of an expression and the 'G' is used if the word appears later in the expression.

Ashi 'Legs'. See *Body*, *Legs*, *Feet*.
— **Ashi-barai (-harai)** *Judo*. A sweeping movement in which *Tori* takes *Uke's* legs or feet from under him or her using his or her own legs or feet, and throws him or her on to his side.
— **Ashibo-kake-uke** *Karate*. Blocking an opponent's leg by hooking with one's own leg.
— **Ashibumi** *Kyudo*. The first position assumed by an archer, legs placed an arrow's width apart, toes pointing outwards, the centre of the body in a direct line with the centre of the target. The bow is held under the left forearm and the arrow under the right upper arm so that they both point towards the centre-line.

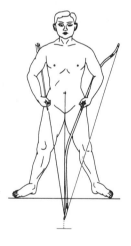

Ashibumi

— **Ashi-garami** see *Kansetsu-waza*, Competition Rules of *Judo*, 18.
— **Ashi-gatame** *Judo*. In groundwork

(*Ne-waza*) techniques a dislocation of a leg using both arms.

Ashi-gatame

Ashi-tori

— **Ashi-gatana** *Karate*. 'Foot-sword', a reaping technique using the foot, to the outside or inside, which acts in a similar way to a sword stroke. Also *Sokuto*.

— **Ashi-guruma** *Judo*. 'Leg wheel'. By turning his or her hips, *Tori* places his or her right leg in front of *Uke* and pulls downwards on Uke's sleeve with the left hand. Uke loses balance in a forward direction and falls over Tori's outstretched leg in a circular or wheel-like shape.

Ashi-guruma

— **Ashi-kubi** 'Ankle'. See *Legs, Feet*.
— **Ashi-kubi Kake Uke** *Karate*. Blocking of the ankle by hooking the leg.
— **Ashi-sabaki** see *Tai-sabaki*.
— **Ashi no Tachi Kata** *Karate*. Method of placing the feet on the ground in anticipation of an attack or in preparation for a counter-attack.
— **Ashi-tori** *Sumo*. Technique of seizing an opponent's leg on the inside, using both hands, in order to throw him or her backwards by pushing with the shoulder on the inside of the thigh. See *Kimarite*.

— **Ashi-ura** 'Sole of the foot'. See *Feet*.
— **Ashi-waza** *Karate*. The name given to all leg and foot techniques.
Tae-kwon-do: *Jokki*.
Judo: A section of the *Tachi-waza* (standing) techniques consisting of three fundamental movements: *Okuri Ashi-barai, Sasae Tsuri-komi Ashi, Uchi-mata*. See *Nage-no-Kata*.
— **Ashizoku** 'Foot strike'. See *Feet*.

Ashikaga. A family of *Daimyo* descended from the *Minamoto*. When, after a civil war, the *Bakufu* of *Kamakura* had been destroyed, Ashikaga Takauji (1308–58) had himself proclaimed *Shogun* by the emperor, thus inaugurating the Ashikaga Shogunate, also known as *Muromachi*, which lasted until 1573, when the general Oda Nobunaga conquered the last of the Ashikaga, Yoshiaki. The Ashikaga line numbered some fifteen Shoguns.

Ashiko. A metal sole with four hooks which the *Ninja* fitted to their shoes to enable them to climb walls more easily. See *Shuko, Ninja*.

Atama 'Head'. See *Body, Kashira, Tsu*.
— **Atama-tsuki** see *Tsu-ate*.

Atari-to see *Omori-ryu*.

Atatamaru 'Warm-up'. Stretching and warm-up exercises performed in the *Dojo* in preparation for actual training.

Atemi 'Body blows' (from *Ateru*, to strike, and *Mi*, body). Atemi are blows aimed at the vital or weak points of an opponent's body in order to paralyse, by means of intense pain. Such blows can produce loss of consciousness, severe trauma and even death, according to which point is struck. A good, all-round knowledge of these vital points is necessary to avoid accidents during training. Knowledge of the location of such points and the way of striking them is generally reserved for *Budoka* of black belt standard or higher, in the empty-hand martial arts. The smaller the striking surface used in Atemi, the greater the power of penetration and thus the greater the effectiveness of the blow. Atemi technique, or *Atemi-waza*, is very ancient and almost entirely based on knowledge of anatomy and the points and meridians used in acupuncture. See *Weapons*, *Kyusho* (vital points).

— **Atemi-waza Wa-jutsu.** A group of fundamental movements (*Kata*) carried out either in *Suwari-waza* (kneeling down, face to face) – *Hakko-dori*, *Kao-ate*, *Hiza-gatame* – or standing – *Hakko Zeme Dori*, *Tachi Hiza-gatame*, *Mae Kata-te Hakko-dori* – and their variations. All these movements focus on seizing the wrists, *Te-hodoki*.

Ato no Sen 'Defensive initiative', an action which forestalls an attacker's intention as soon as it is perceived, by means of a simultaneous block and counter-attack. Sometimes, if the defender's perception is adequate, he or she may attack first. Also called *Ato-no-Saki*, *Go-no-sen*. See *Go-no-sen*, *Sen-no-sen*.

Ato-uchi Kendo. A feinting action carried out during an attack.

Attacks see *Hasso*, *Kumite*, *Kong Kyeu*, Competition Rules of *Judo*, 14.

Awa Kenzo Kyudo. A great archery master (1880–1939) who taught his art to Eugen Herrigel from 1923 to 1929 and awarded him 5th *Dan*. One of his most famous disciples was *Anzawa Heijiro* (1887–1970).

Awasete-ippon see *Waza-ari*, Competition Rules of *Judo*, 22.

Awase-tsuki Karate. A straight punch,

Drawing illustrating the vital points or Atemi points:
1. Tendo, point at the junction of the bony sutures between the parietal and frontal bones.
2. Uto, the point at the root of the nose.
3. Kasumi, the point on the temple.
4. Jinchu, the point on the upper lip.
5. Dokko, the point on the maxillary or jaw bone.
6. Kachigake, the point on the end of the chin.
7. Suigetsu, the point on the solar plexus.
8 and 9. The two points on the lateral and upper areas of the abdomen.
10. Myojo, the point close to the umbilicus, or navel.
11. Tsurigane, the testicles.
12. Shitsu-kansetsu, the point on the knee joint.

delivered and also withdrawn at top speed.

Awase-waza *Judo.* A score of no points to either contestant when one is held down by the other, but when he or she in turn is strangling the opponent effectively. The contest may begin again, in a standing position, on the referee's command.

B

Bach-dai see *Kyu, Kyudan*.

Back see *Ushiro*.

Ba Gua Quan Wushu. 'Eight hexagram' boxing of China (see *Yijing*), which belongs to the 'internal' methods (*Nei-jia*). The techniques of this style of 'boxing' are practised alone but have an application to fighting. They consist of a series of successive movements performed round an imaginary circle about 2.5 metres in diameter. When performed with a partner they take on three forms: expanding (*Kai*), pushing and raising (*Peng*) and holding (*Chan*). Vietnamese: *Bat Quai*. See *Kung-fu, Wushu*.

Bai see *Bai To, Bo*.

Bai Hok Taidu see *Taidu*.

Bai Su see *Bai To*.

Baito Qwan-ki-do. Salutes (see *Rei*) used in various ways:

facing a teacher, hands in front (*Bai Su*)
before beginning a *Quyen*, hands joined in front of the neck (*Le To*)
before beginning an advanced *Quyen* (*Vu Bai*)
kneeling, traditional (*Bai*), with the head placed on the hands, which rest palms down on the floor.

Ba-ji Quan Wushu. Chinese school of combat using violent punching and strong shoulder strokes.

Ba-jutsu. 'Methods of horsemanship', formerly considered to be a martial art method (*Bu-jutsu*) and used in conjunction with the art of the sword (*Ken-jutsu*) and the bow (*Kyu-jutsu*) by all those Samurai who followed *Kyuba no Michi*, the forerunner of *Bushido*. This art of horsemanship associated with archery still plays a part in the performance of *Yabusame* techniques.

Formerly in Japan, a rider mounted his horse from the right and settled the weight of his body towards the rear, the opposite of present-day practice. The mounted Samurai would hook the reins through a ring on his armour to keep his hands free for fighting or firing his bow. He would direct his mount by using his legs or his body weight. The saddle was made of wood covered in fabric or leather, and included a backrest. The stirrups were large and deep to give a stable seat at any speed. *Ba-jutsu* included a complete course in horsemanship, with and without armour, leaping over obstacles, crossing rivers, as well as the use of various weapons which could be used on horseback: long swords (*Jin-tachi, No-tachi, O-dachi*), bow (*Yumi*), *Yari*, Naginata, etc. Every warrior family (*Buke*) had its own Ba-jutsu techniques. One of the most ancient schools (*Ryu*) of Ba-jutsu was created in the fifteenth century and called *Otsubo-ryu*. Its followers used the long bow (Yumi) and a very long sword with a curved blade (O-dachi).

Bakufu. 'Government from the tent', a type of Japanese military rule installed by *Minamoto no Yoritomo* in 1185. The emperor nominated a *Shogun* who governed the country in his name. There were three *Bakufu* or Shogunates in the history of Japan: the *Kamakura* (1185–1333), the *Ashikaga* (or *Muromachi* 1336–1573) and the *Tokugawa* (or *Edo*, 1603–1868). See *Bushi*.

Bando see *Thaing*.

Bang-o Tae-kwon-do. Defensive techniques using evasion (*Pihag-gi*) or blocking (*Makki*) with the hands, forearms or legs. See *Uke*.

Bang-xie Bo see *Bo*.

Bankoku-choki. A Japanese weapon of ancient times consisting of a metal ring armed with spikes, used for striking the vulnerable *Atemi* points. It could be easily hidden in the clothing and is identical to the *Vajramushti* of India. This little-used weapon was mainly for brigands, *Ninja* or rebellious peasants. The *Bushi* rarely made use of them, for they were not considered weapons worthy of the nobility, as they belonged in the category of concealed weapons (*Kakushi*). However, one school (*Ryu*) of martial arts followed by the people, *Nagao-ryu*, taught the use of them. This school appeared during the Edo era (1603–1868). Also known as *Tekkan-zu*. See *Kakushi*.

'Bansenshuka'. 'A hundred thousand rivers', a work produced in 1676 by Fujibayashi. It dealt with the art of *Ninjutsu* and with the *Ninja*. Fujibayashi was a Ninjutsu expert belonging to the *Iga-ryu*, a school in the Iga region, and in his work he described the physical and philosophical aspects of *Ninjutsu*.

Banshay see *Thaing*.

Banzuke see *Sumotori, Sekitori, Seki-wake*.

Bao-zi Taidu see *Taidu*.

Ba Quan *Wushu*. Chinese martial arts style created during the Ch'ing (Qing) dynasty. It belonged to the 'internal' style (*Neijia*) of the *Shaolin-si* tradition. See *Ba Gua Quan*.

-barai see *Harai*.

Bara-te *Karate*. Reverse punch using the fingers. See *Weapons*.

-basami see *Hasami*.

Bassai (from *Hasamu*, to insert; *Sai*, fortress). 'To storm the fortress.' *Karate*. Name given to several *Kata* 'offensives', typical of the *Tomari-te* of Okinawa.

Bat Ho see *Phong Duc*.

Bat Phong Son see *Thu Phap*.

Bat Quai see *Bagua Quan*.

Batto see *Omori-ryu*.
— Batto-jutsu *Iai-do*. Style of swordfighting, based on the speed of drawing a sword, created by *Hayashizaki Shigenobu*, a seventeenth-century warrior. It is the ancient name for *Iai-jutsu*. See *Iai-do*.

Begin see *Ushiro*.

Belly see *Hara, Tanden*.

Belts see *Obi, Mawari, Kyu, Kyudan*, Competition Rules of *Judo*, 3, 28; *Karate*, 2.

Benkei see *Bo-jutsu, Yoshitsune*.

Bersilat. Malaysian style of martial arts named after an Indonesian woman called Minangkabau, from Sumatra, who transmitted her art to Malaka. Bersilat closely resembles the *Pentjak-Silat* of Java, as it imitates the movements of animals, after the fashion of Chinese *Wushu*. It is possible that the Chinese exported their techniques to Indonesia, where they had a profound influence on the styles which grew up in the archipelago. Bersilat, in consequence, divided into many schools; some placed the accent on unarmed combat, others on the use of weapons. Over the centuries, two forms of Bersilat developed. One was a kind of sport used in demonstrations; the other was a system of real combat. The sporting form is known as *Sila-pulat*, the combat form as *Sila-buah*. See *Penchak-silat, Kundao*.

Bikime see *Ikiwake*.

Bisen-to. A Japanese weapon resembling a *Naginata* with a short thick blade; a type of slash-hook, used mainly by the peasants and the *Ninja*.

Bitei 'Coccyx'. See *Body, Kyusho*.

'Bleeder'. Name given by the Americans to a new weapon which is in fact a *Nunchaku* armed with razor-sharp blades. Its purpose is not to attack; it is a test of the user's skill during demonstrations on electronic targets. The use of this terrible weapon demands speed and great precision. See *Nunchaku*.

Blows see *Atemi, Ate, Tsuki*.

Blue see *Aoi*.

Bo. A long staff (1.60 to 2.80 m approximately) made of wood; nearly always round in section but occasionally hexagonal. The most common long staff is cylindrical but some weapons schools use a tapered *Bo*. It is made of hardwood, most often of oak.

Various staffs are included in this category of weapon: long staff (*Kyushaku-bo*, *Bo* of 9 *shaku*, 2.80 m approximately) and the medium staff (*Rokushaku-bo*, *Bo* of 6 shaku, 1.90 m approximately), sometimes called *Tambo*. The art of handling this long staff is *Bo-jutsu*. The police staff or baton is called a *Keibo*, and metal staffs are known as *Kanabo*. A favourite weapon of the *Ninja* is a short staff called a *Han-bo* (half-staff). Vietnamese: *Bong*.

Bo (Bai) *Wushu*. Fundamental postures used principally in *Kung-fu*:

Ma-bo, 'horse-riding stance', feet wide apart, knees bent.
Gong-bo, feet apart, legs stretched, fists on hips.
Mao-bo, 'cat stance', weight carried on the toes, hands open, trunk turned to the side.
Lau-ma-bo, front leg crossed over rear leg, weight carried on the toes.
She-bo, 'snake stance', squatting down

sideways on.
Yang-ma-bo, 'hourglass stance', legs apart, knees and toes turned in.
Pak-hok-bo, 'crane stance', weight on one leg, one leg raised.
Banxie-bo, 'crab stance', somewhat similar to *Yang-ma-bo* but with the fists on the hips.

Bodhidharma. A Buddhist religious teacher who is thought to have lived from 460 to 534 and is considered to have been the twenty-eighth patriarch of the pure meditation sect (Dhyana). He came to China from India and installed himself at the Small Forest Temple (*Shaolin-si*), where he created the *Chan* Buddhist sect. When the Chan teaching was introduced into Japan it became known as *Zen*. Bodhidharma is credited with the creation of a system of unarmed fighting, but this is debatable. The system, intended to strengthen the monks' bodies and to increase their determination, became the basis for the majority of Chinese martial arts. Stories concerning events in the life of the founder abound in the form of legends, the dates being always uncertain. Chinese: *Damo*; Japanese: *Daruma*. See *Shaolin-si*, *Shorinji Kempo*, *Zen*.

Body. Words which describe the body (*Tai*, *mi*) play a crucial role in the vocabulary of martial arts, whether in descriptions of movement or in pinpointing the weak spots (*Kyusho*) which are targets for *Atemi* blows:

Chest: *Mune* (middle level, *Chudan*)
Belly: *Hara* (low level, *Gedan*)
Shoulders: *Kata*
Hips: *Koshi* (-*goshi*)
Pit of the stomach: *Suigetsu*
Clavicle: *Sakotsu*
Top of the sternum: *Kyototsu*
Solar plexus: *Kyosen*
Testicles: *Kinteki*.
Points on the back:
Point between 4th and 5th ribs: *Kyoei*
7th cervical vertebra: *Soda*
7th dorsal vertebra: *Chelang*
Lumbar vertebrae: *Kodenko*
Small of the back: *Hizo*
Coccyx: *Bitei*.

See also *Arms*, *Legs*, *Head*, *Feet*, *Hands*.

Ma-bo   Yang Ma-bo   Banxie-bo

Lauma-bo   Mao-bo   She-bo

Gong-bo   Pak-hok-bo

Bo-jutsu. The art of using the long staff (*Bo*), studied either as a separate discipline or complementary to the techniques of *Kendo, Karate* and *Aikido*. The use of the Bo is very similar to that of the long staff used in Europe in the Middle Ages by the peasants. In Japan, *Bo-jutsu* is almost always practised in the open air, with no special means of protection. Its techniques are based on *Kata*, but even so it is not regarded as a sport. The art of the *Bo* was particularly favoured by the religious warriors of the sixteenth century, in their struggles with the troops of *Oda Nobunaga* and *Toyotomi Hideyoshi*, but the Bo, sometimes tipped with iron, had already been in use for a long time. Legend tells how, in the twelfth century, the monk *Benkei* had faced the young *Minamoto Yoshitsune* with this weapon. The young man, who was the brother of the Shogun *Minamoto no Yoritomo*, defeated Benkei and then took him into his service. Yoshitsune eventually became one of the most famous generals in Japanese history. Stories are told of certain very strong monks who wielded Bo made entirely of iron. Later, during the *Tokugawa* period (1603–1868), the wooden Bo was often used by the shogunate police for dealing with brigands and *Ronin* armed with swords. Vietnamese: **Bong.** See *Bo*.

Boken (Bokken). 'Wooden sword', generally 1.05 m long, shaped like a real *Katana* and made of very hard wood such as red oak (*Akagi*) or white oak (*Shiragashi*), medlar (*Biwa*) or ebony (*Kokutan*). Its use is identical to that of a steel sword. The story is told of how *Miyamoto Musashi* killed his personal enemy *Sasaki* using a *Boken* shaped from a branch. Also called *Bokuto*.

Bokuden see *Tsukahara Bokuden*.

Bokuseki. The Japanese art of calligraphy, considered to be one of the seven traditional martial arts since it demands profound concentration as well as total precision combined with great swiftness of movement. Every practitioner of a school of *Budo* or *Bu-jutsu* in Japan, China, Korea or Vietnam, where a system of writing using ideographs is still in use, must train himself in producing sentences or poems with a brush. This practice aims at disciplining simultaneously the mind, the vision and the stability of the body muscles. According to one Zen theory, the rapid flight of brush on paper evokes the almost instantaneous leap of the sword from its scabbard seen in *Iai*, or the release of the arrow (*Hanare*) in *Kyudo*. 'It is said that it is the inner serenity which guides the brush. The brush brings forth the depths of the unconscious. It calls upon the wisdom of the eye, which relates things to one another . . . the ego to the ten thousand things of the universe, the present moment to beyond time' (M. Random). It is the same principle which must guide the brush of the painter of *Sumi-e* (Chinese ink painting), for in the Far Eastern mind there can be no division between these two acts, as both are seen as springing from the same source, the human spirit. Thus an expert in the martial arts must also be a good poet and an excellent calligrapher. In the *Buke Sho-hatto*, a text dealing with the rules which warriors had to follow in the seventeenth century, it is written from the outset: 'The literary arts (*Bun*), the arts of weaponry (*Buki*), of archery (*Kyu-jutsu*), and of horsemanship (*Ba-jutsu*) must be the chief pursuits of the warrior.' Also called *Shodo*.

Bokuto see *Boken*.

Bo Linh (*Mot, Hai*) see *Quyen*.

Bonno 'Disturbed feeling'. That moment, sometimes very brief, in which the mind of a *Budoka* 'freezes' and loses its calm. If an opponent knows how to make use of this loss of concentration – by sensing or 'reading' it (*Yomi*) for instance – he or she will easily win. In fact it is of paramount importance that the Budoka maintains an alert, calm presence, so that the opponent is given no chance of profiting from such a crucial moment. Also called *Suki*. See *De-ai*.

Bo Phap *Qwan Ki Do*. Fundamental postures of a fighter. They can be high (*Thong Bo*), medium (*Trung Bo*) or low (*Ha Bo*):

High:
    feet together: *Lap Tan*
    feet slightly apart: *Chuan Bi*

Drawing by Hokusai showing two men using the Boken.

in a walking position: *Doc Han Vu Tan*
'like a crane', on one leg: *Hac Tan*
Medium:
leg joints slightly bent: *Lien Hoa Tan*
legs spread wide apart: *Trung Binh Tan*
leaning forward: *Dinh Tan*
'as if riding a horse', oblique with hands on thighs: *Am Duong Tan*
bent walking position: *Xa Tan*
in a walking position on the toes: *Chao Ma Tan*
'like a cat' (see *Neko-ashi*): *Tieu Tan*
Low:
leaning well back: *Nhi Tan*
squatting down, one knee on the floor: *Ho Diep Tan*
one knee on the ground: *Quy Tan*.

Bo-shuriken see *Shuriken*.

Bow see *Arrows, Inu-oi Mono, Kasagake, Kyuba no Michi, Kyudo, Kyu-jutsu, Kisha, Ninja, Reisha, Togasagake, Yabusame, Yumi, Yumitori-shiki*.

Boxe française. Although this discipline does not form part of the martial arts, it is included on account of its defensive possibilities. It is a style of boxing derived from 'Savate' or street fighting, which was codified around 1820 by Michel Casseux. The style makes great use of whiplike kicks, and points are awarded merely for contact. Knockouts are rare.

Breaking see *Hishigi, Shiwari*.

Bu 'Combat'. *Bu* presupposes a confrontation but also includes the art of evasion. It is equally synonymous with harmony (*see Ai, Wu*) and with the reconciliation of man and the universe. The word appears in the martial arts vocabulary as a frequent syllable in other words such as *Budo, Bu-jutsu*, etc.

Budo 'The Way of combat'. A name adopted in the twentieth century for martial arts in general, with an emphasis on their peaceful aspects. In addition to the physical discipline and the techniques of movement, it implies an attitude of mind and a certain ethic. *Budo* is distinct from *Bugei* (arts of combat) and from *Bu-jutsu*

(techniques of combat). These latter approaches are concerned with real fighting, whereas Budo is concerned with the physical and spiritual training offered through the study and practice of the martial arts. To make this distinction, the new approach of Budo was given the name *Shin-Budo* after 1868, and later became known simply as Budo. All Budo is now regarded as a sporting enterprise and has a system of grading called *Kyudan* which aims at determining the degree of technical proficiency attained by the *Budoka*. See *Bugei, Bu-jutsu, Kyudan, Menkyo*.

— **Budoka.** Name given to all those who follow a school of Budo, whatever their grade. Each branch of Budo has its own name: *Judo, Aikido, Karate*, etc. A Budoka within a particular branch is thus also a *Judo-ka, Aikido-ka* or *Karate-ka*, the suffix *-ka* denoting 'a practitioner'.

— **Budo-kai** see *Koizumi Gingyo*.

— **Budokan.** A martial arts centre, built in Tokyo in 1962 to replace the old *Kodokan*, where different branches of Budo are taught and practised. This place has become the 'Mecca' of students of the martial arts of Japan. See *Kodokan*.

— **Budokukai.** A paramilitary Japanese school founded in 1895 to toughen up future soldiers and prepare them for war. This school of martial arts warriors was disbanded in 1945.

— **Budo-seishin** 'Martial spirit of Budo'. See *Bushido*.

— **'Budo Shoshin-su'** *Elementary Readings in Budo*. This is a Japanese work on martial arts and *Bushido* written by *Daidoji Yusan* (1639–1730). It consists of forty-four chapters and deals with education, filial piety, respect, moral dignity, and above all with death. It inculcates those principles dear to the ruling *Samurai* class of the Tokugawa shogunate, who were permeated with neo-Confucian philosophy.

Bugei. 'Art of combat' in the form practised by the *Samurai* of old, mainly concerned with the effective use of weapons. This warrior art includes the laws governing the behaviour of Samurai *vis-à-vis* their opponents, according to the code of *Bushido*. All the techniques relevant to *Jutsu* fall within the art of *Bugei*. Bugei took the name *Budo* towards the end of the nineteenth century, when it was transformed into a physical and spiritual discipline. It is the equivalent of *Bu-jutsu* or 'warrior techniques'.

— **Bujin** 'Warrior'. See *Bushi*.

— **Bu-jutsu** 'warrior techniques or techniques of combat' used by the *Bushi*, or warriors of ancient Japan, whose aim was to achieve maximum effectiveness in warfare. Chinese: *Wushu*; Vietnamese: *Vo-Thuat*. See *Budo, Bugei, Ryu*.

— **Buke** *'Warrior family'*. The name given to a class of warriors whose profession and techniques were transmitted from father to son, and from teacher to student.

— **'Buke-jiri'** see *Yamaga Soko*.

— **'Buke Sho-hatto' 'Rules of the warrior families'**. A code of thirteen articles composed on the orders of the *Shogun Tokugawa Ieyasu* in 1615 by the Zen Buddhist Suden and other learned men. It emphasized the study of the arts of literature, weapons, archery and horsemanship: 'In times of peace and social order, we must not forget that trouble can arise. Furthermore, we must not neglect the practice of martial arts.' This text was revised by *Tokugawa Iemitsu* in 1635, and on several other occasions by the Tokugawa Shoguns to meet the requirements of the moment. See *Bushido*.

— **Buki**. General term used for all weapons of war.

— **Bukinobu**. Attack with an armed hand, as opposed to *Toshunobu*, an attack with empty hands. See *Goshin-jutsu*.

— **Bukyo-ryu**. Ancient tradition of handling the *Naginata*, used by female warriors and for purposes of attack.

— **Bukyo** 'Code of the warrior'. See *Bushido*.

Bushi 'Warrior'. This was the name given to all the warriors who made up families (*Buke*) with a warrior tradition. It distinguished them from the noble families (*Honke*). The *Bushi* class developed mainly in the provinces in the north of Japan where landowners had to defend themselves against the Ainu. They formed themselves into powerful clans who, from the twelfth century, opposed the noble families which were grouping in support of the imperial family living in Kyoto. The *Bushi* fought among themselves for supremacy. A famous example is that of the *Minamoto* or *Genji* clan against the *Taira* or *Heike*. The victorious Minamoto set up a *Bakufu* or 'government from a military camp' in 1185 at Kamakura. They held the reins of power under the aegis of the Shoguns or 'Generals fighting the barbarians', a type of regime which remained vigorously in force until 1868. This period covered three 'dynasties' and was subject to some interruptions, but it ended only with the emperor's return to direct power and establishment in Tokyo. Also called *Bujin*. See *Buke*.

— **Bushido** 'Way of the warrior'. A code of honour and social behaviour. It took shape in the seventeenth century as a successor to the unwritten code of *Kyuba-no-Michi* (Way of the bow and the horse) which dated from the thirteenth century. The term *Bushido* (from *Bushi*, warrior and *Do*, moral Way) was used for the first time in the writings of Yamaga Soko, a learned Confucian

Japanese print of Bu-jutsu exponents.

(1622–85). It was popularized by the work of Nitobe Inazo (1862–1933) called *Bushido*, published in 1905: a book whose contents reverberated around the world. This code of Bushido demanded from the warrior, *Bushi* or *Samurai* a single-minded existence, contempt for death, loyalty to one's lord through thick and thin, courage, politeness, sincerity of heart and self-control, above and beyond that demanded by the martial arts. Nitobe Inazo defined seven virtues which a Bushi must possess: a sense of justice and honesty, courage and contempt for death, sympathy towards all people, politeness and respect for etiquette, sincerity and respect for one's word of honour, absolute loyalty to one's superiors and finally, a duty to defend the honour of one's name and clan. This list of virtues was simplified in the form of Duty (*Giri*), Resolution (*Shiki*), Generosity (*Ansha*), Firmness of soul (*Fudo*), Magnanimity (*Doryo*) and Humanity (*Ninyo*).

The first written code of Bushido was the *Buke Sho-hatto*. Another famous code was the *Hagakure* ('Hidden beneath the leaves') by *Yamamoto Tsunetomo* (*c.* 1716). According to these works, Bushido is a code of honour directing the Bushi – and more particularly the Samurai – to follow a severe etiquette and to devote their lives and spirits to one or several activities 'beyond the level of an ordinary man', transcending considerations of life and death (*Seishi-o Choetsu*). It is a way of being, of behaving towards one's fellows, and an absolute fidelity to a line of life (formerly to a lord, or superior), which demands the giving up of self when necessary (see *Sutemi*), It implies respect for oneself and for others – whoever they may be, weak or strong – as well as perfect control of the mind, the impulses and passions, in order to leave the spirit in harmony (*Wa*) with the universe.

It is evident that this ideal was rarely attained. In the majority of cases, Bushido was regarded merely as a collection of fastidious rules of etiquette and behaviour used to guide the relationships between the Bushi class, the *Daimyo* (heads of a province or clan), the *Shogun* and the common people (peasants, artisans and merchants). Japanese society was grouped in this way during the Edo period (1603–1868). Bushido was tailored for a dominant class whose ordinary members gave themselves free rein, producing an outburst of numerous abuses of power. The principal aim of the Bushido code was to 'civilize' the Bushi and make them follow a prescribed course of behaviour simultaneously warlike and courteous. Also called *Bukyo*.

— **Bushi no Nasake** 'Gentleness of the warrior'. This expression of *Bushido* meant that the strongest and bravest men must also be those who are in closest touch with feelings such as compassion, gentleness and justice, not only towards their peers but towards all beings. For according to Bushido, the force and knowledge derived from the arts of war should ultimately be used, in times of peace, only to protect the weak and enlighten the ignorant.

Butokuden. 'Hall of martial virtues', centre for training in martial arts founded in 1899 near the Heian sanctuary at Kyoto by the *Dai Nippon Butoku-kai* (Association for the Martial Virtues of Great Japan) established in 1895. Its purpose was the teaching of the principal forms of *Budo*.

Butsukari *Judo, Aikido.* An exercise involving the study of particular movements through repetition. The number of repetitions may vary. The idea is that one's partner provides minimum resistance to the technique but does not accept being thrown to the floor (*Nage*) unless the performance of the movement against him or her is carried out perfectly. Also called *Uchi-komi*.

C

Cadence see *Hyoshi*.

Calligraphy see *Bokusei*.

Caltrop see *Tetsu bishi*.

Canh see *Jikan*.

Capoeira. African system of empty-hand combat, brought to Brazil by slaves from Angola. It was transformed into a ritual dance but retained clear vestiges of combat, demonstrating the wide use of kicking techniques in the art.

Cau Liem see *Kama*.

Chan see *Bodhidharma*, *Zen*, *Zazen*.

Changes (Book of) see *Yijing*. (The old transliteration, *I-Ching*, is better known.)

Chanko Sumo. Special meal eaten by the *Sumotori*, consisting of a mixture of meat, vegetables and boiled fish. Also called *Chanko-nabe*.

Cha-no-Yu. 'Tea ceremony', in the course of which the participants try to maintain a state of collectedness while bitter green tea is prepared in a ritual fashion by the tea master, who is often also a martial arts expert. This intimate ceremony always unfolds in a simple, quiet atmosphere, frequently within the *cha-no-ya* (house of tea), a small, rustic pavilion specially designed for it and built in a garden. The rules for the ceremony were elaborated by two adherents of *Zen*, Juko (1422–1502) and Sen-no-Rikyu (1520–91). Their aim was to restore to the great warriors of the period an inner peace and enable them to return within themselves, so that they could more easily control their minds and outward behaviour. Although *Cha-no-Yu* is not included among the martial arts as such it may be considered an indispensable 'external' element.

Chao see *Rei*.

Chao-lin Szu see *Shaolin-si*, *Shorinji-kempo*.

Chao Ma Tan see *Tan Phap*, *Bo Phap*.

Cha Quan Wushu. A Chinese style of martial art related to the 'internal method' (*Neijia*) of the *Shaolin-si*, and practised by the Moslems of Yunnan. It was established during the Ming dynasty (1368–1644).

Chatan Yara. An inhabitant of Okinawa who went to China in the eighteenth century and learned some of the techniques of *Wushu*. When he returned to his native village of Chatan, Yara created a school of martial arts using weapons and empty-hand techniques, with the emphasis on *Kata*. From among the latter, the best-known are the *Sai Kata*, *Chatan Yara no Sai* and the *Bo Kata*, *Chatan Yara no Bo* (staff). These *Kata* are now taught as part of the syllabus of the *Shorinji-ryu*.

Chau Quan Khi. Vietnamese name of a Chinese weapons master (1895–1969) born in Guangdong (Canton) province. He was the student of a Buddhist from the *E-Mei-Shan* of *Shaolin-si*. In 1936 he fled to Hong Kong and then to Vietnam, where he became a herbalist and acupuncturist in Cholon (Saigon) in 1956. There he created a Vietnamese martial arts school and became a naturalized citizen. Before his death he installed his disciple *Pham Xuan Tong* as his legitimate successor. The latter came to France in 1968; in 1981 he created a new martial discipline known as *Qwan-ki-do*.

Chelang '7th dorsal vertebra'. See *Body*, *Kyusho*.

Chem, Chem Mang-tang, Chem Xuong, Chem Ngang . . . see *Hands*, *Fists*, *Dong Trung Cap*.

Chen Yuanbin see *Ju-jutsu*.

Cherry (flowers of). In Japanese tradition, the beauty, fragility and above all the impermanence of the cherry blossom (*Sakura*) symbolize the precarious life of the *Samurai*. It was adopted as the emblem of the *Kodokan*. See *Kodokan*.

Cheun Kwon see *Poom-se*.

Chi (Ch'i) see *Ki*.

Chibana Choshin *Karate*. An Okinawan martial arts master (1885–1969), born in Shuri. He was a disciple of *Itosu Anko* and *Matsumura Sokon* in 1900, becoming a teacher himself in Shuri and Naha. He also taught the police. In 1956 he established the *Okinawa karate-do Renmai*, an association which brought together all the styles of *Karate* practised in Okinawa. In 1920 he changed the name *Shuri-te* to *Shorin-ryu*.

Chiba Eijiro (1832–62). A notable *Samurai*, son of *Chiba Shusaku* (1794–1855) and famous for the whiplike action of his *Shinai* strokes.

Chiba Shusaku see *Chiba Eijiro, Hokushin Ittor-ryu, Kumi-tachi, Otani Shi-mosa*.

Chiburi *Iai*. A sharp movement of the sword-hand used to shake off the blood from a blade after a sword-fight, before replacing (*Noto*) it in the scabbard (*Saya*). See *Omori-ryu*.

Chidori-ashi *Shorinji-kempo*. The action of sliding the feet along the ground when moving sideways.

Chigiriki. A weapon consisting of a wooden staff to which is attached a chain with an iron ball on the end, formerly used by the peasants in Japan to disarm warriors or brigands armed with a sword. It is a type of *Kusari-gama*, without a blade.

Chika-ma see *Ma, Keri*.

Chikara *Judo*. A movement executed with force.

Chikara-gami *Sumo*. Special paper napkin used by the *Sumotori* to wipe the body and face clean before and after a contest. See also *Tenugui, Hachimaki*.

Chi-kung see *Ji-gong*.

Chi-mei *Karate*. A dangerous and decisive blow (*Atemi*) which can be fatal if performed with force and accuracy.

Chinese Boxing see *Wushu, Kung-fu, Quan*.

Chioken *Shorinji*. Defensive and counter-techniques against an opponent who is using kicking attacks.

Chireug-gi see *Kong Kyeuk*.

Chiri see *Shikiri*.

Cho see *Don Trung Cap*.

Cho-ichi-ryu. The title given to *Otani Shimosa Kami Seiichiro*, meaning 'superman of the sword'.

Choi-gar see *Shaolin-si, Shin Li Fu*.

Choku-tsuri (Chokuzuri) *Karate*. A punch directed at the face.

Chon-gake *Sumo*. A sweeping action against the heel of an opponent, from the inside to the outside, using the inside edge of the foot, accompanied by a simultaneous pull with both hands on the arm on the same side as the leg which is being swept.

Chon-gake

Chon-mage see *Sumotori, O-Icho-mage*.

Choshu see *Satsuma*.

Choy Lee Fut see *Shin Li Fu*.

Chu 'Middle', 'Centre'. See *Space*.

Ch'uan see *Quan, Ken.*

Chuan-bi Tan see *Tan Phap, Bo Phap.*

Chuan Bi see *Ki-o-tsukete.*

Chuan-fa see *Shaolin-si, Quan-fa.*

Chudan 'Middle level', chest height. Korean: *Chung-dan*; Vietnamese: *Trung-dang.*

— **Chudan no Kamae** *Kendo.* Middle-guard position with the point of the *Shinai*, held in both hands, directed towards the chest of the opponent.

— **Chudan Mae-geri** *Karate.* Forward front kick delivered at the height of the opponent's chest.

— **Chudan Shuto Uke** *Karate.* Blocking technique, chest high, using the 'sword-hand' (*Shuto*).

—**Chudan-tegatana Uke** *Karate.* Defensive technique, middle level, at chest height, using the hand palm open like a sword. See *Weapons, Shuto, Tegatana.*

— **Chudan-tsuki** *Karate.* Middle-level attack with the fist.

— **Chudan-ude Uke** *Karate.* Blocking technique against an opponent's forearm.

Chuden see *Hasegawa Eishin-ryu.*

Chui. Minor warning given by the referee when one of the fighters is in danger of infringing a rule. When a light call is made, this is known as *Shido*. A more severe call is referred to as *Keikoku*. When a *Chui* is given, the referee may ask the opinion of the judges, a *Hantei*. Two Chui bring about disqualification (*Hansoku-make*) of the offender. Vietnamese: *Phat.* See Competition Rules of *Judo*, 25, 28, 29; *Karate*, 24, 27.

Chui-zi Quan see *Quan.*

Chujo-ryu *Ken-jutsu.* A tradition of sword-fighting introduced by Chujo Naga-hide around 1400. It gave birth to various styles of *Ken-jutsu*, notably:

Itto-ryu, founded by Ito Ittosai Kagehisa (*c.* 1600)
Tomita-ryu

Toda-ryu
Kanemaki-ryu, founded by Jisai Michiie (1576–1615)
Muto-ryu
Hasegawa-ryu, founded by Hasegawa Soki (1568–95)
Nikaido-ryu, founded by Matsuyama Mondo (*c.* 1600)
Gan-ryu, founded by Sasaki Kojiro (*c.* 1600).

Chukitsu see *Kyusho.*

Chun no Kon *Bo-jutsu.* A fundamental *Kata* using the long staff (*Bo*), employing slanting blows and thrusting techniques.

Chung Dang see *Chudan.*

Chuo-jiao-quan *Wushu.* A style of Chinese martial arts emphasizing attacks with the legs.

Chuong Mon Dai see *Obi.*

Chusen 'Drawing lots'.

Chushingura see *Ako-gishi.*

Chusoku see *Feet.*

Chuto see *Kyusho.*

Chuyen Than see *Than Phap.*

Cloth see *Hachimaki, Tenugui, Chikara-gami.*

Competition see *Shiai, Randori.*

Contrary, reverse see *Gyaku.*

Control see *Osae, Katame.*

Courtesy see *Miyabi.*

Co Vo Dao. The traditional weapons of Vietnamese martial arts. The principal ones are sticks (*Bong, Tien Bong*), flails (*Long Gian, Tham Thiet Gian*), swords (*Guom, Duan Guom*), straight sword (*Kiem*), scimitar (*Ma Dao*), halberds (*Dai Dao, Kich*), lance (*Thuong*), dagger (*Yen Dao*), sickle or long-handled bill-hook (*Cau Liem*), and the cutlass (*Song Dao*).

Cung Tan see *Than Phap*.

Cung Thu *Qwan-ki-do*. Basic blocking techniques performed on three levels: low (*Ha-dang*), middle (*Trung-dang*), and high (*Thuong-dang*), using the arms or the legs.

Cuoc Phap *Qwan-ki-do*. Kicking techniques:

> straight kick: *Truc Cuoc*
> side kick: *Song Cuoc*
> roundhouse kick: (*Mawashi-geri*): *Hoanh Cuoc*
> external foot-sword kick: *Dao Phuong Cuoc*
> internal foot-sword kick: *Tao Phuong Cuoc*
> back kick: *Ho Vi Cuoc*
> turning side kick: *Hau Cuoc*
> turning round kick: *Luu Van Cuoc*.

jumping kicks:
> forward jumping kick: *Phi Tieu Cuoc*

side jumping kick: *Phi Bang Sat Cuoc*
jumping round kick: *Phi Hoanh Sat Cuoc*

Cuong see *Go*.

Cuong Dao *Qwan-ki-do*. Techniques using the 'sword-hand' (see *Tegatana*, *Shuto*):

> horizontal, used against the side of the head: *Tram Xa*
> vertical, against the top of the head: *Tram Tach*
> vertical, against the arm; *Phat Moc*
> reverse: *Hoanh Chi*
> with both hands at once: *Sat Tich*.

Cuong Nhu Tuong Thoi *Qwan-ki-do*. The Vietnamese Taoist principle of harmony between the physical polarities (*Duong*, *Yang*) and the vital energy (*Am*, *Yi*), flowing from the laws of Changes as expressed in the Chinese Book of Changes, the *Yijing* (*I-Ching*). According to this principle, a combination of force and softness is necessary in order to perfect one's physical movements and the knowledge of the Self.

The symbol of the Dao (Tao);
union of the Yin and Yang.

D

a Bat see *Don Trung Cap*.

Dae see *Dai*.

Da Hu Yuan Jiao see *Jiao*.

Dai 'Great, big'. Also *O*, *Oki*. Korean: *Dae (Tae)*. See *Obi*, *Space*.

Dai Dao see *Naginata*.

Daidoji Yuzan see *Budo Shoshin-shu*.

Daido-ryu. School of martial arts founded by *Goto Tamauemon Tadayoshi* (1644–1736) of the Aizu clan. He taught *Ken-jutsu*, *Kyuba* (archery on horseback), *So-jutsu*, and *Kajutsu* (musket-firing).

Daigo Tettei see *Zen*.

Daimyo 'Great name'. A head of a province carrying an income (during the Edo period, 1603–1868) of at least 10,000 *Koku* or 1,800,000 litres of rice. These *Daimyo* lived in the castles of their province or else in Edo (Tokyo), the *Shogun*'s capital. They maintained a great number of *Samurai* in their service, who all swore an oath of allegiance to them according to the rules of *Bushido*.

Daisan see *Kyudo*, *Zanshin*.

Daisho. Pair of swords. The name given to the two swords carried in the belt by *Samurai* and *Bushi* of high degree. These swords generally consisted of a *Katana* (or *O-dachi*) and a *Wakizashi* (or *Kodachi*). This custom lasted until 1876, when the carrying of swords was forbidden except by members of the armed forces and the police. People of other classes were sometimes authorized to carry a short sword in certain circumstances.

Daito 'Large sword'. See *Katana*.
— **Daito-aikido** see *Genji-no-heiho*, *Aikido*.
— **Daito-ryu Aiki-jutsu.** A traditional school of *Aiki-jutsu*, created at the end of the nineteenth century at Aizu by *Takeda Sokaku Minamoto no Masayoshi* (1858–1943), a swordsman who excelled in the techniques of the schools of *Ono-ha Itto-ryu* and *Jikishin Kage-ryu*. *Ueshiba Morihei*, the creator of *Aikido*, had followed the teaching of this school. See *Aikido*, *Genji no Heiho*.

Daki-te *Karate*. A hand position resembling a hook, used in attacking the *Atemi* located on the face. See *Weapons*.

Dalyeun-ju see *Makiwara*.

Damo (Ta-mo) see *Bodhidharma*.

Da Moc see *Don Trung Cap*.

Dam Muc, Dam Thang see *Don Can Ban*.

Dan. The higher grades of *Budo* conferred on those qualified to wear the black belt (see *Obi*). Such men or women have successfully progressed through the *Kyu* grades, and are sufficiently technically qualified to move on towards an expert level. Depending on the schools and techniques, there are between five and twelve *Dan* grades. In the martial arts of Vietnam, these grades are called *Dang*. See *Kyudan*, *Obi*.

In the field of *Budo* or traditional martial arts, the *Dan* grades correspond to either technical awards or honorary awards:

First Dan: that of the 'student' (*Sen*).
Second Dan: corresponds to the title of 'disciple' (*Go-no-sen*).
Third Dan: that of the 'confirmed' disciple.
Fourth Dan: that of the 'expert' (*Sen-no-sen*).
Fifth and Sixth Dan: these are the 'spiritual experts' (*Kokoro*).
From seventh Dan to tenth Dan the experts specialize and are called *Iro-kokoro*.
Only ninth- and tenth- *Dan* grades are entitled to the title 'Master'.

The honorary grades are those of *Hanshi* (which corresponds to spiritual control), *Kyoshi* (given to experts of sixth and seventh *Dan* grade to indicate the degree of their inner perfection), and *Renshi*, given to practitioners of fifth *Dan* grade to symbolize that they have reached a degree of perfect self-control.

Dang see *Dan, Kyudan.*

Dang Mon see *Quyen.*

Da Ngang see *Don Can Ban.*

Dankyu see *Kyudan.*

Dansha. A man or woman who is entitled to wear a *Dan* grade insignia, in the shape of a belt or other item of clothing, having successfully passed the required grading in a martial art. See *Kyudan, Shingitai.*

Dantian see *Taiji Quan, Hara, Tanden.*

Dan Tsuki *Karate.* An attacking technique with the fist, consecutive to another attacking technique or as a counter-attack.

Dao. A Chinese word, equivalent to *Do* (*Michi*, the 'Way') in Japanese. Also written *Tao.* It is the name given to the sign symbolizing the interaction of the *Yin* and the *Yang*, (see *Yin-Yang*) and the *Taiji* 'Supreme Ultimate'. Korean: *Taegeug*; Vietnamese: *Do.* See *Taiji, Yin-Yang, Do, Si, Yijing.*
Wushu. In the training and practice of Chinese martial arts the *Dao* constitute the fundamental movements, equivalent to the *Kata* of Japanese *Budo.* Also *Tao*, 'Knife', 'Dagger'.

Dao Phong Cuoc see *Cuoc Phap.*

Dao Son see *Thu Phap.*

Dap Chan see *Don Trung Cap.*

Da Quay, Da Quay Vong see *Don Trung Cap.*

-dare see *Tare, Do, Kendo, Men.*

Da Thang see *Don Can Ban.*

Da Vong see *Don Can Ban.*

-de see *Te.*

De (*Deru*, to go out, to advance).
— **De-Ai.** A counter-attack, launched the moment an opponent loses his or her state of alertness (*Hontai*). See *Bonno.*
— **De-ai Osae Uke** *Karate.* A blocking technique delivered as one moves forward, pressing rather than hitting the opponent's attacking limb.
— **De-ashi-barai** *Judo.* A technique of sweeping the front foot of an opponent (from *Deru*, to go out; *Ashi*, leg; *Harai*, to sweep). It is performed as the opponent is about to place his or her foot on the ground. *Tori* uses a leg and foot in a movement which is flush with the floor to upset *Uke*'s balance backwards to the right or left, depending on which leg is attacked.

De-ashi-barai

Death (Contempt for) see *Enryo.*

Decision see *Kime.*

Defeat see *Make, Hansoku-make.*

Denko see *Kyusho.*

Densho A so-called 'secret' document to which numerous martial arts schools (*Ryu*) of Japan appeal as a basis for their existence. Such documents usually contain certain special techniques peculiar to the school; techniques handed down from the days of the ancient clans and jealously guarded by the weapons masters. They are transmitted from father to son or from master to disciple.

Di Anh see *Than Phap.*

Diem see *Ippon.*

Dinh Tan see *Tan Phap, Bo Phap*.

Diplomas see *Gaku*.

Disciples see *Juku-gashira, Kanshusai, Vo Sinh, . . . ka*.

Di Son see *Thu Phap*.

Di-tang-quan Wushu. A school of Chinese martial arts distinguished for its acrobatic movements, surprise attacks and ground techniques.

Di Than see *Than Phap*.

Do *Kendo*. A piece of *Kendo* armour which protects a practitioner's lower thorax and stomach. It is strong and rigid. Also called *Mune-ate, Ken-dogu*. See *Dogu, Kendo*.
— **Dogu** *Kendo*. The complete outfit used by *Kendoka* during training. It consists of a breastplate (*Do*), a helmet with a grille for protecting the face while enabling the wearer to see (*Men*), a head-cover made of cloth and worn under the helmet for comfort and sweat absorption (*Tenugui, Hachimaki*), padded gloves (*Kote*) and pieces of thick material to protect the hips and pelvic area (*Tare* and *Tare-obi*). See *Kendo*.

Do 'Way'. The spiritual path followed by adepts of a discipline, be it martial, religious or artistic. The concept of *Do* is an integral part of *Budo*, and without it the latter would, as it were, revert to an assemblage of mere techniques of fighting (*Jutsu*). The purely Japanese word for the Sino-Japanese one is *Michi* (Chinese *Tao* or *Dao*), which means 'path'.

Such a concept implies the multiplicity of ways of being and of behaving both morally and socially to reach the ultimate goal of mankind: harmonious integration with the laws of the universe. The *Dao* of the Chinese and the *Marg* of the Indians are both moral, ethical and aesthetic concepts which guide the seeker in the direction of serenity of mind, absolute equanimity. Such conditions of being are paramount to the Way, whether in the practice of martial arts (Budo) or in other disciplines. However, the Japanese concept of the Do is different from that of the Chinese in the sense that it contains no religious or superstitious connotation. It is merely a 'path' (*Michi*) to be followed by those who truly wish to live the life of a free human being, with all the difficulties which such a wish may bring. In this, the Japanese compare favourably with the Greeks, who maintained that to reach the fullness of oneself it was necessary first of all to know oneself, and become capable of using the mind to tame the reactions and emotions. It is the Do, the Way, which leads to the 'light', to the awakening of the self to its own true nature; a nature identical to that of the universe. The Way, therefore, is a constant search for self-perfection, implying the practice of numerous virtues, which must lead the individual to perfect union (*Ai*) with himself and his environment. The Do is in fact a sort of religious education whose sole aim is spiritual harmony with all beings, and mutual accord of self and the universal energy, so it is not surprising to find that the philosophy of the Do has become inseparable from that of *Zen*, representing its 'active' aspect. The Do is the symbol of Wisdom, distinct from simple knowledge although not excluding the latter, for 'To believe and to act are one and the same thing'. See *Budo, Kokoro, Shin, Jutsu*.

Doan Guom see *Guom*.

Do Bok see *Keikogi, Obi*.

Doc Han Vu Tan see *Bo Phap*.

Doc Nhan Vietnamese school of martial arts, nicknamed 'one-eyed'.

Dogen see *Zen*.

Dohyo *Sumo*. 'Sacred circle', the arena in which Sumo contests take place, made up of a platform some 5.7 m square and about 0.60 m from the floor. In the centre is a circular area, 4.55 m in diameter, made of earth covered in fine sand, with a border of thick straw 'rope', tightly woven and half buried in the surface. Above the *Dohyo* hangs a roof with two sloping sides, calling to mind the sanctuaries of *Shinto*. From each angle of the roof is suspended a

Maku-uchi in the Dohyo. Sumotori come together in the sacred circle of Sumo. These senior Sumotori are wearing the huge ceremonial loin-covering or pagne.

huge pompon; each pompon bears a colour symbolizing one of the seasons of the year. Within this circle the bouts between the *Sumotori* are staged. One of the wrestlers (*Rikishi*) must either throw his opponent to the ground or cause him to touch the earth outside the circle to be declared the victor. Each man enters the Dohyo from either the west or east side. Before each series of contests, the contestants are presented (*Dohyo-iri*), and for this occasion the Sumotori wear a long ceremonial apron, the *Kesho-mawashi*.

On the day before the tournament opens a special ceremony, the *Dohyo-matsuri*, takes place in the Dohyo itself. Here, the master judge (*Tate-gyoji*) officiates in the role of a *Shinto* priest, reciting invocations to the *Kami* to bring peace to the tournament. Auspicious objects such as sweet chestnuts (*Kachiguri*), seaweed (*Kombu*) and purified rice (*Senmai*) are placed on the Dohyo, and offerings of salt and *Sake* are made to the divinities. Then a man with a drum (*Furedaiko*) walks around the Dohyo.

At the end of each day a commemorative ceremony known as *Yumitori-shiki*, or dance of the bow, is performed on the Dohyo. A *Maku-uchi* is handed a bow by one of the *Gyoji* and dances with it in memory of a similar dance, in 1575, when a wrestler, having been honoured for his victories, thus showed his appreciation. His reward was in fact a bow, given to him by the renowned *Oda Nobunaga*, the military chief of the period. Hence the dance of the bow. See *Yobidashi*.

— **Dohyo-iri** see *Dohyo*.

— **Dohyo-matsuri** see *Dohyo*.

Do-jang see *Dojo*.

Do-jime *Judo*. Technique in which *Tori* squeezes *Uke*'s body using his legs. This technique forms part of the training in groundwork or *Ne-waza*.

Dojo 'Place for studying the Way'. The training hall of all martial arts (*Budo*) or equally the place where competitions take

place. The floor is often covered with *Tatami*, arranged in a square whose sides are 8 to 10 metres long, in the centre of the hall; or the entire hall may be so covered. The side where the teachers are is called the *Kamiza*, 'seat of the *Kami*', behind which is generally found an altar or shrine for the divinities. On the left of the Kamiza stand the highest grades and on the right the lesser grades (*Joseki* and *Shimoseki*). According to the official rules, the surface surrounding the Tatami must be about 15 centimetres below the surface covered by the Tatami. It may, however, be on the same level as the latter provided that a broad coloured line defines the surface covered by Tatami. In former times the word Dojo was used for the meditation hall in Buddhist monasteries. Korean: *Dojang*; Vietnamese: *Vo-duong*.
— **Dojo-arashi** see *Yaburi-dojo*.
— **Dojo-yaburi** see *Yaburi-dojo*.

Dokko see *Kyusho, Head*.

Doken-jutsu see *Tai-jutsu*.

'Dokukodo'. A work composed of twenty-one sections, written by *Miyamoto Musashi* and devoted to advice of an ethical nature for warriors. It places emphasis on being unattached to one's actions, a sense of honour, contempt for death, austerity, and the subjugation of self-interest.

Dol-lyeu Cha-gi *Tae-kwon-do*. A round-house kick. See *Mawashi-geri*.

Don Can Ban *Viet Vo Dao*. The fundamental techniques of empty-hand combat, including:

fist techniques:
   direct fist techniques: *Dam Thang*
   circular fist techniques: *Dam Vong*
   rising fist techniques: *Dam Muc*
foot techniques:
   direct foot techniques: *Da Thang*
   side foot techniques: *Da Ngang*
   circular foot techniques: *Da Vong*
blocking techniques:
   low: *Do Xuong*
   external: *Do Ra*
   internal: *Do Vo*

See *Don Trung Cap*.

Don Song Luyen (Dam, Chan, Chem) see *Song Luyen, Quyen*.

Don Trung Cap *Viet Vo Dao*. Advanced techniques of empty-hand combat, rounding out the fundamental techniques (*Don Can Ban*). They consist of:

hand-sword techniques (*Chem*):
   horizontal, to the head of neck of an opponent: *Chem Mang-tang*
   vertical: *Chem Xuong*
   reverse side: *Chem Ngang*
elbow blows (*Cho*);
kicking techniques:
   direct returning: *Da Quay*
   circular returning: *Da Quay Vong*
   hooking: *Da Moc*
   reverse techniques using the outside of the foot: *Da Bat*;
blocking techniques:
   low with the forearms crossed: *Do Treo Xuong*
   high with the forearms crossed: *Do Treo Len*
   techniques with the sole of the foot: *Dap Chan*
   techniques using the tibia: *Doong Quyen*.

See *Don Can Ban*.

Doong Quyen see *Don Trung Cap*.

Do Ra see *Don Can Ban*.

Doryo see *Bushido*.

Dosha see *Reisha*.

Dosoku Kata Sode-tori *Aikido*. 'Second sleeve-hold.' When *Uke* grasps *Shite* by the sleeve (*Sode*) with his or her left hand, Shite takes a big step to the right and uses his or her left arm to make a large circle to the side. With the right hand Shite then seizes Uke by the elbow and draws back, delivering an *Atemi* blow to Uke's elbow. See *Sode-tori*.
— **Dosoku Te-dori** *Aikido*. 'Third arm-hold.' When *Uke* seizes *Shite*'s left wrist with his or her left hand, Shite takes hold of Uke's left elbow from underneath with his or her right hand and lifts it, finishing off with

an *Atemi* blow. See *Te-dori*.

Do Treo Len, Do Treo Xuong see *Don Trung Cap*.

Do Vo see *Don Can Ban*.

Do Xuong see *Don Can Ban*.

Dozukuri *Kyudo*. The second position of the archer, legs apart, right fist on the right hip, holding the bow and arrows in the left hand. It is the 'stabilization' posture. See *Kyudo*.

Duit-cha-gi *Tae-kwon-do*. A kick delivered backwards.

Dui Quan see *Quan*.

Du-bal Dang-sang *Tae-kwon-do*. A straight, forward jumping-kick.

Duong see *Yin-Yang*.

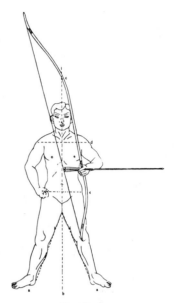

Dozukuri.
Act of stabilizing the posture.

E
bi 'Prawn'.

— **Ebi-garami** *Judo*. 'Prawn wrapping or winding technique', a groundwork movement (*Ne-waza*), the eighth strangulation technique.

— **Ebi-jime** *Judo*. From the groundwork techniques (*Ne-waza*), the sixteenth strangulation technique.

Eboshi. Plaited horsehair cap, lacquered black, displayed in former times by the *Samurai* and the *Bushi* and peculiar to them. It still forms part of the ceremonial costume of certain martial arts, such as *Kyudo* and *Sumo*. This cap was reserved for adults, after the ceremony of 'replacing the hat' or *Genpuku*, during which a young man was given a new name (*Eboshi-na*). The Eboshi of the Samurai was somewhat triangular in shape (*Ji-eboshi*) while the nobility and *Shinto* priests wore a bonnet-shaped hat (*Nae-eboshi*). See *Gyoji*.

Edo. The ancient name for the city of Tokyo. See *Tokugawa*.

Eido-tsuki *Karate*. A front punch using both fists in such a way that they simultaneously move in from both sides of an opponent's chest to strike him or her. Also *Eido-zuki*.

Eido-tsuki

Eight Directions see *Happo*.

Eisai see *Zen*.

Eishin. A master of sword and *Iai-jutsu* at the beginning of the eighteenth century. His family name was Hasegawa Chikara-no-Suke Hidenobu. He studied the techniques of the *Hayashizaki* school at Edo and created his own style of *Iai-jutsu*, the *Hasegawa Eishin-ryu*. He was the Seventh Master of the *Muso Shinden-ryu*.

Shinto archer Master Nakano, 10th Dan Hanshi, wearing Eboshi headgear.

'Eki-kyo' see *Yijing*.

Ekku. A wooden oar used by the fishermen of Okinawa against the *Samurai* of Japan. Such an improvised weapon was also used by *Miyamoto Musashi*, after he had reshaped it, to defeat his enemy *Sasaki Kojiro*. It now forms part of the Ko-budo armoury.

Elbow see *Empi*, *Hiji*.

Embu *Shorinji*. Exercises giving two opposing students the opportunity of working together on a particular movement.

E-mei Shan Pai. Chinese style of *Shaolin*, created on the sacred mountain of the same name. Vietnamese: *Nga Mi Phai*.

Emmei-ryu *Ken-jutsu*. School of swordmanship founded by *Miyamoto Musashi* (*c.* 1584–1645) based on the principle of *Fudoshin*. It is also referred to as *Nito-ryu*, or 'Two-sword school'.

Portrait of a Samurai of the Emmei-ryu, by Miyamoto Musashi.

Empi 'Elbow'. In the language of former times: *Hiji*. Vietnamese: *Phuong Duc*.
Karate. 'Flying swallow', a *Kata* expressing the lightness and swiftness of such a bird.
— **Empi-uchi *Karate*.** An attack delivered with the elbow.

Encho-sen. 'Prolongation' of a period of combat.

En-no-Irimi *Aikido*. A turning technique of *Irimi*, which is difficult to master and must lead to the fall of an opponent. This technique was invented by *Ueshiba Morihei*. See *Irimi*.

Empi-uchi.

Enryo. Contempt for death, a feeling cultivated by all the *Samurai* with the full approval of their lords, who could have complete confidence in their total fearlessness during combat with the warriors of enemy clans. The feeling of the impermanence of all things, as taught by Buddhism, was not far removed from that of contempt for death, man often being compared in Japan to the cherry blossom, whose flowering lasts only a few hours.

Ensho 'Heel'. Also called *Kagato*. See *Feet*.

Entanglement see *Garami, Maki*.

Eri 'Lapel'.
— **Eri-jime *Judo*.** One of the groundwork techniques (*Ne-waza*), strangulation using the lapels of the *Judo-gi*.
— **Eri Seoi-nage** see *Ippon Seoi-nage*.
— **Eri-tori *Aikido*.** A series of nine defences against grips on the collar or lapels of the clothing:

> *Hiji Nobashi Eri-tori*
> *Hiji Nage Mae Eri-tori*
> *Ryo-te Eri-tori*
> *Mae Ryo-te Shime Age*
> *Tsukomi-jime*
> *Eri-tori Yokomen Uchi*
> *Eri-tori Tsuki-age*
> *Ushiro Eri Obi-tori*
> *Ushiro Katate Tori Eri-jime*.

See *Te-hodoki, Rofuse, Kote-geashi, Kansetsu-waza*.

— **Eri-tori Tsuki-age *Aikido*.** Seventh grip on the lapel. *Uke* seizes *Shite*'s lapels with his or her left hand and delivers a right uppercut. Shite blocks the punch with his or her left forearm as he or she

31

turns to the right; then thrusts his or her right arm under Uke's left wrist, raising it sharply and 'wrapping' around it, finishing the movement with an *Atemi* blow to Uke's face. See *Eri-tori*.

— **Eri-tori Yokomen Uchi** *Aikido*. Sixth lapel hold. *Uke* seizes both Shite's lapels with his or her left hand. Shite steps forward half a pace and delivers a sword-arm attack to an *Atemi* point, using his or her forearm on Uke's right arm. Then, with a twist of the whole body, he or she passes under Uke's arms, draws back and delivers an Atemi strike to Uke's face. See *Eri-tori*.

Erlang Men. A Chinese martial art style (*Wushu*) developed during the Ming dynasty (1279–1644) and belonging to the 'internal' (*Neijia*) styles of the *Shaolin-si* tradition.

Exercise see *Randori*.

External see *Soto*.

F

Fan see *Gyoji, Uchiwa, Tessen.*

Fanzi Quan Wushu. School from the north of China, using rapid successions of hand or foot techniques.

Feet (*Ashi, Keri, -geri, Soku*). Korean: *Tae*; Vietnamese: *Cuoc*; Chinese: *Jiao.* Great use of the feet is made in all the martial arts where striking plays a big part; in *Karate,* for example.

Ankle: *Ashi-kubi*
Kicking: *Haisoku (-baisoku), ashi-zoku*
Top of the foot: *Kori*
Base of the toes: *So-in*
Heel: *Kakato (Kagato), Ensho*
Sole of the foot: *Teisoku, Ashiura*
Ball of the foot: *Koshi, Chusoku*
External 'cutting' edge of the foot: *Ashigatana, Sokuto*
Achilles tendon: *Akiresuken*
Toes: *Tsuma*
Point of the toes: *Tsumasaki*

Feng Taidu see *Taidu*

Ferozue. A type of long, hollow bamboo enclosing a chain weighted with an iron ball, characteristic of the armoury of the practitioners of the *Hozo-in-ryu* and the Shinden *Fudo-ryu.*

Firearms see *Juken-jutsu.*

Fists. Japanese: *Ken*; Korean: *Kwon*; Vietnamese: *Cuong*; Chinese: *Quan.*

Foot sweeps see *Harai.*

Force see *Go.*

Forearm see *Kote, Ude.*

Forms see *Kata, Quyen.*

Fudo see *Bushido, Fudoshin.*

'Fudochi Shimmeiroku'. A divine book on imperturbable wisdom, written by the Buddhist monk *Takuan* (1573–1645) for the instruction of *Yagyu Munenori* (1571–1646),

a celebrated sword-master. The book expresses the state of mind which a warrior must have, according to the doctrines of *Zen*: 'Penetrate the mystery of nature, by the grace of an open mind, and, through non-action, master the principles of Change.' According to Takuan, calm and serenity in combat must lead to victory: 'The one who is truly prepared for combat seems to be the one who is not at all prepared.' See *Fudoshin.*

Fudoshin 'Immutable in heart'. That state in which the mind is not troubled by anything external. A person knows no fear when faced with danger, aggression or unexpected events. It is a total impassivity before the hazards of life. This concept, expressed by Takuan, was developed by *Miyamoto Musashi,* who gave it the name *Iwa-no-mi,* 'Body-like-a-rock'. It applies to a warrior who remains calm and imperturbable in all circumstances. Also *Fudo no Seishin.* See *Fudochi Shimmeiroku.*

Fudo no Seishin see *Fudoshin.*

Fudo no Shisei no Kata. Basic *Kata* of all martial arts training. See *Fudotachi.*
Wa-jutsu. The name of the first Kata of this style of *Budo.*
Karate. See *Fudotachi.*

Fudotachi 'Firm posture', still and serene, imperturbable, descriptive of the state of a warrior before the attack. See *Fudoshin.*
Karate. In the *Wado-ryu* style of Karate, when the feet are joined together, the posture is known as *Fudo no Shisei.*

Fugatami Misanori Han-no-Suke see *Sosuichi-ryu.*

Fugul Seug-gi see *Seug-gi.*

Fujiwara. A noble family allied with the imperial family. They governed Japan from the ninth to the twelfth century.
— Fujiwara no Nobutsuna see *Shinkage-ryu.*

Fujubun *Karate.* A term used by the

referee to describe a contest in which no technique has been used.

Fukko-gamae Shorinji. Defensive position, one knee on the ground perpendicular to the front leg.

Fukuno-ryu see *Kito-ryu.*

Fukuno Shichiroemon see *Kito-ryu.*

Fukuro Shinai Kendo. A wooden sword covered with fabric or leather, formerly used in schools teaching swordsmanship instead of the *Shinai.*

Fukushen-shugo Karate. The gesture made by a referee when he calls the judges from the four corners of the contest area to listen to their comments on something which has just occurred in a tournament.

Fukushiki Kokyu see *Kokyu.*

Fukushiki Kumite Karate. A double attack during a combat *Kata.*

Fukushin An assistant judge at a *Budo* competition.

Fukuto see *Kyusho.*

Full Contact. A form of *Karate* which has grown up in the United States. Blows from the hands and feet are delivered with full power, just as in a boxing match. The aim of each fighter is to knock his opponent out, and none of the restraints and niceties which govern a *Budo* competition enters the Full Contact ring. Competitors wear gloves, foot protectors, headguards, groin guards and gum shields. The nearest European styles to Full Contact are *Savate* and its more formal descendant *Boxe Française.* The nearest Asian style is *Thai Boxing.* Full Contact was invented in 1974 by Mike Anderson, a promoter of American competitions, in response to the needs of the cinema which had witnessed the overwhelming success of the *Bruce Lee* movies. He was assisted by Jhoon Rhee, and both saw their brainchild flourish. The first championships were held in Los Angeles. There are no *Kata* in this sport, and all Japanese terminology has been replaced by American words. A wave of worldwide enthusiasm for the sport brought forth similar types of all-out competitions with different names such as Kick Boxing and Knock-down Karate, containing variations on the theme. The precise rules of some of these sports are often controversial. Contests in Full Contact are generally of ten rounds, and in the USA almost all competitors are professionals. There is no sense of the aesthetic here; only effectiveness.

Full-nunch (Full-nunchaku). A martial arts discipline born in the United States which uses the *Nunchaku* as a weapon (see *Kobudo*) but in this case delivers real blows to an opponent. The fighters wear a protective helmet which covers the entire face. Contests last several rounds and end if one of the competitors is knocked out. There are three weight categories in this new discipline: less than 60 kg, from 60 to 70 kg and over 70 kg. A softer form of fighting using a light, flexible Nunchaku which is comparatively harmless also exists. In this type of competition points are awarded for accurate striking techniques; injuries of any sort are rare.

Fumibari see *Shuriken.*

Fumi-kiri Karate. A blow delivered with the 'cutting' edge of the foot.
— **Fumikomi** 'Crush to the ground'. See *Fumi-waza.*
— **Fumikomi Age-uke Karate.** A high, blocking movement with a forward action.
— **Fumikomi Shuto-uke Karate.** A blocking movement using the 'sword-hand' (*Shuto*).
— **Fumikomi Ude-uke Karate.** A forearm block.
— **Fumitsuki** see *Fumi-waza.*
— **Fumi-waza Karate.** A technique of crushing, either by a blow or by pressure. It is delivered on any part of an opponent's body by the fist or the foot. See *Fumikomi*, *Fumitsuki.*

Funakoshi Gichin (1869–1957). The founder of modern *Karate* and creator of the *Shotokan* style of Japanese Karate. Born in

Fumikomi

Okinawa, where the practice of martial arts is traditional, he began to study *Okinawa-te* at the age of eleven and became a pupil of *Itosu Anko*. In turn he himself became a teacher, and in 1902 he gave a demonstration to a number of men in authority in Kagoshima (Kyushu). From that time onwards he acquired a certain reputation, which grew. He was invited to Tokyo in 1917, and with the assistance of his pupils gave a demonstration of Karate. He went again in 1922, and became a close friend of *Kano Jigoro*. Then he decided to make his home in Japan and spread his art as widely as possible. He wrote numerous articles on Karate, then published an important book, *Karate-do Kyohan*, which was later translated into other languages including English, in a modernized form. He decided at this time to change the meaning of the word Karate by substituting for the character *Kara* ('Chinese') the one meaning *empty*. His unceasing activity led to the creation of more than

thirty Karate *Dojo* in Japan in 1936, as those found in the universities and big institutions were private affairs. His activity eased off during the war, but afterwards began again under the aegis of the American authorities. From then on Karate expanded rapidly. His son, Funakoshi Yoshitaka, who died in 1953, succeeded him as head of the main dojo, the Shotokan.

Funakoshi Yoshitaka see *Funakoshi Gichin*.

Fundoshi A type of loincloth consisting of a long, narrow cotton strip, worn by the Japanese.

Furedaiko see *Dohyo*.

Furi-kaburi *Iai-do.* The act of lifting a sword above the head, following the gesture of threatening intent (*Seme*), before the delivery of the final blow (*Kiri-tsuke*).

Furi-uchi A blow given in a diagonal direction, downwards, with the hand in a 'sword' position (*Shuto*), as if it were a weapon.

Furumaru see *Hakakure*.

Fusegi *Karate.* A defensive technique.

Fusen-gachi 'Victory by default'. See Competition Rules of *Judo*, 30.

Fusensho 'Default'. *Fusensho* is declared against a competitor who in the course of a contest, refuses to fight, or stops fighting, or even fails to present himself for a contest for which he is entered. Korean: **Kikwon**. See *Fusen-gachi*.

The Torii Shinto of Miyajima.

G

achi see *Kachi*.

-gaeshi 'Counter-attack'. See *Kaeshi*.

Gaiwan. Outer edge of the arm. See *Arms*, *Wan*.

-gake see *Kake*.

Gaku. A written diploma awarded when a grading is passed in a style of *Budo*. See *Kyudan*.

Gaman Kamae *Kendo, Karate*. The attentive position taken before the beginning of a contest.

Gamen-tsuki *Karate*. A blow with the fist delivered in a backward direction using a circular action.

Ganka see *Kyusho*.

Gankaku *Karate*. 'A crane on a rock', the name of one of the advanced *Kata* of the *Shotokan* school.

Gan-ryu see *Chujo-ryu*.

Garami *Judo, Aikido*. A 'wrapping, winding, and holding' action used in immobilizing an opponent (*Osae-waza*).

-gari 'Sweeping'. See *Kari*.

Gashi *Karate*. The term used by a referee at the end of a contest, denoting the winner.

Gassan-ryu. A nineteenth-century school of *Naginata* in which a 'universal wisdom' was sought by means of practising with this weapon.

Gassho-gamae *Shorinji*. The saluting posture of the style, given at the beginning and end of training sessions. The hands are joined, palms facing, fingers separated wide from one another, at eye level.

-gatame 'Keeping under control'. See *Katame*.

Ge 'Low', 'Inferior' (in the sense of space and rank). Also *Shimo*. See *Space*.

Gedan 'Low level'. This term is used in martial arts to indicate the height of an attack or defence. In *Kendo* it means level with the abdomen; in *Karate* it can extend to mean level with the ground. When used with the word for punch or kick it denotes the region at which the attack is aimed; when used with the word for block, the same applies. It can also mean a defensive movement with the forearm, followed by a punch delivered with a twist of the body. Korean: *Ha-dan*; Vietnamese: *Ha-dang*. See *Space*.

— **Gedan-barai** *Karate*. An action of sweeping the feet from under an opponent, used with frequent success in modern *Karate* contests; action of blocking an attack using a downward-sweeping movement of the arm.

Gedan-barai

— **Gedan Choku Tsuki** *Karate*. A punch delivered straight to the lower abdomen.
— **Gedan no Kamae** *Kendo*. Low guard, with the *Shinai* held in front of oneself, the tip lowered. See *Kamae*.
— **Gedan Kake Uke** *Karate*. A hooking block.
— **Gedan Kekomi** *Karate*. A kick delivered straight to the lower abdomen.
— **Gedan Tensho Uke** *Karate*. A defensive action delivered low, using the heel of the hand.

— **Gedan Tsuki** *Karate.* A low punch, usually in the region of the lower abdomen.

— **Gedan Uke** *Karate.* A low defensive block.

-geiko see *Keiko, Kangeiko, Shochu-geiko.*

Gekken *Kendo.* The former name for *Kendo* used during the Meiji period (1869–1912) in Japan. The practitioner of this type of swordplay was called a *Gekkenka.* Today the word is used to describe a strongly executed attacking technique with the *Shinai.*

Gekon see *Kyusho.*

Genji no Heiho 'The warrior art of the Genji'. Genji was the name given to the warrior clan of the Minamoto who destroyed the power of the rival Taira, or Heike, clan in 1185 and established the first shogunate in Kamakura. The name *Genji-no-heiho* was given to the methods of war used in this epoch, relying more on strategy than on the art of individual proficiency in combat. It included methods of constructing fortifications, *Ken-jutsu, Ju-jutsu,* and the use of the lance (*Yari*). This array of battle techniques was comprehensively augmented by the Takeda family, and thenceforth took the title of *Takeda Heiho,* probably in the fifteenth century. According to Minamoto tradition, Genji no Heiho was created by Prince Teijun, the sixth son of Emperor Seiwa (859–77). In the seventeenth century the techniques of the Takeda gave birth to several *Ryu,* amongst which is the *Daito-ryu Aiki-jutsu* (or *Daito Aikido*), the forerunner of present-day *Aikido.*

Genshin. An acute sense of the intended action of an opponent, which can be acquired only after long years of martial arts training. A martial artist who possesses *Genshin* can thus anticipate an attack a fraction of a second before it takes place and counter-attack immediately with maximum effectiveness. See *Yomi.*

-geri see *Keri.*

Gesa-gatame *Judo.* 'Scarf-hold', a technique from *Osae-komi* (holding down on the ground). *Tori* 'lies' across *Uke*'s body; Uke is on his back. Tori presses his or her right ribs area against *Uke*'s chest and side, spreading his or her legs wide and pushing against the floor with the soles of his or her feet to prevent escape. There are two forms of *Gesa-gatame*: controlling the side of the body around the rib cage (*Hon Gesa-gatame*) and *Ushiro Gesa-gatame*, which consists of controlling across the chest by the arm and the belt. In the second technique, Tori lies on his or her left side, facing in the opposite direction. There are two variations on these two techniques. The first is *Kuzure Gesa-gatame* or 'broken scarf-hold', in which Tori lies on his or her right side. The second is *Makura Gesa-gatame*, in which Uke is controlled from the rear. Also called *Kesa-gatame.*

Geta. Light wooden clogs, worn by the Japanese in wet weather. In *Karate* training, heavy metal *Geta* are sometimes worn to perform kicking techniques in order to strengthen all the muscles involved in such techniques.

Gi see *Keikogi.*

Giao Long Cuoc *Qwan-ki-do.* A scissor technique in which both the attacker's legs are used in a scissor-like action on the opponent's legs to bring him or her down, at low level (*Ha-dang*) or middle level (*Trung-dang*).

Gi-in *Karate.* A *Kata* employing various fist attacks and blocks, and only one kicking technique, the *Mae-geri.*

Gino-sho see *Torikumi.*

Giri see *Bushido.*

-giri see *Kiri.*

Give up see *Ma-itta,* Competition Rules of *Judo,* 21.

Giwaken *Shorinji.* Fundamental techniques of offence and defence, used in training. Also called *Tenchiken.*

Go 'Five'. Chinese: *Wu.* 'Principle of force.' Vietnamese: *Cuong.* 'Protection.' Korean: *o.* See *Numbers.*

Gobu no Tsume *Kyudo.* The five final parts of applying tension to the bow.

Gohei see *Shinto, Tsuna.*

Goho *Shorinji.* The 'active' techniques of blocking, attacking and foot blows, as distinct from the 'passive' techniques or *Juho.*

Gohon-kumite *Karate.* A series of five attacks made with five steps; a form of prearranged sparring. See *Kumite, Ju-Ippon Kumite.*

Goju-ryu *Karate.* A school founded by *Miyagi Chojun* (1888–1953) in 1930. *Yamaguchi Gogen* (1909–), nicknamed 'the Cat', carried on the line, and taught an approach blending force (*Go*) with softness (*Ju*). The techniques of this school originated in Okinawa, where Miyagi's teacher, Higaonna, taught them. Among the techniques especially emphasized in *Goju-ryu* are those of *Sanchin*, performed with small steps and close arm movements combined with breathing exercises, and of *Tensho*, performed in a relaxed posture somewhat analogous to *Zazen.*

Goju-shi-ho *Karate.* A technique known as the 'fifty-four steps', in which each of the steps taken during the performance of the *Kata* displays one or several movements.

Gokaku-geiko *Kendo.* Training between pupils who possess the same strength and are at the same level.

Gokuhi. Special techniques which are taught by a martial arts master to his most gifted students having the highest grades. The techniques are sometimes described as 'secret' (*Hiden*, hidden science, or *Hi-jutsu*, hidden techniques). See *Hi-ho.*

Go-kyo *Judo.* 'Five principles.' This is a series of five groups of standing techniques (*Tachi-waza*), each of which contains eight throws. In each group the movements of

throwing are listed in order of difficulty; this order having been decided by the masters of the *Kodokan*. Each group of throws is part of the syllabus studied in Europe by those wishing to qualify for a higher grade or differently coloured belt:

First Kyo (yellow belt):
 De Ashi-barai
 Hiza-guruma
 Sasae Tsurikomi Ashi
 Uki-goshi
 O Soto-gari
 O-goshi
 O Uchi-gari
 Seoi-nage.
Second Kyo (orange belt):
 Ko Soto-gari
 Ko Uchi-gari
 Koshi-guruma
 Tsurikomi-goshi
 Okuri Ashi Harai
 Tai Otoshi
 Harai-goshi
 Uchi-mata.
Third Kyo (green belt):
 Ko Soto-gake
 Tsuri-goshi
 Yoko Otoshi
 Ashi-guruma
 Hane-goshi
 Harai Tsurikomi Ashi
 Tomoe Nage
 Kata-guruma.
Fourth Kyo (blue belt):
 Sumi-gaeshi
 Tani Otoshi
 Hane Mikikomi
 Sukui Nage
 Utsuri-goshi
 O-guruma
 Soto Makikomi
 Uki Otoshi.
Fifth Kyo (brown belt):
 O Soto-guruma
 Uki-waza
 Yoko Wakare
 Yoko-guruma
 Ushiro-goshi
 Ura Nage
 Sumi Otoshi
 Yoko-gake.

These movements do not make up the

complete syllabus, but they are fundamental.
Aikido. The fifth principle using techniques of stretching the arms (*Ude-nobashi*), used against a blow from above (*Shomen-uchi*) or a sideways blow (*Yokomen-uchi*). See *Kyo, Ude-nobashi*.

Gokyu see *Kyu, Kyudan*.

Gong Bo see *Bo*.

Gongfu see *Kung-fu*.

Gonin 'Five people'.
— **Gonin-gake** *Karate*. One man or woman fighting against five attackers.
— **Gonin-nuki** *Karate*. A contest in which five consecutive attacks must be made to score a point.

Gorei. Group training in a martial art under the direction of an expert. A form of collective training.

'Gorin no Sho' *Book of Five Rings*, a work about martial arts concentrating on swordplay (*Ken-jutsu*), attributed to *Miyamoto Musashi*. He would have written it in about 1643. This work is split into five scrolls – hence its name – which are known respectively as: Concerning Earth, Concerning Water, Concerning Fire, Concerning Wind and Concerning Heaven (Sky), the five elements of the philosophy of the Far East. The 'Way' which he puts forward is that of the *Hyoho*, a global concept of the way of the sword. He advocates the use of the large sword as well as the small sword in one hand; a difficult technique, the reasons and movements of which he explains. This book is considered a classic among works dealing with the martial arts. Above all it is important because it emphasizes the spirit of *Budo*, as distinct from merely teaching the techniques of swordplay, *Ken-jutsu*. See *Miyamoto Musashi, Hyoho*.

Go no Sen. A technique of seizing the initiative at the moment of an attack by an opponent, and moving into a counter-attack immediately. Also called *Ato no Sen, Ato no Saki*. See *Sen, Sen no Sen, Kyudan*.

-goshi see *Koshi*.

Goshin-do see *Goshin-jutsu*. A form of self-defence study (*Go*, protection; *Shin*, the Self, the Body) against possible attack, taught at the *Kodokan*. In fact it deals with the application of the techniques of *Judo* in a self-defence context. *Tori* is confronted by *Uke*, variously armed with a stick, a knife and a pistol. The methods of dealing with such an armed assailant are learned in the form of a *Kata* series. *Goshin-jutsu* therefore represents the practical as distinct from the sporting uses of Judo against an unarmed (*Toshunobu*) or armed (*Bukinobu*) assailant. This teaching includes counters to twenty-one basic situations. See *Tanaka Goshin-jutsu*.
Karate. Likewise in this discipline, *Goshin-do* is a collection of purely defensive techniques.

Goto Tamauemon Tadayoshi see *Daido-ryu*.

Grades see *Dan, Kyu, Kyudan, Obi*.

Great see *Oki, O, Space*.

Grip see *Kumi-kata, Temoto*.

Guando see *Kwan-do*.

Guards see *Kamae, Taidu, Thu Phap*.

Gun see *Jo*.

Guom. A long Vietnamese sword. The short sword is called *Doan Guom*. See *Swords*.

Guoshu see *Wushu*.

-guruma see *Kuruma*.

-gusari see *Manriki-gusari*.

Gyaku 'Contrary, reverse'. *Karate*. A counter-attacking term signifying that a contrary movement is made, as well as meaning simply reverse or contrary.
— **Gyaku-ashi** *Karate*. Opposite foot or rear foot.

— **Gyaku Mawashi-geri** *Karate*. A roundhouse kick describing a semicircle beginning from the opposite direction to a *Mawashi-geri* and often called a reverse roundhouse kick.

— **Gyaku-tsuki** *Karate*. See *Tsukomi*.

— **Gyaku-gaeshi-jime** *Judo*. A strangling technique in reverse leading to a possible dislocation, part of the groundwork or floor fighting of the art.

— **Gyaku-gamae** *Aikido*. The natural posture at the beginning of a contest, where one competitor stands with the opposite foot forward to that of the opponent.

— **Gyaku-geri** *Shorinji*. A kicking technique begun from a distance.

— **Gyaku-Han-mi** see *Ai-Hanmi*.

— **Gyaku-hineri** see *Kimarite*.

— **Gyaku-juji** *Judo*. Immobilization in which the attacker crosses the arms.

— **Gyaku-juji-jime** *Judo*. One of the groundwork (*Ne-waza*) techniques in which the attacker's arms are crossed under the opponent's throat.

Gyaku juji-jime

— **Gyaku kata Te-dori** *Aikido*. The second arm-gripping technique. *Uke* seizes *Shite* by the right wrist with his or her left hand and pulls him or her forward; whereupon Shite takes a big step to the right, seizes Uke by the left wrist with his or her left hand, and abruptly raises Uke's left arm, pulling him or her at the same time. Shite ends the technique with an *Atemi* blow to the base of Uke's rib cage. See *Te-dori*.

Gyaku Kesa-garami *Judo*. Holding *Uke* down on the ground, by lying across his or her body.

— **Gyaku Kesa-gatame** *Judo*. Holding *Uke* down on the ground, by lying across his

or her body.

— **Gyaku Okuri Eri** *Judo*. In groundwork (*Ne-waza*) this technique uses a twisting grip on *Uke*'s lapels to bring about strangulation.

— **Gyaku Te-dori** *Aikido*. A grip on *Uke*'s wrist by *Tori*, twisting it inwards and across the arm using either the thumb or the fingers.

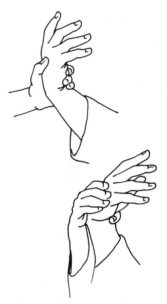

Gyaku Te-dori

— **Gyaku Te In-yo Shintai** see *Omori-ryu, In-yo Shintai*.

— **Gyaku Tekubi** *Judo*. In groundwork (*Ne-waza*), a technique which could dislocate *Uke*'s wrist.

— **Gyaku-to** see *Omori-ryu*.

— **Gyaku-tsuki (Gyaku-zuki)** *Karate*, *Aikido*. A punch delivered with a twist of the body. If the right leg is in front the punch is with the left hand; if the left leg is in front the punch is with the right hand.

— **Gyaku-tsuki no Ashi** *Karate*. A leaning-forward posture with the pelvis twisted towards the front leg.

— **Gyaku no Tsukomi** *Karate*. A punch delivered after a sideways movement of the pelvis and a thrusting forward of the upper chest.

Gyaku-tsuki

— **Gyaku no Tsukomi Ashi** *Karate*. A standing position with a sideways lunge, the rear leg stretched and the front leg bent.

Gyoji. *Sumo.* A general term for the referees. The first referee of *Sumo* was *Shiga Seirin*, a former *Sumotori*, who was given the name of *Hote* (Judge) by the emperor in 704. The *Gyoji* are dressed like *Shinto* priests, in rich costumes (the colour varying according to their grade) dating from the period of the Ashikaga *Shoguns* (1336–1573). They wear a conical *Eboshi* typical of the *Shinto* priests. Their symbol of office is a fan (*Uchiwa*), also coloured according to their grade, which is used to give emphasis to their decisions in the form of an appropriate gesture. The chief referee is called *Tate-gyoji*. It is he who signals the start of contests and referees the matches between a *Yokozuna* and another *Rikishi*. See *Shobu-shimpan, Sechie-zumo.*

H

a (1) *Kendo.* The edge of the *Shinai* used for striking; also the name of the cutting edge of a sword blade. See *Mune, Habaki-moto.*
— 'Branch' of a school (*Ryu*) of martial arts. See *Ryu.*

Ha (2) see *Ge, Gedan.*

Habaki-moto *Ken-jutsu.* The thick part of a sword blade, used not for cutting but for parrying cuts. The *Ha,* or cutting edge, damages more easily. See *Mune, Ha.*

Hachiji Tachi. The firm attention-posture assumed before a contest, and also used in *Kata.*
— **Hachiji Uchi** *Karate.* An attack made with the back of the hand (*Haishu*).

Hachiji Tachi

Hachimaki. A white cotton strip which fighters fasten round their heads as a sign of their firm resolve. It stops sweat from flowing into their eyes. In *Kendo* the *Hachimaki* is worn under the helmet (*Men*). The use of the Hachimaki is current in Japan, and shows the wearer's determination to persist in whatever trade he or she follows. See *Tenugui.*

Hac Ho. A Vietnamese school of martial arts called 'Black Tiger'.

Hac Tan see *Tan Phap, Bo Phap.*

Hadaka-jime *Judo.* Strangulation made with the bare arms (*Hadaka*) as distinct from a strangulation using the opponent's lapels or collar. One of the techniques of groundwork (*Ne-waza*). See *Shime-waza.*

Hadaka-jime

Hadako. A type of *Kempo* originating in China.

Ha-dang see *Gedan.*

'Hagakure'. 'Hidden beneath the leaves', a Japanese work on the martial arts and the spirit of *Bushido.* It exalted the idea of self-sacrifice in the service of one's lord, and was written in about 1716 by *Yamamoto Tsunetomo* a *Samurai* from the province of Saga, who sometimes signed his poems with the name *Furumaru. See Bushido, Budo.*

Hai-rei see *Rei.*

Hair see *Kami.*

Hairstyle see *Chon-mage, O-icho-mage.*

Haishin-undo *Aikido.* Exercises for loosening the back.

Haishu 'Backhand'.
— **Haishu-uchi** *Karate.* A backhand blow rising diagonally.
— **Haishu-uke** *Karate.* A backhand block.

Haisoku (-baisoku). The instep of the foot. A rising kick delivered to the side of an opponent with the top inside edge of the foot. See *Feet, Karate.*

Haishu-uchi

Haito 'Sword-hand'. See *Shuto, Tegatana*.
— **Haito Uchi** *Karate*. A blow delivered with the index finger edge of the hand, like a sword cut. Sometimes known as 'ridge hand'.

Haito Uchi

Haiwan. The upper edge of the arm. See *Arms*.
— **Haiwan Nagashi Uke** *Karate*. A blocking technique using the upper edge of the arm.

Hajime. 'Begin!'. The command given at the beginning of a contest by the referee to the two opponents. Korean: *Sijak*; Vietnamese: *Vo, Dau*. See Competition Rules of *Judo*, 12, 27; *Karate*, 5, 22.

Hakama. Very wide trousers which look like a skirt, part of the ceremonial costume

traditional in Japan. Also worn by certain groups of women such as the *Miko* (priestesses) in *Shinto* sanctuaries. Though it was formerly worn by both men and women, the *Hakama* was reserved for men at the beginning of the seventeenth century. At the outset of the Meiji period, however, certain women who were in the universities adopted the garment again. Similarly, women who train in the martial arts wear a Hakama in preference to the *Kimono*, which is hardly practical. The Hakama has a large pleat at the back and five pleats in front. It is attached by a belt with a rigid knot at the back (*Koshi-ita*), and is worn over a light jacket. Sometimes a *Haori* completes the outfit. In present-day martial arts, principally those of *Kendo, Kyudo, Aikido* and *Iai-do*, different-coloured *Hakama* are worn, signifying technical ability and grade: black, navy blue, dark brown and white.

Hakke-yoi *Sumo*. 'Very good!' A shout of encouragement sometimes given by a referee (*Gyoji*) to point out the perfection of a movement during a contest.

Hakko see *Sochin*.

Hakko-dori *Wa-jutsu*. A basic training principle (*Suwari-waza*) in which *Uke* kneels down opposite *Tori* and seizes his or her wrists, and Tori tries to free him(her)self from the grip.
— **Hakko-zeme-dori** *Wa-jutsu*. A standing *Kata* in which *Uke* seizes *Tori* by the wrists and Tori frees him(her)self by extending his or her arms outwards, pushing Uke away and striking him or her on the neck. See *Mae Katate Hakko-dori*.

Hakko-ryu *Ju-jutsu*. A school of combat created by *Okuyama Yoshiji*, of the *Daito-ryu* school, in 1938. It was the inspiration for the creation of *Shorinji-kempo*. The school specializes in the study of the application of oriental medicine to the martial arts.

Hakuda 'Period of training'. See *Kempo, Yoshin-ryu*.

Hana-michi *Sumo*. 'Path of flowers', a corridor or passage connecting the vestibule of the arena to the *Dohyo*, through which the *Sumotori* go to take part in the tournament. In theatres the expression is used for the path between the wings and the stage.

Hanare *Kyudo*. The seventh position of archery, that of releasing the arrow. The fingers open naturally, freeing the bowstring, at a moment when the aim is perfect and the mind and body are in complete harmony. This act should ideally take place without the imposed will of the archer. The arm which draws the bow comes to rest in a backward position, relaxed. The completed posture must be maintained for a few seconds, with the mind united with the arrow and the target: this is *Zanshin*. See *Zanshin*, *Daisan*.

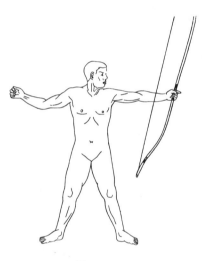

Hanare
Releasing or letting fly an arrow.

Han-bo see *Bo*.

Hando no Kuzushi. Loss of balance due to a contrary reaction. When one of two fighters resists a pull or push which affects his or her balance, if the attacker stops his or her action then the defender will tend to lose balance in the direction of his or her own resisting movement. It will only be necessary to reinforce this contrary movement to make

him or her lose balance completely. See *Kuzushi*.
Judo. The fundamental principle is to push when pulled and to pull when pushed.
Aikido. The fundamental principle is to turn (*Tai-sabaki*) inwards when pushed, to unbalance the attacker forwards, and to 'enter' or advance when pulled, to unbalance him or her backwards.

Hands *Te, -de, Shu*. Fist: *Ken*. In all hand-to-hand combat the hands play a very large part, either for seizing an opponent or for striking him or her with an *Atemi* blow. Here are the principal relevant terms:.

Wrist: *Tekubi*
Heel of the hand: *Teisho*
Palm: *Shuwan*, *Shotei*
Top of the hand: *Haishu*
Cutting edge of the hand (hand-sword): *Shuto*, *Tegatana*
Palm with hooked fingers: *Kumade*
Cutting edge of the hand with fingers clenched (hammer-fist): *Tettsui*
Fingers: *Yubi*
Two-finger thrust: *Nihon Nukite*
One-finger thrust: *Ippon Nukite*
Internal cutting action using the outside of the thumb: *Haito*
Top side of the wrist: *Kakuto*
Fingers joined to make a point (eagle's beak): *Washide*, *Keiko*
Front of the fist: *Seiken* or *Kento* (fist-sword)
Half-fist: *Hiraken*
Closed fist with biggest finger knuckle protruding beyond the rest: *Ippon-ken*, *Nakayubi*
Strike using four rigid fingers closely joined: *Nukite*
One hand: *Katate*
Both hands: *Ryote*, *Morote*.

Hane 'Wing', 'To leap'.
— **Hane-age** *Kendo*. A movement consisting of raising the *Shinai* after having forced the opponent to lower his or hers, and then striking him or her downwards.
— **Hane-goshi** *Judo*. Known as the 'spring hip throw'. *Tori* presses his or her bent leg against *Uke*'s legs and, leaning forward, lifts Uke and throws him or her for-

Hane-goshi

ward, pulling his or her sleeve downwards.
— **Hane-maki-komi** *Judo.* Known as
'winding hip throw'. Same technique as
Harai-goshi, but *Tori* brings more force to
the movement by letting him(her)self fall
forward, drawing *Uke* off balance and on to
the floor. See *Sutemi.*

Hangetsu-dachi *Karate.* The posture of
Sanchin-dachi with feet and knees turned in.
See *Sanchin.*
— **Hangetsu Kata** *Karate.* 'Half-moon
or crescent *Kata.*' The legs and feet move in
the *Hangetsu-dachi* stance, describing semi-
circles.

Hang Quan see *Quan.*

Hangetsu-dachi

Hanmi. A defensive posture used in *Karate, Aikido* and *Kendo,* which leads into a
counter-attack. The front leg is bent and
the upper chest half-turned to one side. See
Ai-hanmi.

Hanshi 'Master'. An honorary title given
to the highest black belt grades, signifying
their understanding (*Kokoro*) of their art.
See *Kyudan, Obi.*

Hansoo (Hansu) see *Poomse.*

Hansoku-make. The words used by a referee in a contest or competition of *Budo* to
indicate defeat by disqualification. See also
Shikaku, Chui, Make, Competition Rules
of *Judo,* 20, 21, 28; *Karate,* 24, 27, 29.
Vietnamese: *Loai.*

Hansu (Hansoo) see *Poomse.*

Hantai. An expression used to describe
a position or posture opposite that of an
opponent.

Hantei 'Decision'. A referee in a contest or
competition utters this word while raising an
arm vertically in the air, to indicate to the
judges that he or she wishes them to make
a decision. Vietnamese: *Diem.* See *Chui,*
Competition Rules of *Judo,* 8, 20.

Hao Pai *Wushu.* A school of *Kung-fu*
derived from the postures of the heron,
and using the fingers in the shape of this
bird's beak in order to attack. The foremost
posture in the school is the 'iron horseman'.

Haori. A jacket with large sleeves, worn
over the *Hakama* and decorated on the back
with the family crest (*Mon*) or that of the
Dojo. It may equally well be worn over the
Kimono, especially by the referees in *Sumo*
(*Gyoji*). See *Hakama.*

Hap-ki-do. An eclectic Korean martial arts
style using kicks, punches, locks, throws,
and so forth, giving an all-round fighting
method with practical self-defence applications.

Happo 'Eight directions', 'Eight laws'.

Korean: *Palgwe (Palgue)*.

— **Happo-giri** *Ken-jutsu*. Art of cutting with the sword, using eight directions.

— **Happo no Kuzushi** 'Loss of balance in eight directions': backwards, forwards, right, left, diagonally forwards right, diagonally forwards left, diagonally backwards right, diagonally backwards left.

— **Happo-moku** *Shorinji*. A technique of gazing into space, taking in the whole field of vision and beyond (in eight directions) without moving the head and without focusing on any particular object.

— **Happo Undo** 'Exercise in the eight directions', in which practitioners of *Budo* must learn to throw their partners in eight directions (see *Happo no kuzushi*) in relation to their centre of gravity (*Hara*).

Hara 'Belly'. The human body's inner centre of gravity and the source of breath (energy), which is traditionally located about four centimetres below the navel, between the latter and the vertebral column. According to Japanese belief, it is here that profound vital forces reside. Through the *Hara* men and women can communicate with the universal energy, and there *Ki* is found. 'Deep' breathing must take place from the *Hara*, for it is from there that all the individual's physical and psychic forces emanate. The art of concentrating all mental and physical forces on this point is called *Haragei*. In Buddhism, Hara is called *Tanden*, the Japanese translation of the Chinese word **Dantian**, 'cinnabar field', the focal point for adepts of the *Dao (Tao)*. Also called *Seika-no-itten*. See *Ki, Aiki, Kime, Ibuki, Tanden*.

— **Hara-gatame** *Judo*. One of the techniques of groundwork (*Ne-waza*), involving the bending of an opponent's arm against the lower abdomen.

— **Haragei** 'Art of the belly'. The art of concentrating one's thought, mind and energy in the *Hara*, of meditating so as to collect one's vital energies (*Ki*) in the Hara; indispensable for achieving perfect control of the self. Through *Haragei* it becomes possible to be at one with the universe, to 'read' (*Yomi*) the very thoughts of a potential assailant, and to feel in harmony with other beings and with the environment. See *Hara, Hyoshi, Ma-ai, Sakki, Yomi*.

Correct position for executing Harai-goshi.

Hara-gatame

Harai (-barai). Sweeping or reaping the feet from under an opponent using a driving movement of the foot or leg, producing a loss of balance on one side.

— **Harai-goshi** *Judo*. The sweeping hip throw in which *Tori*'s hip makes close contact with *Uke*'s abdomen and Tori sweeps Uke off balance with a leg action. Uke loses balance in a forward direction. See *Yama-arashi*.

— **Harai Maki-komi** *Judo*. A counter-move against the *Harai-goshi* throw.
— **Harai-te** *Karate*. A rapid sweeping action executed with the hand.
— **Harai-tsurikomi Ashi** *Judo*. The sweeping, drawing ankle throw in which *Tori* sweeps *Uke*'s foot and lifts him or her with the arms to bring about loss of balance directly forward.

Harai-tsurikomi Ashi

Hara-kiri see *Seppuku*.

Harau *Kendo*. A turning movement using the *Shinai* to deflect a blow from an opponent.

Hari-te *Karate*. A blow delivered with the palm of the hand.

Hariya Seki-un (1592–1662). A Japanese sword master reputed to have fought fifty-two contests undefeated.

Harmony see *Wa, Ai, Cuong Nhu*.

Hasami (-basami) 'Scissors', a scissor-like action using either the arms or the legs.
— **Hasami-jime** *Judo*. One of the techniques of groundwork (*Ne-waza*), involving squeezing with the legs.
— **Hasami-tsuki** *Karate*. A blow given with both fists in a scissor-like action.

Hasegawa Eishin-ryu *Iai*. A *Kata* of *Iai*, characteristic of the *Muso Shinden-ryu* school, consisting of ten movements carried out in a standing position. Also called *Chuden* 'middle teaching'. They are:

Hasami-tsuki

Yoko-gumo
Tora-i Soku
Inazuma
Uki-gumo
Yamashita Oroshi
Iwanami
Uroku-gaeshi
Nami Kaeshi
Taki Otoshi
Batto Nuki Uchi.

See *Omori-ryu, Oku-iai, Eishin*.

Hasegawa Chikara no Suke Hidenobu see *Eishin*.

Hasegawa Soki see *Choju-ryu*.

Hasen-kata *Karate*. A series of *Kata* carried out one after another, 'in waves'.

Hasso 'Attack'.
Judo. A blow given with the 'sword-hand' (*Shuto*) or (*Tegatana*), travelling downwards. See *Waki*.
— **Hasso no Kamae** *Kendo*. A position in which the *Shinai* is held vertically with the hands at shoulder level on the right or left side.

Hat see *Eboshi*.

Hataki-komi *Sumo*. An evasive movement using a turn of the body as an attack is launched, allowing the opponent to fall as a result of his or her own impetus, but if necessary giving a push with the palm of the hand on his or her back. See *Kimarite*.

Hataki-komi

Hatsu-geiko. Training which takes place at the beginning of the New Year, lasting several days and ending with competitions between clubs or international tournaments. See *Keiko.*

Hayashizaki Jinsue (Jinnosuke) Shigenobu, Hojo *Iai-do*. A sixteenth-century sword master (see *Ken-jutsu*) who created and gave his name to a school of *Iai-jutsu* in 1560. The techniques of this school were brought to a high state of perfection by *Eishin,* and it was renamed *Muso Jikiden Eishin-ryu.*

Hayashi Teruo see *Kenshi-ryu, Batto-jutsu.*

Haya-uchi see *Kyusho.*

Head. Since it is a part of the human body, the head plays an important part in the martial arts, mainly as the target for *Atemi* blows; it has numerous vital points (see *Kyusho*). The head (*To, Tsu, Atama*) makes up the upper level (*Jodan*) of the body.

Face: *Men, Kao*
Hair: *Kami*
Top of the skull: *Tento*
Neck: *Kubi*
Frontal nasal point: *Choto*
Fontanelle: *Tendo*
Point of the jaw: *Kachikake*
Adam's apple: *Hichu*
Back of the neck: *Keichu*
Ears: *Mimi*
Temples: *Kasumi*
Mastoid process: *Dokko*
Angle of the jaw: *Mikazuki*
Right carotid artery: *Murasame*
Left carotid artery: *Matsukaze.*

Heian Kata *Karate*. 'Forms of peace and calm.' The name given to the five fundamental *Kata* of the *Shotokan* style; created by Itosu Kensei from among the techniques and Kata of former times. It is obligatory to learn these Kata to obtain 8th and 4th *Kyu*. The study of the other Kata or *Tekki* begins with 3rd *Kyu* training. Certain *Karate* schools use the Chinese word *Pinan* to designate these fundamental Kata:

Heian Shodan (first level)
Heian Nidan (second level)
Heian Sandan (third level)
Heian Yondan (fourth level)
Heian Godan (fifth level)

Heido see *Hyodo.*

Heiho The name given to *Ken-jutsu* by *Ito Ittosai* of the *Itto-ryu* school. This was done to show that the art of the sword must not be merely one of the techniques of combat (*Jutsu*) but must include an attitude of mind which is calm and pure. Such an attitude enables one to take advantage of the movements (*Katsujin-no-Ken*) of an opponent. Thus *Heiho* became purely defensive. Also called *Seiho.*

'Heiho Kadensho' see *Yagyu Munenori.*

Heijo-shin. This is the firm state of mind which must be maintained when one is under attack: tranquil and free from passion. This condition should be accompanied by a relaxed attitude, steady regular breathing and totally fearless self-confidence. See *Munen Mushin, Kokoro, Fudoshin.*

Hei-ken *Karate*. A blow given by the first and second fingers closely joined together.

Heiko-dachi *Karate*. The 'ready' position, feet parallel.
— **Heiko-tsuki *Karate*.** Punch with the fist 'parallel'.

Heisoku-dachi. A standing posture, feet joined together.

Helmet see *Armour.*

Henka 'Change of side': for example, in

Heisoku-dachi

a stance with the right foot forward and right arm back one would change to left foot forward and left arm back.

Het see *Ki-ai*.

Hexagrams see *Bagua Quan, Yijing*.

Heya see *Sumotori*.

Hichu 'Adam's apple'. See *Kyusho, Head*.

Hidari 'Left'. Korean: **Oenchok**. See *Space, Sa*.

— **Hidari Ashi-jime** *Judo*. One of the techniques of groundwork (*Ne-waza*), employing the left leg to produce strangulation.
— **Hidari-do** *Kendo*. A blow from the *Shinai* on the left side of the *Do* of an opponent.
— **Hidari Ippon Seoi-nage** see *Ippon Seoi-nage*.
— **Hidari Shizen-tai** *Karate*. Left natural posture.
— **Hidari Teiji-dachi** *Karate*. Left T-shape posture.

Hiden 'Concealed', 'Secret'. See *Gokuhi*.

Hideyoshi see *Toyotomi Hideyoshi*.

Higaonna Kanryo (1853–1915). A master of Okinawan martial arts, *Naha-te* style, the teacher of *Funakoshi Gichin*. See *Mabuni Kenwa*.

Hi-gi *Wa-jutsu*. The study of the relationship between the material world and the divine plan. An esoteric subject reserved for *Kyoshi* grades and for the *Taishi* of this discipline.

Hi-ho 'Hidden method', meaning instructions taught by a master only to his closest Chinese disciples.

A. Hidari-do: blow to the left side. B. Migi-do: blow to the right side.

Hiji 'Elbow', in the language used by the *Bushi*. Also *Empi*.

— **Hiji-ate** *Karate, Aikido*. An attacking technique using the elbow.

— **Hiji-dori** *Aikido*. A blow delivered by *Shite* with the fist when *Uke* seizes his or her left sleeve at elbow level. The blow is aimed at the face.

— **Hiji-maki-komi** *Judo*. Known as 'elbow entanglement'.

— **Hiji-nage Mae Eri Tori** *Aikido*. The second lapel grip, a variation of *Hiji-nobashi*. *Shite* passes his or her right arm above that of *Uke*, steps with the right leg behind Uke's left and upsets his or her balance backwards. Shite finishes with an *Atemi* blow with the foot.

— **Hiji-nobashi Eri Tori** *Aikido*. The first lapel grip. When *Uke* seizes *Shite*'s left lapel with his or her left hand, Shite steps to the right to avoid the accompanying blow and grips his or her own lapel with the right hand close to Uke's grip. He pulls Uke to the right and makes a wide turning movement, rising from left to right, with the left arm, finishing with an *Atemi* blow to the face. See *Eri-tori*.

— **Hiji-otoshi** *Judo*. A defensive move using the elbow.

— **Hiji-shime** see *Ude-hishigi*.

— **Hiji-suri Uke** *Karate*. A sliding block using the shoulder.

— **Hiji-uchi** *Karate*. An elbow attack.

— **Hiji-uke** *Karate*. A defensive movement using the elbow, brought about by turning the body or by bringing the elbow upwards.

— **Hiji-waza** *Aikido*. Techniques of attacking *Uke*'s elbows, when practising

Hiji-waza

either key arm techniques (*Ude-hishigi*) or strong locking movements such as *Oshi-taoshi*, twisting movements like *Ude-garami*, pulling (*Hiki-taoshi*), twisting (*Uke-hineri*) or bending back (*Ude-gaeshi*). See *Kansetsu-waza*)

Hi-jutsu see *Gokuhi*.

Hiki 'To pull', 'To evade'.

— **Hiki-age** *Kendo*. The action of lifting the *Shinai* high after making a cut, to be ready to make another downward cut.

— **Hiki-otoshi** *Sumo*. An evading movement in response to a low frontal attack, followed by a downward push on the attacker's back to make him fall forward. See *Kimarite, Omote*.

— **Hiki-mi** *Shorinji*. A technique of avoiding a blow to the stomach by rapidly drawing back the midsection of the body.

Hiki-otoshi

— **Hiki-taoshi** *Aikido*. Key arm technique (*Ude-hishigi*) involving a pulling action, from the techniques of *Hiji-waza*. See *Kansetsu-waza*.

—**Hiki-tate**. A technique of drawing an opponent closer to oneself in order to control him or her more easily.

— **Hiki-te** *Karate*. A series of movements (*Kata*) in preparation for a counter-attack. These involve a simulated blow with the open hand or fist, accompanied by a twist of the pelvis to increase the speed of the action. The undelivered blow is pulled back immediately. The total effect is to give extra power to any real blow which follows.

— **Hiki-tori** *Kyudo*. The action of raising the arms holding the bow and arrow before assuming *Hikiwake*.

Hikiwake *Kyudo.* The fifth position of the archer, consisting of two parts in succession: the movement of raising the bow above the head (*Hiki-tori*) and standing in a state of mental and physical stability (*Dai-san*, great third), with growing tension before the condition of maximum tension, or *Kai*.

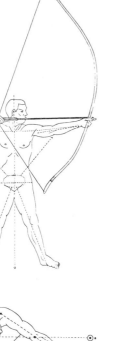

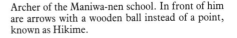

Hikiwake

Kendo. The limit of a period of attack, without a decision.
Judo, Karate. A draw, equal score. When he or she makes this announcement, the referee stretches out both arms in front at an angle of 45 degrees, then spreads them apart, palms upwards, before pointing them at the opponents. See Competition Rules of *Judo*, 8, 20, 21, 31; *Karate*, 28.
— **Hiki-waza** *Kendo.* When one of the contestants draws back, either to feint or

to give him- or herself more space in which to attack.

Hikida Bungoro see *Hikida-ryu.*

Hikida Kage-ryu see *Hikida-ryu.*

Hikida-ryu *Kendo.* A school of *Kendo* founded by Hikida Bungoro (*c.* 1537–*c.* 1606), a celebrated swordsman of the *Shinkage-ryu.* This school introduced for the first time a training sword made of wood, which was very heavy and dangerous, analogous to the *Bokken.* Also called *Hikida Kage-ryu.* See *Kage-ryu.*

Hikime *Kyudo.* An arrow with a wooden

Archer of the Maniwa-nen school. In front of him are arrows with a wooden ball instead of a point, known as Hikime.

ball instead of a point, to avoid serious injury. It is used in *Yabusame*, *Kasagake* and *Inu-oi-mono*. The *Kabura-ya* belong in the *Hikime* class of arrows.

Hikita Kagekane, Hikita Kage-ryu see *Kage-ryu*.

Hikiwake *Kyudo*. See *Hiki*.

Hikkomi-gaeshi *Judo*. This expression is used when two opponents roll to the ground at the same time. It can equally describe *Sutemi*, when one contestant seizes the opponent's belt at the back to bring about the fall.

Himo *Kendo*. A cord used to fasten the armour (*Do*).

Hineri 'Twisting'.

Aikido. Twisting of the hand: *Hineri-te*. Twisting back of the elbow: *Hineri Yoko Empi*.
— **Hineri-nagashi** *Karate*. An evasion made by turning the body obliquely inwards, in contrast to *Hiraki Uke*.
— **Hineri-uchi** *Aikido*. An elbow blow. See *Keri-goho*.

Hips see *Koshi*.

Hira 'Flat', a general word to describe the flat of the hand, the top of the foot, and all plane surfaces.
— **Hira-ken Tsuki** *Karate*. A direct punch (*Tsuki*) with the front of the fist facing the target.
— **Hiraki Uke** *Karate*. An evasion made by turning the body sideways and inwards, in contrast to *Hineri Nagashi*.

Hirai see *Korindo*.

Hisami-ashi see *Kimarite*.

Hisamori-ryu see *Takenouchi-ryu*.

Hishigi *Karate*. The technique of 'breaking' by which the *Karateka* or practitioner can prove the power of his or her blows, using the fist (*Ken*), the 'sword-hand' (*Shuto*) or the feet. To increase his or her effective-

ness the Karateka must spend a long time training at hitting the *Makiwara* to harden the striking edge of the hand (*Tegatana*), the outer edge of the foot (*Sokuto*) and the fists. It is then possible to break wooden planks, tiles, and even bricks with powerful, trained blows. Certain Karateka go to the extent of breaking objects with the head. Although this is a spectacular sight, it is not necessary for the execution and application of the techniques of *Budo*. Korean: *Kyok-pa*; Vietnamese: *Nghanh*. See *Shiwari*.

Hishiryo see *Satori*.

Hitsui 'Knee'. See also *Hiza*, *Legs*.
— **Hitsui-geri** *Karate*. A blow delivered with the knee.

Hitsui-geri

Hiza 'Knee'. Also *Hiza-gashira* (kneecap), *Hitsui*. See *Legs*.
— **Hiza-gatame** *Judo*. A groundwork (*Ne-waza*) technique, bending the arm over the knee.
Wa-jutsu. A basic *Kata* performed in a kneeling (*Suwari*) position. It shows methods of freeing the wrists and is identical to *Hakko-dori*, except that it ends with *Tori* delivering two successive *Atemi* blows to *Uke*: 1. with the right fist on Uke's rib cage, at the *Kyoei* point between the fourth and fifth ribs; 2. with the 'sword-hand' (*Tegatana*, *Shuto*) in reverse at the side of Uke's neck, at the *Matsukaze* point on the left side at the base of the carotid sinus, or on the right side

Hiza-gatame

at the corresponding point called *Murasame*.

— **Hiza-geri** *Karate*. A blow using the knee. Also called *Hitsui-geri*.

— **Hiza-guruma** *Judo*. 'Knee-wheel.' *Tori* places his or her foot on *Uke*'s knee, turned inwards so that the sole of the foot is flat, and blocks *Uke*'s forward movement; then pulls and turns so that *Uke* loses balance to the front (right or left).

Hiza-guruma

— **Hiza-jime** *Judo*. A strangulation groundwork (*Ne-waza*) technique using the knee.

— **Hiza-makuzu** *Kendo*. A salute from a kneeling position.

— **Hiza-tsui** *Karate*. A 'hammer' blow delivered with the knee.

— **Hiza-tsuki** *Kendo*. A kneeling position.

— **Hiza Uke** *Karate*. A blocking movement in which the bent knee is raised and used in a similar fashion to a blocking arm.

Hizo The small of the back. See *Body*.

Hoanh Chi see *Cuong Dao*.

Hoanh Cuoc see *Cuoc Phap*.

Hoanh Phong, Hoanh Xa see *Phuong Duc, Thu Phap*.

Ho Diep Tan see *Bo Phap*.

Ho-gu see *Tae-kwon-do*.

Hogu-jutsu A school of close-quarter combat (*Ju-jutsu*), akin to *Hokusai-ryu* and using various techniques to overpower an opponent. These techniques are part of *Kobudo*.

Hojo Hayashizaki Jinsuke Shigenobu see *Muso Jikiden-ryu*.

Hojo-jutsu 'Art of tying up'. Methods of binding an adversary with cord or rope, quickly and effectively, formerly used by the *Ninja* and still used today by the Japanese police force.

Ho-jutsu. An ancient school of martial arts (*Kobudo*) using techniques of the *Yo-ryu* (handling of the arquebus), created in the sixteenth century. Also called *Ka-jutsu*. See *Firearms*.

Hoki-ryu *Kyu-jutsu*. One of the oldest schools (*Ryu*) of archery as used in warfare, created in the tenth century by *Zensho Masatsugu*, who was one of the first to study and codify the postures and techniques of the bow and the arrow.

Hoko-in-ryu. An ancient martial arts school specializing in the use of the lance and hand-to-hand combat.

Hokusai-ryu *Ju-jutsu*. An ancient school of hand-to-hand combat. See *Hogu-jutsu*.

Hokushin Itto-ryu *Ken-jutsu*. A school of martial arts dating from the end of the Edo period (eighteenth to nineteenth centuries) which promoted an art of using the sword which was less warlike and more spiritual than the simple *Ken-jutsu*; created by *Chiba Shusaku* (1794–1855). This school used a straight *Bokken* in training (*Kumitachi* style), which was the ancestor of the *Shinai*, and long-sleeved gloves for protecting the forearms. Followers of the art used to hold competitions in which the Bokken was used against women wielding a Naginata with a wooden blade. See *Kumi-tachi*.

Hon 'Origin', 'Root', 'Foundation'.
— **Hon Kesa-gatame** *Judo*. A technique of holding down on the floor by immobilizing the upper side of the body. See *Ne-waza, Osae-waza*.

Hon Kesa-gatame

— **Hon-mokuroku** *Aikido*. The title given to those *Aikidoka* with 4th and 5th *Dan* grades. See *Kyudan*.
Wa-jutsu. The title given to the 'experts' (black belt with four violet bands) and to the 'true disciples' (black belt with three violet bands). It indicates that such practitioners have 'true knowledge' of the techniques of the style.

Hong Bach Dai see *Kyudan*.

Hong Quan A Chinese style of martial art (*Wushu*) created during the Sung dynasty (1127–1279). It belongs to the 'internal' method (*Neijia*) of the *Shaolin-si* tradition.

Honke see *Bushi*.

Hontai. The permanently awake and alert state of a fighter whose mind is unattached and remains clear and in control of all his or her faculties. This condition is reached only after long training and brings perfect control of body, will and mind. According to the *Zen* monk Takuan it is the Wisdom which 'reflects the unmoving mind; a mind clinging to no object'. See *Takuan Zenshi, Bonno, Kito-ryu*.

Hormat see *Setia-hati, Terate, Salutes*.

Horse see *Ba, Ma, Yabusame*.

— **Horse-riding stances** see *Kiba, Mabo*.

Hoshino Kanzaemon see *Wasa Daiichiro*.

Hoshin-ryu A school of *Naginata*, created in the nineteenth century with the aim of producing in its followers a 'perfect intelligence'.

Hoshi Tetsuomi see *Kobu-jutsu*.

Hosokawa-ryu see *Takeda-ryu*.

Hote see *Gyoji, Sechie-zumo*.

Ho Tan see *Tan Phap*.

Ho Vi Cuoc see *Cuoc Phap*.

Hozan-ryu *Kendo*. A school of swordplay created at the end of the nineteenth century, using the *Shinai* for training.

Hozo-in-ryu *Kendo*. A school of swordplay which was restored to popularity at the end of the nineteenth century. The most famous expert in modern times was *Takeda Sokaku Minamoto no Masayoshi* (1858–1943). The school was originally founded by the Buddhist monk Hozo-in Ei (1521–1607), a guardian of the temples of Nara. His successors were all monks. The *Hozo-in-ryu* school was closely connected to the *Shinden Fudo-ryu*.

Hua-quan *Wushu*. A school of Chinese martial arts with the accent on suppleness and swiftness of movement.

Hu Jiao see *Jiao*.

Hung-gar Kung-fu *Wushu*. A style of *Kung-fu* coming from the *Shaolin-si* tradition, using various *Dao* (*Tao, Kata*) which imitate the movements of animals such as the tiger, leopard, heron, monkey and dragon. Techniques of the staff and *Nunchaku* are included in the style.

Huyen Dai see *Kyudan*.

Huyet see *Kyusho*.

Hu-zi Taidu see *Taidu*.

Hwa-rang see *Tae-kwon-do*.

Hyodo. The name given to Japanese martial arts at the beginning of the Edo period (early eighteenth century). Also called *Heido* or military Way. The name was used by *Tsuji Getten Sakemochi* (1650–1729) to describe his own school of martial arts. He was a peasant who invented his own style of fighting with a sword, the *Mugai-ryu*, in 1695, resorting to techniques from the *Yamaguchi-ryu* school.

Hyoho 'Method of strategy', a term which included a certain conception of the world. It was used by *Miyamoto Musashi* to define that state of mind which is favourable for fighting. In the study of Hyoho, one must seek a relationship between the mind and the technique. Theoretically, these cannot be separated from the man himself or the woman herself. When this relationship is found it confers complete confidence in oneself: 'one must respect the gods and the Buddha, but not depend upon them', Miyamoto wrote in his *Gorin-no-sho*. He wrote several works on Hyoho as he understood it, notably the *Hyoho-kyo*, 'Mirror of the Way' (in twenty-eight parts) on the art of strategy, followed by the *Hyoho Sanjugo Kajo*, 'Thirty-five articles on Hyoho'; the forerunners of his major work, the *Gorin-no-sho*, 'Book of Five Rings'. According to Miyamoto Musashi, the concept of Hyoho can be applied to all those disciplines which come under the heading 'Arts of living and dying'. This concept is equivalent to the modern concept of the *Do*.

Hyong *Tae-kwon-do*. A method of training alone enabling the student to learn and assimilate the principle movements of attack and defence against one or several opponents. This solo performance, comparable in this respect with *Taiji Quan*, can bring technical progress. It is the equivalent of Japanese *Kata*. The *Hyong* (also spelt '*Hyung*') round off a student's apprenticeship in the basic movements, or *Ki-bon*. They are numerous and their performance varies with the style and the school concerned. Also called *Poomse*. See *Dao*.

Hyoshi 'Cadence'. According to Tokitsu Kenji, in his book ('The Way of *Karate*' La voie du Karate, Seuil, Paris, 1979), 'when cadences are integrated in a certain way, they give a kind of rhythmic relationship between one or several subjects and their environment. This takes place within the framework of a culturally constituted activity and results in the equilibrium or harmony of the whole.' A cadence can thus be described as a sequence of intervals separating space and time which conditions the body–mind rapport of two opponents. See *Ma-ai*, *Yomi*.

Iai-do. A technique of sword-fighting (*Ken-jutsu*) with the primary aim of drawing the sword from its scabbard (*Saya*) at lightning speed and striking the enemy before he has time to completely draw his own sword or make use of any other weapon he may have. *Iai-do* is a complement of *Ken-jutsu*. The forerunner of *Iai-do* was known as *Iai-jutsu*, and the latter was given its name because it was used in real fighting. Tradition states that it was created in 1560 by *Hayashizaki Jinnosuke Shigenobu*, who founded a school of *Iai-jutsu*. His techniques were perfected by *Eishin* in the eighteenth century (see *Muso Jikiden-ryu*). This discipline, born of the ancient Ken-jutsu, has become a technique of concentration, precision and swiftness of movement. Under the name *Iai-do*, 'Way of Iai', the art of drawing the sword has become a *Budo* in its own right, most of the time combined with the teaching of *Kendo*. Leaving aside the ceremonial gestures and bows, it includes a series of *Kata* and symbolic actions (such as shaking blood from the surface of the sword blade after a duel, so that when the sword is replaced in its sheath the blood will not 'glue' the blade to the sheath and so impede the next swift *Iai* [draw]; see *Chiburi*). All these movements and the Kata are performed standing, kneeling, sitting or even lying down. The movements of Iai-do are today restricted to twenty for 'drawing the sword' and fifty for cutting and slicing, for it is not simply a matter of drawing the sword swiftly from the scabbard, but of striking the enemy *in the same movement*. Iai-do is taught in martial arts schools which specialize in Kendo and Ken-jutsu, but it is also taught in other schools such as the *Katori-Shindo-ryu*, which teach disciplines other than the use of the sword. It is also referred to as *Batto-jutsu*.

In addition to the general martial arts schools, the principal *Ryu* of Iai-do are those belonging to the *Shinto-ryu*, *Chujo-ryu*, *Kage-ryu* and *Nen-ryu*. See also *Batto-jutsu*, *Muso-Shinden-ryu*, *Seitei-gata*.

— **Iai-goshi.** A squatting position used in training for *Iai-do*.

Master Shiokawa demonstrates the art of drawing the sword.

— **Iai-jutsu** see *Iai-do*.

Ibaragi Sensai see *Kito-ryu*.

Ibuki. A technique of sonorous breathing initiated by the muscles of the abdomen (see *Hara*). This technique is mainly used by *Karate* practitioners (see *Goju-ryu*) and helps them to withstand pain and shock when struck by an *Atemi* blow, as well as that experienced when executing *Hishigi* (a breaking technique). It is somewhat akin to the practice of *Kiai*. See *Yoi-ibuki, Nogare*.

Ichiban. 'First', in Japanese. It is used to describe anything which is of the highest quality, and can be applied to things as well as to the techniques of a fighter or contestant.

Ichiden-ryu. A school of sword-fighting created in the nineteenth century.

Ichikawa Mondaiyu see *Kowami*.

I-ching see *Yijing*.

Idori *Judo*. A series of eight fundamental movements (*Kime-no-Kata*) used for self-defence. In this *Kata*, *Tori* and *Uke* face each other in a kneeling position:

Ryo-te-dori: when Uke seizes Tori's wrists, Tori strikes him with his knee in the testicles and applies an armlock.
Tsugake: Tori evades a punch and counters with a punch between Uke's eyes, followed by an armlock.
Tsuri-age: Tori evades a blow from Uke's palm, aimed directly at him or her, by raising Uke's arm from underneath, ending the movement by applying an armlock on Uke across the knee.
Yoko-uchi: Tori evades a punch from Uke, aimed at the temple, by upsetting Uke's

Ibuki breathing performed by a Karate man.

Ibuki breathing technique giving the power to control pain, Shito-ryu Karate school.

balance backwards, finishing the defence with an elbow strike (*Empi-uchi*) to the solar plexus.

Ushiro-dori: Tori counters a rear attack from Uke by grabbing Uke's sleeve and delivering a backward elbow strike to the solar plexus.

Tsukomi: Tori evades a knife thrust at his abdomen by turning to the right. [N.B. All *Kata* are done in a highly stylized form, with large, unrealistic movements on the part of Uke. Readers should not think that a mere body turn is an effective defence against a knife attack.] Tori then strikes Uke between the eyes, ending the movement with an armlock across the knee.

Kirikomi: Tori evades a downward attack with a knife by lifting Uke's arm from underneath, at the same time giving a knee attack to the genital area, finishing the movement with an armlock.

Yoko-tsuki: Tori evades a sideways knife thrust by turning and at the same time turning aside Uke's knife arm, ending with a blow between the eyes and an armlock. See *Tachi-ai, Kime-no-Kata*.

Iga-ryu see *Togakure-ryu, Bansenshukai*.

I-gyeong see *Yijing*.

Iizasa (Choisai) Ienao. *Samurai* (Iizasa Ienao, 1387–1488?) with the title Yamashiro-no-Kami, who created a school of swordsmanship (*Ken-jutsu*) and lance (*So-jutsu*) in the *Shinto* sanctuary of Katori-jingu, in Chiba province. He did this to fulfil a vow. He named the school *Tenshin Shoden (Seiden) Katori Shinto-ryu*, which is better known by the simplified name *Katori Shinto-ryu*. This is the oldest martial arts school in Japan. Iizasa Choisai was the teacher of the *Shogun Ashikaga Yoshimasa*, then he retired from active life and became a Buddhist monk in order to preserve his ethical teaching in a pure state. His favourite weapon was the *Kodachi* or short sword (see *Katana*).

Ikaku-ryu. A school of martial arts created in the seventeenth century which mainly taught the use of the *Jutte*, or short iron truncheon (ancestor of the police truncheon) and of the *Keibo* (short truncheon), combined with the techniques of *Taiho-jutsu*.

Iki-tsuki see *Keri-goho, Tsuki*.

Ikiwake *Judo*. Drawn contest. Korean: *Bikime*.

Ikkyo *Aikido*. 'First principle'. Also called *Ude-osae*, immobilization of *Uke*'s arm by *Shite* as follows:

Ryote-dori, by seizing both wrists.
Katate-ryote-dori, by seizing one wrist with both hands.
Shomen-uchi, by a blow delivered downwards against Uke.
Shomen-tsuki, by striking with the fist.
Ushiro-ryotekubi-dori, by seizing both wrists from behind.
Ushiro-tekubi-kubi-dori, by seizing one wrist from behind with the intention of strangling Uke.
Ushiro-eri-dori, by seizing the neck from behind.

See *Ude-osae, Katame-waza*.

Ikkyu see *Kyu, Obi*.

Iko-kokoro *Wa-jutsu*. A study of states of spiritual consciousness, reserved for those qualified in *Kyoshi* grade in this discipline. See *Kyudan*.

Ilmu see *Setia-hati Terate, Ki*.

Ilyeo see *Poomse*.

Immobilizations on the ground *Judo*. In order that an immobilization on the ground (*Osae-waza*) should count as one point (*Ippon*), it is imperative that *Uke* should not be able to change position for thirty seconds. See *Katame, Kesa-gatame, Kami-shiho-gatame, Yoko-shiho, Shiho-gatame, Osae-waza, Ne-waza*.

In see *Yin-Yang, Mudra*.

Inazuma see *Kyusho*.

Inferior see *Ge, Ha, Shita, Space*.

Initiative see *Sen*.

Interior see *Uchi*.

Intuition see *Genshin, Kan, Sakki, Yomi*.

Inugami (Gubei) Nagayasu see *Kushin-ryu*.

Inu Oi-mono. A sport for training *Samurai* in *Kyuba* (horsemanship combined with archery) which was mainly practised during the Kamakura period (1185–1333). The horsemen had to fire muffled arrows (*Hikime*) at dogs roaming an enclosure some twenty metres in diameter. The 'game' consisted of knocking the dogs down without actually injuring them. Before this period, a similar 'game' was in favour using deer or monkeys. Several variations on this sport existed, depending on the number of Samurai on horseback who were taking part. It was also called *Taka-inu*, 'dog-hunting'. See *Yabusame, Kyuba*.

In-yo see *Yin-Yang*.
— In-yo-shintai see *Omori-ryu*.

Ippon 'One point'. During a contest, when this point is awarded, the referee raises his arm high in front of him. In *Judo* and *Aikido*, this point is scored by one of the following: cleanly throwing *Uke* on to the mat, immobilizing him or her on the mat for at least thirty seconds, a submission on the part of Uke following a stranglehold or an armlock, disqualification of one of the contestants, the scoring of two *waza-ari* by *Tori* or *Shite*, or by the scoring of one *waza-ari* plus an immobilization lasting twenty-five seconds. *Ippon* is worth ten points, *waza-ari* seven points and *uze-gaeshi* five or three, depending on the officials' decision. *Ippon* is scored in **Kendo** by a clean stroke delivered by the *Shinai*; in *Karate* by a recognized blow or a clean throw followed by a recognized blow at an accepted target on the body. Vietnamese: ***Mot-diem***. See *Koka, Yuko*; Competition Rules of *Judo*, 8, 14, 20, 21; *Karate*, 8.
— Ippon-ken Tsuki *Karate*. A straight punch delivered with the clenched fist, either the index or middle finger knuckle protruding beyond the rest. Also called *Nakayubi Ippon Ken*.
— Ippon-kumite *Karate*. A conventional attack using only one technique.
— Ippon-nukite *Karate*. A stabbing attack using only the extended index finger.
— Ippon-Seoi-nage *Judo*. 'Shoulder throw'. *Tori* turns into *Uke* with a hip movement so that his or her right shoulder is under Uke's right armpit at the same time gripping Uke's right arm by the sleeve with both hands. By bending his or her own body forward and tipping Uke in the same

Ippon Seoi-nage

59

direction, Tori throws Uke over his or her shoulder to the mat. This technique can be done on the right side (*Migi Ippon Seoi-nage*) or the left (*Hidari Ippon Seoi-nage*). *Eri Seoi-nage* is an almost identical technique, but in this case Tori lowers his or her hips further to make contact with Uke, so that Uke falls more easily. This is especially useful when Uke is much heavier than Tori. See *Seoi-nage*.

Irimi. This is the positive aspect (*Omote*) of any defensive technique. The aim is to allow an opponent's force to be used against him or her, by yielding. This manoeuvre produces a simultaneous counter-attack. It is also called *Tenkan, O-irimi*.
— **Irimi-nage** *Aikido*. These are throwing techniques belonging to the *Nage-waza* series, performed by *Shite* in response to attacks by *Uke*:

Katate-Ryote-dori, by gripping one wrist with both hands.
Shomen-uchi, by a blow from the fist delivered downwards.
Yokomen-uchi, by a sideways blow.
Shomen-tsuki, by a straight, forward blow.
Ushiro-ryotekubi-dori, by seizing both wrists from behind.
Ushiro-ryo-Kata-dori, by seizing both shoulders from behind.

— **Irimi-tsuki** *Aikido*. A throw carried out by *Shite* on *Uke* in response to an elbow grip (*Hiji-dori*) or a downward blow from above (*Shomen-uchi*). See *Nage-waza*.
— **Irimi-uke** *Karate*. An evasive movement, in a diagonal direction, in response to a blow. The evasion takes place in an outward direction.

Iko no Kokoro see *Kyudan*.

Ishin-den Shin see *Yomi*.

Ishizuki. A steel point fixed to the collar of the shaft of a lance (*Yari*) or a *Naginata*; used in times gone by to pierce the armour of an enemy with a straight thrust.

Iso Mataemon see *Tenjin Shin-yo-ryu*.

Itami-wake. A 'no contest' score given during a team contest if one of the contestants is injured or if the contest is stopped by the doctor.

Itto Ittosai Kagehisa see *Itto-ryu, Chujo-ryu, Heiho*.

Ito Kagehisa see *Ito Ittosai Kagehisa*.

Ito Magoi see *Oku-iai*.

Itosu Anko (1830–1915). A *Karate* master from Okinawa. He developed Karate by adding to the existing technique the Chinese *Kata* known in Japanese as *Pinan* or *Heian*, and also modifying other Kata. His influence was decisive in the evolution of modern Karate as conceived by *Funakoshi Gichin*. See *Jigen-ryu, Shorin-ryu*.

Itosu Kensei see *Heian Kata*.

Itosu Yasutsune see *Mabuni Kenwa*.

Itsusai Chozanshi *Ken-jutsu*. A sword master (*Niwa Jurozaemon*) who lived from 1659 to 1741 and wrote a famous work on martial arts called *Tengu Geijutsu-ron* (Treatise on the martial arts of the *Tengu*); its philosophy was influenced by that of *Zen* and Neo-Confucianism.

Itsutsu no Kata *Judo*. 'Five (principles) of *Kata*'. They are based on:

a push by Tori against *Uke*'s chest, producing a backward fall or a step backwards;
the seizure of Uke's sleeve by Tori, producing a sideways fall on the former;
a turning movement with outstretched arms. This is carried out by Tori on Uke with a *Sutemi* technique, so that Uke falls forward;
a counter-attack by Tori against a rear attack by Uke, causing Uke to lose his balance and fall backwards;
the blocking of a swift attack from Uke, in which Tori makes a barrier of his body parallel to the ground;

These five manoeuvres should be practised in succession, then repeated in reverse order. They end with a salute to the *Kamiza*, as do all *Kata*.

Itto-ryu 'One-sword school', created by Ito Ittosai Kagehisa (1560–1653). He used only one sword, held in both hands. The school had a profound influence on the development of *Kendo*. Its students learned to master the spirit-heart (*Shin*), the spirit-breath of the internal energy (*Ki*) and the energy of the body (*Ryoku*). Through such training they learned to act only when the emotions were quiet and free from any fear or evil intent (see *Makoto*). See *Heiho*, *Hyoho*.

Itto-ryu Seiunkan see *Ken-bu*.

Itto Shoden Muto-ryu see *Muso*.

Iwa-nami see *Ura*.

Iwao no Mi see *Fudoshin*.

Izumo no Kanja see *Shinden Fudo-ryu*.

J

ayu-dae Ryeun see *Randori*.

Jiang A Chinese straight double-edged bladed weapon; used in Chinese and Vietnamese martial arts. Also *Guom*.

Jiao Wushu. Foot techniques used in *Kung-fu*:

Hu Jiao, a very high back-kick.
Yue-liang Jiao, 'a crescent kick', in which the sole of the foot describes a semicircle to the side and then upwards to strike the face.
Yuan Jiao, a circular kick aimed at the side of the body.
Bang Jiao, a side-kick aimed at the face.
Quan-bian Jiao, a straight front-kick.
Xia-lai Jiao, a descending-kick, which brings the foot into a similar finishing position as that reached in *Quan-bian Jiao*.
Da Hu Yuan Jiao, a big kick to the rear similar to a reverse roundhouse kick (see *Mawashi-geri*).

Yue-liang Jiao   Hu Jiao   Bang-jiao

Quan-bian Jiao   Xialai Jiao

Da Hu Yuan Jiao   Yuan Jiao

Jiaodishu see *Kempo*.

Jibun no Tsukuri *Judo*. The preparation of a movement by *Tori*, opposite *Uke*.

Ji-geiko *Kendo*. Freestyle fighting, used in training.

Jigen-ryu. An ancient art of cutting with the sword which gave birth to a particular school in Okinawa, the *Jigen-ryu*. One of the most famous experts of this traditional school was Matsumura Sokon (1809–99), who also created the *Karate* style known as *Shuri-te*, which later became the *Shorin-ryu* school. His direct successors, who also came from Okinawa, were *Itosu Anko* (1832–1916), *Chibana* (1885–1969) and Miyahira Katsuya (1916–). See *Shorin-ryu*, *Tameshi-giri*.

Ken-jutsu. A school of sword-fighting created by *Togo Shigekura Bizen no Kami* (1563–1643). Its techniques were followed by the famous Japanese rebel Saigo Takamori (1827–77) at the time of his revolt on the island of Kyushu in 1877 against obligatory conscription decreed by the Emperor Meiji.

Ji-gong (Chi-kung) *Wushu*. Techniques of *Kung-fu* which call upon the internal energies (*Neijia*). This descipline is practised in China, where adepts claim to be able to cure certain illnesses such as intestinal cancers using the power of *Ji-gong*. The exercises involved are related to those of *Taiji-Quan*.

Jigotai (Jigo-hontai). A basic defensive posture. It may be assumed in the standing posture (*Tachi*), sitting posture (*Za*), on the right (*Migi*) or on the left (*Hidari*).

Ji-in *Karate*. An ancient *Kata* handed down by Buddhist monks who used it in their military training.

Jikan 'Time'. During competitions this is the time deducted from the time-clock. Vietnamese: **Canh**. See Competition Rules of *Karate*, 22.

Jikishin Kage-ryu *Ken-jutsu*. A school of

sword-fighting created by *Yamada Heizae-mon*, who died in 1578. He used it to train the *Bushi*, using a kind of primitive wooden *Shinai* or *Bokken*.

Jikishin-ryu *Judo*. A school of *Ju-jutsu* founded by *Terada Kan-emon*, a low-ranking *Bushi* who belonged to the *Kito-ryu* school. This school was already using the term *Judo* to describe those techniques which did not aim at killing one's opponent. It was the first school of *Budo* to use exclusively empty-hand techniques (unarmed combat).

Jiman *Kyudo*. The sixth position of the archer: holding the bow at full stretch, betraying no sign of effort or strain. This position precedes the *Hanare* or release of the arrow. Also called *Kai*.

-jime see *Shime-waza*.

Jinchu see *Kyusho*, *Head*.

Jin-tachi see *Ba-jutsu*, *Swords*.

Ji-on *Karate*. 'Gratitude for the Buddha', a name given to an ancient *Kata* handed down by Buddhist monks.

Jisai Michie see *Chujo-ryu (Kanemaki-ryu)*.

Jitae see *Poomse*.

Jita-kyo-ei. The principle inherent in the concept of *Wa*, which desires that all beings should be united in a spirit of reciprocal fellowship, for their mutual benefit and prosperity.

Jite A kind of Japanese lance (*Yari*). This consisted of a straight 'spearhead' with two metal blades fixed at the base at right-angles to it, forming a cross. The weapon was used in former times by the foot soldiers (*Zusa*). Training was carried out with a *Jite* which had muffled points, made entirely of wood. The techniques were similar to those of the lance and the long staff. The Jite is no longer regarded as part of the martial arts arsenal and is largely a forgotten weapon, replaced by the *Naginata*.

Jitte see *Sai*, *Jutte*.

Jiu-jitsu see *Ju-jutsu*.

Jiu-kumite (Jiyu-kumite) *Karate*. Freestyle practice without a referee.

Jiyu-renshu Freestyle training.

Jo (1) 'Principle':

Ikka-jo: first principle
Nika-jo: second principle
Sanka-jo: third principle
Yokka-jo: fourth principle
Goka-jo: fifth principle

See also *Kyo*.

Jo (2) 'Surface' on which a contest takes place. See *Dojo*.

Jo (3) 'High', 'Upper'.
— **Jodan** Upper level, as high as the head or higher. Korean: **Sang-dang**; Vietnamese: **Thuong-dang**.

Jodan Age Uke *Karate*. A high block using the rising arm to parry a face punch.
— **Jodan no Kamae** *Kendo*. Position of holding the *Shinai* above the head with one or both hands, before striking straight downwards or to the side.
— **Jodan Kekomi** *Karate*. A straight kick to the face, with a penetrating quality.
— **Jodan Mae-geri** *Karate*. A straight kick to the face or neck areas.
— **Jodan Tensho-uke** *Karate*. A defensive blow to the face of an opponent, using the palm of the hand.
— **Jodan Tsuki** *Karate*. A fist attack to the face of an opponent.
— **Jo-mokuroku** *Aikido*. The name given to those awarded 2nd and 3rd *Dan* grades. See *Kyudan*.
Wa-jutsu. 'Higher studies'. Those who have reached this grade wear a white *Keikogi* and a black belt with two violet-coloured bands.
— **Joseki** see *Kamiza*, *Dojo*, *Body*.
— **Jo-sokutei** *Karate*. A blow delivered with the sole of the raised foot.

Jo (4) Short staff (1.20 m approximately), round in section, made of very hard wood,

Drawing of Jite techniques by Hokusai.

Demonstration of a Jo attack against a Boken in a Karate Dojo.

used in the practice of *Jo-jutsu* and *Jodo*. Vietnamese: **Tien-bong**; Chinese: **Gun**.

Joints see *Kansetsu*.

Jo-jutsu. A technique of martial arts using the short staff (*Jo*), invented in the seventeenth century by *Muso Gonnosuke*. He found that the long staff (*Bo*) was not successful enough against an enemy armed with a sword, so he invented a different technique. Legend tells that using the Jo he was able to defeat Miyamoto Musashi in combat, and in so doing inflicted upon him the only defeat of his entire life. Thus Muso Gonnosuke created the *Shindo Muso-ryu*. *Jo-jutsu* does not aim to kill an enemy but to disable him so that he is harmless. Its techniques were brought to a level of maximum efficiency by the *Shindo Muso-ryu* school, which taught sixty-four basic movements. The *Katori Shinto-ryu* school teaches in its own syllabus only twelve techniques using the Jo, of which six are in the domain of 'Higher studies' (*Jo-mokuroku*). These twelve basic movements (*Kata*) were

codified in 1955 and Jo-jutsu thus became *Jodo*, 'the Way of the short staff'. Both in training and in combat the students wear no form of protection. They wear *Hakama* and *Haori* and in general practice in the open air. A practitioner of this art is called a *Shijo*. The Japanese police make use of a type of short staff (*Keijo*) to deal with street incidents. See also *Bo*, *Bo-jutsu*.
— **Jodo** see *Jo-jutsu*.

Jogai. This describes a situation in which two contestants go beyond the limits of the mat area or floor area in which they are competing.

Jokki see *Ashi-waza*.

Jo-no-kuchi see *Sumotori*.

Jo-nidan see *Sumotori*.

Joran-zumo see *Sumo*.

Joseki see *Dojo*, *Kamiza*.

Joshi Judo Goshinho *Judo*. Techniques of self-defence for women, created by the experts of the *Kodokan* in Tokyo. These techniques concentrate on methods of escaping from grips (*Ridatsu-ho*) and on counter-attacks (*Seigo-ho*).

Joza see *Kamiza*.

Ju 'Soft', 'Pliant', 'Adaptable', 'Yielding', 'Harmonious'. This Sino-Japanese written character has often been translated as 'Gentle'. The interpretation of the meaning of 'gentle' in relation to the practice of martial arts is frequently misleading. Many people have equated gentle with weak, when in fact the character contains more an idea of flexibility, in both mind and body. When a bamboo or willow branch is laden down with snow, it yields; it is flexible towards the new 'circumstances', and by yielding it allows the snow to fall to the ground, preserving its own existence and springing back into place with more force and speed than was employed in its yielding and bending action. The concept of *Ju* therefore implies flexibility and suppleness in direct proportion to subsequent speed and force. It is the direct opposite of hardness, or *Go*. Thus, whatever word is used to translate '*Ju*', that word in itself will be insufficient without a practical explanation of its meaning. Vietnamese: **Nhu.** See *Ju-no-ri*, *Judo*, *Ju-jutsu*.

Juban no Ma-ai see *Ma*, *Ma-ai*.

Judo. 'Way of gentleness', a nonviolent, basically defensive martial art created in 1882 by *Kano Jigoro* (1860–1938). It is mainly based on the techniques of unarmed combat used in *Ju-jutsu* as practised by the *Bushi*. The word *Judo* itself had already been used by the *Jikishin-ryu* of *Ju-jutsu* to describe their own art of combat, which relied on techniques which were not fatal. It was revived and used by Kano Jigoro, who wished to turn Ju-jutsu into a 'martial sport', to train and educate the young. He said: 'the aim of Judo is to understand and demonstrate the living laws of movement.' To this end, Kano Jigoro codified a certain number of body, arm and leg movements used in Ju-jutsu which had shown themselves very effective in hand-to-hand combat. They covered fighting on the floor and standing up. Kano Jigoro used those aspects of these techniques which could upset an opponent's balance (*Kuzushi*) and also immobilize him or her. The overall aim was to be able to neutralize an opponent. He thus created an art of self-defence which is learned in conjunction with a study of the fundamental movements, with a partner. This is expanded into training in freestyle combat known as *Randori*, in which the opponent, or 'the one who submits' (*Uke*), is thrown to the mat and immobilized by 'the one who throws' (*Tori*). Training and contests take place in a *Judojo* (shortened to *Dojo*), on a surface covered with *Tatami* to soften the falls (*Ukemi*). As in all the martial arts, the practitioners of Judo (*Judoka*) seek to acquire suppleness of body and limbs, speed of body shifting (*Tai-sabaki*), perfect balance through the control of the breath and the concentration of the energies in the *Hara*, as well as a thorough knowledge of the techniques of the art. A spirit of detachment and serenity should prevail throughout. Students must aim to be in a state of permanent alertness (*Hontai*), without allowing any 'dead moments' (*Bonno*). Armed with a disciplined mind, calm and serene, with controlled body and reactions, such students will then be able to bring about the downfall of any adversary with ease.

Judo was created in Tokyo in the Buddhist temple known as Eiho-ji in 1882. It developed rapidly and the first black belt grade (see *Obi*, *Kyudan*) was conferred by Kano Jigoro on Taira Shiro in 1883. When Kano Jigoro came to Europe in 1889 to teach his techniques, his Dojo numbered some 600 pupils. After a demonstration which he gave in Marseilles during the same year, the first Dojo were established in France, notably in Paris under the direction of Jean-Joseph Renaud and Guy de Montgrillard. Back in Japan, the founder continued his work and in 1922 he established the *Kodokan*, which was to become the official centre of Judo.

From the end of the nineteenth century, Great Britain received visits from various Japanese Ju-jutsu instructors. (The name used was not *Ju-jutsu* but *Jiu-jitsu*.) By 1918 the influence of Kano Jigoro's relatively new Judo was growing stronger, and in this year *Koizumi Gunji* founded the *Budokwai* martial arts school in London. At about the same time two British Judoka, W.E. Steers and E.J. Harrison, were awarded black belt grades in Japan, and they strengthened the ranks at the Budokwai. In 1920 Kano Jigoro visited London and absorbed the Judo and Jiu-Jitsu fraternities into his International Kodokan Affiliates. During the next two decades, until the outbreak of the Second World War, Judo grew steadily in popularity, urged on by Koizumi Gunji, visiting Japanese instructors and an increasing band of skilled British exponents.

After the war the first international Judo tournament between Great Britain and France was won by the British, in 1947. In 1951 the first European Championship was won by the French team. By 1956 Judo had become an obligatory sport in all Japanese schools and for a time the Japanese dominated all world championships, with Judoka such as Natsui and Yoshimatsu in the first world event, and Sone and Kaminaga in the second. But in 1961 the giant Dutchman Anton Geesink defeated the Japanese champion Sone, and from then onwards it appeared that the advantage lay with the biggest and heaviest competitors. The recognition of this fact led to the creation of weight categories such as those used in boxing. This step was contrary to the concept of Judo, as formulated by Kano Jigoro, but in the postwar period Western Judo organizations began to see Judo more and more as a competitive sport and less and less as an approach to life itself. This gradually led to an ideological split between the sport-orientated Judoka and those who still clung to the ideals of the founder, and to Japanese martial arts traditions. A similar dichotomy can be found in all martial arts which have left their native shores and put down roots in Western countries. The division into weight categories had come at the same time as the 1964 Olympic Games in Tokyo. It was timely to say the least, for the Japanese did not want to see themselves totally defeated in their own country. Although Geesink and later his fellow Dutchman, Ruska, dominated the heavyweight division, the Japanese were still the champions in the other divisions, in world championships. It was not until 1969 that a Japanese heavyweight, Shinomani, took the title by beating Ruska in Mexico. Since its debut as an Olympic sport in 1964 Judo has seen several changes in rules, but the weight categories have finally been fixed as follows:

	Men	Women
Super-lightweight:	– from 60 kg	– from 48 kg
Semi-lightweight:	– from 60 to 65 kg	– from 48 to 52 kg
Lightweight:	– from 65 to 71 kg	– from 52 to 56 kg
Semi-middleweight:	– from 71 to 78 kg	– from 56 to 61 kg
Middleweight:	– from 78 to 86 kg	– from 61 to 66 kg
Light-middleweight:	– from 86 to 95 kg	– from 66 to 72 kg
Heavyweight:	– over 95 kg	– over 72 kg

The World championships were created in 1956 and take place every two years.

The men's European championships were inaugurated in 1951; the women's European championships in 1982.

There is also a European Cup for clubs, created in 1974, as well as numerous international tournaments.

When Kano Jigoro created Judo he was resolutely opposed to all public competitions, as he considered that it must be a personal art of training the mind and body. One of the last and memorable French representatives of the true Kodokan spirit, Yves Klein (1928–62), worked exclusively on the gentle aspect of Judo, never giving way to the temptation to use force. He was a 4th *Dan* black belt grade who qualified at the Kodokan in Tokyo. It would be untrue to say that Judoka with the same spirit no longer exist, but they are the exception rather than the rule.

The essence of Judo is encapsulated in an oath which Judo students at the Kodokan must take on admission to the Dojo:

> Once I have entered the Kodokan, I will not end my study without reasonable cause.
> I will not dishonour the Dojo.
> Unless I am given permission, I will not disclose the secrets which I have been taught.
> Unless I am given permission, I will not teach Judo.
> Pupil first, teacher second, I will always follow the rules of the Dojo.

For Judo was, in the spirit of Kano Jigoro, not only an art of unarmed self-defence but, more emphatically, a philosophy, an art of daily living: 'The study of the general principles of Judo', he said, 'is more important than the simple practice of Ju-jutsu.'

Unfortunately, present-day Judo competition grows further and further away from the spirit of the founder. It becomes, in fact, a trial of strength between opponents, and belongs more to the field of wrestling than to true Judo. This is why, perhaps, some other martial arts disciplines such as *Aikido* or *Karate* have progressively won favour among the followers of the martial arts; though Karate also has degenerated into a

Throwing technique known as Sumi-otoshi.

contest largely emphasizing aggression. In spite of everything, Judo is currently one of the most widespread sports in the world, with several million students. In England there are 2,382 black belt grades, and approximately 60,000 licensed practitioners. Judo training is done in stages. It covers standing techniques (*Tachi-waza*) and floor fighting techniques (*Ne-waza*).

Each of the stages (*Kyo*) is marked by the award of a coloured belt. This indicates to others the grade (*Kyu*) which the wearer has attained. The black belt grades and above (*Dan*) are the higher grades. The belts also serve to keep the *Judogi* or uniform closed. See also *Keikogi, Kyudan, Gokyo*.

The competitions (*Shiai*) take place under the auspices of a referee and judges. A certain number of Japanese terms which apply to the conduct of such competitions have been retained. Judo techniques rely heavily on body shifting (*Tsugi-ashi, Tai-sabaki*), on repetition of movements (*Uchi-komi*) during training, and on freestyle fighting (*Randori*). In addition to the action of gripping the *Judogi* (*Kumi-Kata*), the principal movements of Judo are:

a series of throws (*Nage-waza*)
techniques of control (*Katame-no-Kata*)
immobilizations on the ground (*Osaekomi-waza*)
strangulation techniques (*Shime-waza*)
techniques of bending and locking the joints (*Kansetsu-waza*)

They also include some techniques of self-defence against an armed attacker (*Kime-no-Kata*). It goes without saying that the study of 'formal movements', the *Kata*, is carried out in detail.

— **Judogi.** The clothing worn specifically for *Judo* training (*Keiko*). It is made of

Hold-down or immobilization known as Makura-kesa-gatame.

thick, white cotton, or unbleached cotton. It consists of a pair of large, baggy trousers (*Zubon*), a wide-fitting jacket (*Uwagi*) with wide sleeves coming halfway down the forearm (*Sode*), and a belt (*Obi*), which is white, black or a colour conforming to the grade of the wearer. *Judoka* train in bare feet on the *Tatami* or mats. The place where they study is called a *Dojo*. See *Kyudan, Obi*.

— **Judojo.** The training hall for *Judo*, its floor covered with *Tatami*. The term is generally shortened to '*Dojo*'.

— **Judoka.** A practitioner of *Judo*.

The Rules of Judo Based on the Contest Rules of the International Judo Federation

Article 1. COMPETITION AREA

The competition area shall measure between 14 × 14 m and 16 × 16 m. It must be covered with *Tatami* or similarly accepted material, generally green in colour. The competition area shall be divided into two zones, surrounded by a border of red *Tatami*, approximately 1 m wide, attached to the mat and parallel to it, which will also divide the two contest areas. The demarcation area between the two zones shall be called the danger area.

All that area between the danger zones and including them shall be called the contest area and shall be between 9 × 9 m and 10 × 10 m. The area outside the contest area shall be called the safety area, between 2.5 m and 3 m wide.

In the centre of the contest area shall be fixed a red and a white strip of adhesive tape, 4 m apart. Both tapes shall be 6 cm wide and 25 cm long. They indicate the points at which contestants must start and end the contest. The red tape shall be on the right of the referee and the white on his left.

The competition area must be fixed to a resilient floor or platform (see Appendix).

If there are two or more adjacent competition areas, a common safety zone is permitted, at least 3 m wide.

A free zone of at least 50 cm must be maintained around the competition area.

Tatami

Traditionally, *Tatami* should be rectangular units measuring 1.83 m × 91.5 cm or slightly smaller, according to the regions of Japan. Today, they generally measure 1 × 2 m and are made of pressed straw, or more frequently from pressed foam. They must be firm and be capable of absorbing shock during '*Ukemi*'.

They must be covered with a plasticized material which is neither too slippery nor too rough, and coloured green or red.

These units making up the surface of the competition area must be juxtaposed, without a space between them, giving an unbroken surface and fixed so that they will not be displaced.

Platform

The platform is optional. It must be made of solid wood which also gives some resilience, and measure approximately 18 m from side to side and at least 50 cm high.

Article 2. EQUIPMENT

(a) Chairs and flags (judges)

Two lightweight chairs must be placed on the safety area at diagonally opposite corners of the contest area, placed in such a way that they do not obstruct the view of the judges and recorders when they need to see the scoreboard. A red flag and a white flag shall be placed in a holster fixed to each chair. (See the International Judo Federation sporting code.)

(b) Scoreboard

Two scoreboards for each contest area shall be placed diagonally outside the competition area, so that they can easily be seen by the judges.

When electronic scoreboards are used, manual scoreboards must be available in reserve (see Appendix).

(c) Timing clocks

There shall be timing clocks as follows:
one to time contest duration; one to time *osaekomi*; one in reserve.
When electronic timing clocks are used,

manual timing clocks must be used for checking and others kept in reserve (see Appendix).

(d) Flags (Timekeepers)

Timekeepers shall use flags as follows:
yellow for the duration of a contest; blue when *osaekomi* is in progress; green for injuries.

When electronic display clock(s) are in use, the yellow, blue and green flags shall not be necessary, but should be kept available.

(e) Signal for the end of the contest

A bell or similar audible device shall indicate to the referee that a contest has ended.

(f) Red and white sashes

Every contestant shall wear a red or a white sash at least 5 cm wide and long enough to go once round the waist, on top of the belt. When tied, the sash should protrude at each end by 20 to 30 cm. (The first competitor called shall wear red, and the second white. See the IJF sporting code.)

(g) Medical examination batons

Two crosses, one red and one white, shall be displayed on the scoreboard to indicate the need for medical attention (see Appendix, Articles 8 and 31).

(h) Position of recorders/scorers/timekeepers

As far as possible the scorers and the timekeepers should face the referee and be well in view of the recorders.

(i) Distance of spectators

Spectators should be allowed no closer than 3 metres from the competition area.

(j) Reserve manual timing clocks

The clocks must be close at hand and checked for accuracy at the start of the competition.

(k) Reserve manual scoreboards

The scoreboards must correspond to IJF requirements (see below) and be readily available to officials if needed.

PÉNALITÉ PENALTY	POINTAGE SCORE		POINTAGE SCORE	PÉNALITÉ PENALTY
		WAZA-ARI		
		YUKO		
		KOKA		

Article 3. UNIFORM

The contestants must wear a *Judogi* (*Judo* uniform) complying with the following stipulations:

(a) Strongly made of cotton or similar material and in good condition (without rent or tear).

(b) White or offwhite, without excessive markings.

(c) The jacket must be long enough to cover half the thighs.

(d) The jacket sleeves must cover over half the forearm but not extend beyond the wrists. There must be a space of 5 to 8 cm between the sleeve and the forearm (including bandages) along the whole length of the sleeve.

(e) The trousers must be free of any markings and long enough to cover more than half the calf, without going beyond the ankles. There must be a space of 5 to 8 cm between the leg (including bandages) and the trouser leg.

(f) A strong belt, 4 to 5 cm wide, of a colour corresponding to the grade of the competitor, shall be worn over the jacket at waist level, and tied with a flattened knot. It must be tight enough to prevent the jacket from being too loose and long enough to go twice around the waist, leaving between 20 and 30 cm protruding from each side of the finished knot.

(g) Female contestants shall wear a plain white or offwhite T-shirt under the jacket, with short sleeves and long enough to reach inside the trousers.

Should a female contestant need to leave the contest area to change any part of her uniform, and the judges are not female, the organizing committee shall designate a female official to accompany the contestant.

If a competitor's *Judogi* does not conform to this article, the referee must order the competitor to change into one which does so conform, as quickly as possible.

If the referee considers that the sleeves of a competitor's jacket are too short or too narrow, he must ask him or her to extend the arms to a horizontal position in order to verify his judgement.

Any competitor who will not comply with the requirements of articles 3 and 4 shall be refused the right to compete (see Article 30).

Article 4. HYGIENE

(a) The *Judogi* must be clean, dry and without an unpleasant smell.

(b) Toenails and fingernails must be cut short.

(c) The personal hygiene of the contestant shall be satisfactory.

(d) Long hair must be tied to avoid causing inconvenience to the other contestant.

Any contestant who refuses to comply with Articles 3 and 4 shall be refused the right to compete (see Article 30).

Article 5. OFFICIALS

As a rule, the contest shall be conducted by one referee and two judges, assisted by recorders and timekeepers.

The timekeepers and recorders, as well as other technical assistants (used at British Judo Association – BJA – events), must have *judo* experience. For all BJA events recorders must be at least sixteen years of age. (This varies in different countries. In France, for instance, it is given as twenty-one years of age.) For national events timekeepers must be at least sixteen and for all other BJA events at least fourteen. The organizers of a national event must ensure that all officials have been thoroughly trained. There shall be a minimum of two timekeepers: one to register the real contest time and one to specialize in *osaekomi*. If possible there should be a third person to supervise the two timekeepers to avoid any errors due to mistakes or forgetfulness. At all other BJA events the table should be manned as per the Tournament Handbook.

The overall timekeeper (real contest time) starts his watch on hearing the words *hajime* or *yoshi* and stops it on hearing the words *matte* or *sonomama*.

The *osaekomi* timekeeper starts his watch and lifts the blue flag on hearing *osaekomi*, stops it on *sonomama*, and restarts it on hearing *yoshi*. On hearing *toketa* he stops his watch, lowers the blue flag, and indicates the number of seconds elapsed to the referee, or on expiry of the time for *osaekomi* (thirty seconds where there has been no previous score or twenty-five seconds where the person being held in the *osaekomi* has had a *waza-ari* or *keikoku* awarded against him) indicates the end of the *osaekomi* by means of a signal.

The overall timekeeper (real contest time) shall raise a yellow flag whenever he stops the watch on hearing the command and seeing the signal of *matte* or *sonomama* and shall lower the flag when he restarts the watch on hearing *hajime* or *yoshi*.

When the time allowed for the contest has expired, the timekeepers shall warn the referee with a clear, audible signal (see Articles 12 and 13 of the competition rules).

The contest recorder must be sure that he is completely informed of all the current gestures and signals used to indicate the result of a contest.

In addition to the above persons there shall be a list-writer to record the overall course of the contests.

If electronic systems are used, the procedure shall be the same as that described above. Nevertheless, manual recording devices must be available.

Any competitor who fails to take his place on the contest area after three calls at one-minute intervals shall forfeit the match.

Article 6. POSITION AND FUNCTION OF THE REFEREE

The referee shall generally stay within the contest area. He shall conduct the contest and administer judgement. He shall ensure that his decisions are correctly recorded.

When the referee announces his appraisal of a contest, he shall do so without losing sight of the contestants while maintaining his signal, and also be in a position to observe if the judge whose position allows him to assist him better is indicating a different appraisal, showing in this way his disagreement.

In cases where both contestants are in *ne-waza* and facing outwards, the referee may observe the action from the safety area (extract from the IJF sporting code).

Before they officiate at a competition, the referees and judges must familiarize themselves with the sound of the bell or other means of indicating the end of the contest on their particular mat (as they may vary).

When the referee and judges assume control of a contest area they must ensure that the surface is clean and in good condition, with no gaps between the mats (See Article 1 – Appendix); that the chairs and flags to be used by the judges are in place; and that the contestants comply with Articles 3 and 4 of the competition rules. The referees must ensure that there are no spectators, supporters or photographers in a position to cause nuisance or injury to the contestants. (See Appendix of Article 2.)

Article 7. POSITION AND FUNCTION OF THE JUDGES

The judges must assist the referee and sit opposite each other at the corners, outside the contest area. Each judge must indicate his opinion by making the official, appropriate signal each time he disagrees with the referee on technical appraisal or with a penalty announced by the referee.

If the referee expresses an opinion of a higher degree than that of the two judges on a technical result or a penalty, he must adjust his appraisal to that of the judge with the higher appraisal.

If the referee expresses an opinion which is lower than that of one judge and higher than that of the other, the referee's opinion may stand.

If the referee expresses an opinion of a lower degree than that of both judges on a technical result or penalty he must adjust his appraisal to that of the lower of the two judges.

Should both judges express a judgement different from that of the referee and the referee not notice their signals, they must stand up and maintain their signals until the referee is informed and rectifies his appraisal.

If, after a few seconds, the referee has not noticed the standing judges, the judge who is closest to him must immediately approach him and inform him of the majority decision.

The judge must express, by the appropriate gesture, his opinion on the validity of any action on the edge or outside of the contest area.

Discussions between the referee and judges are possible and necessary only if one of them has witnessed something which the other two have not seen which could change the decision. Nevertheless, the one in the minority must be sure of what he has seen so as to avoid useless discussion. The judges must also observe that the scores recorded by the contest recorder tally with those announced by the referee.

If a contestant temporarily leaves the competition area for any reason considered necessary by the referee, it is obligatory for a judge to accompany him to see that no irregular behaviour occurs. Only in exceptional circumstances shall such authorization be given (to change uniform which does not conform to the competition requirements.)

The referee and the judges should leave the competition areas during presentations or for any lengthy delay in the programme.

A judge should sit with both feet placed on the mat in front of his chair, and with his hands palm down on his knees.

A judge must not make any alteration to the scoreboard unless directed to do so by the referee. However, should a judge notice that the scoreboard is incorrect he should draw the referee's attention to the error.

A judge must be quick to remove himself and his chair if his position endangers the contestants.

If a judge disagrees with the opinion of the referee, or if the referee does not signal an opinion, the judge must signal his own opinion.

A judge should not pre-empt the referee's signal for a score.

If an action takes place on the edge of the contest area, the judge must first signal whether the action is 'in' or 'out' – then signal (if necessary) whether the subsequent action is 'in' or 'out'.

If his or her contest area is not in use and there is a contest in progress on an adjacent area, the judge should remove the chair if it could endanger the contestants in that area.

If a judge signals that an action is 'out' – for example if the referee signals 'ippon' and the other judge a lesser score – a majority decision should first decide if the action was 'in' or 'out' and then, if it is judged 'in', a majority decision should decide the score.

Article 8. GESTURES BY THE REFEREE

The diverse announcements of the referee must be accompanied by the following actions:

(I) *Ippon*: raise one arm high above the head, palm facing forward.

(II) *Waza-ari*: raise one arm horizontally, sideways, palm down.

(III) *Waza-ari awasete ippon*: signal for *waza-ari* followed by signal for *ippon*.

(IV) *Yuko*: raise one arm sideways, palm

down, to an angle of 45 degrees.

(V) *Koka*: raise one arm with the thumb close to the shoulder and the elbow close to the chest.

(VI) *Osaekomi*: point his arm towards the contestants, palm down, while bending towards them, and facing them.

(VII) *Toketa*: raise one arm to the front and wave it from right to left, thumb uppermost, two or three times.

(VIII) *Hiki-wake*: raise one arm high in the air, then lower it in front of him, thumb edge uppermost, holding it there for a while.

(IX) *Matte*: raise one arm to the horizontal, towards the timekeeper, palm vertical.

(X) *Sonomama*: bend forward and touch both contestants with the palms of his hands.

(XI) *Yoshi*: press firmly with the palms of his hands on both contestants.

(XII) To indicate a technique which is not considered valid: raise one hand in front of him and above his head and wave it from right to left two or three times.

(XIII) To indicate the cancellation of an opinion: repeat the signal which indicated his opinion with one hand, and raise the other in front of himself and above his head and wave it from right to left two or three times.

(XIV) *Hantei*: raise one arm high above the head, palm facing inwards.

(XV) To indicate the winner of a contest (by *yusei-gachi*, *kiken-gachi*, *fusen-gachi* or *sogo-gashi*): raise one hand, palm in, above shoulder height in the direction of the winner.

(XVI) To indicate to the competitor(s) the need to adjust *judogi*: cross the left hand over the right, palms inwards, at belt level.

(XVII) To indicate failure to fight: rotate the forearms at chest height, then point with the index finger at the contestant concerned.

(XVIII) To award a penalty (*shido, chui, keikoku, hansoku-make*): point towards the offender with the index finger extended and the fist closed.

(XIX) To indicate the recording of a medical examination by the doctor, the referee shall signal with the hand opened towards the doctor and with the other hand raise the index finger towards the recorder

for the first examination and the index and middle finger for the second examination, palm of the hand facing the table.

Having made the official gesture or signal the referee may, if the need arises, point to the red or white strip of adhesive tape to indicate which competitor has scored or was penalized.

If a lengthy delay in the contest occurs, the referee signals to the contestants that they may sit cross-legged at their respective starting positions by pointing to those positions with hands open, palms up.

Yuko and *waza-ari* signals should start with the arm across the chest, then move sideways to the correct finishing position.

The referee must maintain the signals for *koka, yuko* and *waza-ari* while he makes a 90-degree turn so that he is sure that his signals are seen by the judges. Even so he must take care that he has both contestants in view as he does this.

Should both contestants be given a warning for failure to fight, the referee shall point alternatively at both of them (left index finger for the one on his left; right for the one on his right).

If a rectification gesture is needed it should immediately, or as quickly as possible, follow the annulment gesture.

When cancelling a score or penalty no announcement should be made.

All gestures should be maintained for at least three seconds.

To indicate a winner the referee should return to his starting position, take one step forward, indicate the winner, then take one step back.

Article 9. CONTEST (location – control – judgement)

The contest shall take place on the contest area (see Article 1). It shall be controlled and judged on the basis of Articles 16 to 32 inclusive.

Article 10. LOCATION (valid areas)

The contest shall take place on the contest

area. No technique is valid if it is performed with one of the contestants outside that area. Furthermore, a contestant shall be adjudged outside if his or her foot, hand or knee is outside during a *tachi-waza*, or if more than half his or her body crosses outside during a *sutemi-waza* or during *ne-waza*.

Exceptions:

(a) When one contestant throws the opponent outside the contest area and he or she stays within the contest area long enough for the effectiveness of the technique to be recognized and clearly apparent.

(b) When *osaekomi* has been announced, the contest may continue until the time allowed for the *osaekomi* has expired, until one contestant submits, or *toketa* is announced, so long as at least one contestant has any part of his or her body touching the contest area.

(c) If during the course of an attack such as *o-uchi-gari* or *ko-uchi-gari* the foot or leg of the thrower (*Tori*) leaves the contest area and goes over the safety area, the action shall be considered valid (for scoring purposes) so long as the thrower does not place any weight on the foot or leg while it is outside the contest area.

Uke may apply a *shime-waza* or a *kansetsu-waza* after the anouncement of *osaekomi* even if more than half his or her body is outside the contest area. However, *matte* must be announced if the *osaekomi* is broken or if both the contestants move completely out of the contest area.

In the case of '*osaekomi* on the edge', if that part of the contestant's body touching the contest area is raised clear of the mat, the referee must announce *toketa* and then *matte*.

If, during the course of a throw, *Tori* leaves the actual surface of the combat area – that is, becomes completely 'airborne' and is not in contact with any part of the floor – the technique is valid from the point of view of scoring if *Uke* makes contact with the mat before any part of *Tori*'s body touches the exterior surface of the contest area.

As the coloured danger area which defines the contest area from the safety area is immediately inside the boundary of the contest area, any contestant whose feet are still touching the coloured danger area in the standing position should be considered to be within the contest area.

During the performance of a *sutemi-waza*, a throw is considered valid if at least half *Tori*'s body is within the contest area. (Thus *Tori*'s feet must not leave the contest area before either his or her back or hips touch the mat.)

In *ne-waza*, the action is valid and may continue so long as both contestants have at least half their bodies inside the contest area.

If *Tori* falls outside the contest area whilst executing a technique, the action is considered valid from a scoring point of view if *Uke*'s body touches the mat before *Tori*'s. Therefore if any part of Tori's body, including hand or knee, touches the safety area before any part of Uke's body, the result should be disregarded.

Once the contest has begun, the contestants may not leave the contest area unless the referee gives permission. Such permission is given only in very exceptional cases (to change a *judogi* which does not conform to Article 3, or has become damaged or soiled).

Article 11. DURATION OF CONTEST

The duration of a contest must be that laid down in the sporting code (see Appendix on periods of recuperation).

During World Championships and the Olympic Games, the duration of contests is determined by the IJF sporting code.

The referee should be made aware of the duration of a contest before he comes on to the mat.

The contest ends at the expiry of the allotted time and not when the referee announces *sore-made*.

The duration of the contest and its form shall be determined by the rules of the tournament.

Any contestant is allowed to rest between contests for a time equal to the anticipated duration of his next contest.

Article 12.   TIME OUT

The time which elapses between the calls of *matte* and *hajime* and between the calls of *sonomama* and *yoshi* shall not count as part of the duration of the contest.

The referee may interrupt a contest following an acceptable minor incident which befalls a contestant (e.g. a nose bleed, broken nail, disarranged bandages, etc.). The same applies if a contestant is injured, and a doctor may be called if the referee thinks it necessary. Even so, the length of the interruption should be kept to a minimum. If the referee notices that a contestant is injured or indisposed, he may interrupt the contest and ask for a doctor to proceed with a quick examination.

If the doctor considers that the contestant cannot continue with the contest immediately, he must so inform the referee and judges.

The referee then stops the contest and a decision is given according to Article 32.

Article 13.   SIGNAL FOR THE END OF THE CONTEST

The end of the time allotted to the contest shall be indicated to the referee by the ringing of a bell or similar audible device.

In the case of simultaneous use of several contest areas, the use of varying audible devices is necessary.

The sound of the signal indicating the end of the contest should be sufficiently loud to be heard above the noise of the crowd.

Article 14.   IMMOBILIZATION TIME – OSAEKOMI

(I) *Ippon*: total of 30 seconds.

(II) *Waza-ari*: 25 seconds or more, but less than 30 seconds.

(III) *Yuko*: 20 seconds or more, but less than 25 seconds.

(IV) *Koka*: 10 seconds or more, but less than 20 seconds.

An immobilization of less than 10 seconds will be counted the same as an attack.

If *osaekomi* is announced before or at the same time as the signal indicating the end of the contest, the time allotted to the contest is prolonged until the award of *ippon* (or its equivalent) or the announcement of *toketa* or of *matte* by the referee.

Article 15.   TECHNIQUE WHICH COINCIDES WITH THE TIME SIGNAL

Any technique applied successfully at the moment at which the time signal is given shall be considered valid.

Any technique applied after the time signal from the bell or any other audible device which indicates the end of the contest is not valid, even if the referee has not announced *sore-made*.

Although a throwing technique may be applied simultaneously with the bell, if the referee decides that it will not be effective immediately, he should announce *sore-made*.

Article 16.   START OF THE CONTEST

The contestants must stand face to face on the contest area at the place indicated by the strips of coloured adhesive tape corresponding to the colours of the sashes they are wearing (red or white). After the contestants have performed the standing bow and stepped forward one pace, the referee shall announce *hajime* to start the contest.

The contest must always begin from a standing position.

Before the start of each contest, the three officials (referee and two judges) shall stand together inside the limits of the competition area (in the centre) and shall bow together towards the *joseki* before taking their places.

The referee and the judges must always be in their respective places on the mat and ready to start the contest before the competitors arrive in the contest area.

The referee must stand in the centre, about two metres back from the starting and finishing positions of the contestants. He must face the timekeeper's table.

The contestants must bow at the beginning and end of the contest. If they fail to do so the referee must call them back, saying 'rei', then begin the contest by saying 'hajime'.

The referee must not bow with, or to, the contestants.

Before the contest starts, the referee must be sure that 'all is correct': contest area and surface, material, uniforms, hygiene, officials, etc. (extract from the IJF sporting code).

The first three officials (referee and two judges) who 'open' the mat before the first contest of the session (morning, afternoon, evening) must bow together towards the *joseki* before taking their respective places. The three officials who 'close' the mat after the last contest must repeat this action of bowing to the *joseki*. Between the first and the last contest of the same session, the referee and judges must discreetly take their places on the mat as quickly as possible.

Article 17. ENTRY INTO NE-WAZA (Groundwork)

The contestants may pass from standing positions and enter *ne-waza* in the following cases, although the referee may bring them back to a standing position if he considers that the technique which brings *ne-waza* about has not been a continuous one.

(a) When a contestant has obtained a certain result from a throwing technique and changes without a break in movement into *ne-waza* and takes the offensive.

(b) When a contestant falls following an unsuccessful attempt at a throw, the other may follow him down to the mat; if he merely loses his balance and is in danger of falling, the other may take advantage of his loss of balance to follow him to the mat.

(c) When a contestant obtains a telling result through *shime-waza* (strangulation) or *kansetsu-waza* (a lock) in a standing position and follows this through without interruption into *ne-waza* (groundwork).

(d) When a contestant takes the opponent down into *ne-waza* by the clever use of a movement which, although resembling a throwing technique, does not qualify as such.

For example, when a contestant performs *hikomi-gaeshi* (a locked-together rolling action), if the contestants separate at the end of the action, the result shall be considered as a throw and counted as such.

(e) In any other case not mentioned in this article where a contestant may fall down or be about to fall down, the other may take advantage of the situation to bring his opponent down into *ne-waza*.

Article 18. APPLICATION OF 'MATTE' (Wait)

In the following cases, the referee must announce '*matte*' to stop the contest temporarily, and 'hajime' to restart it:

(a) When one or both contestant(s) leave the contest area.

(b) When either or both of the contestants perform a forbidden action.

(c) When either or both of the contestants are injured or become ill.

(d) When either or both of the contestants need to adjust the *judogi*.

(e) When no apparent progress is made in *ne-waza* and the two contestants find themselves in a position leading to no result, such as *ashi-garami* (entangled legs).

(f) When one contestant regains a standing position with the other clinging to his back, following *ne-waza*.

(g) When one contestant is standing already, or regains a standing position from *ne-waza*, with the other holding on to any part of the standing contestant's body with his legs, and the standing contestant lifts his opponent clear of the mat.

(h) When a contestant applies or tries to apply *shime-waza* or *kansetsu-waza* in a standing position without an immediately apparent result.

(i) In any other case which the referee deems necessary.

When he has announced '*matte*' the referee

must keep both contestants clearly in sight to ensure that they have understood his call and are not carrying on the contest.

The referee must not announce '*matte*' to stop the contestants leaving the contest area, unless there is danger of injury.

The referee should not announce '*matte*' without valid reason when a contestant has escaped from *osaekomi*, or *shime-waza* or *kansetsu-waza* and calls for or appears in need of a rest.

The referee should not announce '*matte*' if, in doing so, the interruption to the contest would put the contestants in danger. Refer to Article 28 (xxx).

The referee must announce '*matte*' when a contestant who is flat on his stomach with his opponent gripping his back manages to get to his feet without his hands touching the mat.

If the referee announces '*matte*' by mistake during *ne-waza* and as a result the two contestants separate or release their *kumi-kata* (grip), the referee and judges shall attempt, if possible, to replace both contestants in the positions they were in before the '*matte*', so that they may continue to fight, if by so doing they will rectify any injustice done to one of the contestants.

After the call of '*matte*', both contestants shall return to their starting positions as soon as possible.

When the referee announces '*matte*', the contestants must take a standing position if they are being spoken to or to adjust the *judogi*, and take a sitting position if a lengthy delay is expected. They are not authorized to take any other position unless receiving medical attention.

(j) The referee may announce '*matte*' following a minor incident involving one of the contestants such as a nose bleed, broken nail, slipped bandage, brief pain, etc., and authorize the doctor to come rapidly to assist, (cf. Appendix Article 31).

The referee may announce '*matte*' if one of the contestants is injured or indisposed and call on the accredited doctor to come on to the contest area to make a quick examination (cf. Article 31). See the Sporting Code for a definition of 'team doctor'.

The referee may announce '*matte*' if an injured contestant indicates to him that he is in need of a medical examination from an accredited doctor. Such an examination must be carried out as quickly as possible (cf. Article 31.)

The referee may announce '*matte*' if the jury (cf. Sporting Code), at the request of the team doctor, authorize the doctor to make a rapid examination of an injured contestant (cf. Article 31).

Article 19. SONOMAMA (Do not move)

The referee must announce '*sonomama*' each time he wants to stop the contest temporarily (for instance to speak to one of the contestants without either of them changing position or to award a penalty without the contestant losing his advantage). He must call out '*yoshi*' to indicate that the bout is to continue.

Sonomama can be applied only to *ne-waza*.

Each time the referee announces '*sonomama*', he must be careful that there is no change in the positions or grips of the contestants.

If a contestant shows signs of injury during *ne-waza*, the referee may announce '*sonomama*', assess the injury situation, then replace the contestants in the position they were in before his announcement; then he calls out '*yoshi*'.

Article 20. END OF CONTEST

The referee must announce '*sore-made*' (that is all) and end the contest:

(a) When a contestant scores *ippon* or *waza-ari awasete ippon* (Article 21, Article 22).

(b) In the case of *sogo-gachi* (compound win) (Article 23).

(c) In the case of *fusen-gachi* (win by default) (Article 30), or of *kiken-gachi* (win by withdrawal) (Article 30).

(d) In the case of *hansoku-make* (disqualification) (Article 29).

(e) When a contestant cannot continue due to injury (Article 31).

(f) When the time allotted to the contest has expired (see *hantei*).

When '*sore-made*' is announced by the referee, the competitors must return to their starting points.

The referee awards the contest as follows:

(1) If a contestant has obtained an *ippon* he shall be declared the winner.

(2) In the absence of an *ippon* or its equivalent, the winner is declared on the following basis:

A *waza-ari* prevails over any number of *yuko*.

A *yuko* prevails over any number of *koka*.

(3) Where there is no recorded result, or when the results are identical under each heading (*waza-ari*, *yuko*, *koka*), the referee shall announce '*hantei*' and make the appropriate gesture.

Before the announcement of '*hantei*', the referee and the judges must decide who is the winner, taking into account the evident difference in attitude during the contest as well as the skill and effectiveness of the techniques.

The referee must combine his own opinion with that of the judges and give the resulting score according to the majority of the three opinions.

If the opinions of the judges differ, the referee shall make the decision.

If the referee has a different opinion from that of the judges after the announcement of '*hantei*', he can delay his decision in order to talk to the judges about their reasons. Then he must announce '*hantei*' again and this time give a decision based on the majority of the three.

Once the referee has given his decision and left the contest area, he cannot change his decision.

If the referee gives a wrong decision, attributing the contest to the wrong contestant, the two judges must make sure he changes this decision before he leaves the contest area.

(4) The decision *hiki-wake* (contest void) must be given in the absence of a score or if it is impossible to decide on the superiority of one or other of the contestants in the time allotted to the contest, in conformity with this article.

As soon as the referee has indicated the result of the contest, the contestants must take one step back to their respective places (red or white tapes), give a standing bow and leave the contest area.

After he has announced '*sore-made*', the referee must keep the contestants clearly in view to be sure that they have heard him correctly and that they do not continue fighting.

The referee must indicate to the contestants if they need to adjust their *judogi* before the result is given.

Even if a throw seems possible at the very moment when the time signal is given, the referee must announce '*sore-made*' if he considers that it would not be effective immediately.

Article 21. IPPON

The referee must anounce '*ippon*' when he considers that the technique conforms to the following criteria:

(a) When a contestant throws his opponent with control, largely on his back, with force and speed.

(b) When a contestant holds his opponent in *osaekomi* for thirty consecutive seconds.

(c) When a contestant gives up by tapping twice or more with his hand and says '*maitta*' (I give up), generally as a result of a grappling technique, a *shime-waza* (strangulation) or a *kansetsu-waza* (armlock).

(d) When the effect of a strangulation technique or an armlock is sufficiently apparent.

Equivalence: if a contestant is penalized with a *hansoku-make*, his opponent is automatically declared the winner.

When both contestants obtain *ippon* simultaneously, the referee must announce '*hiki-wake*' (draw) and if necessary the contestants shall have the right to continue with their contest. If only one contestant exercises this right, and the other refuses, the contestant who wishes to continue shall be declared the winner by *ippon*.

Simultaneous techniques: when both contestants fall to the mat as a result of attacks which appear to be simultaneous, and the referee and the judges cannot decide which technique was dominant, the referee shall give no score, indicating his decision by the gesture which means 'not valid'.

If the referee announces '*ippon*' by mistake during *ne-waza* and the contestants separate or release their grips (*kumi-kata*), the referee and the judges shall try – to the best of their ability, and following the rule of 'majority of the three' – to restore the contestants as closely as possible to the positions they were in before and cause the contest to continue, in order to avoid giving the advantage to one of the contestants.

If one of the contestants falls, deliberately making a 'bridge' (head and heels in contact with the mat and the rest of the body arched above it) after being thrown, the referee in order to discourage this action may none the less award an *ippon*, or any other score which he judges appropriate, even if the criteria needed for it are not all present.

Ippon can be given for a throwing technique only if that technique began from a standing position.

Article 22. WAZA-ARI AWASETE IPPON

If a contestant obtains a second *waza-ari* in the same contest (see Article 24) the referee must announce '*waza-ari awasete ippon*' (two *waza-ari* make one *ippon*).

Article 23. SOGO-GACHI (compound win)

The referee must announce '*sogo-gachi*' in the following cases:

(a) When one contestant obtains a *waza-ari* and his opponent is subsequently penalized with a *keikoku* (see Article 28).

(b) When a competitor whose opponent has already been penalized with a *keikoku* is subsequently awarded a *waza-ari*.

Article 24. WAZA-ARI

The referee must announce '*waza-ari*' when in his opinion a technique conforms to the following criteria:

(a) When a contestant throws his opponent by means of a technique which lacks in its execution one of the three elements necessary for obtaining an *ippon*. (See Article 21a and the Appendix).

(b) When a contestant holds his opponent in *osaekomi* for twenty-five consecutive seconds but less than thirty seconds.

Equivalence: if a contestant is penalized with a *keikoku*, his opponent automatically benefits with a *waza-ari* at the end of the contest.

In general, in relation to *waza-ari* (and *yuko*), the interpretation of 'partially lacking' in 'largely on the back' can also mean that the contestant's 'side of body' is in contact with the mat.

Although the criteria for *ippon* (largely on the back with speed and force) may be evident in a throw such as *tomoe-nage*, if there is any interruption in the performance of the technique, *waza-ari* is the maximum score that can be awarded.

Article 25. YUKO

The referee must announce '*yuko*' when he considers that a technique conforms to the following criteria:

(a) When a contestant throws his opponent by means of a technique which lacks two or three elements necessary to obtain *ippon*:

(i) The fall is not 'largely on the back' and the throw lacks to some degree one of the two elements of 'force' or 'speed'.

(ii) The fall is 'largely on the back' but lacks to some degree one of the two elements of 'force' and 'speed'.

(b) When a contestant holds his opponent in *osaekomi* for twenty seconds or more, but for less than twenty-five seconds.

Equivalence: if a contestant is penalized with a *chui*, his opponent automatically benefits by a *yuko* at the end of the contest.

Regardless of how many *yukos* are announced, no amount will be considered equal to a *waza-ari*. The total number announced will be recorded.

Article 26. *KOKA*

The referee must announce '*koka*' when he considers that a technique conforms to the following criteria:

(a) When a contestant throws his opponent on to his thighs or buttocks with force and speed.

(b) When a contestant holds his opponent in *osaekomi* for ten consecutive seconds or more, but for less than twenty seconds.

Equivalence: if a contestant is penalized by a *shido* his opponent automatically benefits with an award of *koka* at the end of the contest.

However many *koka* are announced, their total will never be considered equal to a *yuko* or a *waza-ari*. The total number announced will be recorded.

The fact that a throw on an opponent brings him down on to the front of his body, his knees, his hands or his elbows is registered as a simple attack. Likewise, an *osaekomi* of less than ten seconds is also registered as a simple attack.

Article 27. *OSAEKOMI*

The referee will announce '*osaekomi*' when, in his opinion, the technique applied conforms to the following criteria:

(a) The contestant who is being held must be under the control of his opponent and have his back, both shoulders or one shoulder in contact with the mat.

(b) The control must be exercised from the side, the rear or from above.

(c) The contestant effecting the hold must not have his leg(s) controlled by the leg(s) of his opponent.

If a contestant changes his *osaekomi* technique without losing control of his opponent whilst so doing, the immobilization time

count shall continue without a break until the announcement of '*ippon*' (or '*waza-ari*' or the equivalent in the case of '*waza-ari awasete ippon*') or of '*toketa*'.

The *osaekomi* is valid as long as one of the contestants remains within the contest area and is in contact with the mat.

When *osaekomi* is being applied, if it is the contestant who is in an advantageous position who commits an infringement meriting a penalty, the referee shall announce '*matte*', return the contestants to their starting positions, award the penalty (and any score from the *osaekomi*), then restart the contest by announcing '*hajime*'.

When *osaekomi* is being applied, if the contestant who is in a disadvantageous position commits an act meriting a penalty, the referee shall announce '*sonomama*' (consulting quickly with the judges to ascertain if the act deserves a penalty of *keikoku* or higher), award the penalty, then restart the contest by touching both contestants and announcing '*yoshi*'. However, should the penalty be awarded by '*hansoku-make*' the referee shall act in accordance with Article 29, paragraph 3.

The referee must announce '*toketa*' when he considers that the contestant is no longer controlling his opponent.

If the two judges think that an *osaekomi* has been effected which the referee has not announced, they must indicate this to him with the appropriate gesture and the referee must announce '*osaekomi*', in conformity with the rule of the 'majority of the three'.

Likewise, if the referee announces '*osaekomi*' and the judges think that there is no immobilization, they must indicate this with the signal of 'not valid'.

When he is held down and immobilized, *Uke* may try to use *shime-waza* or *kansetsu-waza* even if his body is afterwards brought outside the contest area. However, the referee must announce '*toketa*' and '*matte*' if the *osaekomi* is broken or if the contestants leave the contest area entirely.

The referee must announce '*toketa*' and '*matte*' in the case of '*osaekomi* on the edge', when that part of the contestant's body which is still touching the mat within the contest area is lifted up and no longer touches it.

Article 28. PROHIBITED ACTS

All the actions mentioned below are prohibited:

(a) *Shido* is given to a contestant who has committed a slight infringement:

(i) Intentionally to avoid taking hold in order to prevent action in the contest.

(ii) To adopt an excessively defensive posture.

An award of failure to fight should be made if a contestant produces actions which give the impression of attacking techniques, but show clearly that he or she has no real intention of throwing the opponent.

The warning for failure to fight should not be given merely for the absence of attacking techniques, provided that the referee considers that the contestant(s) is (are) waiting for the right moment to attack.

With the exception of the first warning given for failure to fight, before the penalty itself, there shall be no 'free' warnings given.

A condition of failure to fight can be said to exist if, during a period of between twenty and thirty seconds, no positive attacking movement has been made by either contestant. This period of time can be lengthened or shortened according to the circumstances.

If the referee considers that a contestant is culpable of failure to fight, the first warning given (Article 8, XVII) shall not confer a penalty on the culprit, but simply be regarded as a warning.

On the other hand, if a warning has already been given, for whatever reason, any subsequent warning of failure to fight must bring a penalty equal or superior to *shido*.

(iii) In a standing position, continually to hold without attacking:

— with one or both hands on the belt or bottom of the opponent's jacket

— the opponent's lapel or jacket on the same side with both hands

— one sleeve of the opponent's jacket with both hands.

A contestant must not be penalized for holding with both hands one side of his opponent's jacket if this has been caused by the latter's ducking his head under underneath the holder's arm. However, if a contestant repeatedly ducks his head under his opponent's arm the referee should consider whether he should be penalized for adopting an 'excessively defensive attitude'. (See Article 29, II.)

(iv) In a standing position, a contestant continually holds on to one or both of his opponent's sleeve ends for defensive purposes.

(v) To insert one or more fingers into the sleeve or trouser bottom of his opponent, or 'screws up' his sleeve with a twisting grip.

(vi) In a standing position, continually to keep the fingers of one or both of his opponent's hands interlocked, in order to prevent action in the contest.

(vii) Without the referee's permission to tie or retie the belt, or the trousers; intentionally to disarrange his or her *judogi*.

(viii) To wrap the end of the belt or jacket round any part of the opponent's body.

The term 'wrap round' implies that the belt or jacket makes a complete circle round any part of the body. The act of using the belt or jacket as an 'anchor' (without wrapping round) to block the arm of an opponent, for example, should not be penalized.

(ix) To seize an opponent's *judogi* between the teeth.

(x) To place the hand, arm, foot or leg on an opponent's face. The face area is designated as the top of the forehead, the ears and the lower jaw; i.e. the area within those limits.

(xi) In a standing position, to take hold of the opponent's foot/feet, leg(s) or trouser leg(s) with the hand(s), unless simultaneously attempting a throwing technique.

(xii) While lying on the back, to hold on to an opponent's neck and armpit with the legs, when the opponent succeeds in standing up or reaching a kneeling position from which he could lift the opponent up.

(b) *Chui* is awarded against any contestant who commits a serious infringement (or repeats a minor infringement after being given *shido*).

(xiii) To apply a 'scissors grip' (feet crossed, legs extended) around the trunk (*dojime*), neck or head of an opponent.

(xiv) To strike an opponent's hand or arm with the knee or foot to oblige him or her to release a grip.

(xv) To insert the foot or the leg into an opponent's collar, lapel or belt.

(xvi) To twist an opponent's finger(s) to loosen a grip.

(xvii) To drag an opponent to the mat in order to enter *ne-waza* in a fashion not conforming to Article 17.

(xviii) In a standing position, to go outside the contest area while applying a technique begun inside the contest area.

(c) *Keikoku* is awarded against any contestant who commits a grave infringement (or repeats a serious infringement after being penalized with *chui*).

(xix) To go out of the contest area intentionally or force an opponent out intentionally (see Article 10 for exceptions to this rule).

Any contestant who intentionally goes out of the contest area during *ne-waza* shall be penalized with a *keikoku*. If the referee has announced '*osaekomi*' and *Uke* deliberately moves out of the contest area, the *osaekomi* shall continue until *ippon* is scored or until he or she frees him(her)self from the immobilization. The referee shall then penalize *Uke* and award, if it applies, the score of the *osaekomi* to *Tori*.

(xx) To attempt to throw the opponent by winding one leg around his leg, while facing more or less in the same direction as the opponent, and falling backwards on top of him (*kawazu-gake*).

(xxi) To apply *kansetsu-waza* (joint lock) on any joint other than the elbow.

(xxii) To apply any technique which might injure the opponent's neck or vertebrae.

(xxiii) To lift an opponent from the mat in order to throw him back down on the mat.

(xxiv) To sweep an opponent's leg, if it is the supporting leg, from the inside whilst he is applying a technique such as *harai-goshi*, etc.

(xxv) To apply or try to apply any technique outside the contest area (see Appendix to Article 27 for exceptions).

(xxvi) To ignore the referee's instructions.

(xxvii) To make unnecessary remarks or gestures of a disturbing, pointless or derogatory nature to the opponent during the contest.

(xxviii) To commit any act which might be injurious or dangerous to the opponent or any act contrary to the spirit of *judo*.

(xxix) To fall directly to the mat while applying or attempting to apply techniques such as *waki-gatame*.

(d) *Hansoku-make* is awarded against any contestant who has committed a very grave infringement (or who, having been penalized *keikoku*, commits a further infringement of any kind).

(xxx) To 'dive' headfirst towards the mat, by bending forward and downward while attempting to perform or performing techniques such as *uchi-mata*, *harai-goshi*, etc.

The referee will call out '*matte*' only if he considers that an interruption to the contest will not endanger the contestants.

(xxxi) Intentionally to fall backwards when the other contestant is clinging to his or her back, and when either contestant has control of the other's movement.

(xxxii) To wear any hard or metallic

article, whether covered over or not.

In accordance with paragraph (ii) of this article, the state of failure to fight shall be said to exist if, during a period of twenty to thirty seconds, no attacking movement has been carried out by either contestant. This period may be lengthened or shortened according to circumstances.

If the referee considers that a contestant is guilty of failure to fight then the first warning given (Article 8, XVII) shall not carry a penalty to the contestant in question, but be regarded simply as a warning.

On the other hand, if a penalty has already been awarded, for whatever reason, any subsequent warning of failure to fight must bring a penalty which is equal or superior to *shido*.

Article 29. PENALTIES

The division into four groups of infringements mentioned in Article 28 is intended as a guide, to give a clearer understanding to all of the relative penalties normally awarded for committing the applicable prohibited act. Referees and judges are authorized to award penalties according to the 'intent' or the circumstances, bearing in mind the best interests of the sport.

If the referee decides to award a penalty against a contestant (except in the case of *sonomama* during *ne-waza*), he must temporarily stop the contest, bring the contestants back to their starting/finishing points and announce the penalty while pointing to the guilty contestant.

If the penalty awarded is *hansoku-make*, the referee must bring the contestants back to their starting/finishing points, step forward between them, turn to face the guilty party, point to him and announce 'hansoku-make'. He must then step back to his appointed place, announce 'sore-made' and indicate the winner.

Before awarding *keikoku* or *hansoku-make*, the referee must consult the judges and make a decision according to the rule of 'a majority of the three'. If the two contestants

infringe the rules at the same time, each of them must be penalized according to the gravity of the infringement committed. If both contestants have already been penalized with *keikoku* and they subsequently receive another penalty, they must both be declared 'hansoku-make'. However, the officials must make a final decision in conformity with Article 32, 'situations not covered by the rules'.

If a contestant pulls his opponent down to the mat in a way not in accordance with Article 17, and the latter does not take advantage of the situation to enter *ne-waza*, the referee must announce 'matte', stop the contest temporarily and award a *chui* against the contestant who has infringed Article 17.

Penalties are not cumulative. Each penalty must be awarded at its own value. The awarding of a second or subsequent penalty automatically cancels an earlier penalty. Furthermore, any contestant who has already been penalized and commits an infringement meriting another penalty must receive one which is at least in the next higher value than his existing penalty.

Every time a referee awards a penalty, he should if necessary demonstrate with a simple action the reason for the penalty.

A penalty may be awarded after the announcement of 'sore-made' for any forbidden act during the time allotted for the contest or, in certain exceptional cases, for grave acts committed after the signal for the end of the contest, provided that no decision has already been given.

Article 30. DEFAULT AND WITHDRAWAL

The decision of *fusen-gachi* (win by default) shall be given to any contestant whose opponent does not appear for his contest.

Before he awards *fusen-gachi*, the referee must be sure that he has received authority to do so from the director of the tournament.

The decision of *kiken-gachi* (win by withdrawal) shall be given to any contestant whose opponent withdraws from the contest, for any reason whatsoever, during the course of the contest.

Any contestant who does not conform to the requirements of Articles 3 and 4 will find himself or herself refused the right of competing, and the opponent will be declared the winner of the contest by *kiken-gachi*, in accordance with the rule of 'a majority of the three'.

Article 31. *INJURY, ILLNESS OR ACCIDENT*

If a contestant sustains an injury which is sufficiently serious to require treatment outside the contest area, or if an injury sustained by a contestant needs more than two examinations by the team doctor (cf. Sporting Code: definition of an accredited doctor) then the referee, after consulting the judges, will put an end to the contest and announce the result in accordance with the other provisions of this article.

If the team doctor, after examining an injured contestant, informs the referee that the contestant cannot continue the contest, then the referee, after consulting the judges, will put an end to the contest in accordance with the other provisions of this article.

If the type of injury sustained by a contestant is such that it requires treatment by an accredited doctor on the contest area, then the referee, after consulting the judges, will put an end to the contest in accordance with the other provisions of this article.

When an injury has been sustained by one or both contestants, and the referee and the judges think that the contest should not continue, the referee will bring the contest to an end and announce the result in accordance with the other provisions of this article.

The decision of *kachi* (victory), *make* (defeat), *hiki-wake* (draw) must be given by the referee after consultation with the judges when one of the contestants is unable to continue the contest following an injury, illness or accident sustained during the course of the contest. This decision shall be made according to the following criteria:

(a) *Injury*

(i) If the responsibility for the injury is attributed to the injured contestant, he or she loses the contest.

(ii) If the responsibility for the injury is attributed to the uninjured contestant, he or she loses the contest.

(iii) If it is impossible to determine who is responsible for the injury, a decision of *hiki-wake* can be given.

(b) *Illness*

In general, if a contestant becomes ill during a contest and cannot continue, he or she loses the contest.

(c) *Accident*

If an accident occurs, due to an external cause, the decision *hiki-wake* (draw) must be given.

The referee must be certain that the number of interruptions to the contest, for purposes of medical examination, is registered for each contestant.

As a general rule, only one doctor per contestant is allowed on to the contest area. If a doctor needs assistance, the referee must be informed first.

The recorder shall display one cross to indicate the first medical examination and two crosses to indicate the second medical examination. The background of the display area should be green and the crosses red and white, to correspond to the belt of the contestants.

Exceptions to treatment of injuries:

— The referee himself may instruct a doctor to attend to a contestant on the mat if the injury has been caused by his or her opponent. This action must not be registered as a medical examination.

— If a minor incident such as a nose bleed, broken nail, pain of brief duration, slipped bandage, etc., needs attention, then this must be performed as quickly as possible.

Article 32. *SITUATIONS NOT COVERED BY THE RULES*

When any situation arises which is not covered by these rules, it shall be dealt with and a decision given by the referee after consultation with the judges.

Jugo Awase. A technique combining soft-ness (*Ju*) with hardness (*Go*).

Juho 'Method using softness' or 'pas-sive, yielding'. It is solely employed for evasion and defensive action, in contrast with *Goho* or 'hard method', which is used for attacking or counter-attacking action. It is the training system used in the art of *Shorinji-kempo*.

Ju-ippon Kumite *Karate*. A series of eight fundamental *Kata* practised in the *Shotokan* style, and codified by Master Kanazawa Hirokasu in the 1970s. They are used in counter-attacks against:

> *Jodan Tsuki*
> *Chudan Tsuki*
> *Chudan Mae-geri*
> *Chudan Yoko-geri Kekomi*
> *Chudan (Jodan) Mawashi-geri*
> *Ushiro-geri*
> *Jodan Kisami Tsuki*
> *Chudan Gyaku Tsuki.*

Juji-garami *Aikido*. 'Keeping in the shape of a cross'. This is a type of control-ling movement which makes a cross-shape (*Juji*). It is applied in *Kata-dori* (shoulder grip), *Ushiro-ryotekubi-dori* (gripping both wrists from behind), and *Ushiro Tekubi Kubi-dori* (strangulation from behind with a single wrist grip). See *Nage-waza*.

— Juji-gatame *Judo*. In groundwork (*Ne-waza*) techniques, this is a technique of gripping, extending and locking the arm of *Uke* by *Tori*. The arm forms a cross-shape, lying across *Tori*'s pubic region.

Juji-gatame

— Juji-uke *Karate*. A block against an arm attack using the crossed wrists.

Ju-jutsu. 'Science of softness', techniques of combat elaborated by the *Bushi* during the Kamakura period (1185–1333) in Ja-

Juji-uke

pan. It was intended for disarmed warri-ors, so that they could defend themselves against enemies who were still armed. This art developed from the ancient techniques of *Kumi-tachi* (or *Yawara*) as described in the *Konjaku-monogatari*, a Buddhist work dating from the thirteenth century. Over the centuries, various schools of *Ju-jutsu* developed such as *Wa-jutsu*, *Yawara*, *Kogu-soku*, *Kempo*, *Hakuda* and *Shubaku*; each be-ing a part of the 'Way of archery and horse-manship' (*Kyuba-no-michi*). They improved on the more primitive techniques and com-bined them with movements and countering grips taken from Chinese methods of combat (see *Shaolin-si*) as well as specific techniques used by the peasants of Okinawa. A recip-rocal movement took place when Ju-jutsu was exported to China by *Chen Yuanbin* (1587–1671), a Chinese poet and diplomat sent to Japan, when he returned to his native land around 1638. Ju-jutsu became a martial art only in the Edo period, when Japan was at peace. Numerous schools created by the *Ronin* (or masterless *Samurai*) spread their techniques throughout the country. These were codified only with the dawn of the Meiji period (1868–1912), from the time when the Samurai were no longer permit-ted to carry swords and the fighting feuds between noble families were forbidden.

The essential principle of Ju-jutsu is to conquer the enemy with any and all means, minimal force. This demands from its fol-lowers a strict conformity to various disci-plines. They must:

be able to judge the force of an opponent's

Drawing of an armlock by Hokusai.

attack and use it against him before it takes effect;

in the course of a confrontation, be able to bring an opponent off balance;

if possible, evade an attack;

know how to attack without necessarily being able to reach the weak points;

know how to topple an opponent by making use of leverage;

know how to immobilize an opponent by holding him down on the ground, twisting his limbs, bending his limbs or strangling him;

know how to strike the vital points of the body in such a way as to produce loss of consciousness, serious injury and even death.

In actual fact, the older art of Ju-jutsu for warriors, as distinct from its modern descendants, aimed to annihilate the enemy and render him powerless. This principal intention led warriors to use all kinds of dangerous – often fatal – techniques. Ju-jutsu was first practised by the Samurai, then by the *Ninja*, and finally spread among the rest of the populace, to become an offensive technique mainly used by bandits. From this stems the bad reputation which it has never lost. This is why Kano Jigoro, in adapting the 'gentle' techniques of Ju-jutsu to create a new sporting system, called this system *Judo*, to distinguish it from the deadly art of Ju-jutsu.

Around 1922, the date of the official creation of the *Kodokan*, only Ju-jutsu was recognized and taught in innumerable *Ryu* or 'schools', in Japan as well as abroad. The armed forces and the police in Western countries were interested in this particular art, to give them some advantage in fighting situations. Even today, the majority of the armed forces of the world teach their recruits some techniques of 'close combat' which are inspired by Ju-jutsu, *Karate* and various types of combat from local sources such as boxing, wrestling, *Savate*, etc.

To a large extent Ju-jutsu has been dethroned by *Judo*, *Karate* and *Aikido*. This fall from favour has led to its being no longer widely considered as a sport, only as a number of techniques for real fighting. In recent years some variations have appeared, mainly in the West, and followers of such systems have devised sporting contests with rules and methods of scoring. International Ju-jutsu tournaments have been staged in Canada and in Great Britain. This relatively new trend is reversing the first one and demonstrating the prevailing state of flux in martial arts. However, it is from the ancient schools of Ju-jutsu that almost all the current techniques used in martial arts flow. Also referred to erroneously as *Ju-jitsu* and as *Jiu-jitsu*.

Ju no Kata *Judo*. 'Forms of softness'. A series of fifteen formal exercises, or *Kata*, which may eventually be used outside the *Dojo*. They are divided into three *Kyo* (principles or lessons) of five movements each:

First Kyo (Ikkyo):
   Tsukidashi, to pierce with the hand.
   Kataoshi, to push the shoulders.
   Ryote-dori, to seize both hands.
   Kata-mawashi, to make the shoulders turn.
   Age-oshi, to drive back the jaw.

Second Kyo (Nikyo):
   Kiri-otoshi, to cut down.
   Ryo-kata-oshi, to push both shoulders back.
   Naname-uchi, to cut down diagonally.
   Katate-age, to raise the hand to strike.

Third Kyo (Sankyo):
   Obi-tori, to seize by the belt.
   Mune-oshi, to push the chest back.
   Tsuki-age, rising punch or 'uppercut'.
   Uchi-otoshi, a descending blow with the fist.
   Ryogan-tsuki, to stab at both eyes.

Juken-jutsu. A martial arts method using the musket and bayonet, created at the beginning of the seventeenth century. It was developed mainly in the Meiji period (1868–1912) by the military. Soldiers trained with wooden muskets (*Mokuju*) in the techniques of *Juken-do*, a system which was not intended for real fighting in battle (see *Do*). The techniques of musket and bayonet mainly comprise thrusting actions with the point (*Shitotsu*).

Juku-gashira. This is the title given to the leading disciple of a 'professor' or 'doctor' of a martial art; someone of such a calibre and skill that the founder of a martial arts system, the 'professor', imparts to him all his secrets. This disciple might be the founder's son or even one of his pupils.

Ju-kumite *Karate*. An attack during free-style training, which must be carried out and sustained with 'softness' or 'gentleness' (*Ju*).

Jumbi-undo. Warming-up and stretching exercises performed by students before a training session in a martial art (*Budo*). These exercises generally include wrist-stretching (*Tekubi-undo*), breakfalls (*Ukemi*), breathing exercises (*Kokyu*), body-turning (*Tenkan-ho*), and back-stretching exercises (*Haishin-undo*). However, every school and every master has their own favourite movements. Also *Junbi-undo*, *Junbi-taisho*.

Junan Shin see *Nyunan Shin*.

Junbi-undo, *Junbi-taisho* see *Jumbi-undo*.

Junin-gake *Judo*. Training which involves fighting against ten opponents, one at a time, in unbroken succession.

Jun Kata Sode-tori *Aikido*. 'First sleeve-hold.' *Uke* seizes *Shite*'s right sleeve with his or her left hand. Shite raises the right arm in a circle, taking a big step to the left. He or she seizes Uke's left wrist with his or her left hand, lifts Uke and strikes an *Atemi* blow in the side, using the right elbow. See *Sode-tori*.
— **Jun Kata Te-dori** *Aikido*. 'First arm-hold'. *Uke* seizes *Shite*'s right wrist, thumb on top. Shite frees his or her wrist by turning to the left and raising the captured arm high, completing a circular body movement, finishing the technique with an *Atemi* blow to the face with the right arm. See *Te-dori*.
— **Jun-tsuki (Jun-zuki)** *Karate*. This is the name used in *Wado-ryu* for the same movement in *Shotokan*, where it is called *Oi-tsuki (Oi-zuki)*. It consists of a straight, forward punch using body weight and the thrust of the rear leg. The same arm is used as the advancing leg; right arm punch with right leg in front, left arm punch with left leg in front.
— **Jun-tsuki no Ashi** *Karate*. Position of inclining forward.

Jun-to see *Omori-ryu*.

Ju no Ri. Principle of softness and flexibility (see *Ju*). It requires a firm and adequate posture, with no brutality. *Tori* does not resist *Uke*'s force; on the contrary, he or she yields to it, using it to upset Uke's balance and at the same time preserving his or her own balance. The principle is well expressed in the five *Kata* of the *Kito-ryu* school of *Ju-jutsu* and in the *Koshiki-no-Kata* of *Judo*, as taught by the *Kodokan*. See *Ki*.

Juru see *Penchak-silat, Setia-hati Terate*.

Juryo see *Salt, Sumotori*.

Ju-tai-jutsu see *Tai-jutsu*.

Jutsu 'True', 'Technique'. This means an art (*Gei*), a science or a technique rooted in the tradition of a school (*Ryu*). One can ac-

quire it only after long years of training and study. The term applies to all the 'violent' martial arts, just as the term *Do* applies to the martial arts which are not meant for real fighting. Apart from *Ju-jutsu*, all the other martial arts with the element '*jutsu*' in their names include also the name of the weapon which they employ. Examples are *Kyu-jutsu, Ken-jutsu, Jo-jutsu*, etc.

Jutte see *Sai, Ikaku-ryu, Jitte*

Ju-yeok (Ju-yeog) see *Yijing*.

Ju-yoku-go-o-sei-suru 'Gentleness controls force'. The concept found at the root of all *Budo*. Tradition maintains that it was first formulated by the Chinese sage Lao-tzu (fourth century before Christ). See *Ju*.

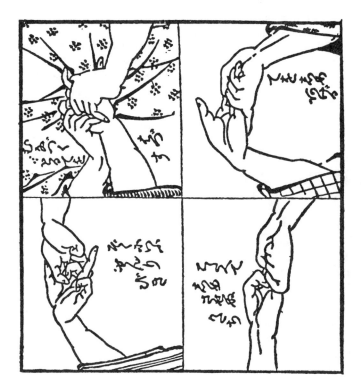

Drawing of some Jutsu fingerlocks, by Hokusai.

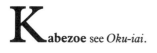

Kabezoe see *Oku-iai*.

Kabuki. A style of 'heroic' theatre created in Japan at the beginning of the seventeenth century. Its highly colourful performances are still presented today. Some of these stories contain scenes in which *Samurai* display all the facets of martial arts in a stylized form which meets the needs of the theatre without destroying the realism. Among the pieces of this kind are the *Chushingura* and the *Kokusenya*, the most famous and most worthy of mention. These two have been the subject of numerous screen adaptations, in which the battle scenes are really memorable.

Kabura-ya *Kyudo*. An arrow armed with a wooden tip 'in the shape of a turnip'. In flight it emits a keen whistling sound. The sound is supposed to frighten away both evil spirits and enemies alike. They were fired without fail before every conflict, and today are used ceremonially. Muffled or 'safe' arrows which do not emit a whistle are called *Hikime*. See *Kyudo, Kasagake, Reisha, Yabusame, Ya*.

Kachi (-gachi) 'Victory'.

Kachiguri see *Dohyo*.

Kachikake 'jaw'. See *Head*.

Kachi-make *Karate*. A contest during a competition or demonstration in which one of the contestants must win by scoring *Ippon*. The winner is called *Kachite*.

Kachinuki *Kendo*. A contest-cum-exercise in which one *Kendoka* takes on one opponent after another, in succession, until he or she suffers a defeat. The winner in turn fights in a similar fashion, and so on. The final winner of this training method or exercise is the one who has obtained the highest number of wins.

Kachite see *Kachi-make*.

Kachu see *Yoroi*.

Kaeshi (-gaeshi) 'Exchange', 'Transformation', 'Counter-attack'.
— **Kaeshi-jime** *Judo*. Strangulation technique in reverse.
— **Kaeshi-waza** *Judo, Aikido*. Counter-attack.
Karate. Succession of counter-attacks, in

Archery with a Kabura-ya.

90

'waves'.

Kendo. A technique of parrying a *Shinai* blow (with another Shinai) in such a way that the Shinai which parries also bends to some extent, and the 'rebound' sends the striking Shinai back and turns it aside.

Kagato-jime *Judo.* Strangulation using the foot; a part of groundwork (*Ne-waza*) technique. See *Kakato.*

Kage-ryu *Ken-jutsu.* A school of sword-fighting, created according to tradition by *Aizu Iko* (1452–1538), from Aizu province. It is also referred to as *Aizu Kage-ryu.* It gave birth to numerous other schools and styles:.

Shin Kage-ryu, founded by Fujiwara no Nobutsuna (*c.* 1520–77).

Yagyu Shin-kage-ryu, founded by Yagyu Muneyoshi (*c.* 1527–1606).

Yagyu-ryu, founded by Yagyu Muneyoshi in 1603.

Taisha-ryu, founded by Marume Kurando (1540–1629).

Shinkan-ryu, founded by Okuyama Tadenobu.

Hikita Kage-ryu, founded by Hikita Kagekane (1573–92).

Okuyama-ryu, founded by Okuyama Magojiro (1525–1602).

Kashima Shinto-ryu, which belongs equally to the *Shinto-ryu* tradition.

Kagi 'Hook'. Also *Kake.*
— **Kagi-tsuki (Kagizuki)** *Karate.* A punch delivered in a curve. A 'hook' similar to that used in boxing.

Kagi-tsuki

Kagura *Sumo.* These are forms of sacred dance and music, as found in *Shinto* cer-emonies, which used to accompany *Sumo* events. At the time, *Sumo* was regarded as a religious rite. See *Shinto, Sumo.*

Kaho see *Kata.*

Kai *Kyudo.* The sixth position of the archer, in which he or she has drawn the bow to its fullest extent. It immediately follows the position of *Hikiwake,* which is the moment of stabilization (union of mind and body), with the bow held high above the head. Also called *Jiman.*

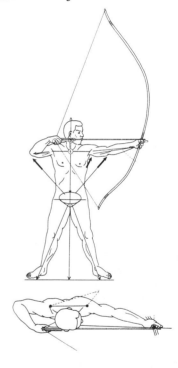

Kai

Kaiden *Aikido.* A high grade (see *Kyudan*) equal to that of a master who teaches.

Kaiken. A small dagger without a guard, often carried by the wives of the *Bushi,* who could carry it, easily hidden, in the pleats of the *Kimono.* They used it to defend themselves, and in extreme circumstances they cut open their own necks with it in an act of ritual suicide. See *Swords, Kakushi.*

Kaiko see *Kempo*.

Kaikyu-shiai. A competition organized in lines or groups as part of training in martial arts techniques.

Kaina-hineri *Sumo*. A technique very similar to *Ippon Seoi-nage* in *Judo*, but performed with more force.

Kaina-hineri

Kaishaku-to see *Omori-ryu*.

Kaisho *Karate*. 'Open hand'. This refers to the type of blow which is delivered with the open palm. It can be used to describe other hand blows in which the fist is not fully clenched.

Kaiten-nage *Aikido*. A series of throws using a turning action. These throws (*Nage*) are used against *Ryote-dori* (seizing the wrists), *Shomen-uchi* (vertical downward blow) and *Shomen-tsuki* (punch to the face). See *Nage-waza*.

Ka-jutsu. Technique of using a firearm and explosives, developed mainly by the *Daido-ryu* school. See *Ho-jutsu*.

Kakari-geiko *Kendo*. Fundamental attacking techniques which are studied as a part of essential training.
Judo. Continuous *Randori* used to test the endurance of *Judoka*.
Aikido. A series of successive attacks against one partner by other members of a class, one after the other, used as a training exercise.
Wa-jutsu. The continuous series of attacks carried out by *Uke* against *Tori*.

Kakato (*Kagato*) 'Heel'. See *Body*, *Feet*, *Ensho*.

Kake (-gake) 'Hook'. Also *Kagi*.
Judo. A technique in which *Tori* hooks *Uke*'s legs with his or her own legs or feet. It also refers to the last phase of a push taken by *Uke*, leading to loss of balance and a fall. It is in fact the preliminary act of a throw executed by Tori.
— **Kake-dameshi** *Kendo*. A strong attack.
— **Kake-nage** *Sumo*. The same movement as in *Kote-nage*, but including a hook with the leg inside the leg of an opponent.

Kake-nage

— **Kake-uke** *Karate*. A blocking movement in the form of a hook, made with the 'sword-hand' (*Shuto*). Also *Kake Shuto Uke*.

Kake-uke

— **Kake-waza** *Karate*. Variations of hooking techniques.

Kaki-wake-Uke *Karate*. A blocking technique carried out with the arms, making a rough X-shape.

Kakushi 'Hidden weapons'. The name

given to all weapons of small dimensions, such as the *Shuriken, Bankokuchoki,* daggers (*Kaiken*) and small knives in general. The art of using these weapons is called *Kakushi-jutsu*. See *Nagao-ryu*.

Kakutei-jutsu see *Kung-fu*.

Kai-wake-Uke

Kakuto *Karate*. The bent wrist position taken when delivering an *Atemi* blow.
— **Kakuto-bugei** 'Fighting martial arts'. This name is given to the entire array of martial arts techniques (*jutsu*) involving the use of weapons only, and excluding all unarmed combat techniques. They are very numerous (more than fifty) when one takes into account the number of weapons available for use. The main *Kakuto* are:

> *Ba-jutsu,* fighting on horseback
> *Kyu-jutsu,* archery used in warfare
> *Ken-jutsu,* sword-fighting techniques
> *So-jutsu* fighting with a halberd,
> *Yari-jutsu,* fighting with a lance
> *Naginata-jutsu,* fighting with a *Naginata*
> *Bo-jutsu,* long-staff techniques
> *Jo-jutsu,* short-staff techniques
> *Tanto-jutsu,* fighting with a dagger.

— **Kakuto Uke** *Karate*. Blocking an attack using the flexed wrist.

Kalaripayat 'The Path of the Field of Battle'. A very ancient Indian martial art originating in the state of Kerala in South India. It includes unarmed techniques (*Suvasu*) somewhat similar to those of *Karate*

and *Aiki-jutsu*, and armed techniques. The latter make use of such weapons as the *Otta*, a kind of pointed club made of hardwood; the *Modi*, a double dagger with gazelle horns; the *Urimi*, a highly flexible sword with two edges; lances, sticks, daggers, small round shields made of willow or metal, etc. Movements are accompanied by controlled breathing exercises (*Pranayama*) and in general attacks are carried out against the weak points (*Marman*) of the body. These number 108, according to tradition. It is also part of the traditional beliefs that the style is the same as that brought to China from India by *Bodhiarma*, and taught at the *Shaolin* temple. In India, *Kalaripayat* is regarded as a ritual form of combat, dedicated to the goddess Kali. Some authorities on martial arts history suggest that the Indian art of *Vajra-mushti*, 'Diamond Fist', had some technical influence on *Kalaripayat*.

Kama (-gama). A kind of sickle used to cut rice straw, with a long handle. It was used at one time by the peasants of Okinawa to defend themselves against bandits and *Samurai*. Vietnamese: *Cau liem*. See *Kusari-gama*.

Kamae (-gamae) 'Guard', 'Posture', 'Stance'.
Kendo. There are three types of guard holding the *Shinai*: high guard (*Jodan-no-Kamae*), middle guard (*Chudan-no-Kamae*), and low guard (*Gedan-no-Kamae*). See also *Waki-gamae, Postures*.
Aikido. 'On guard' position, with body turned sideways on to the opponent. It may be taken with the left side forward (*Hidari*), right side forward (*Migi*), high (*Jodan*), low (*Gedan*), or in a 'natural' middle (*Chudan*) position.
Viet-Vo-Dao see *Thu Phap*.
Wushu see *Taidu*.

Kamakura. A small city to the south of present-day Tokyo. It was here that the first *Shogun, Minamoto no Yoritomo,* established himself in 1185, after he had defeated the rival *Taira* clan. This shogunate (*Bakufu*) was destined to last for almost 150 years. It was overthrown in 1333 by rebellious *Daimyo*. This led to the setting

Two exponents of Kalaripayat performing leaping technique. (Photograph: François Gautier)

Contest between Kama and Bo (long staff) in a Dojo on Okinawa.

up of the *Ashikaga* shogunate in Kyoto. It was during the Kamakura period that the Mongols from China and Korea tried twice, unsuccessfully, in 1274 and 1281, to invade Japan.

Kami 'Above', 'Those who are above'; also 'Spirit'. This is the general name given to all the divinities and spirits of *Shinto*, who personify the elements, trees, mountains and other natural phenomena. They also play a part in the supernatural experiences of exceptional human beings. See *Shinto*.
— **Kamidana** see *Kamiza*.
— **Kami Hiza-gatame Judo.** Joint lock using the knee to enforce it.
— **Kami Izumi Ise no Kami.** The *Samurai* (1508–78) who created the *Shinkage-ryu*.
— **Kami Sankaku-gatame Judo.** A triangular form of hold by *Tori* on *Uke*. It is part of the groundwork (*Ne-waza*) techniques.
— **Kami Shiho Ashi-jime Judo.** Upper strangulation of the four 'quarters'.
— **Kami Shiho-basami Judo.** Upper strangulation of the four 'quarters' using a 'scissors' hold. Part of the groundwork (*Ne-waza*).
— **Kami Shiho-gatame Judo.** Locking of the upper four 'quarters'. *Tori* holds *Uke* largely by pressing his or her body down on

Uke's. One of the techniques of groundwork (*Ne-waza*) techniques.
— **Kami Shiho-jime Judo.** Strangulation of the upper four 'quarters' in groundwork (*Ne-waza*).

Kami Shiho-gatame

— **Kami Ude Hishigi Juji-gatame Judo.** An upper armlock on the outstretched arm.
— **Kamiza** 'Seat of the *Kami*'. The name of the bow which begins and ends all *Kata* performances. It is made by turning in the direction of the *Kamidana* (altar of the *Kami*) where the master of the *Dojo* is sitting. The *Kamidana* is always placed at a specific point in the Dojo, and the bows are made whether the master of the Dojo is present or not. In Japan, the same place is used to locate the altar of the ancestors. It is also called *Joza* (higher seat) or *Joseki*.

Kami 'Hair'.
— **Kami-tori Ju-jutsu, Aikido.** 'To seize by the hair'. The defensive techniques used against this form of attack are as follows; they are called *Mae Kami-tori* and *Ushiro Kami-tori*:

Mae Kami-tori: 'To seize by the hair from the front'. *Shite* wards off an *Atemi* blow to the face from *Uke*'s right arm. Most frequently, however, Uke seizes Shite by the hair. In reply, Shite grips Uke by the right wrist with his or her left hand and bends it back (*Kote-gaeshi*).
Variation: Shite steps back one pace with his or her left foot and blocks an Atemi blow from Uke's knee, using the right forearm, then grasps Uke by the left ankle and delivers an Atemi blow to the thigh with his or her right elbow.
Ushiro Kami-tori: 'To seize by the hair from the rear'. Shite turns quickly to his right, if Uke is holding him or her with

the left hand, and delivers an Atemi blow to the face with his or her right hand, then seizes Uke's right wrist with both hands and passes under Uke's right arm, giving a second Atemi blow to the stomach with his or her elbow.

Variation: Shite steps back with the right foot and turns to the right to deliver an Atemi to Uke's face. He or she seizes Uke's right wrist with his or her right hand and inflicts a wristlock (*Kote-gaeshi*).

Kamikaze Literally, 'divine wind'. This expression was used to describe the storm which destroyed the Mongol invasion fleet in 1281 when it was sailing towards the island of Kyushu, Japan. 'Divine wind' was the name given to the Japanese suicide pilots who deliberately crashed their aeroplanes, loaded with high explosives, on to the decks of American warships towards the end of the Second World War. In general, the amount of petrol in these aeroplanes was insufficient for them to be able to return to base. By extension, the expression is used to describe anyone who undertakes a spectacular enterprise or risks his life. In fact, the ideal of all the *Samurai* through the ages was to become a kind of '*Kamikaze*'.

Kan (-gan). An intuitive faculty which enables a combatant to foresee the movements of his adversary. See *Yomi*.

'*Winter*'. See *Kangeiko*.

Kanabo. An iron club, formerly used by warriors, but in particular by monks.

Kanemaki-ryu see *Chujo-ryu*.

Kangeiko 'Winter (*Kan*) training (*Keiko*)'. Training in which the practitioner of an art (*Gei*) or of a technique (*Jutsu*) strives to overcome the cold, so that he learns to discipline his bodily reactions and achieve much greater ease of movement. Such training often lasts for a week, and the body is pushed to the extreme limits of its resistance to cold and fatigue. *Kangeiko* takes place during the hardest winter months. See also *Shochu-geiko*.

Kani-basama *Judo*. (*Kani*, crab; *Ha-sami*, scissors). A *Sutemi* technique called 'crab-scissors throw'.

Kanjin-sumo *Sumo*. A *Sumo* tournament which was held in bygone days to raise funds for the building of a Buddhist temple or a *Shinto* sanctuary. The first such events were held in Kyoto between 1596 and 1615 to support the rebuilding of a temple. Others were subsequently held in Osaka and Edo (Tokyo) after 1620.

Kanku *Karate*. 'To Look At The Sky'. The ancient *Kata* from which the *Heian* and *Pinan* Kata were derived. There are two distinct *Kanku*: *Kanku Dai* (Great) and *Kanku Sho* (Small).

Kano Jigoro (1860–1938). One of the most famous martial arts masters of modern times, and founder of *Judo*. He was born in the village of Mikatse in the province of Hyogo (Kobe). His family belonged to a class of high imperial functionaries, and he himself studied Political Science at the university of Kyoto from 1881 to 1884. He was at the ministry of the Imperial Household. He was very attached to the study of martial arts, practising *Ju-jutsu* of the *Tenjin Shin-yo* school under the direction of Fukuda Hachinosuke. When the latter passed away in 1879, Kano became a pupil of Iso Masachi and Iikudo Tsunetoshi of the *Kito-ryu*.

In 1882 he created his own *Dojo*, which had only twelve *Tatami*, in the Eisho-ji temple in Tokyo with the assistance of his own pupils, Saigo Shiro, Yokoyama Sakujiro and Yamashita Yoshiachi. They received from his hands the first 'black belts'. He then began to synthesize the various, differing techniques which had until that time been used only in the schools of Ju-jutsu. His aim was to create a sporting discipline which was much less dangerous, and more likely to meet the wishes of the people in a period of peace. Parallel with this undertaking he pursued his official career, and was named Dean of the Central High School in Tokyo in 1893. He made use of his official position to come to Europe where, in 1899, he gave demonstrations of *Judo* in Marseilles. Subsequently, he was sent on official missions to China and Europe (notably in 1902, 1905 and 1912) to spread and teach the principles of Judo. In 1915 the king of Sweden gave him the Olympic medal in recognition of his efforts to promote sport in an idealistic spirit. After a period of retreat in 1920 he devoted himself exclusively to spreading Judo throughout the world, and trained numerous instructors in his advanced school of Judo, the *Kodokan*. In his day he produced thousands of *Judoka*. As the founder of Judo, he alone is entitled to the name of *Sensei* in this discipline. He died in 1938 while returning from Cairo, where he had been the Japanese delegate to the International Committee for the Olympic Games.

Kansetsu 'Joints', 'Knuckles'. See *Body*, *Arms*, *Legs*.

— **Kansetsu-waza** *Aikido*. Techniques of twisting and locking the joints of the arms; in particular the elbow and wrist joints. The include the elbow techniques (*Hiji-waza*), armlocks (*Ude-Hishigi* and *Ude-garami*) and the wristlocks (*Tekubi-waza*) divided into *Kote-hineri* and *Kote-gaeshi*.
Judo. Techniques of bending the joints of *Uke*'s limbs during groundwork (*Ne-waza*) using locks, and thus immobilizing him or her. Typical techniques are:

> *Ude-garami*, twisting the arms
> *Ude-gatame*, twisting locks, arms bent
> *Ude-hishigi*, locks in a position of hyper-extension
> *Hiza-gatame*, locks in a position of hyper-extension, using the knee
> *Waki-gatame*, locks in a position of hyper-extension, using the armpit
> *Hara-gatame*, locks in a position of hyper-extension over the stomach
> *Ashi-garami*, leg locks.

See also *Kami* . . .
— **Kansetsu-geri** *Karate*. A side-kick (*Yoko-geri*) against an opponent's knee.

Kanshusai *Judo*. A pupil who takes part in special courses at the *Kodokan*. These bring together the best students, selected after special competitions, and give them very advanced instruction.

Kansetsu-waza
(Oshi-taoshi)

Kanto-sho see *Sechie-zumo*.

Kanzashi. Large wooden needles, sometimes metal, which are generally forked so that the 'shafts' run parallel to one another. They are 12 to 20 cm long and served to keep the characteristically styled hair of Japanese women in place, in bygone days. They were also ornamental and in addition had a possible martial use: as a thrusting weapon in an emergency when no other weapon was to hand. Single needles, without the fork, are more frequently referred to as *Kogai*.

Kao 'Face'. See *Head*.

Kao-ate *Wa-jutsu*. Basic *Kata* performed in kneeling positions (*Suwari-waza*), identical to *Hakko-dori* but ending with an *Atemi* blow from *Tori* to *Uke*'s temple (*Kasumi*), using a 'sword-hand' technique (*Te-gatana*). See *Tachi-ate*.

Kappo. Technique of resuscitating people who have succumbed to a shock to the nervous system rendering them unconscious, unable to breathe, dizzy, etc. The method of resuscitation uses finger pressure (see *Shiatsu*) and percussive actions of the fists or fingers (*Kuatsu*) on vital points (*Kyusho*) or on points found along the meridians of acupuncture.

Karate (-do) *Kara*, empty; *Te*, hand): Art of the empty hand. Overleaf is the calligraphy for the modern name '*Kara-te*'. Formerly, the name was '*Kara* (Chinese) *Te* (hand)': Chinese hand art (also called *Tode*;

KARATE-DO:
| Kara | Te | Do |
| Empty | Hand | Way |

same meaning). The change was made by Funakoshi Gichin in 1936.

Karate (or, more exactly, *Karate-do*) is a fighting art using only the bare hands (and feet) which has developed over the centuries. It began when the Chinese occupied Okinawa, part of the Ryukyu chain of islands in the sixteenth century, and forbade the inhabitants to possess weapons; this interdict was repeated later under a Japanese occupation. This style of fighting was inspired by similar Chinese techniques, which originated from those practised at the *Shaolin* temple by Buddhist monks. It was intended as a means of defending oneself against brigands and armed invading troops. At that time the peasants trained in secret and, little by little, they invented various techniques which enabled them to defend themselves against attack to good effect. Their centuries of contact with the Chinese also brought the Okinawans some knowledge of the rules and techniques of Chinese Boxing, known as *Kempo*. This was another system of fighting with the feet and hands, using striking techniques without actually grappling with an opponent. It was very effective in putting him out of action. Efficacy was indeed the order of the day in this martial art; the aesthetic and moral aspects played little or no part.

The followers of *Full Contact* fighting cite the tough and rough-and-ready methods of these early Karate techniques as a justification for their own equally hard approach. On the other hand, in the early days the fighting techniques were meant for real combat, *Jutsu*; they are hardly justifiable in times of peace. There were also several styles of *Karate* named after the places in which they were practised: *Shuri-te*, *Naha-*

te, *Tomari-te*, etc. Then came *Funakoshi Gichin* (1869–1957), a Karate student and later a teacher who tried to unify the diverse styles of *Okinawa-te* (as the styles were collectively known) and spread them throughout Japan as a form of *Budo*. To this end, he staged demonstration tournaments in the main towns of Japan to show Karate techniques; notably in 1917 and 1922. The young people of Japan responded with enthusiasm to this new *Okinawa-te*. They saw in it a method of acquiring a kind of invulnerability, or at least a superior physique. Such possibilities lent themselves to a wave of ultra-nationalistic feeling which was being promulgated by those who were directing Japan's future.

The exercises and contests which took place in the *Dojo* at that time were extremely violent. Blows were actually delivered, not 'pulled'. The contestants wore no protective armour of any kind. It was then that Funakoshi Gichin's son, Funakoshi Yoshitaka, in friendly opposition to his father, developed from the deadly Okinawa-te a sporting method which he called *Karate-do*. This was completely separate from *Karate*, the *-do* suffix expressing the idea that this new approach was not intended for a warrior but had the aim of physical and spiritual development. He transformed the techniques of *Okinawa-te* imported by his father into gentler techniques; blows were not delivered fully. He codified them along the lines already followed in *Judo*. Thus Karate became a discipline analogous to Judo, but maintained its own characteristics: using the feet, hands and legs to deliver *Atemi* blows to the vital points(*Kyusho*) of an opponent, and refraining from the grappling and throwing methods typical of Judo and Ju-jutsu. Funakoshi Yoshitaka was the true 'father' of *modern* Karate. After the fall of Japan in 1945, the American authorities banned all Japanese combat sports with the exception of Karate, as they regarded it as a form of Chinese gymnastics. According to certain writers, the fact was that American soldiers wanted to learn some Karate techniques to improve their own close-combat fighting skills. Karate grew in popularity, conquering the USA, Canada, Australia, Europe, and many other countries. Today, most countries have Karate instructors from Japan or from among their own populations. In Europe, Henri Plée is noteworthy, since he imported the art into France in 1955, having gained *Godan* (5th grade of black belt). Students from Britain and other European countries went to learn from him and from the Japanese instructors whom he brought to France from time to time. Among them was Tom Morris from Glasgow, who was one of the promoters of the *Shukokai* style. In the late 1960s and early 1970s various styles of Karate flourished in Britain. Tatsuo Suzuki led the teaching of *Wado-ryu*, Hirokasu Kanazawa the *Shotokan* style, Steve Arneil the Kyokushinkai style, and Steve Morris the *Goju* style. Later, other styles made their appearance but these were the 'big four'.

After 1974, the *Bruce Lee* phenomenon took Western film audiences by storm. Lee displayed electrifying kicking and punching techniques on the screen. Some commentators on the martial arts scene regard his influence as an important factor in the rise of *Full Contact* fighting. Europeans, and Americans in particular, wanted to see more real fighting, and Full Contact gave them what they wanted. But Karate-do remains an art and a sport whose motto is to 'never strike the first blow'; that is, it is a defensive, 'peaceful' art. The essential principles are:

1. Powerful blows requiring a well-developed musculature.

2. Concentration of force to maximize its effect.

3. Utilization of the force of reaction, which gives greater power of penetration and of 'breaking'. (See *Hishigi*, *Shiwari*).

4. Breath control (*Kokyu*) and the development of a low, strong centre of gravity (*Hara*).

5. Speed of movements and good 'timing' of attacks.

Karate technicians wished to keep abreast of and be compatible with the other schools of *Budo*, and added spiritual training and mind control (*Mizu-no-Kokoro*) to their study, as well as the development of an all-round, global vision of the environment (*Tsuki-no-Kokoro*). Thus, practical physical development went hand in hand with psychological development, producing a wider field of perception of both oneself and the world at large. A long and sometimes severe training is needed to achieve good technique. Very soon after the appearance of the *Shotokan* style of Funakoshi, other schools of Karate sprang up, stressing different aspects of technique and modifying others. These include the ones already mentioned, to which may be added: *Shito-ryu* in 1948, and *Sankukai*. The first Karate-do World Championships took place in Tokyo in October 1970, when delegates from thirty-three nations met to create the international Karate federation (WUKO – World Union of Karate-do Organizations). The second world event took place in Paris in 1972. Japan took the titles and one of the foremost European *Karateka*, Dominique Valera of France, came third in the individuals, with his colleague Sauvin. Other championships for the world crown followed under the auspices of WUKO and brought it complete recognition: the USA in 1975, Tokyo in 1977, Madrid in 1980, Taipei in 1982, Maastricht in 1984 and Sydney in 1986. Although Karate-do is not yet a recognized Olympic sport, WUKO officials hope that this will change in 1992. In championship events, weight categories exist, as in *Judo* (see *Judo*.) Championships for women were established in 1981. Championships in Full Contact began in 1980, with an additional weight category; that of Super-Heavyweight.

Karateka may obtain the same grades as *Judoka* (see *Kyudan*). Their training uniforms (*Keikogi*) are called *Karate-gi*. Figures of between 50,000 and 100,000 are given for the number of Karateka training in Great Britain, but as there is no single body in complete control of Karate-do, such figures are unreliable. It is estimated that in the world as a whole there are some fifteen million Karateka.

Competition Rules of Karate-do

CONTESTANTS' EQUIPMENT

Article 1. The competition area (*Shiai-jo*) will in general be a square measuring no less than 8 × 8 m and no more than 10 × 10 m.

If an area of these dimensions is not available, then the conditions in paragraph 1 need not be strictly adhered to.

The surface must be flat, smooth, and made of polished or painted wood, very firm *Tatami* (*Tatami-omote*), or covered with stretched canvas, according to the possibilities of the location.

However, the demarcation line between the contest area and the surroundings must be clearly marked in red or white.

Competition area

Article 2. A contestant must wear a white Karate uniform (*Karate-gi*) and an extra belt or tape in red or white.

The belt must be tied in a correct knot, sufficiently tight to prevent the jacket from coming loose too easily and long enough to go around the waist twice, with at least 15 cm protruding from the tied knot.

The belt must correspond to the grade of the contestant.

Jackets may bear the national badge or insignia, provided this is not too ostentatious.

The Karate-gi must be clean, pressed and not torn or with unravelled stitching.

Article 3. Contestants will wear a groin protector made of an effective material.

Shin-guards, forearm-guards, knee-guards and elbow-guards of any material whatsoever are forbidden, except in the case of an injury which justifies such protection in the opinion of an official doctor.

Article 4. Contestants will keep their toenails and fingernails short, and must not wear any metallic object, etc. . . . , which might cause injury.

The wearing of spectacles is forbidden.

Contact lenses are permitted, at the risk of the contestant wearing them.

COMPETITION

Article 5. The contestants will stand facing each other at a distance of about 5 m apart, in the centre of the contest area, where they will exchange bows. On the command '*Hajime*' the contest will begin.

In team contests the whole team will bow to the opposing team while standing in an orderly line on opposite sides of the contest area. The opposing team will bow at the same time.

Article 6. At the end of the contest(s), the individual contestants or the entire team will return to the position(s) taken at the beginning of the contest(s) and stand face to face. Following the indications and declarations of the referee, they will bow at the same time.

Article 7. The result of the contest will be judged on the basis of a sound and decisive win in which the contestant who delivers an 'effective' blow is the victor.

Article 8. The result of a contest will be decided on the basis of an '*Ippon*' (one point) scoring a win.

Article 9. The time or duration of a contest shall be fixed beforehand, but in certain cases the allotted time may be extended.

Article 10. When the duration of the contest has expired, the referee must be alerted by a double sound signal or by some other means.

Thirty seconds before the end, the contestants and the referee will be alerted by a single sound. In both cases the sound signal shall be sufficiently sonorous or penetrating to be heard above the noise of the crowd.

Article 11. A technique which is delivered at the same time as the signal which indicates the end of the contest shall be judged as valid.

Article 12. A technique which is delivered when the attacker is inside the contest area and the defender is partly outside will be valid, but such an attack shall be void if the attacker has one foot outside the contest area.

JUDGEMENT OF THE COMPETITION

Article 13. The decisions of referees are final; there is no appeal.

Article 14. In principle there must be four judges and one referee. However, according to the circumstances and the type of competition, there may be two judges only, and one referee. It is equally permissible for there to be only a referee and no judges.

Article 15. The referee alone will have responsibility for the conduct of the contest. He will stay within the contest area and manage the progress of the contest.

Article 16. The judges will help the referee. The four judges will take up their positions at the four corners of the contest area, outside and in full view of the area.

Article 17. When a contestant wins with a sound and effective technique, the referee will announce 'Ippon' (one point), stop the contest, return the contestants to their starting positions, and indicate the winner by raising his arm in his or her direction.

Article 18. When a contestant scores *Waza-ari* (80–99 per cent of a point), the referee will announce '*Waza-ari*'. If the same contestant scores another *Waza-ari*, the referee will announce '*Waza-ari Awasete Ippon*' (one whole point from two techniques); he will stop the contest, return the contestants to their starting positions and indicate the winner by raising his arm in his or her direction.

Article 19. If a judge has a different opinion from the referee, the latter may adopt the opinion of that judge after consultation with the other judges. The decision he then indicates or announces shall be final.

Article 20. When the time limit for a contest has expired, and if no *Ippon* is scored, the referee shall announce '*Yame*', stop the contest and return the contestants to their starting positions. The referee must then withdraw from the contest area to a position from which he can see all the judges at once.

He will then raise his hand and call to the judges, '*Hantei*' (judgement).

On this call, the judges will select one of the contestants as the superior of the two and raise a red or white indicator corresponding to the extra belt or tape worn by that contestant. In the case of *Hikiwake* (drawn match), both indicators will be raised at the same time.

Article 21. The referee may then add his own decision to that of the judges concerning the superiority of one of the contestants, following the principle of a majority of the five, and declare 'Yusei-gachi' (winner by superiority), or he may agree with the judges and declare '*Hikiwake*' (draw).

In the event that the opinions of the five officials differ, the judgement of the referee shall prevail.

Even so, the referee will not overrule the absolute majority decision of three judges who are in agreement.

Article 22. In the following cases the referee will announce '*Yame*' and may stop the contest temporarily. To restart the contest he will announce '*Hajime*'. In this instance, if the referee announces '*Jikan*', the time taken up by the stoppage will be deducted from the contest time:

(a) When a contestant goes out of the contest area.

(b) When a contestant commits a prohibited act.

(c) When a contestant is injured, overcome by illness or sustains an accident.

(d) When a contestant is required to readjust his uniform.

(e) In any other case not covered by the above mentioned, when the referee deems it necessary.

The chief referee is the only official authorised to bring the contest time to a stop.

PROHIBITED ACTS

Article 23. In relation to the actions and techniques of the contestants, the following acts are forbidden:

(a) To strike without proper control any of the vital points of an opponent. Any touch to the head, even a light one, will be considered a grave offence.

(b) .To attack or simulate an attack to the eyes using a stabbing action with the open hand, fingers extended.

(c) To bite and scratch.

(d) Wilfully to use a technique to injure an opponent.

(e) To call out without reason, make remarks or gestures disrespectful to the opponent with the aim of making him lose self-control and therefore be at a disadvantage.

(f) To fail to carry out the referee's instructions immediately.

(g) To lose one's temper to such an extent that the opponent is in danger and there is a likelihood of prohibited acts being committed.

(h) To show a lack of sporting spirit, leading to the expression of an opinion or protest which contradicts the referee.

(i) To display an attitude contrary to the spirit of Karate.

(j) To seize, encircle with an arm or leg, hold on to the opponent without an immediate follow-up action.

(k) To avoid in any way a genuine confrontation with the opponent obviously in order to arrive at the expiry of time without further fighting; by running, for example.

(l) Deliberately to leave the contest area.

(m) To adopt an unpleasant attitude, in order to avoid defeat through systematic obstruction.

(n) To unfasten and refasten the belt or the tapes of the trousers of the Karate-gi without the referee's permission.

(o) To speak for any reason, other than in an emergency.

(p) To strike with the head.

All the preceding paragraphs are regarded as 'infringements of the rules of Karate'.

Article 24. The referee may himself make a 'remark' to the contestants. He should give a warning (*Chui*) if one of the contestants has made or has tried to make an action which constitutes a grave infringement of the rules. If, after this warning, he notices that a further infringement is made, he may, after consultation with the judges, announce that the culprit has lost the contest on the basis of infringement. In the case of a very grave infringement, he may directly disqualify the contestant by announcing '*Hansoku*'.

JUDGEMENT OF A CONTEST

Article 25. The judgement '*Ippon*' will be delivered on the basis of the following:

(a) An 'effective blow' constitutes an attack delivered at a vital point (Article 31). This attack must be:

Correct as to form
Correct as to attitude
Correct as to distance
Delivered with force, speed and decisiveness.

However, if the technique does not seem sufficient, the referee may, at his own discretion, bring the contestants back to their starting positions.

(b) When one of the contestants gives up.

Article 26. The judgement '*Waza-ari*' will be delivered on the basis of the following: in the case of an effective technique, when a contestant strikes an opponent with good form and good attitude almost meriting an '*Ippon*.

Article 27. The judgement '*Yusei-gachi*' may be delivered on the basis of the following:

(a) If a score of *Waza-ari* has already been given, the referee does not ask for *Hantei*, but must obligatorily award a win.

(b) If a warning of *Chui* has already been given, the referee asks for *Hantei*.

(c) If both a *Waza-ari* and a *Chui* have already been given, the referee asks for *Hantei*.

(d) If a contestant has already received two warnings of *Chui*, he or she loses by *Hansoku-make*.

(e) If a contestant has obtained two *Waza-ari*, he or she wins by *Waza-ari Awasete-an Ippon*.

Article 28. The judgement *Hikiwake* (match drawn) will be given when no decisive result has been obtained during the standard time limit of a contest, and when the superiority or the inferiority of one of the contestants has not been judged apparent.

Article 29. The referee may give *Hansoku-make* (losing through violation of the rules) against a contestant on the basis of the following:

(a) When an action is performed which might possibly be dangerous to the other contestant or if unnecessary words are spoken or if any behaviour is such that it falls under the heading of 'very grave'.

(b) If a contestant repeats a violation, thus flouting a warning already given by the referee (see Article 24).

(c) When a contestant leaves the contest area for the first time, on purpose, the referee will draw his attention to the fact, immediately. The second time, the referee will deliver a warning. The third time, the referee must award a disqualification (*Hansoku-make*).

It is important to note that the movement out of the contest area must be for reasons of 'running away' or evidently a refusal to fight.

Article 30. When a contestant does not present him- or herself ready for the contest, the opponent may be awarded *Yusei-gachi* (winner through superiority).

VITAL POINTS

[Translator's note: the importance or otherwise of vital points in the scoring of points in a Karate contest varies. If all the other considerations for the awarding of a point are present, then the question of the area of focus is often disregarded.]

Article 31. These are the vital points accepted in contests: the face, the neck, the lower abdomen, the solar plexus, the lumbar region of the back, the floating ribs.

Article 32 (amended). No distinction will be made between opponents over the question of height, reach, strength or weight (as regards training only).

Article 33. In the case of a contestant not being able to continue with a contest following some incident, injury or illness, the referee will declare, after consultation with the judges, a win, a defeat or a draw, on the basis of the following:

(a) In the case of injury:

If the responsibility for the injury lies with the injured party, then he or she will lose.
If the responsibility for the injury lies with the opponent, then the opponent will lose.
If the responsibility for the injury cannot be attributed to either party, then the injured contestant will lose on the grounds of withdrawing from the contest.

(b) If the contest cannot be continued due to the illness of one of the contestants, then the latter shall be declared the loser.

Article 34. If a situation arises which is not foreseen by these rules, the referee and the judges will settle the matter between them.

— **Karate-do.** All practitioners of traditional *Karate-do*, of whatever style, owe respect to the *-do* added to the *Karate*. They observe the significance implicit in this, to show that it is a 'Way' of *Budo*. This differentiates it from the diverse forms of Karate which are merely training for fighting purposes.

— **Karate-gi.** The training uniforms worn in *Karate-do*, consisting of a wide-fitting jacket made of cotton, white cotton trousers long enough to reach halfway down the lower leg but frequently almost ankle length, a belt coloured according to the grade, and during competitions either a red or white tape round the belt. Also called *Keikogi*.

— **Karateka.** Anyone who trains in *Karate-do*, whatever his or her grade.

— **Karate-shinto.** A school of Japanese *Karate*, founded by *Yamaguchi Gogen* around 1955, combining the principles of *Zen*, Yoga, *Shinto* and *Karate-do*. It brought the practice of Karate into the realms of 'spiritualist' religion.

Kari (-gari) *Judo*. Technique of sweeping away the opponent's legs. See *O Soto-gari, O Uchi-gari, Ko Uchi-gari, Ko Soto-gari*.

Karimata see *Ya*.

Kasagake *Kyudo*. An exercise performed during archery training on horseback. Arrows were fired at hats mounted on stakes, at close range. It was formerly practised by *Samurai*. They had to knock off the hats (*Kasa*) with muffled arrows (*Hikime*) while passing in front of them at full gallop. See *Togasagake, Inu-oi-mono, Yabusame*.

Kashima Shinto-ryu. An ancient school of martial arts similar to *Katori Shinto-ryu*, created by *Bokuden*, the son of a *Shinto* priest of the sanctuary of Kashima (prefecture of Ibaraki). See *Kage-ryu*.

Kashinuki-shiai. A type of competition 'in line'.

Kashira (-gashira) 'Head', 'Column', 'High'.

Kassatsu see *Kyusho*.

Kassei-ho see *Kuatsu*.

Kasumi 'Temples'. See *Head, Oku-iai*.

Kata 'Form', 'Sequences'. Also see *Kaho*. In all the martial arts, the *Kata* are made up of 'imaginary combats' against, in most cases, relatively slow-moving real or imaginary opponents. They are constructed of sequences of basic, intermediate or advanced techniques which are meant to be performed with technical accuracy. They are studied so that their nature, purpose and the teaching implicit in them may be understood. They are practised as much for the perfecting of technique as for the aesthetic experience to be derived from 'beautiful movements'. They may be described as a choreography of attack and defence, a 'ritual' of technique and movement; the *Waza* are the application of the latter and the *Do* their spiritual aspect.

All the *Kata* must be begun and ended with a bow to the master and his assistants, in front of the *Kamiza* (*Joseki*). Korean: **Hyong**, **Poomse**; Vietnamese: **Thao Quyen, Quyen, Song Luyen**: Indonesian: **Juru**.

Judo. In the *Judo* of the *Kodokan* six main Kata are generally studied:

> *Nage-no-Kata*, Standing forms
> *Katame-no-Kata*, Forms of control
> *Kime-no-Kata*, Self-defence forms
> *Ju-no-Kata*, Forms of gentleness
> *Koshiki-no-Kata*, Ancient forms
> *Itsutsu-no-Kata*, Ancient forms
> *Seiryoku Zen-yo Kokumin Tai-iku-no-Kata*.

Karate. Today, as in former times, the Kata learned in Karate consist of the 'Kata of power' (*Go*) or 'Kata of victory' (*Shobu-no-Kata*) consisting of ten techniques used for real fighting. Also called *Kaho*. See *Kanku, Heian, Pinan*.

Kendo. In this discipline the Kata are performed not with the *Shinai* but with a real sword (*Katana*).

Kata 'Shoulder'.
— **Kata-ashi-dori *Judo*.** A grip on the leg.
— **Kata-dori *Aikido*.** A defensive sequence. *Uke* seizes *Shite* by the shoulder. Shite avoids with *Tai-sabaki* and throws Uke.
— **Kata-gatame *Judo*.** Controlling an opponent at the shoulder in a technique of groundwork (*Ne-waza*).

Kata-gatame

— **Kata-guruma *Judo*.** 'Shoulder wheel.' *Tori* lowers his or her body, slides an arm between *Uke*'s legs, head below the armpit, and lifts him or her across his or her shoulders with the help of the back of the neck,

Demonstration of Kata (Shito-ryu style) by Master Shiokawa.

throwing *Uke* down on to his or her back.

— **Kata-ha-jime** *Judo.* Strangulation technique combined with control of the shoulder. A groundwork (*Ne-waza*) technique.

Kata-ha-jime

Kata-guruma

— **Kata-jime** *Judo.* Strangulation using the shoulder.
— **Kata-juji-jime** *Judo.* Strangulation technique in which the forearms make a cross shape resulting from a cross grip in which the left hand holds the left collar of an opponent and the right hand the right collar.

Kata-juji-jime

— **Kata-mawashi** see *Ju-no-kata*.
— **Kata-osae-gatame** *Judo*. Controlling an opponent by the shoulder in groundwork (*Ne-waza*).

Kataki 'Opponent'.

Katame no Kata *Judo*. In the techniques of the *Kodokan*, these are the forms (*Kata*) concerned with control of an opponent, or *Katame*. These Kata consist of three techniques (*Waza*) of five movements each:

Osae-waza (techniques of immobilization)
Shime-waza (techniques of strangulation)
Kansetsu-waza (techniques of bending the joints). See *Goshin-jutsu, Kata*.

The *Osae-waza* (or *Osae-komi*) are carried out across the body (*Kesa-gatame*) or 'by controlling the four limbs' (*Shiho-gatame*).
The *Shime-waza* are carried out face to face (*Shimeai*), from the rear (*Ushiro-shime*), without the aid of the *Judo-gi* (with bare hands, *Hadaka-jime*) or with the aid of the Judo-gi (*Kesa-shime*).
The *Kansetsu-waza* are carried out by bending the joints of an outstretched limb (*Ude-hishigi-gatame*) or a bent limb (*Ude-garami-gatame*). To control or immobilize an opponent, two principles are brought into play: *Ju*, which consists of changing to another technique when necessary, to maintain or complete an immobilization, and *Go*, which consists of controlling the focal point of a technique by using force.
The *Katame-no-Kata* 'techniques' are also called *Katame-waza*, and *Ne-waza* (lying-down techniques, on the ground).
— **Katame-waza** *Judo* see *Katame-no-*

Kata, Ne-waza.
Aikido. These are also forms of control carried out:

against the elbows of an opponent (*Ikkyo, Ude-osae*)
by twisting of the wrist(s) (*Nikyo, Kote-mawashi*)
by a different form of twisting the wrist(s) (*Sankyo, Kote-hineri*)
by painful pressure on the wrist (*Yon-kyo, Tekubi-osae*)
by stretching the arm (*Gokyo, Ude-nobashi*)
by locking the arm under the armpit (*Ude-hishigi*)

Katana. A slightly curved sword with one cutting edge (the convex one), used from the beginning of the Ashikaga period (1333–1474). It was one of the weapons used by the *Bushi*, particularly the *Samurai*, who carried it thrust into the belt (*Obi*), with its 'companion sword', the *Waki-zashi*. The Waki-zashi was the shorter of the two. The *Katana* or 'long sword' (*Daito* or sometimes *O-dachi*) was worn in the belt with its cutting edge uppermost, so that it could be drawn (see *Iai-do*) in a position ready for cutting. The blade was 61 cm or more, while the blade of the Waki-zashi or *Shoto* varied from 31 to 61 cm. The Katana was a fighting sword *par excellence*, endowed with a sacred element since it came from the workshop of a swordsmith who was also a member of the *Shinto* priesthood. The two swords together were called *Daisho* (large and small) and were worn by Samurai of all ranks.
Three groups of sword are recognized. These are the *Koto* or 'Ancient swords', produced from around 900 to around 1530; the *Shinto* or 'New swords', produced from 1530 to 1867; and the *Shin-Shinto* or 'Very new swords', forged after 1867. The children of the Bushi also carried a type of Katana, but smaller, called *Mamori-gatana*, or 'Protective sword'. When a Samurai entered a friend's house, he put his *Katana* on a special rest constructed for that purpose at the doorway, but he was allowed to keep his Waki-zashi. In the presence of the emperor or *Shogun*, Samurai were obliged to leave both swords at the entrance

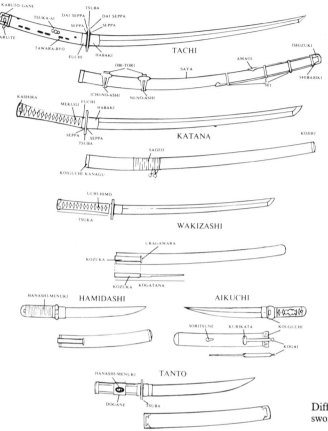

Different types of Japanese sword.

to the audience chamber. When a Katana was not being used or worn it was taken to pieces and its blade replaced by a similar one made of wood. The original blade was then cleaned, and a hilt of magnolia wood was fixed to it. The whole was placed on a special support also made of magnolia wood, the *Katana-kake*, cutting edge uppermost. The cutting edge was often protected by a sheath of the same wood, without a guard. A Katana is composed of a blade (*To*), a hilt (*Tsuka*), a sheath (*Saya*) and a worked guard (*Tsuba*). The blade has a flat tang pierced with two holes (*Mekugi-ana*) which serve to fix the hilt. The blade itself, often a very precious object, is sometimes decorated with etched designs (*Horimono*) and with Sino-Japanese characters. A blade was

recognized by the undulating lines left by the process of tempering on the cutting edge (*Ha*), the *Yakiba*. The back of the blade varied in thickness and was called the *Mune*, the point *Kissaki*, and the line separating the cutting edge from the back, *Shinogi*. The tang (*Nakago*) was often streaked with lime (*Yasuri-me*) to prevent the hilt from slipping. It often bore the engraved name (*Mei*) of the swordsmith (*Kaji*).

The techniques of forging and tempering steel were the jealously guarded secrets of the swordsmiths, but it is known that the blade was generally forged using a sandwich method in which the soft iron ingot was used to enfold a piece of hard steel. The whole was heated a number of times and hammered into shape, undergoing various

107

stages of tempering in which the cutting edge was protected by a glaze which left a wavelike pattern (*Yakiba*). Next the blade was polished for a long time. Perfect balance was given to the blade by the weight of the guard (*Tsuba*), which was also made of iron. The Samurai who had ordered the blade could then replace the original guard with another, of the same weight, specially made for him by a smith specializing in precious metals. The tang consisted of two pieces of wood held in place and joined by two *Menuki* (or pegs) and covered with sharkskin (*Same*) held down by crisscross threads. The pommel (*Kashira*) of the tang was in decorated copper or bronze. Finally, a copper ring, *Fuchi*, completed the fixing of the tang and kept the guard in place. The guard was fixed to the side of the blade by another copper ring, the *Habaki*. The sheath too was made of two pieces of wood, either simply lacquered or more profusely decorated. It was composed of a 'mouth ring' (*Ko-guchi*) made of horn and a chape or tip (*Kojiri*) of decorated copper or other metal. On the side of the sheath was a ring (*Kurikata*) designed to take a cord (*Sageo*) and to prevent the sword from slipping in the belt. See *Wakizashi*, *Swords*, *Tsuba*, *Kaiken*, *Tanto*, *Tachi*.
— **Katana-kake** see *Swords, Katana*.
— **Katana-zutsu** see *Swords*.

Kata Oshi see *Ju-no-Kata*.

Kata-sukashi *Sumo*. The action of wrapping the arm round the shoulder of an opponent, from under the armpit, while he or she is off balance, to throw him or her forwards. See *Kimarite*.

Katate 'A single hand'.
— **Katate-age** see *Ju-no-Kata*.
— **Katate-dori** *Aikido*. A technique in which *Uke* grasps *Shite*'s left wrist with the right hand, from the front, or the right wrist with the left hand. When the right hand grasps the right wrist or the left the left wrist it is called *Gyaku Katate-dori*.
— **Katate-jime** *Judo*. Strangulation with one hand.
— **Katate Ryote-dori** *Aikido*. Seizing both wrists from the front.

Kata-sukashi

— **Katate-uchi** *Karate*. A blow delivered with the edge of the open hand, known as sword-hand.
— **Katate-waza** *Kendo*. A technique of using the *Shinai* with one hand, requiring a lot of strength in the wrist.

Katori Shinto-ryu. A school of *Ken-jutsu* (sword-fighting) created by *Iizasa Choisai* (1387–1488) in which the principles of *Zen* are applied to the use of the sword. In this school, diverse disciplines are studied and practised in addition to the sword. These are the use of the staff, *Naginata*, *Iai-do*, and most other weapons. Great emphasis is placed on the use of *Mudra* (mystical hand gestures) which are incorporated into the *Kata*. This school is classed as a 'Cultural Treasure of Japan'. Such a title is conferred on any institution which is regarded as part of the national heritage and worthy of preservation. Also called *Tenshin Shoden Katori Shinto-ryu*. See *Kashima Shinto-ryu, Mudra*.

Katsugi *Kendo*. A shoulder movement which allows a blow with the *Shinai* to be delivered at an opponent or an evasion to be made when attacked.

Katsujin no Ken see *Heiho*.

Katsuya Miyahira see *Shorinji-ryu*.

Kawaishi Mikonosuke. A master of martial arts specializing in the *Judo* of the *Kodokan*. He came to France in 1935 and

Members of the Katori school during a Shinto ceremony.

founded a Franco-Japanese club which fused with the Ju-jutsu Club of France in 1938. He also created a *Judo* method, peculiar to France, which bears his name. The names of the movements are French, as are the names of the belt (grading) system. He left for Japan at the outbreak of the Second World War and returned to France in 1949 to take up residence and concentrate on the teaching of Judo. The *Kawaishi* system differs only slightly from that of the Kodokan; the main difference being the use of French terminology. Refer to the entry on *Kodokan* for an outline of the basic techniques of Judo.

Kawashi *Aikido, Karate.* An evasion against a blow or attacking movement, usually effected by a turn of the body (*Tai-sabaki*).

Kawazu-gake. A technique of moving which is not officially recognized by the sporting federations of martial arts. See Competition Rules of *Judo*, 28.

Ke-age *Karate.* A type of kick involving a 'whipping' action in which the foot lashes down and is equally quickly withdrawn. See *Tachi-ai*, *Keri*.
— **Ke-banashi** *Karate.* An 'outside' kick

in which the foot is quickly withdrawn.
— **Kega** 'Injury'.

Keibo see *Bo, Sticks.*

Keibo-soho see *Taiho-jutsu.*

Keichu See *Kyusho, Head.*

Keijo see *Jo.*

Keijo-jutsu see *Ju-jutsu.*

Keiko see *Kyusho.*

Keiko (-geiko) 'Training' designed to perfect oneself in an art or technique in order to surpass (*Kei*) whatever has gone before (*Ko*).
Aikido. *Keiko* consists of three phases: *Randori, Tai-Sabaki* and *Kokyu*. See *Kangeiko, Hatsu-geiko, Shochu-geiko, Kakarigeiko.*
Sumo. Training takes place in the heart of a *Heya* or 'schoolhouse' (also called 'Stable'), starting at five o'clock on the morning, seven days a week. The basic exercises are striking a pole with the palms of the hands (*Teppo*), stretching exercises on the ground (*Koshiwari*), throwing the leg to the side, high in the air, before stamping down on the ground

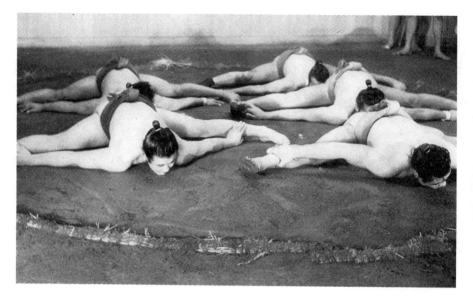

Stretching exercises in a Sumo school.

with the sole of the foot (*Shiko*). See *Ji-geiko*, *Weapons (hands)*.

— **Keikoba.** Training place.

— **Keikogi.** Uniform for training in the martial arts in the *Dojo*, called by different names according to the art concerned: *Judogi*, *Karate-gi*, *Aikidogi*, etc.
Korean: ***Do-bok.*** The uniform for *Viet Do Dao* is called *Vo Phuc*.

Keikoku see *Chui*, Competition rules of *Judo*, 23, 24, 29.

Keirei *Kendo.* Simple bow, inclining the upper body forward.

Keito *Karate.* That part of the top of the thumb used in striking. See *Weapons*.

— **Keito-uke** *Karate.* A blocking technique in which the hand is held in the *Keito* position.

Kekomi *Karate.* A 'forcing in' or penetrating kick. See *Keri*.

Kempo 'Way of the fist'. A Chinese martial art, originally a fighting method, using no weapons, introduced into Okinawa just before 1600. Known in China as *Quanfa*

Keito-uke

(Ch'uan-fa), it was probably practised in that country from the seventh century by Buddhist monks of the *Shaolin-si* and later became known as *Jiaodishu*, then *Kaiko* (under the influence of the Mongols) and finally *Kenyu*, 'art of the fist'. It is characterized by powerful and fast fist techniques, the feet being used only to move the combatants around. The techniques of *Kempo* profoundly influenced those of *Okinawa-te*, which developed into a modified form known as *Karate-do* at the end of the nineteenth century. Also called *Hakuda*, *Shuhaku*. See *Shorinji-kempo*.

Ken 'Fist'. See *Kento*, *Kempo*. Also *Seiken*. Korean ***Kwon***; Chinese: ***Quan*** (The older

English spelling of 'Quan' was 'Ch'uan'); Vietnamese: *Qwan (Kwan)*.

Ken 'To hook'. *Kendo*. The moment when one of the combatants waits for the opponent to attack, or seeks to provoke the opponent into attacking him or her. During this brief period he profits from the *De-ai* (loss of concentration) of the opponent when the latter is deciding to attack but has not actually carried out the attack and strikes with the *Shinai* to score a point.

Ken 'Sword'. The name given to the ancient, straight, double-edged weapons. See *Katana, Swords, Kendo, Ken-jutsu*.

Ken-bu. Dances performed as homage to the *Kami*. The *Samurai* danced in this fashion before they departed for combat and on their return in celebration of their exploits. The dance was accompanied by a poem, which was sung. *Ken-bu* probably came from certain movements used in the *Noh* theatre and in performances of *Kabuki*, as well as from the *Yumitori-shiki* of the *Sumotori*. The Japanese school of *Itto-ryu Seiunkan* works to preserve this tradition in Japan. The dances are performed in large ceremonial costumes, with a drawn *Katana*.

Kendo 'Way of the sword'. A martial art (*Budo*) of using the sword (*Ken*), formerly called *Ken-jutsu, Ken-no-michi*, and *Gekken* during the Meiji period (1868–1912). This art was developed from the earliest times by the warriors (*Bushi*) of Japan, and from the thirteenth century onwards by the *Samurai*. Ken-jutsu was prohibited in 1876, when the Samurai were forbidden to carry swords, but was transformed into a martial sport (*Kendo*) by *Sakakibara Kenkichi* (1830–94) for physical and mental training of the young. The term Kendo was invented in 1900 by *Abe Tate* to replace the term Ken-jutsu, which was considered too 'warlike'. The first Kendo academy was founded in Tokyo in 1909, and the art continued to flourish and grow in Japan, where it is practised by men and women alike. The aims of Kendo were defined by the Japanese Kendo Federation, founded early this century: 'The aim of Kendo training is to mould the mind and the body, to cultivate a steady and firm attitude, to work with perseverance in order to progress in Kendo through true and rigorous training, to hold courtesy and honour in high esteem, to deal with others with sincerity, and finally always to pursue the perfecting of oneself.'

Kendo is one of the foremost and most respected of Japanese Budo disciplines, because it is based on the classical art of the sword. For centuries it represented the spirit of the governing class of the Bushi. About the year 1600, which saw the dawn of the Tokugawa period, hundreds of schools and styles of sword-fighting existed in Japan, and each family or *Buke* of warriors had its own instructors. Sakakibara Kenkichi was inspired by the techniques of these schools (see *Ken-jutsu*) when he formulated the rules of Kendo. These are based on blows delivered with speed and precision using a bamboo *Shinai* instead of a 'live' blade. The combatants wear special armour (*Dogu*) which includes a mask with a steel grill (*Men*) and shoulder flaps, a rigid breastplate of lacquered bamboo (*Do*), firmly padded gloves or mitts, protectors for the abdomen (*Tare*) and the lower abdomen (*Tare-obi*). Under the armour the *Kendoka* wear a jacket (*Keikogi*) and a *Hakama* or wide split 'skirt' reaching the ankles. This conceals from the opponent the movements of the feet during combat. Training and contests usually take place in a room with a smooth floor; contestants are barefoot. Contests begin with the command '*Hajime*' (Begin!) and end with a call of 'Yame' (Stop!) or '*Shobu-ari*' (End of contest). In the case of a win (*Shobu*) or a draw (*Hikiwake*) the contest simply stops. The fighting usually lasts for five minutes, but the referee may order a three-minute extension when no score has been made. The winner is the one who has either scored two points (two *Ippon*) during the five-minute period or a single point (*Ippon*) during the extension. Time for stoppages – such as after the first *Ippon*, during a consultation with the judges, or a momentary stop brought about by the referee – is not included in the time allotted for the contest, but the time needed by the referee to separate the contestants from a *Tsuba-zeri-ai* (*Tsuba* touching) is included in the time allotted for the contest.

Training exercise of raising and lowering the sword (Suburi). School of Master Takano at Kamakura.

For one of the contestants to score a point, he or she must attack cleanly, using the body, the Shinai and energy expressed with a *Kiai* all at the same time; this is known as *Kikentai-no-uchi*. The scoring blow must be made with the point of the Shinai or with the upper third of the bamboo blade. Only certain points on the body give scoring results:

the head: on the forehead (*Men*), on the right side (*Migi-men*) or the left side (*Hidari-men*)
the forearms (*Kote*), right (*Migi-kote*) or left (*Hidari-kote*)
the trunk (*Do*), on the right side (*Migi-do*) or left (*Hidari-do*)
the throat (*Tsuki*).

The blows must be clean and accurate, the Shinai held in both hands (*Ryote*) or in one hand (*Katate*). A blow may be struck and counted as a scoring blow on a contestant who has dropped his Shinai or fallen. A scoring blow may also be struck by a contestant who has just fallen, provided that it is delivered immediately. If a blow is struck at the instant the time is given it is valid. For a blow to be counted as a scoring blow, the contestant delivering it must call out at the same time as he or she strikes the name of that part of the opponent's body which is the target. In performing the *Kata* of Kendo a real sword (*Katana*) is used, not a Shinai. This is why *Iai-do* is a natural complement to the study of Kendo. Until 1955, the sport was virtually confined to Japan. In

Training exercise of Kendo. Forward strike.

1955 it was introduced on an organized scale to France and the USA, and in the same year the first international tournament took place in the USA. The sport was first taken up in Britain in the early 1960s and the first world championships were held in Tokyo in 1970. Since that time Kendo has gained a high reputation internationally and is practised in numerous countries. There are about 550 Kendoka in Britain, affiliated to the British Kendo Association. See *Dogu, Ken-jutsu, Iai-do, Shinai*.

Suburi, from left to right.

Kendo equipment.

Rules of Kendo Competition

CONTEST AREA

Article 1. The dimensions of the contest area are from 9 to 11 m, including the line.

Article 2. Another line must be drawn 1.50 m outside the first line.

Article 3. Every line must be 5 to 10 cm wide and in principle coloured white.

EQUIPMENT

Article 4. The size classification, length and weight of the *Shinai* is shown in the table below. The weight of the *Tsuba* is not included in that of the Shinai.

Size	Length	Weight
37 (1)	112 cm	375–450 g
38 (2)	115 cm	450–485 g
39 (3)	118 cm	485 g+

Guide to age relative to size:

(1) 13, 14, 15 years
(2) 16, 17, 18 years
(3) 19 years and older.

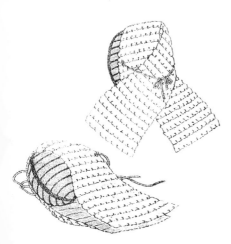

Kendo helmets drawn by Hokusai.

Article 5. If two *Shinai* are used, the first must be no longer than 1.10 m and no lighter than 375 g; the second must be no longer than 60 cm and no lighter than 265 g.

Article 6. The construction of the *Shinai* and the names of its different parts are indicated in Figure 2.

Article 7. The *Tsuba* is usually made of hide, but may also be plastic. It is round; its maximum diameter is 8 cm. It must be firmly attached.

Article 8. The equipment used in *Kendo* consists of: *Men, Do, Kote, Tare.* The articles of clothing are: *Keikogi, Hakama* or simply some kind of sports outfit.

DIFFERENT TYPES OF CONTEST AND THEIR METHODS

Article 9. Individual combat

1. Individual combat or a contest between two persons only should in principle follow the rule of *Sanbon-shobu.*

2. The rule of *Sanbon-shobu* prescribes that the first contestant who scores two points, within the time limit, is the winner. However, if a contestant scores only one point within the time limit then that contestant is the winner.

3. If no point has been scored within the time limit, or if the standard of each contestant has been equal, then the time limit may be extended until one of them scores a point. In any case, it is possible to decide a winner either by a decision of the referee or by drawing lots.

Article 10. Team contests.

1. Team contests are primarily contests between individual team members selected to fight in a definite order. The contestants line up and take their places one at a time on the contest area. The total number of points scored by each team is totalled and the winning team is the one with the most points.

2. Contests take place according to the Winner System or the Elimination System.
— Winner System:

The team with the highest number of winning contestants is declared the winner.

However, when two teams have an equal number of winners, the team with the highest number of points prevails. If it happens that two teams have an equal number of points, then a contest must take place between a representative from each team. The victory of one of them decides the winning team.

— Elimination System:

In this system a contestant who wins his first bout continues to fight until he loses.

BEGINNING, INTERRUPTION AND END OF A CONTEST

Article 11. A contest begins with an announcement from the chief referee of '*Hajime!*' and breaks off when he calls '*Yame!*'.

Article 12. A contest comes to an end when the chief referee announces '*Shobu-ari*' (end of contest) or '*Hikiwake*' (drawn match).

DURATION OF CONTEST

Article 13. The normal duration of a contest is five minutes.

Article 14. The normal duration of extension or extra time is three minutes.

Article 15. Time spent as listed below is not included in the time allotted for the contest:

(a) in restarting the contest after the chief referee has announced that a point has been scored;

(b) when accidents, and consultations between judges occur;

(c) between an order to stop a contest and begin it again.

However, the time spent by the referee in separating two contestants in a situation of *Tsubazeriai* (they are too close to each other, their *Shinai* and *Tsuba* touching) is included in the time allotted to the contest.

POINTS OF ATTACK

Article 16.

Men – forehead
Sho-men – middle of forehead
Migi-men – right side of forehead
Hidari-men – left side of forehead

Article 17.
Kote – forearm(s)
Migi-kote – right forearm
Hidari-kote – left forearm

Article 18.
Do – side of the body
Migi-do – right side of the body
Hidari-do – left side of the body

Article 19.
Tsuki – throat (a point of attack which is not permitted to contestants under sixteen).

EVALUATION OF BLOWS

Article 20. Scoring blows are given when they strike the designated points of the body with the top third of the *Shinai*. The side of the Shinai which makes contact must be the side opposite the cord (*Tsuru*). Thrusting blows to the throat (*Tsuki*) are delivered with the tip of the Shinai. Blows delivered with one hand (*Katate*) must be especially accurate. In all circumstances a contestant must show an intense, attacking spirit and keep his or her body in a suitable attitude.

A scoring point may be awarded also in any of the following cases:

1. A blow given immediately after a contestant has dropped his or her Shinai or fallen to the ground himself (or herself). Furthermore, a contestant who has fallen to the ground may deliver a scoring blow to the opponent provided it is carried out immediately, without pause.

2. A blow given at the same moment as a contestant leaves the contest area.

3. A blow given at the same moment as the signal for the end of the contest.

WARNINGS

The following actions or behaviour are considered to merit warnings:

Article 21. Words or actions showing disrespect to the other contestants or to the judges.

Article 22. Jogai (leaving the contest area). When a contestant's foot goes completely outside the contest area, or when a contestant loses his or her balance and supports him- or herself outside the contest area, or if he or she leans on the *Shinai* outside the contest area, all these actions shall be judged as *Jogai*.

However, if both contestants leave the contest area, the one who leaves first receives a warning. If they both leave the contest ares at the same time, both receive a warning. If one of the contestants falls, and only part of his or her body is outside the limits, this is equally an act of *Jogai*. If both contestants fall outside the contest area, the first to do so receives a warning. If they fall outside at the same time, both receive a warning.

Article 23. Ashigarami (hooking the leg).

Article 24. A push which is not an acceptable part of an encounter, whether it is given with the body or with the *Shinai*.

Article 25. Blows which are deliberately struck against those parts of the opponent's body which are not protected by his or her *Kendo-gu*.

Article 26. Holding the opponent with the hand or introducing the *Tsuba* between his or her hands when the hands are gripping the *Shinai*.

Article 27. When a contestant drops his or her *Shinai* and seizes the opponent's *Shinai* above the *Tsuba* (that is, by the blade).

Article 28. Various actions considered detrimental to the good conduct of the contest.

PENALTIES

Article 29. A contestant who is guilty of the faults described in Article 21 loses the contest. He or she forfeits two points to the opponent and must leave the contest area. The points scored up to this moment are cancelled.

Article 30. A contestant who is guilty of the acts described in Articles 22 to 28 receives a warning for each infringement; infringements are announced every time they are committed. The contestant who commits three infringements forfeits a point to his or her opponent. However, if the two contestants obtain one point each and commit a third infringement simultaneously, the infringement will not be counted.

The warnings in Articles 22 to 28 remain in force during the whole of the contest, including any extra time.

INJURY OR ACCIDENT DURING THE CONTEST

Article 31. Following an accident, the contestant who cannot continue may ask for an interruption in the contest time.

Article 32. If a contestant refuses to fight on or asks for the contest to be ended, even though his or her injury is light and not bad enough to prevent the contest from continuing, then that contestant is declared the loser.

Article 33. If a contest cannot be continued because of injury, and if the injury has been caused intentionally by the opponent or as a result of some act of the opponent, the latter loses the contest. If the cause of the injury cannot by determined, the contestant who cannot continue loses the contest.

Article 34. A contestant who cannot continue or asks for an interruption in the contest for any reason other than an injury loses the contest.

Article 35. According to Articles 32, 33 and 34, the winner receives two points. If the loser has already scored one point, it remains valid.

OBJECTIONS

Article 36. No objection to the judges' decisions is admissible.

Article 37. If there is any doubt about the

application of a rule, objections may be presented to the president of the judges by a representative, before the beginning of the next contest.

OFFICIALS

Article 38. The president of the judges has total authority over the good conduct of the contests.

Article 39. When there are two contest areas or more, a vice-president of the judges is assigned to each of them, to help the president, and he or she is responsible for the rulings in that area.

Article 40. A chief judge and two assistant judges are assigned to each contest area. They have complete authority for evaluating blows and giving warnings. The chief judge co-operates with the other officials concerned and makes sure that the contests are being conducted properly. It is he or she who announces the winner.

Article 41. In principle there must be two line judges for each contest area. It is their task to indicate an infringement when one of the contestants crosses the line limiting the contest area.

Article 42. In principle, a chief time-keeper and two assistants or more control the time of a contest and signal its end.

Article 43. In principle, a chief scorer and two assistants or more display the decisions of the referees.

Article 44. In principle, a chief recorder and two assistants or more take note of the valid blows, the number and type of warnings, the duration of the contest, etc.

Article 45. In principle, a chief controller and two assistants or more call the contestants to their places, check their equipment and make sure that the contest takes place without delay.

JUDGES' FLAGS

Article 46. The make-up of the flags used by the judges is indicated on page 184. See *Referees and judges.*

Rules for Judging Kendo Contests

Article 1. The judges decide the winners according to the rules of *Kendo* competition.

Article 2. For each contest area there is a chief judge and two assistants.

Article 3. The functions of the judges are as follows:

(a) The chief judge has full power over the good conduct of the contest; he decides and indicates the valid blows; he indicates the winner.

(b) The assistant judge possesses the same powers as the chief judge concerning the validity of blows and assists him over the good conduct of the contest.

Article 4. When two or three judges decide that a blow is valid, a point is recorded. However, if one of them acknowledges the validity of a blow and the two others decline to make a judgement, the point is recorded.

Article 5. The judges base their decisions on the following rules:

1. The chief judge announces '*Hajime!*' and starts the contest after the two contestants have bowed, taken guard, and are ready to fight; that is, the contestants are standing or crouching with *Shinai* drawn or sheathed.

2. When a judge announces a valid blow, the other judges must take up their positions.

3. When a judge notices that an infringement has been committed by a contestant, the contest is interrupted, and after consulting together the judges will give him or her a warning. However, if the infringement is clearly evident, no consultation is necessary.

4. If, in the course of a contest, one of the contestants falls or lets drop his or her *Shinai* and the opponent does not strike him or her immediately, the chief judge interrupts the contest, brings the contestants back to their starting points and restarts the contest.

5. When two contestants find themselves in a position of *Tsuba-zeriai* and this situa-

tion is prolonged, with no intention of making an attack in evidence, the chief judge separates them and orders the contest to continue.

6. When the chief time-keeper announces that the time of the contest is finished, the chief judge stops the contest and brings the contestants to their starting point. If the contest goes into extra time, the chief judge announces it by calling 'Encho' and begins the extra time by calling 'Hajime!'.

7. If the victory or defeat has to be decided by consultation between the judges, the chief judge stops the contest and signals 'Hantei'. Then the three judges announce their decisions together.

8. Use of the flags:

(a) To indicate a valid blow, the flag which is the same colour as that of the contestant who has scored the point is raised obliquely upwards, at the side of the body, at an angle of 45 degrees.

(b) To indicate that a blow is not valid, both flags are waved in front, low down, with a crossing action.

(c) To refrain from giving judgement, the two flags are crossed in front.

(d) To announce a valid blow the same procedure as in part (a) is followed.

(e) To indicate the interruption of a contest, both flags are raised vertically above the head, arms parallel. The assistant judges can also, if the need arises, take the place of the chief judges and announce an interruption of the contest ('Yame') to avoid danger, give a warning or indicate that the allotted time of the contest has ended.

(f) To separate the contestants in the position of *Tsuba-zeriai*, the two flags are raised in front to a horizontal position, spread apart and lowered, at the same time as the call of 'Hajime!'.

(g) When there is a consultation, both flags are raised in the right hand, high in the air, and at the same time a call of 'Gogi' (consultation) is made.

(h) If one of the contestants leaves the contest area, a line judge signals by raising vertically the flag which corresponds to the colour of the contestant who has done so. At the same time he announces 'Jogai'. If both contestants leave the contest area at the same time, he raises both flags and announces 'Doji-jogai'.

Article 6. Announcements.

(a) Beginning of a contest: 'Hajime!' (the two contestants have drawn their *Shinai* and are ready to fight).

(b) Announcement of a valid blow: 'Men, Kote, Do, Tsuki, Ari' (the contestants are at the spot where the blow has been struck).

(c) Resuming the contest after a score has been made: 'Nihon-me' (the contestants are standing at the line which indicates their starting point).

(d) Resuming the contest after each of the contestants has scored a point: 'Shobu' (both at the starting point).

(e) Announcement of the winner: 'Shobu-ari' (both at the starting point).

(f) Announcement of extra time: 'Encho . . . Hajime' (both at the starting point).

(g) Announcement of the winner who has scored a single point, when the time allotted to the contest has expired: 'Ippon-gachi' . . . Shobu-ari' (both at the starting point).

(h) Announcement of a contest won by forfeit: 'Fusensho . . . Shobu-ari' (both at the starting point).

(i) Announcement of a decision: 'Hantei-gachi . . . Shobu-ari' (both at the starting point).

(j) Interruption of a contest: 'Yame!'.

(k) Separation of the contestants who are in *Tsuba-zeriai* position: 'Wakare . . . Hajime!' (the contestants are in place).

(l) Warnings: announcement of the colour of the contestant who is at fault (red or white) and of the total of the faults committed (both at the starting point).

(m) Announcement of a point awarded after a warning given to the opponent: 'Ippon-ari' (both at starting point).

The chief judge indicates to the penalized contestant the total of the faults committed, using his or her hand to show the colour, then with the other hand he or she lifts the flag of the winner and announces '*Ippon-ari*' or '*Shobu-ari*' accordingly.

(n) Announcement of the winner after proclaiming three warnings against one of the contestants: '*Shobu-ari*' (both at the starting point).

(o) Announcement by the chief judge: '*Yame!*', after a contestant asks for 'time' (momentary interruption of the contest).

The chief judge lifts the flaps high, announcing '*Yame!*', and asks the contestant why he or she has asked for 'time'.

(p) Announcement of a drawn match: '*Hikiwake*' (both contestants at the starting point). The chief judge crosses the two flags high in front of him or her and announces '*Hikiwake*'.

Article 7. Situations may arise which are not dealt with in the rules. The judges will discuss these among themselves and after they have consulted the president of the judges about their decisions, he or she will settle the matter.

— **Kendogi** *Kendo*. Training jacket, made of thick white cotton, worn underneath the armour (*Dogu*).

— **Kendogu** see *Dogu*.

— **Kendoka** A practitioner of *Kendo*.

— '**Kendo Ron**' see *Yamada Jiro-kichi*.

— **Kendo Shugyo no Shiori** see *Makino Toru*.

— **Kengi** 'Techique of the sword'.

— **Kengo** 'Expert in sword technique'. Also *Kenkaku*, *Kenshi*.

Ken-jutsu 'The warrior art of the sword'. This is the art of using the sword as soon as it is drawn from the scabbard, in order to attack the enemy. *Iai-do* is thus included in the techniques of *Ken-jutsu*. It was the warrior art *par excellence*, studied and practised by all the *Bushi*, and by the *Samurai* in particular, from at least the tenth century. There were during this period and up until 1876 (the date at which the carrying of swords was prohibited) more than 2,000 schools (*Ryu*) of swordsmanship in Japan, and more than 400 dedicated to the study of *Iai-jutsu* alone (now called Iai-do). These schools shared numerous traditions. The main ones were: *Jigen-ryu*, *Katori Shinto-ryu*, *Chujo-ryu*, *Ito-ryu*, *Kage-ryu*, *Nen-ryu*, *Maniwa-nen-ryu*, etc.

Ken-jutsu was known by various names during its long history: *Heiho*, *Toho*, *Gekken*, *Hyoho*, *To-jutsu*, *Tachi-uchi*, *Hyodo*, etc. Fi-

nally it was transformed into a harmless art, *Kendo*.

—**Ken no Michi** 'The way of the sword'. See *Kendo*.

Kenkaku see *Kengo*.

Kensaki see *Kissaki*.

Kensa-yaku see *Shobu-shimpan*.

Kensei. The technique of uttering a silent *Ki-ai*, related to the practice of meditation. See *Ki-ai*.

Kenshi see *Kengo*.

Kenshin-ryu A modern style of *Karate* founded by Hayashi Teruo, of *Kito-ryu*.

Kenshikan Karate. A style of *Karate* which is similar to *Shito-ryu*, mainly practised in the Kyoto region of Japan. It was created by *Kusano Kenji*, 8th *Dan*, and brought to Europe in 1972 by the 6th *Dan* Tsukada (born in 1949). *Kenshikan* places the accent primarily on *Kata* and their applications, harking back to the old styles *Naha-te*, *Shuri-te* and *Tomari-te* of Okinawa.

Ken no Sen. To take the initiative during the launching of an attack. See *Sen*.

Ken no Shinzui see *Muto, Tsukahara Bokuden*.

Ken-jutsu demonstrated by Master Kuroda Ichitaro.

Kensho see *Zen*.

Kensui *Judo*. 'Seized by both hands'. Also *Mochi*.
— Kensui-jime *Judo*. Strangulation by 'hanging' technique in groundwork (*Newaza*).

Kento *Karate*. 'Sword fist'. The fist is clenched and only the knuckles of the index and middle fingers are used to strike, directly forward.

Kentsui *Karate*. 'Hammer fist'. A blow dealt with the little-finger side of the clenched fist.
— Kentsui-kuchi *Karate*. A blow with the fist in the *Kentsui* formation, used in an attack.

Kenyu *China*. Ancient type of Chinese boxing derived from *Jiaodishu*, which is the origin of *Kempo*.

Keri (-geri) *Judo*. Application of *Tori*'s foot on *Uke*'s knee, to upset his or her balance.
Karate 'Kick'. Different foot techniques (*Keri-waza*):

Mae-geri, a straight front kick
Yoko-geri, side-kick
Mawashi-geri, roundhouse kick
Ura-mawashi-geri, back roundhouse kick
Ushiro-geri, back kick
Kesa-geri, diagonal kick. See *Sokuto*.

These Keri may be straight out (*Toma*), medium (*Ma*), short (*Chickama*), simple (without a jump), jumping (*Tobi*), whiplike (*Keage*), or penetrating (*Kekomi*).
— **Keri-age** *Karate*. A rising knee-kick; striking with the knee.
— **Keri-gaeshi** *Karate*. A returning kick.
— **Keri-goho** *Aikido*. Techniques of punching and kicking against the vital points (see *Kyusho*) of an opponent, including direct punches with the fist or palm (*Iki-tsuki*, *Tsuki*), reverse punches (*Gyaku-tsuki*), elbow strikes (*Hineri-uchi*), straight front kicks (*Mae-geri*), side-kicks (*Yoko-geri*), back kicks (*Ura-geri*, *Ushiro-geri*) and roundhouse kicks (*Mawashi-geri*).
— **Keri-komi** *Karate*. Beginning an attack with a kick.
— **Keri-waza** *Karate*. Kicking techniques. See *Keri*.

Kesa (-gesa). 'Lapels', 'Across'; also translated as 'Scarf' (see *Kesa-gatame*).
— **Kesa-garami** *Judo*. Control and immobilization of *Uke*, across his or her body.
— **Kesa-gatame** *Judo*. Scarf hold. Control across *Uke*'s body.

Kesa-gatame

— **Kesa-geri** *Karate*. An 'across' (diagonal) kick.

Kesho-mawashi *Sumo*. The ceremonial apron, embroidered with silver and gold, with a fringed border, worn by the grand champions (*Yokozuna* and *Ozeki*) during their ritual presentation (*Dohyo-iri*) before the tournament. This type of apron is generally a gift offering from their 'fans', and is often worth a considerable sum of money. See *Mawashi*.

Keta-guri see *Kimarite*.

Keuman see *Sonomama*.

Keup see *Kyu*.

Keupso see *Kyusho*.

Khi see *Ki*.

Khi Phap see *Kokyu*, *Ibuki*.

Khoa Go Qwan Ki Do. Various methods of locking the arms, in front and behind, divided into 'static techniques' and 'moving techniques'. In both types the final result is a throw (*Vat*).

Khoa Hau see *Thu Phap*.

Ki. The concept of *Ki* is one of the most important in Japanese philosophy. It directly concerns everyone's daily life, since it is nothing less than the vital energy of that life. In Chinese philosophy, the equivalent concept is known as *Qi* (*Ch'i*); an energy whose 'home' is the *Dantian* (*Tan T'ien*) point, located in human beings below the navel. *Dantian* is often translated as 'cinnabar field'. A similar concept is found in Indian philosophy in the idea of Prana, and in the Judaeo-Christian tradition the word 'soul' has some affinity to these three Far Eastern expressions. Although the Chinese and Japanese concepts are very close to one

Spirit   Essence   Breath

Calligraphy expressing the essence of the K (identical to that of the Dao).

Demonstration of Ki by Master Aoki of the Shintaido school.

another, the equivalence of the other two is very much open to question, and represents merely a convenient peg on which to hang the concept rather than an exact counter-part. As the concept of Ki is found at the root of all Japanese activities, it is also found at the root of all the martial arts (*Bujutsu* and *Budo*). The nature of this universal and fundamental energy is such that it penetrates everywhere, uniting all the manifestations of the universe, visible or invisible. It is a creative energy, the divine 'breath' in every being, which appears as active attention, concentration, mental force and can, according to certain writers, be 'projected' outside oneself – by means of the *Ki-ai*, for example. M. Random writes: 'Thought energy or "conscious energy" produces a vi-

bratory field which operates in an alchemical way, in the sense that it "crystallizes" or manifests certain subtle properties which are characteristic of this vibrating field'. Thus: 'To take in oxygen from the air is a spontaneous act, but to bring a particular form of attention of the mind to this act means that the attention potentializes the air molecules more intensely, giving them a different quality. It is indeed the "art of the Breath".' The Ki, then, results from a potentiality of the universal energies. Whoever uses the power of Ki may do so in a positive or negative way, for its manifestation is what man makes of it. Nowadays one would say that a man or woman has a weak Ki (*Yowaki*) or a strong Ki (*Tsuyoki*) depending on whether the personality was weak or strong. To unite the Ki (see *Aiki*) with the *Hara*, the physical and psychological centre of an individual, is thus synonymous with concentrating a subjective form of this universal energy in oneself. The result of such a concentration is to produce both a great psychic force (personality, character, determination) and, at the moment when it is released, instantaneous physical power. It is accepted that the concept of Ki, whatever its scientific basis, is, for the Japanese, a day-to-day reality. The use of Ki is primary in achieving results in very diverse aspects of life, notably in the martial arts. Vietnamese: **Khi**; Indonesian: **Ihru**. See *Aiki, Ki-ai, Hara, Haragei, Kokyu, Ki-no Michi*.

Ki-ai 'The meeting together of energy'. This is 'the cry which gives life', sometimes regarded as the manifestation of the Active Principle (*Aiki*) of the universe. According to E.J. Harrison, it is 'the art of perfectly concentrating all one's energy, physical and mental, upon a given object, with unremitting determination, so that one achieves one's goal' (see *The Fighting Spirit of Japan*, London, 1913). It is the shout made at the moment of attack, akin to the sound uttered by a lumberjack, butcher or any tradesman who uses blows in his work; when a particularly difficult piece of material has to be dealt with, he may utter a sound to give added force to the blow. When the Ki-ai is uttered by a martial artist, the vibration of the sound may momentarily paralyse the opponent's functioning and render him or her more susceptible to an attack. Although reports of the effectiveness of the Ki-ai have been published, its action has never been clearly demonstrated except to show that it has the effect of surprising an opponent. This fact should not lead one to conclude that the claims made concerning the Ki-ai are invalid. The Ki-ai enables a person carrying out a violent movement to purify his mind of extraneous thoughts, leaving simply the pure energy (*Ki*) which causes him to act, and confers upon him all its intensity. The efficacy of the shout depends upon the mastery of certain appropriate breathing exercises (see *Kyoku*), analogous to the Pranayama of the Hindus.

The contention by Japanese martial arts experts that the Ki-ai enables one to liberate mental and physical force very rapidly, and so influence another who is in close proximity, explains why the Ki-ai is sometimes used in resuscitation techniques (*Kuatsu*). Kuatsu can be employed by black belt martial artists to bring back to consciousness anyone who has been strangled or subjected to a sudden shock. Certain martial arts masters maintain that there are three or four kinds of Ki-ai: low and weightly at moments of action, high and piercing with a cry of victory, normal for purposes of resuscitation, and silent (*Kensei*) in certain meditation exercises. It is thus very similar to *Aiki*. Vietnamese: *Het*; Korean: *Kihap*. See *Ki, Aiki, Hara, Haragei, Kokyu, Nogare, Kotodama*.

Kiba-dachi *Karate*. A posture called 'horse-riding stance', with the legs wide apart and slightly bent, toes pointing inwards. See *Sochin-dachi, Zenkutsu-dachi*. **Wushu**: *Ma Bo*.

Kiba-dachi

— **Kiba-sen.** The art of fighting on horseback against someone on foot (*Toho-sen*).

Ki-bon see *Ki-hon, Kata*.

Kich. A Vietnamese lance with a metal blade resembling the blade of a sword.

Kick-boxing. Boxing using the feet as well as the hands. An American expression to describe a type of combat which is in no way a form of *Budo*. It is widely appreciated in Japan, the USA and many other

Western countries, and contains a mixture of *Savate*, *Thai Boxing* and elements of *Kyokushinkai Karate*. This type of realistic training is popular among various groups including the armed forces, who have included it in their 'close-combat' training syllabuses. As in *Full Contact*, the blows are really struck, not pulled, and the aim is to knock the opponent out, by almost any possible means, apart from blows with the head and biting. Contestants wear gloves, groin protectors and ankle guards. They fight for ten three-minute rounds, and continue until there is a knockout. Contestants are frequently injured and some have been paralysed or handicapped for life, such is the violence of the combat. Nevertheless, the spectacular nature of the contests brings in a large audience.

Kiem. A type of Vietnamese sword; very narrow, with a guard.

Ki-hap see *Ki-ai*.

Ki-hon. A basic movement or a fundamental movement of a martial arts system. *Ki-hon* involves the study of one or several fundamental movements of a technique. These are repeated until the movement becomes almost instinctive, at the same time achieving a perfect action. Also *Kata*. Korean: **Ki-bon**.
— **Ki-hon Kumite.** The study of one or several movements (*Ki-hon*) performed alone, without a partner, which simulate an attack (*Kumite*).

Kikai. The moment which separates two movements of attack or defence during a contest, when one of the contestants experiences a state of uncertainty. At this moment the opponent has a potential advantage. See *Tanden*.

Kiken *Judo.* The act of giving up, submission, by *Uke*, to an immobilization, strangulation or locking technique. Uke signifies this by tapping several times with his or her hand or foot on the mat or on *Tori*'s body.
— **Kiken-gachi** 'Victory by submission, giving up'. See Competition Rules of *Judo*, 30.

Kikentai no Ichi *Kendo.* '*Ki*', energy; '*Ken*', sword; '*Tai*', body. A contest rule in which these three elements must be present, used and combined during an attack. They must be present in a harmonious way; if they are not, an '*Ippon*' may not be given. See *Kendo*.

Kikitori see *Kyudo, Uchi-okoshi*.

Kikwon see *Fusensho*.

Kimarite *Sumo.* The range of techniques used by the *Sumotori* to throw an opponent during a contest. Also called *Shijuhatte* (forty-eight techniques). They are:

1. *Oshi-dashi*, a simple push or final push.
2. *Oshi-taoshi*, a push followed by a fall.
3. *Yori-kiri*, a strong forward push, without a fall.
4. *Yori-taoshi*, a strong downward push.
5. *Tsuki-dashi*, a simple push with the palms of the hands.
6. *Tsuki-taoshi*, a push with the palms of the hands leading to a fall.
7. *Tsuki-otoshi*, a push with the hands resulting in turning the opponent over.
8. *Uwate-nage*, a simple throw.
9. *Uwate-hineri*, a throw brought about by a lift under the arms.
10. *Shitate-hineri*, a throw using a lift under the arms.
11. *Shitate-nage*, a sideways throw.
12. *Uwate-dashi-nage*, a forward throw with pressure on the arms.
13. *Shitate-dashi-nage*, a throw using pressure under the arms.
14. *Kote-nage*, a sideways throw using an armlock.
15. *Sukui-nage*, a throw using a lift under the arms.
16. *Kubi-nage*, a throw using a hold round the neck.
17. *Uchi-gake*, hooking inside.
18. *Soto-gake*, hooking outside.
19. *Keta-guri*, a throw using the foot.
20. *Ashi-tori*, a throw brought about by seizing a leg.
21. *Hataki-komi*, a push on the back with both hands, downwards.
22. *Tsuri-dashi*, to lift up by seizing the belt with a 'snatching' action.

Holding the belt in a Sumo contest.

23. *Utchari*, to lift by the belt, turning at the same time.

24. *Hisami-ashi*, movement of the legs.

25. *Tottari*, an armlock accompanied by a push.

26. *Okuri-dashi*, a push on the back.

27. *Okuri-taoshi*, a push on the back followed by a fall.

28. *Maki-otoshi*, a throw by reversing the arms.

29. *Kiri-kaeshi*, turning over on to the thighs.

30. *Kata-sukashi*, to turn over using an armlock.

31. *Yori-kiri*, to lift and pull by the belt.

32. *Hiki-otoshi*, leaning and pressing on the back.

33. *Abise-taoshi*, pushing strongly towards the rear.

34. *Nimai-geri*, blocking the foot with the foot.

35. *Shitate-yagura*, turning over the opponent by lifting the thigh with the knee.

36. *Ami-uchi*, turning over the opponent by the shoulders.

37. *Gyaku-hineri*, a sliding grip on the belt.

38. *Nodowa-zeme*, pushing the neck.

39. *Uwate-yagura*, turning over by the thigh as a result of raising the opponent's

knee.

40. *Komata-sukui*, seizing the thigh on the inside.

41. *Sabaori*, flattening on the ground with a push on both shoulders.

42. *Koshi-nage*, turning over from under the shoulders.

43. *Watashi-komi*, seizing the thigh from the outside.

44. *Yoyi-modoshi*, seizing by the arms and pushing sideways.

45. *Hataki-komi*, evading and pushing on the back.

46. *Soto-komata*, exterior version of *O-mata* (see *Komata-sukui*).

47. *Soto-muso*, blocking the thigh.

48. *Suso-tori*, seizing the ankle.

Kima Seug-gi see *Seug-gi*.

Kime. In the martial arts this is the focusing of all one's physical and psychological forces on one point, whether it be on one's own *Hara* or on a point just beyond the target of attack (a penetrating blow, *Kikomi*). This is the 'ultimate decision' which mobilizes one's entire being in a single instant and in a single movement. Otherwise expressed, it is pure effectiveness.

Kime no Kata *Judo*. '*Kata* of decision'. In the techniques of the *Kodokan* there are in this Kata the following: defence techniques practised in a kneeling position (*Suwari*) or *Idori* (eight movements), defence techniques from a standing position (*Tachi-ai*) (twelve movements). These defensive movements were introduced to the Kodokan by *Funakoshi Gichin*). See *Idori, Tachi-ai*.

Kime Ke. A Vietnamese school of martial arts, the 'Yellow Cockerel'.

Kimono. a typical item of Japanese clothing, long and ample, worn by men and women in former times but now mainly by women. It is held in place by a sash (*Obi*). The Kimono is still worn by judges and referees of martial arts during official ceremonies, notably by the *Gyoji* of *Sumo*. The European version of the Kimono is called a *Yofuku*.

Expressing the Kime while breaking wood with a kick. Shotokan school, Tokyo.

Kin-geri *Karate*. A rising kick delivered with the top surface of the foot at the testicles. It can produce intense pain and even loss of consciousness. The *Kuatsu* technique for reviving a person injured by this kick is to apply pressure to the sole of the foot, with the leg extended.

Kinh-dich see *Qwan-ki-do*, *Yijing*.

Kinteki 'Testicles'. Also *Tsurigane*. See *Body*, *Kyusho*.

Ki no Michi. A new form of *Budo*, 'The Way of the *Ki*', created in Japan in 1979 by Noro Masamichi, a disciple of *Ueshiba Morihei*. It is an idealized version of of *Aikido*, deprived of all aggression.

Ki-o-tsukete *Kendo*. 'Pay attention!', a term generally used to announce the beginning of a training session. Vietnamese: *Chuan Bi*.

Kiri (-giri). A cutting action, an expression used in several martial arts: cutting with a *Katana*, *Shinai* or other weapon; 'cutting' with the arm, open hand, fist or foot as if those parts of the body were sword blades (*Tegatana*, *Shuto*, *Sokuto*).
— **Kiri-kaeshi** *Kendo*. A warming-up exercise using the *Shinai*. Students perform many repeated cuts without stopping, bringing the Shinai high above the head before each one.
Sumo. A hooking action, placing the leg on the inside of an opponent's supporting leg and twisting with the arms in the opposite direction. See *Kimarite*.

Kiri-kaeshi

— **Kiri-komi** see *Tachi-ai*, *Idori*.
— **Kiri-otoshi** see *Tachi-ai*, *Ju-no-Kata*.
— **Kiritsu** 'To stand up straight'. See *Tachi*.
— **Kiri-tsuke** *Kendo*, *Iai-do*. A cutting action using the *Shinai* or *Katana*. See *Omori-ryu*, *Furi-kaburi*.

Kirpinar. Special sports hall for the traditional Turkish form of wrestling, the *Yaghli-guresh*. Tournaments are held every year in the town of Edirne. The wrestlers fight stripped to the waist and wearing cow-hide trousers, tightly fastened below the knee. Both body and trousers are liberally covered with oil. In order to win a bout, a contestant must grip his opponent by the belt, raise him in the air so that his feet are higher than his head, and deposit him on his back. Before the opponent is put down on the ground, he must be held in the inverted position for a few seconds. If one of the contestants tears his trousers, he is eliminated. Bouts take place on dried earth or grass. The champion receives a sheep as a prize in recognition of his valour. See also *Zour Xaneh*.

Kisha see *Yabusame*.
— **Kisha Hasami Mono**. A school of *Yabusame* created as an official rite of the shogunate of Edo by *Tokugawa Yoshimune* (1684–1751). It was performed annually on 15 January at the sanctuary of Asakusa in Edo, during *Sanja-matsuri*, a *Shinto* religious festival. Now this ceremony takes place in the month of May, accompanied by demonstrations of ancient, sacred dances (*Kagura*). See *Yabusame*.

Kissaki *Kendo*. The point of a sword (*Katana*) or of a *Shinai*. The point of a Shinai is covered with a small piece of leather and is then called a *Sakigawa*. Also called *Kensaki*.

Kito-ryu. An ancient school of *Ju-jutsu* which developed from the seventeenth to the eighteenth century. Its five principal *Kata* have been preserved in the *Koshiki-no-Kata* of *Kodokan Judo*. The teachings of this school are to be found in two ancient texts, *Hontai* and *Seiko*, transmitted by the Buddhist priest Takuan. He tried to transform the combat techniques of Ju-jutsu into

Attack with Tonfa against a Bo in a Dojo, Okinawa.

an art and system of aesthetic behaviour. *Kito-ryu* was founded at the end of the sixteenth century by a *Samurai* of low rank, *Ibaragi Sensai*, a product of the *Yagyu Shinkage-ryu*. Kito-ryu taught *Ken-jutsu, Bo-jutsu, Iai-jutsu* and other weapon techniques such as those of the *Kusari-gama*. Later, this school gave birth to numerous others, such as *Teishin-ryu*, founded by *Terama Heizaemon*, and *Fukuno-ryu*, founded by *Fukuno Shichiroemon*. But it was thanks to *Terada Kanemon* that Kito-ryu developed into a specific art of combat using only the bare hands, which he called *Judo*; he created his own school, *Jikishin-ryu*.

Kizami Tsuki *Karate*. A hook punch delivered directly facing an opponent.

KKK see *Kyokushinkai*.

Knee see *Hiza, Hitsui, Legs*.

'Knight' see *Otokodate*.

Ko 'Small'. Also *Sho*. See *Space*. 'Ancient'.

Koan see *Mondo*.

Kobayashi Koemon Toshinari see *Mizuno Shinto-ryu*.

Kobo-ichi 'United in attack and defence'.

Kobore 'Tibia'. See *Legs*.

Ko-budo. The name 'Ancient martial arts' is given to the lesser martial arts such as those of the *Ju-jutsu* school of *Tonshin Shin-yo-ryu, Yanagi-ryu, Sosuichi-ryu*, and *Takeuchi-ryu*. It applies equally to the schools of *Naginata, So-jutsu, Tai-jutsu, Kyu-jutsu* (*Ogasawara* school), *Hogu-jutsu, Rensa-sankaku, Ho-jutsu, and Yoroi-Kumiuchi*. In fact this name applies to all the martial disciplines which use unconventional weapons such as the *Nunchaku, Sai, Jutte, Kusari-gama, Tonfa*, etc., which come from Okinawa. In Japan, the small schools of Ko-budo are united into the Japanese federation 'Ko-budo Shinko-kai'.

Kobu-jutsu *Aikido*. A system of self-defence created by *Hoshi Tetsuomi*, a disciple of *Ueshiba Morihei*.

Kobu-kai see *Aikido*.

Kobushi *Karate*. A standard or normal punch, delivered with the fingers tightly folded and the thumb bent at right angles across the middle segment of the fingers.

Ko-dachi 'Small sword'. See *Katana, Swords, Wakizashi, Daisho*.

Kodansha. Grades of 5th *Dan* and above. See *Kyudan, Obi*.

Ko-daore see *Omote*.

Kodenko 'Lumbar vertebrae'. See *Body*.

Judo training at the Kodokan.

Kodokan *Judo*. 'School for the study of the Way'. A centre for the study of *Judo*, created by Kano Jigoro in 1882, in the grounds of the Eisho-ji temple in Tokyo (*Kita-mari-cho, Shitaya-ku*). At first he had only nine pupils and his *Dojo* no more than twelve mats, or *Tatami*. This Kodokan rapidly became the centre for world Judo, with most of the foreign and Japanese instructors being trained there. The black belts of high rank (*Kodansha*) came there to further their studies and perfect their technical training. The principle of the centre, formulated by Kano Jigoro, is found printed on the back of the black belt diplomas. It reads: Only through mutual help and mutual concessions can an organism, made up of a large or small number of individuals, reach complete harmony and bring about serious progress,' The Kodokan emblem is a cherry blossom (*Sakura*). A new building called the *Budokan* was built in Tokyo in 1962 to replace the old Kodokan. It houses not only the Judo masters but those of other disciplines such as *Aikido* and other schools of *Ju-jutsu*.
Principal techniques of Kodokan Judo.
Kuzushi – disturbing balance
Tsukuri and *Kake* – preparation and attack
Ukemi – breakfalls
Nage-no-Kata – forms of throwing
Katame-no-kata – forms of grappling or holding
Kime-no-kata – forms of decision
Kodokan Goshin-jutsu – forms of self-defence
Ju-no-Kata – forms of gentleness
Koshiki-no-Kata – ancient techniques
Itsutsu-no-Kata – forms of 'Five'
Seiryoku-Zen'yo Kokumin-Taiiku-no-Kata –

forms of national physical education based on the principle of maximum efficiency.

In addition to the techniques and Kata listed above, which are for the most part demonstration forms, there are other techniques used in contest. A published version of the Kodokan Judo techniques, *Illustrated Kodokan Judo*, appeared in 1955, with a preface by Kano Risei, the President of the Kodokan. In 1976 it appeared bearing the seal of approval of the Judo Black Belt Federation of the USA. Indeed, Kodokan Judo is the framework for Judo training all over the world, but the methods of training, emphasis and attitude vary from country to country (see *Kawaishi Mikonosuke*). In Great Britain the British Judo Association largely follows what is basically a Kodokan system, with additional training methods which have been introduced based on the experience of veteran Judo instructors. There have been various attempts, which have met with varying degrees of success, to change the whole approach to Judo training. Even so, Kano Jigoro's techniques and methods remain at the root of all innovations.

Ko-empi *Karate*. A backward elbow blow, travelling only a short distance and therefore delivered close to the opponent.

Kogai. A kind of long, strongly made needle with a short handle, generally kept in the scabbard (*Saya*) of a *Katana*, on the opposite side to the *Kozuka*. This instrument served as an awl to repair saddles and leather items, as well as a means of caring for horses' hooves. It was also used occasionally as a weapon. In the seventeenth century the Kogai was made of two parts, and was used as an implement for eating. It was in fact an all-round tool, like the *Kozuka*. See *Swords*.

Kogai was also the name given to the large wooden or bone needles used by women to keep their hair in place. The Kogai (which decorated the officials' hats, *Kammuri*) were originally used for scratching the scalp. See *Kanzashi*.

Kogeki *Karate*. Free attack.
Kendo. An action of hindering the movements of an opponent's sword.

Kogi-judo. According to Kano Jigoro, this means the form of Judo taken in a wider sense. It includes technique (*Kyogi* or *Shobu-ho*), the physical form (*Rentai-ho*) and the cultivation of the mind (*Shushin-ho*), which are all necessary to reach self-perfection. See *Kyogi-Judo*.

Kohai. A student who practises a form of *Budo*, mainly *Karate*, under the direction of a *Sempai*.

Kogusoku-jutsu. An art of fencing with a short staff or other short weapon, used against the *Bushi* dressed in light armour (*Kogusoku*). It was created in 1532 by *Takenouchi Hisamori* and is also called *Torite-Kogusoku*. See *Takenouchi-ryu, Araki-ryu*.

Ko-haku Shiai *Karate*. A competition between two teams, the 'Whites' and the 'Reds', who stand in two opposing lines.
Judo. A big competition which takes place twice a year, in spring and autumn, at the *Budokan* in Tokyo. Several thousand black and brown belt students take part. They are divided into two 'camps', the Black and the Red, and into teams. See *Suginami-shiai*.

Koizumi Gingyo (Gunji) *Judo*. A disciple of *Kano Jigoro*. Although he crossed over to Judo later in his life, Koizumi Gunji started his martial arts training at the age of twelve by studying the *Tenjin Shin'yo Ryu* in Tokyo at the *Dojo* of Nobushige Tago. There he learned *Ju-jutsu* and some *Ken-jutsu*. He learned other forms of Ju-jutsu in Korea and Singapore, and in 1906 he came to England. After an abortive attempt to build up a Ju-jutsu school in Liverpool he came to London and in 1918 opened a Dojo in Lower Grosvenor Place, which he named the *Budokai*. It is now the oldest Judo club in Europe. He wrote: 'I opened a Dojo for the practice of the Japanese Martial Arts, including Ju-jutsu and Ken-jutsu, and named it the *Budokwai [Budokai]* – The Way of Knighthood Society; constituting it on the principle of amateur sport with democratic control by the members.' The first chief instructor was Yukio Tani. In spite of the fact that the Budokai was initially orientated towards Ju-jutsu, Koizumi Gunji welcomed Kano Jigoro and his *Kodokan Judo*; eventually both the founder of the Budokai and its members devoted almost all their efforts to propagating and preserving the new Judo system.

Koka *Judo*. 'Small advantage'. An expression used to describe a result of a contest when one of the contestants has obtained some 'technical' points (*Yuko*) but has not managed to score an *Ippon* (winning score). *Koka* = 3 points, *Ippon* = 10 points. See Competition rules of *Judo*, 8, 14, 26.

Koken *Karate*. A blow delivered with the back of the bent wrist. The defensive movement made with the same part of the arm is called *Koken Uke*.

Calligraphy for 'heart', expressing the essence of things.

Kokoro. This means the heart, spirit, soul of a person or thing. Also *Shin*. In Chinese and Japanese thinking, the seat of the spirit is in the heart, not in the head, which houses only the intellect. *Kokoro* thus represents the essence of a man or woman or, indeed, of a thing: the absolute reality. In any art, martial or otherwise, a disciple will succeed only if he or she is filled with Kokoro – or, in other words, if he or she has sacred fire and puts his or her heart to work. Kokoro is thus a form of dispassionate passion, or action without looking for beneficial results. If a *Budoka* has fought a good fight, and loses, this should not be a cause for regret but on the contrary a cause for rejoicing; for this defeat, when it is clearly understood, is nothing less than a source of learning. The battle has been waged not to win a prize, not to win at all costs, but to conquer oneself. It is said that then one has Kokoro. This is the essence of pure love, *Ai*. See *Mushin, Ushin, Mizu-no-Kokoro, Tsuki-no-Kokoro, Kyudan*.

— **Kokoro-e.** The true spirit of understanding.

Kokugikan *Sumo.* The 'temple' of Sumo in Tokyo, corresponding to the *Budokan*, where the major tournaments take place, known as *Sechie-zumo*.

Kokutsu-dachi *Karate.* A straight posture with the leading leg bent and most of the weight of the body on the rear leg, which is slightly bent. See *Zen Kokutsu-dachi*.

Kokutsu-dachi

Kokyu. Deep breathing from the *Hara*, which sets the *Ki* in motion. It involves perfect synchronization of breathing and movement. It is also called *Fukushiki Kokyu*, deep abdominal breathing. Vietnamese: *Tam The, Khi Phap*. See *Keiko, Hara, Haragei, Aiki-taiso*.

— **Kokyu-ho.** A force emanating from the *Ki*, enabling someone who has mastered the art of *Kokyu* to influence other people.

— **Kokyu-nage.** A force emanating from the *Ki*, enabling someone who has mastered it to throw an opponent with a 'soft' action. *Aikido*. A series of supple throws, performed in harmony with the rhythm of breathing and designed to counter the following attacks:

Ryote-dori, a grip on both wrists
Katate Ryote-dori, a grip on one wrist with both hands
Kata-dori, a grip on the shoulder
Shomen-uchi, a vertical blow to the front of the head
Shomen-tsuki, a punch to the face

See *Nage-waza*.

Komata-sukui *Sumo.* A big throw to the rear, using a grip on the inside of the thigh underneath the arm. See *Kimarite*.

Komata-sukui

Komi 'Within', 'Against'. See *Space*.

Komusubi see *Sumotori*.

Kong Kyeuk *Tae-kwon-do.* Attacking moves. There are three main ones:

Chireug-gi, punches to the front using a 'corkscrew' action
Tae-rig-gi, with the hand stretched horizontally
Tulkhi, with the hand stretched, above the level of the top of the chest.

See *Kumite*.

Koran-to see *Omori-ryu*.

Kori see *Kyusho, Feet*.

Korindo Aikido. An independent school of self-defence created by Hirai, one of *Ueshiba Morihei*'s disciples.

Koryo see *Poom-se*.

Koshi (-goshi) Judo. Refers to the hips, which act as a support or pivot in certain throws such as *Haraigoshi*.
Aikido. The name given to a certain point below the navel which is the seat of the *Hara*.
Karate. This is the ball of the foot, which is used in certain kicking techniques to the front. Also called 'tiger's tooth'. See *Feet*.
— **Koshi-guruma Judo.** 'Loin wheel or hip wheel', in which *Tori*'s hip is placed against *Uke*'s groin or lower abdomen while his or her arm is wrapped around the back of Uke's neck. Tori then throws Uke in a semicircle over his or her loin or lower right back.

Koshi-guruma

— **Koshi-ita** see *Hakama*.
— **Koshi no Mawari** see *Tai-jutsu*.
— **Koshi-nage Aikido.** A series of throws using the hips against the following attacks:

Ryote-dori, a grip on both wrists
Kata-dori, a grip on the shoulders
Ushiro-ryotekubi-dori, a grip on both wrists from the rear,

See *Nage-waza*.
Sumo. A pivoting hip throw, using a grip on the belt, under the opponent's arm. See

Koshi-nage

Kimarite.
— **Koshi-sabaki** see *Tai-sabaki*.
— **Koshi-waza Judo.** Hip throws using three types of movement: *Uki-goshi, Harai-goshi, Tsuri-komi-goshi*. See *Tachi-waza, Nage-no-Kata*.

Koshiki no Kata Judo. The old forms of *Kata*, which may be done slowly and broken down into sections (*Omote*) or, on the contrary, rapidly executed (*Ura*). They come from the five fundamental Kata of the *Kito-ryu* school of *Ju-jutsu*. They are practised by black belts, who aim to do them perfectly. These Kata were invented by the Kito-ryu school and represent the transition from the old style of Ju-jutsu to the present style of the *Kodokan*. This is because the founder of the Kodokan style, *Kano Jigoro*, had studied the Kito-ryu system and drew from it when compiling his new syllabus. These Kata were formerly the preserve of the *Samurai*, who performed them clad in full armour (see *Yoroi-kumiuchi*). They are the very essence of all Kata. See *Omote, Ura*.

Koshi no Mawari see *Tai-jutsu*.

Koshi-sabaki see *Tai-sabaki*.

Koshiwari see *Keiko (Sumo)*.

Koshti see *Zour Xaneh*.

Ko-soto-gake Judo. 'Minor outer hooking', referring to a hooking action of *Tori*'s leg combined with a push against *Uke*, which sends Uke backwards to the mat (applied on left or right).
— **Ko-soto-gari Judo.** 'Minor outer

KOTE

Ko-soto-gake

reaping', referring to a reaping action of
Tori's foot against Uke's heel. This is
combined with a backward pull outwards
on Uke's arm, which sends him or her
backwards and to the mat (applied on left
or right).

Ko-soto-gari

Kote 'Forearm'. The part of the arm between the elbow and wrist. See also *Ude*.

Kendo. Padded mitts or gloves which protect the forearms and hands, used when
wielding the *Shinai*. Also *Uchi-kote*, *Oni-
kote*.
— **Kote gaeshi** *Aikido, Ju-jutsu*. Movements involving a grip on an opponent's
wrist with the left hand and a push with
the palm of the right hand which bends
the joint of the wrist inwards towards the
forearm. This bending action can be normal
(towards the inside) or reverse (towards the
outside). It is one of the techniques of
Tekubi-waza, and may be applied to all the
other techniques of *Te-hodoki*:

Ryote-dori, a grip on both wrists
Mune-dori, a grip on the lapels
Kata-dori, a grip on the shoulders
Shomen-uchi, a descending blow to the
head
Yokomen-uchi, a sideways blow
Shomen-tsuki, a forward blow to the face
Ushiro-ryotekubi-dori, a grip on both wrists
from the rear.

See *Nage-waza, Kansetsu-waza*.
— **Kote hineri** *Aikido*. The third move
(*Sankyo*) of the *Katame-waza* (twisting the
wrist, to the right on the right wrist or
towards the forearm) used against an attack such as *Hiji-dori, Shomen-uchi, Ushiro-
tekubi-dori* or *Ushiro Ryohiji-dori*. This defence is part of the *Tekubi-waza*. See also
Kansetsu-waza.
— **Kote-mawashi** *Aikido*. The second
move (*Nikyo*) of the *Katame-waza* (twisting
the wrist inwards) used against an attack
such as *Mune-dori, Shomen-uchi* or *Shomen-
tsuki*.
— **Kote-nage** *Sumo*. A throw in *Uwate-
nage* using a hold on the opponent's arm. See
Kimarite.

Kote-nage

— **Kote-uchi** *Aikido*. A blow delivered
on an attacker's forearm to make him or her
drop their weapon.

Koten-shiai *Kendo*. A competition not
using groups of teams.

Kotodama 'True Word'. A science of
sound brought from China to Japan by
the Buddhist monk Kukai, who created
the Shingon sect or 'True word' at the
beginning of the ninth century. This sect
held a theory which aimed to prove that

134

vibration (sound) is the origin of life. From this theory comes the martial arts practice of uttering the *Ki-ai*.

Ko-tsuri-goshi *Judo*. A minor throw in which *Uke* is lifted by *Tori*'s hip.

Ko-uchi-gari *Judo*. 'Minor inner reaping throw'. *Tori* uses a foot to hook the Achilles tendon region of *Uke*'s foot while pushing him or her backwards to the ground. Tori hooks the right foot if it is in front, with his or her right foot, and pushes with the right arm on the left shoulder. The process is reversed if the left foot is in front.

Ko-uchi-gari

— Ko-uchi Maki-komi *Judo*. Minor inner winding (wrapping) throw.

Ko-ugi see *Swords*.

Kowami *Ju-jutsu*. Method of 'tough fighting' and intensive exercises, based on pure strength, created by *Ichikawa Mondaiyu*.

Koyo Gunkan. A work dating from the seventeenth century, in fifty-nine chapters, attributed sometimes to Kosaka Danjo Nobumasa, a *Samurai* in the service of Takeda Shinden, and sometimes to Obata Kagenori (1572–1662), a learned Confucian of the *Bakufu* (military government at Edo). This book concerns itself with all aspects of *Samurai* life. It is sometimes referred to as the 'Bible of the Samurai', although this expression did not exist when it was written. It is considered essential if one is to acquire knowledge of the spirit which is necessary for a good warrior (*Bushi*). It describes that spirit in terms of both the general bearing of

a Bushi and his behaviour in combat.

Kozuka. A small, narrow dagger with no guard (*Tsuba*), which is carried in the scabbard of a *Katana*, along with a kind of needle (*Kogai*). The *Kozuka* had a number of uses. The *Samurai* used it as an all-purpose knife, which could include such diverse purposes as cutting paper, throwing at and fatally wounding an enemy by cutting him or her in a vital spot. See *Swords*.

Kuatsu. *Kuatsu* is the method of resuscitating a person who has lost consciousness; in the martial arts it is usually applied to cases of strangulation or sudden shock. The study of Kuatsu is in the main reserved for black belt grades and has never been widely studied by Western martial artists except in France, where interest has been strong since the earliest days of *Judo* in that country. The actions used in this method are percussion, pressure and massage. They focus on specific points of the body, the stimulation of which produces beneficial effects upon those areas directly or indirectly affected by the trauma.

The specific points of Kuatsu are akin to the points and meridians used in acupuncture therapy and anaesthesia. Percussion is produced by the palm of the hand, the fist, the elbow, the knee or the heel; pressure by the palm of the hand; massage with the ends of the finger or the thumb, the amount of strength used and the number of applications being regulated. The reflexogenic zones which receive the most attention are the spinous process, the paravertebral points of the vertebral column, and the gap between the spinous processes. The effect is to excite the medullary centre and the nerves themselves.

However, the use of Kuatsu is related to the type of injury. In the (frequent) case of pelvic or testicular injury, for instance, the reflexogenic zone stimulated is located on the inside edge of the foot. In the case of failure to respond to Kuatsu, one should call on medical help; indeed, only a properly trained person should resort to Kuatsu. The validity of the method should really be verified by consulting the medical authorities in your country, before any such treatment is

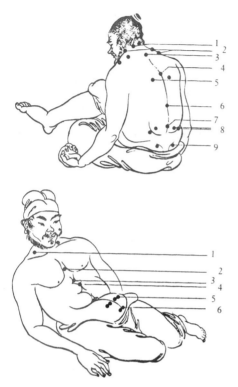

The most commonly used points of Kuatsu:

Above, the dorsal points:
1. The cervical-cephalic points (two)
2. The posterior cervical points (three)
3. The seventh cervical vertebra
4. Percussion point: sixth dorsal vertebra
5. Relaxation point: opposite base of pectoral muscles or nipples
6. First lumbar vertebra
7. Third lumbar vertebra
8. Paravertebral points, at waist height
9. Sacro-iliac points

Below, the ventral points:
1. The median anterior cervical point
2. The respiratory point
3. and 4. The massage and percussion points of the epigastrium
5. and 6. The massage points of the antalgic pelvic-abdominal region

given, or the Kuatsu 'expert' might find him- or herself in court if the 'treatment' goes awry. In fact there have been few scientific studies of Kuatsu, and it is generally classed as one of the methods currently known as 'acupressure' as distinct from acupuncture, which uses needles and pierces the skin. It is advisable to study Kuatsu with an expert, and verify its claims with a qualified Western doctor. Books can only provide a rough guide and are no substitutes for direct tuition.

The particular technique in which the *Ki-ai* is used to resiscitate a person is called *Kappo*; that of the resuscitation method following strangulation takes the name of *Kassei-ho*. See *Shiatsu*.
— **Kuatsu-jin-ken** see *Aikido*.

Kubi 'Neck'. See *Body, Head*.
— **Kubi-nage** *Judo*. A throw using an armhold round the neck and a lifting action of the hip.

Sumo. A throw in *Sukui-nage* using a grip round the neck.

Kubi-nage

Kubotan. This weapon is no more than a short cylinder which looks like a very thick pencil. Sometimes a key ring is attached at one end; this can be used for keys or for attaching the *Kubotan* to a belt or hook. It is used for striking or pressing upon vital spots. A similar weapon was used by the *Ninja*. Additional projections in the form of a cross, or two spikes at right angles to the main shaft, are also found, making the weapon a potential knuckleduster. Other examples were pointed and could be thrown like *Shuriken*. In the 1980s, mainly under the influence of books and magazine articles written by Tak Kubota, the weapon reached a peak of popularity in the West. The name 'Kubotan' was apparently coined by Kubota and is a registered business name. This acquisition of the name led competing manufacturers of a similar article to call their product a 'key-chain'. Originally of metal or wood, it is also made today of an unbreakable, light plastic.

Kue. A hoe used by farmers in Okinawa, sometimes employed as a weapon. It is classed as a part of the *Ko-budo* armoury.

Kuji-kiri. A series of finger movements and positions (see *Mudra*) which belong to the esoteric Buddhism of the *Tendai* and *Shingon* sects. One explanation of their meaning is that they were supposed to endow the men and women who performed them with magic powers, and even invisibility. The interlacing of the fingers was to be accompanied by the chanting of *Mantra* and ritual syllables. The effectiveness of the *Kuji-kiri* (nine symbols) was strongest when they were practised during *Taki-shugyo*, a type of meditation. The *Yamabushi* and the *Ninja* used them as well as Buddhist monks and nuns.

Kukichi-Daoshi *Judo*. 'Dead tree fall'. A throw in which *Tori* seizes *Uke* by the right heel, using his left hand, to bring him down.

Kukichi Tai-otoshi *Judo*. A counter-move against *Hiza-guruma*.

Kukinage see *Mifune Kyuzo*.

Kuk-ki Won. The world centre for Korean martial arts, mainly devoted to *Tae Kwon Do* and situated in Seoul. The immense modern building covers an area of 10,000 square metres and is the equivalent of the *Budokan* in Tokyo.

Kuki-shin Ryu. A secret martial art practised by the *Yamabushi* ascetics in the Kumano mountains. *Ueshiba Morihei* was initiated into the art in his youth. A large part of the training was devoted to the use of the baton and *Ninja* methods.

Kumade (*Kuma*, bear; Te, hand). *Karate*. A 'fist' formation translated as 'bear paw', with the fingers bent on to the palm, used to punch the face. See Weapons.

Kumi-kata *Judo*. A way of seizing (*Kumi*) the *Judogi* by the lapel and by the sleeve; a grip which influences the effectiveness of a movement. Sometimes the English expression 'grip' is used to describe *Kumi-kata*. In contests it is forbidden to grip both sleeves or the lapel and sleeve on the same side of the jacket, unless the taking of that grip is immediately followed by an attack. See *Temoto, Kumi-uchi*.

Kumi-tachi *Ken-jutsu*. A style of sword fighting created by *Chiba Shusaku* (1794–1855), who founded *Hokushin Itto-ryu*. Chiba wanted to make the art of *Ken-jutsu* into a spiritual discipline rather than a true science of fighting. He emphasized silent action and a natural deportment. For training purposes he used a straight *Bokken* rather than the commonly preferred curved weapon, and organized contests against swordsmen using *Katana* or against women armed with *Naginata*. His approach was very popular.

Kumite 'Attack'. Korean: *Kong-kyeuk*. See *Hasso*. *Karate*. Freestyle combat training analogous to the *Randori* of *Judo*.

Kumi-tsuki *Aikido*. A series of four defence movements against attacks involving seizing the belt: *Mae Utate Kumi-tsuki, Mae Shitate Kumi-tsuki, Ushiro Utate Kumi-tsuki, Ushiro Shitate Kumi-tsuki*. See *Te-hodoki*.

Kumi-uchi. Technique of seizing the clothing of an opponent to take part in hand-to-hand combat. Also called *Yawara*. See *Kumi-kata, Temoto, Yoroi-kumi-uchi, Ju-jutsu*.

Kundao. This is the name of several forms of fighting now found in Indonesia but originating in China; it is practised mainly in the Chinese communities of the Malay–Indonesian archipelago. *Kundao* (also transliterated into '*Kuntao, Kuntou, Kuntow*') was inspired largely by the methods and techniques of *Wushu*, with additional influences from *Bersilat* and *Penchaksilat*. This has led to a veritable mixture of styles as widely diverse as *Taiji Quan* and *Karate*.

Kung-fu 'Human effort'. The expression *Kung-fu* is in a sense a misnomer. It is a word from the Cantonese dialect which has become popular during the second half of this century, in preference to the Mandarin word *Wushu*, which means 'martial arts'. The literal meaning of the calligraphy for *Wushu* is 'stop fighting'. *Kung-fu* is sometimes spelled '*Gung-fu*' or '*Gong-fu*'. In Japan it took the name *Kakutei-jutsu*. The Mandarin word for *Kung-fu* is *Quan-fa*. Kung-fu was popu-

larized mainly because of the Bruce Lee films released in the 1960s and early 1970s, and the television series 'Kung-fu' starring David Carradine. A correct understanding of Kung-fu requires lifelong study combined with a wide knowledge of Chinese life, history and customs. Styles of Kung-fu fighting vary enormously, from those which resemble *Karate* to those which imitate the antics of a drunken monkey; from the soft and flowing actions of *Taiji Quan* to the acrobatic feats of the Chinese gymnasts. Styles using weapons are no less varied. At one end of the scale there is the grace and strength of the classical two-edged sword, and at the other the rapid and pragmatic techniques of fighting with a bench! Most Kung-fu styles trace their origins to the *Shaolin-si*. The most important division of styles is the division into hard, external styles and soft, internal styles. See *Wushu*, *Wei-jia*, *Nei-jia*, *Shaolin-pai*, *Taiji-quan*.

Demonstration of Kung-fu at a Shaolin school in China.

Kuni-yuzuri Sumo *Sumo*. A legendary combat related in the *Kojiki* 'History of Ancient Times', dating from 712. The combat was between two *Kami* (gods), or may have simply been a contest between two clan chiefs, elevated to divine status by the passage of time. Their names were Takemikazuchi and Takeminokata, and they fought to settle which of them should rule the kingdom of Yamato, south of Nara. Takeminokata was defeated and fled, but his conqueror was moved by a spirit of reconciliation and gave him the province of Shinshu on the shore of Lake Suwa, near the modern city of Nagano. This combat is regarded as the event which gave birth to *Sumo*. Another legendary contest took place during the reign of the Emperor Suinin (traditional date: 29–70). The contestants were both champions: Nomi-no-Sukune of Izumo, and Taima-no-Kahaya of Nara. Legend tells how they fought using only their feet. Nomi-no-Sukune won and stayed in Yamato, where the emperor made him master of the guild of potters (*Hajibe*). Tradition credits him with the creation of *Haniwa*, tubular decorated pottery which was placed around tombs and sacred spots.

Kuntou see *Kuntow, Kundao*.

Kuntow. A form of *Kung-fu*, indigenous to the Malay–Indonesian archipelago. See *Kundao*.

Kupchagi *Tae Kwon Do*. A leaping back-kick in which the student turns his back on his opponent, jumps into the air, and delivers two kicks in quick succession, or simply one kick.

Kurai. This describes a state of mind free from all sense of pressure, enabling a person to yield to the force of an attacker and turn that force back on the attacker. This non-resistance to a push or pull can act against an attacker, relieving the force of his or her attack and producing maximum efficiency of effort. Also the name of a grade in the martial arts. See *Kyudan, Kuzushi*.

Kuruma (-guruma) 'Wheel'. *Judo*. A vertical turning movement of the body.

— **Kuruma-daore** see *Omote*.
— **Kuruma-gaeshi** see *Ura*.

Kuryeung see *Randori*.

Kuru-run-fa *Karate*. An ancient *Kata* demonstrating 'stopping an attack and "breaking" '.

Kuryeung-opsi see *Randori*.

Kusanagi see *Kyusho*.

Kusano Kenji see *Kenshikan*.

Kusari-gama (*Kusari*, chain; *Kama*, sickle). A sickle formerly used by the peasants of Okinawa for cutting rice straw. They used it as a weapon of self-defence and in some instances added a chain, weighted at the end with an iron or lead ball. The sickle was used to parry a sword blade and the chain to entangle the blade or wrap round the body, arms or legs of the assailant. A skilled protagonist could even pull a sword from an attacker's hand with the help of the chain, but this is a more difficult feat than one might imagine. The blade of the sickle was also used to cut the hocks of a horse and to finish off wounded foes. Later, the weapon was adopted by the *Ninja* and by the police in their struggles with brigands. This weapon is now rarely taught, except in a few rare *Ryu* of Japan; for instance, the *Araki-ryu*. In modern times a wooden sickle is used and a wooden ball or even a rubber one. However, advanced students of the school of *Ryukyu Kobujutsu* still train with a sharp, steel-bladed sickle. See *Chigiriki, Kobudo, Manriki-gusari*.

Kushin-ryu. School of *Ju-jutsu* founded by *Inugami Nagakatsu* and perfected around 1720 in Edo (Tokyo) by his grandson *Inugami Nagayasu* (*Inugami Gubei*). Its teachings are similar to those of *Kito-ryu*.

Ku Yu Cheong. The Cantonese name of a *Wushu* master (1890–1952) famous for his 'iron palm' technique.

Kuzure. From Kuzureru, to fall.
— **Kuzure no Jotai.** State of unbalance. See *Kuzushi*.

Preparation for combat using a Kusari-gama against a Boken. Araki-ryu school.

— **Kuzure-hiji Maki-komi** *Judo*. Upsetting *Uke*'s balance by wrapping one's arms round his or her elbow.

— **Kuzure-kami-shiho-garami** *Judo*. A technique of groundwork (*Ne-waza*) by which an opponent is immobilized by controlling both his or her arms and both legs.

— **Kuzure-kami-shiho-gatame** *Judo*. Control of four points, from on top, used in groundwork (*Ne-waza*).

Kuzure Kesa-gatame

Kuzure-kami-shiho-gatame

— **Kuzure Kesa-gatame** *Judo*. A technique of groundwork (*Ne-waza*) by which an opponent is controlled from the side.

— **Kuzure Tate Shiho-gatame** *Judo*. A groundwork (*Ne-waza*) technique consisting of controlling *Uke*'s four points by 'tucking' his or her head from the front under the arm of *Tori*, who then grips his or her own belt to secure the hold. Tori sits astride Uke as if riding a horse.

— **Kuzure Yoko Shiho-gatame**. A groundwork (*Ne-waza*) technique by which *Uke*'s four points are controlled from the side.

Kuzure Tate Shiho-gatame

Kuzushi 'Loss of balance'. In hand-to-hand combat, to throw an adversary one should, ideally, be able to turn his or her own attacking force against him or her (*Sen-no-sen*). Sometimes it is necessary to use one's own force (*Go-no-sen*) to achieve this, and sometimes a combination of the two methods may be used. It is thus a matter of manoeuvering oneself into a position from which a throwing action (*Kake, Nage-waza*) can be conveniently executed, before one obtains a good *Kuzushi*. The whole art of provoking Kuzushi is of obliging the opponent to lose his or her balance through a shift of the opponent's centre of gravity. The shift of the centre of gravity (*Hara*) is best and most often produced by a turning movement (*Tai-sabaki* in *Aikido*) or an evasive movement in *Judo*. See *Kurai*.

Kuzure Yoko Shiho-gatame

Kwan see *Ryu*.

Kwan-do. A type of Chinese *Naginata*, named after a celebrated third-century general. In general it is heavier than the Japanese weapon, one monster *Kwan-do* weighing almost 50 kg. Also *Guando*.

Kwansu see *Yonhon Nukite*.

Kwon see *Ken*.

Kyeuk-pa see *Kyok-pa, Mishigi, Shi-wari*.

Kyo 'Principle'. (Also used in the expression 'Go-kyo' from *Judo*.) See *Go-kyo*.
Aikido. There are five *Kyo* principles:

Ikkyo (first *Kyo*), or *Ude-osae*
Nikyo (second *Kyo*), or *Kote-mawashi*
Sankyo (third *Kyo*), or *Kote-hineri*
Yonkyo (fourth *Kyo*), or *Tekubi-osae*
Gokyo (fifth *Kyo*), or *Use-hishigi*.

Kyoei. *Kyusho* point situated between the fourth and fifth ribs. See *Body, Kyusho*.

Kyogi Judo *Judo*. According to *Kano Jigoro*'s definition, this means a form of training which aims to prepare the body to be physically apt (*Rentai-ho*), thanks to a preliminary study of technique (*Waza*), for actual contest (*Shobu-ho*). See *Kogi Judo*.

Kyo-jutsu *Karate, Kendo*. An evasive movement or flight, immediately folowing a real attack.

Kyokaku see *Otokodate*.

Kyokushinkai-kai (abridged to KKK) *Karate*. A Japanese *Karate* association; also a particular style of this sport, created in 1955 by *Oyama Masatatsu* (born in Korea in 1923), which is a variant of *Goju-ryu*. It is a very tough and effective form of Karate, based on strength and the *Zen* spirit, in which the positions are natural and the techniques rapidly executed in succession to reduce an opponent's resistance. The *Kyokushinkai* of Oyama puts great emphasis on breathing exercises (*Kokyu*) and on movements which are forbidden in *Karate-do* but are shown to be very effective in real fighting.

Kyosen 'Solar plexus'. See *Body, Kyusho*.

Kyoshi. The grade of 6th and 7th *Dan* in the martial arts. It corresponds to a degree of perfection in the inward sense, and to expert instructors.
Wa-jutsu. The title of 'master': white jacket, black or brown *Hakama*, purple belt with three red tabs. See *Hi Gi*.

Kyoshi no Kamae. The kneeling posture adopted by the Japanese.

Kyoshin Meichi-ryu see *Momono-i, Shunzo*.

Kyotetsu-koge. A dagger with two blades, one of which is curved and may be used as a hook. A long cord is attached to the hilt, weighted by an iron disc. It was used mainly by the *Ninja*, who employed the hook as an aid to scaling walls. The weapon could be held in the hand and also thrown. The weighted cord could knock down or immobilize an enemy. Also *Kyotetsu-shoge*.

Kyototsu 'Top part of the sternum'. See *Body*.

Kyu. The lower grades of the martial arts, below black belt. There are nine in *Karate*, six in *Judo* and other disciplines. People who have *Kyu* grades are called *Mudansha*, 'without *Dan*'. In *Tae-kwon-do* there are ten *Kyu*. Korean: *Keup*; Vietnamese: *Cap*. In ascending order, the Japanese *Kyu* grades are:

Rokkyu (6th *Kyu*), white belt
Gokyu (5th *Kyu*), white belt
Shikyu (4th *Kyu*), white belt
Sankyu (3rd *Kyu*), brown belt
Nikyu (2nd *Kyu*), brown belt
Ikkyu (1st *Kyu*), brown belt

However, the colours are different outside Japan and the most common by far are as follows, in ascending order:

Rokkyu, white belt
Gokyu, yellow belt
Shikyu orange belt
Sankyu green belt
Nikyu blue belt
Ikkyu brown belt

According to style, association and so forth, the grade colours may vary. See *Kyudan*, *Obi*.

Aikido. In Japan the five first *Kyu* grades wear a white belt and the highest, 1st *Kyu*, a brown belt. In Europe the *Kyu* grades wear coloured belts corresponding to the *Judo* system.

Tae-kwon-do. There are ten *Kyu* (*Keup*) grades and their colours in ascending order, prior to attaining black belt status, are:

10th *Keup*: white
9th *Keup*: white with a yellow bar
8th *Keup*: yellow
7th *Keup*: yellow with a green bar
6th *Keup*: green
5th *Keup*: green with a blue bar
4th *Keup*: blue
3rd *Keup*: blue with a brown bar
2nd *Keup*: brown
1st *Keup*: brown with a black bar.

These are followed by ten grades of black belt (*Dan*). See *Kyudan*.

Qwan-ki-do. There are four learning grades (*Cap*) before the five *Dang* (black belts), which constitute the First Level (*Bach-dai*).

The beginners (*So-dang*) wear a large white belt on which the first four grades are marked, one to four, by blue bars. Next is blue belt, and finally the black belt for 1st, 2nd and 3rd ranks. For the 4th, the belt is green and white; for the 5th, the belt is blue and white.

Kyuba. An art combining archery (*Kyu*) and horsemanship (*Ba*).
— **Kyuba no Michi** 'The Way of archery and horsemanship'. See *Bushido*.

Kyudan. The whole range of lower and higher grades in the martial arts. This system of grades is used in all *Budo* to indicate the level of technical ability reached by *Budoka*. When a *Kyu* or *Dan* grade is conferred, a diploma, *Gaku*, signifies its validity, and the name of the student and the grade are recorded in a central register. The Kyu grades are generally considered learning grades; the Dan grades are for improving and perfecting skill. The number of Dan grades varies from five to twelve, according to the style. The highest grade is usually reserved for founder of a school or style, and his successors. He is frequently referred to as *Sensei*, Teacher, meaning *the* teacher; but other instructors are also addressed as *Sensei*. These are the names generally used to describe the ascending progression of *Dan* grades:

1st *Dan*: *Sho-mokuroku*
2nd *Dan*: *Jo-mokuroku*
3rd *Dan*: *Hon-mokuroku* (consisting of one or two grades)
4th *Dan*: *Hon-mokuroku*, *Shi-han*, *Renshi*
5th *Dan*: *Menkyo* or *Tasshi* (recognized as 'master' level)
6th *Dan*: *Menkyo*, *Kyoshi*, etc.

The title *Kyoshi* is given to those who have gained 6th and 7th Dan; that of *Hanshi* to those who have gained 7th or 8th Dan; that of *Shihan*, 'great expert', to 9th Dan grades. The attribution of Shihan sometimes varies from school to school and may be given to other Dan grades, as well as those listed here. Students who are below black belt grade and have only Kyu grades are called *Mudansha*. *Yudansha* and *Kodansha* are the names given to those students who are black belt grade of 3rd Dan and above. The title of *Kaiden* is rarely bestowed on anyone, as it means 'equal to the master'. See *Menkyo, Kyu, Obi* and the titles listed.

Dan grades are themselves qualified or given 'values' as follows:

1st *Dan*: student (*Sen*)
2nd *Dan*: disciple (*Go no Sen*)
3rd *Dan*: accepted disciple
4th *Dan*: expert (*Sen no Sen*)
5th *Dan*: expert (*Kokoro*)
6th *Dan*: expert (*Kokoro*)
7th and 8th *Dan*: expert (*Iko-kokoro*)
9th and 10th *Dan*: master (*Iko-kokoro*)

The title of *Hanshi* is reserved for the *Kokoro* grades, that *Kyoshi* for the expert instructors, and that of *Renshi* as an indication of self-mastery. *Hanshi* is only an honorary title, and is given to the master (*Iko no Kokoro*) by his own pupils or disciples.

Tae-kwon-do. There are ten black belt (*Dan*) grades.

Qwan-ki-do. The *Dang* belts are marked by a picture of the *Dao* in Chinese surrounded by the eight trigrams of the Taoist *Yijing*. They show that the student is a 'confirmed devotee' (*Thuong Dang*). *Thuong Dang* follows the middle grade, *Trung Dang*, which follows the beginner's grade, *So-dang*.

Kyudo 'Way of archery'. The practice of archery, whether for hunting or for war, is a very ancient Japanese art. Lacquered bows dating from the fifth century BC have been found. At least until the sixteenth century *Kyu-jutsu*, or 'warrior techniques of the bow', was considered the primary art of the eighteen *Kakuto-bugei* which all *Bushi* were obliged to study. At first the bow was used on foot, but from the twelfth century onwards it was used equally by horsemen who followed the 'Way of archery on horseback' or *Kyuba-no-Michi* (see *Bushido*). The Japanese bow (*Yumi*) is very long (about 2.20 m) and in this respect is very different from the Chinese or Mongolian version. Its asymmetric shape also distinguishes it from the latter, and obliges the archer to draw from a position one-third along its length. The only advantage afforded by the extra length is that it allows the use of very long arrows (*Ya*). The bowstring is drawn back

beyond the ear, using a 'Mongolian' grip in which the string rests in the hollow of the thumb. Even though stories extolling the accuracy of the bow reach sensational proportions the famed accuracy is in fact relative, because its effective range is no more than 100 m when fired in a straight line. After the sixteenth century, when firearms came into use, the bow was used less and less as a significant weapon of war. Kyu-jutsu was then transformed into an art, a *Budo*, and named *Kyudo*.

Since prehistoric times the bow was used by Shamans as an instrument of invocation. The vibrating string produced a sound which was considered to be in accord with divine vibrations. The bow has always been sacred in Japanese eyes, and surrounded with a quasi-religious respect. It was used mainly in religious ceremonies, and since the seventeenth century it has been an essential feature in *Sumo* tournaments. (See *Yumitori-shiki*.)

However, the bow continued to be used during all the Edo period by the *Ninja*. They used a special bow, of symmetrical Mongolian design with two curves. It was very short, no longer than 0.75 m. Curiously enough, the Japanese armies did not adopt

Archery position. Drawing by Hokusai.

this bow of Mongolian origin, even though the two invasions by combined Korean and Chinese forces in 1274 and 1281 demonstrated both its power and its precision. The Bushi continued to use their traditional bow, regarding it with great veneration. Concurrently with the use of firearms in Japan, bands of archers were used. The latter were sometimes also 'musketeers', and continued to feature in battles throughout the Edo period (1603–1868).

It was mainly from the end of the fourteenth century that the master archers busied themselves with the task of codifying and creating systems for the practice of archery, and creating schools (*Ryu*) which specialized in this weapon. Already, since approximately the tenth century, archery had been practised in times of peace as a diversion or, as we would say today, a 'sport' – as for instance in *Inu-oimono*, *Yabusame* or *Kasagasake*. Certain of these sports were clothed with a religious significance and have lasted until our own times in the form of the Yabusame tradition. But from the end of the Edo period archery was truly outclassed by firearms and became more and more merely a system of training in which hitting the target and having precision were

less important than in ancient *Kyu-jutsu*. The accent was put on ritual during the taking of correct posture and on the attainment of spiritual qualities. The practice of archery must now bring the archer a sense of balance, mastery of the self, elevation of thought, harmony (*Wa*) and effortless serenity.

There was a reassessment of Kyudo at the beginning of the twentieth century and something of its message was conveyed to Western readers in the famous book by Eugen Herrigel, *Zen in the Art of Archery*. This work met with great success in Europe and the USA and brought to public attention the names of the most prestigious Japanese archers, such as Awa and Anzawa. Nearer to our times, in 1940, a renowned *Karateka* and disciple of *Funakoshi Gichin*, *Obata Isao*, carried off the Kyudo honours in a championship in Tokyo. He represented Manchuria, which was then part of the Japanese Empire. The event gave a certain boost to this traditional discipline. Since it is classed as a *Budo*, Kyudo is taught in several *Dojo* outside Japan. In Japan itself there are as many as 500,000 practitioners. The grades consist of *Kyu* and ten *Dan* grades. Competitions usually take place using targets some 60 m away. For training purposes a special *Makiwara* is used and arrows are fired from very close range (two metres or less). Students (*Kyudoka*) wear a *Hakama* and *Kimono*. During certain ceremonies they wear a special *Kimono* and

Opposite: Master Anzawa, one of the truly great masters of Kyudo, at the age of eighty-one, in the Kai posture.

Archery at the school of Master Anzawa.

an *Eboshi*, a cap made of plaited, lacquered horsehair. The act of preparing and firing is a complete ceremony in itself. For training purposes it is broken down into eight parts consisting of eight fundamental positions (*Yugame*): *Ashibumi, Dozukuri, Uchi-okoshi* (or *Kikitori*), *Hikiwake, Kai* (or *Jiman*), *Hanare, Zanshin* (or *Daisan*).

The physical training in *Kyudo* is still called *Kyu-jutsu*, but that part of the discipline which is aimed at spiritual training is given the preferred name of *Shado*.

The All Japan Kyudo Federation (*Zen Nihon Kyudo Renmei*) was founded in 1948. See *Monomi, Yumi, Arrows*.

— **Kyu-ho** see *Yamato-ryu*.
— **Kyu-jutsu** see *Kyudo*.
— **Kyu-ki** see *Yamato-ryu*.
— **Kyu-ko** see *Yamato-ryu*.
— **Kyu-Rei** see *Yamato-ryu*.
— **Kyu-ri** see *Yamato-ryu*.

Kyushaku-bo see *Bo*.

Kyushin-ryu. An ancient Japanese school of defence against lance (*Yari*) attacks, halberd (*Hoko*) or *Naginata*.

Kyusho 'Vital points'. (Korean: *Keupso*; Vietnamese: *Huyet*.) These are the vulnerable points (sometimes called 'vital points') of the human body which a *Budoka* must know so that his or her blows can be as effective as possible (in *Karate* and *Aikido* above all). What are called *Atemi* blows are aimed at these points. Vulnerable points are numerous and are known as *Mato*. They appear all over the body along the lines or meridians used in acupuncture. When struck they can produce severe pain, loss of consciousness and even death. Thus the effect on an assailant can be fatal, disabling or discouraging, and may put him or her completely at the mercy of the defender.

Points which produce death or loss of consciousness:

On the head:

The point of the jaw, slightly to one side, can produce loss of consciousness: *Mikazuki*.

The very tip of the jaw (*Kachikake*): loss of consciousness.
The fontanelle or Bregma (*Tendo*) or (*Tento*): fracture of the skull.
The temples (*Kasumi*): death from brain lesion.
Eyes, upper rim of eye orbit and cheekbones (*Seidon*): temporary or permanent loss of vision and balance.
Between the eyes (*Uto, Chuto*): death.
Below the nose (*Gekon, Jinchu*): fracture and loss of consciousness.
Mastoid process (*Dokko*): death.
Carotid arteries (*Murasame* and *Matsusake*): loss of consciousness.
Larynx (*Hichu*): loss of consciousness.
Seventh cervical vertebrae (*Keichu*): 'rabbit punch': loss of consciousness and death.

On the body:

Testicles (*Kinteki*): loss of consciousness and even death. Also *Tsurigane*.
Navel (*Myojo*): loss of consciousness.
Solar plexus (*Suigetsu*): loss of breathing capacity.
Base of the sternum (*Kyosen*): Paralysis of the nervous system.
Midpoint of the sternum (*Tanchu*): cardiac trauma.
Between the fourth and fifth ribs (*Kyose*):

loss of breathing capacity.
Between the fifth and sixth ribs (*Ganka*): loss of breathing capacity.
Floating ribs (*Denko, Inazuma*): nervous and respiratory paralysis.

On the back:

Base of the shoulder blades (*Haya-uchi*): loss of breathing capacity.
Between the shoulder blades (*Kassatsu*): loss of consciousness.
Kidneys (*Ushiro Denko*): nervous shock.
Coccyx (*Bitei*): lesion of the spinal cord, paralysis.
Below the hip/thigh region (*Ushiro Inazuma*): sciatic nerve damage.

Painful but not traumatic points:

On the arms:

Inside the arm (*Wanju*).
Top of the wrist (*Shuko*).
Top of the hand (*Soto-shakutaku*).
Bend of the arm (*Chukisu*).

Points on the legs:

Inside of the top of the thigh or groin (*Yako*).
Top of the thigh (*Fukuto*).
Base of the calf (*Kusanagi*).
Kneecap (*Shitsu-kansetsu*).
Tibia (*Keiko*).
Ankle (*Naike*).
Top of the foot (*Kori, So-in*).

See *Body, Head, Legs, Arms, Atemi*, Competition rules of *Karate*, 31.

Lan-fa see *Shaolin-si*.

Laofu-shan Wushu. '*Kata* of the old mountain tiger.' One of the oldest *Kata* (*Dao*) of the schools of *Shaolin-si* (Northern style, *Bei Shaolin*), performed alone or with a partner.

Laohu Taidu see *Taidu*.

Lap Tan see *Bo Phap*.

Lapels see *Eri, Hai, Kesa*.

Lathi 'Long stick' popular in India. Although the techniques of using the *Lathi* go back into the most ancient times, its use in the twentieth century has mainly been limited to the police. For training, which usually takes place in an area about 12 m in diameter, the students wear a thick turban and forearm protectors made of padded cotton. To score a point a contestant must touch the head, sternum, ribs, shoulders, hips, knees or ankles. The point or length of the stick may be used to score a point.

Lau-ma Bo see *Bo*.

Le see *Rei, Bow*.

Lee, Bruce. Known mainly as a film actor, Bruce Lee was born in Hong Kong in 1940 and died in 1974. In his early youth he liked to associate with gangs of young hooligans who roamed the streets of Hong Kong looking for trouble. He picked up street-fighting methods and then began to learn *Wing Chun* under the direction of grand master *Yip Man*. He then went to the USA, where he carried on training and also played a memorable role in a television series known as 'The Green Hornet'. On his return to Hong Kong he worked with the film producer Chow, specializing in spectacular roles in *Kung-fu* films from the beginning of 1967. His films had enormous success in Hong Kong and later in many Western Countries. His own martial arts style was called *Jeet Kune Do*; an approach to fighting which concentrated on the practical rather than the classical aspects. He

died in 1974 in circumstances which have never been publicly clarified. His mastery of techniques as shown in his films did much to popularize Kung-fu, and since his death former close pupils such as Daniel Inosanto have continued to teach Jeet Kune Do; the highest concentration of students is found in the USA.

Legs. The legs assure the balance of posture and movement. Their importance in martial arts is obvious; for moving, throwing and striking purposes. They are also vulnerable to attack.

Legs: *Ashi*
Knees: *Hitsui, Hiza*
Kneecap: *Hiza-gashira*
Bend of the knee: *Shitsu*
Inside of the thigh: *Mata*
Tibia: *Kobore*
Base of calf: *Sobi*
Ankle: *Ashi-kubi*

See also *Body, Feet*

Lethwei see *Thaing*.

Le To see *Bai To*.

Lien Hoa Tan see *Bo Phap*.

Li-gar see *Shaolin-si*.

Li Jinglin see *Wudang Pai*.

Li Taidu see *Taidu*.

Liu-gar see *Shaolin-si*.

Liuhe Bafa *Wushu*. Style of Chinese 'boxing' related to the 'internal' (*Neijia*) tradition of *Shaolin-si*.

Loai see *Hansoku*.

Long-dong Taidu see *Taidu*.

Long-nan Taidu see *Taidu*.

Long Tien see *Thu Phap*.

Long-xi Taidu see *Taidu*.

Long Gian see *Nunchaku*.

Long Ho see *Quyen*.

Long-hua Quan *Wushu*. A type of Chinese 'boxing'.

Loss of balance see *Kuzushi*.

Love see *Ai, Aiki*.

Lower Abdomen see *Hara, Tanden*.

Lu-fa see *Shaolin-si*.

Lu Taidu see *Taidu*.

Luu Van Cuoc see *Cuoc Phap*.

Ma. The concept *Ma* is a global one encompassing space, time, an unspecified interval between two things, two volumes of space or two moments. It permeates all Japanese life and the arts of the Far East. According to the concept *Ma*, everything is integrated with nature and is defined by the space–time which is 'right' or proper to it alone. The best painting, the best pottery, the best movement, and so on, exhibit Ma.

—Ma-ai. This is the distance–time which separates two opponents, allowing them to judge the overall timing and distance necessary for each to carry out his or her intentions. If a contestant has a good grasp of *Ma-ai*, he or she will be able to perform a technique near perfectly. A contestant who can, as it were, penetrate the opponent's Ma-ai will outclass that opponent. A perfect distance between two opponents is called *Juban-no-Ma-ai*; too great a distance, *To-ma*; too short a distance, *Chika-ma*. See *Yomi*, *Hyoshi*.

Ma Bo see *Bo*.

Mabuni Kenwa (1889–1952). A martial arts expert who studied in Okinawa at the same time as *Funakoshi Gichin*, under the direction of *Itosu Yasutsune* (c. 1830–1915). The latter was a master of the *Shuri-te* school and of the *Naha-te* school of *Higaonna Kanryo* (1853–1915). He created his own style of *Karate-Ju-jutsu* in Japan in 1928.

Machi-dojo. A private *Dojo* reserved for training in one of the martial arts (*Budo*).

Ma Dao. A kind of Vietnamese scimitar.

Mae 'Front', 'In front'. See *Space*.
— **Mae Ashi-geri** *Karate*. A front-kick, leg travelling directly forwards, with the leading leg.
— **Mae Empi-uchi** *Karate*. A rising blow delivered with the elbow.
— **Mae-gashira** see *Sumotori*.
— **Mae-geri** *Karate*, *Aikido*. A kick to the front.
— **Mae-geri Kekomi** *Karate*. A front-kick which 'penetrates' – one could say a 'driving inwards' front-kick.

Mae-geri

— **Mae Hiji-ate** *Karate*. An elbow blow, delivered through a horizontal plane with a circular action, in a forward direction.
— **Mae Kami-dori** see *Kami-tori*.

Mae-geri Kekomi

— **Mae Katate Hakko-dori** *Wa-jutsu*. A basic *Kata* performed in a standing position in which *Tori* is seized by *Uke*. Uke uses one hand to seize one wrist. Tori delivers an arresting action to Uke's face, focusing on an *Atemi* point, frees him(her)self with a *Tai-sabaki* technique, and strikes Uke with an elbow blow to the face and an elbow blow to the ribs. The same movement using a different grip, from the side, is ended with an Atemi blow using sword-hand (*Shuto*) between Uke's eyes; this is called *Yoko Kata Te*

151

Hakko-dori. The same movement again, this time with a grip from the rear and ending with an Atemi blow to the face, is called *Ushiro Kata Hakko-dori.* When both wrists are gripped from the rear, the technique is called *Ushiro Ryote Hakko-dori.* When one wrist is held with a reverse grip from the rear, the freeing action is called *Ushiro Gyaku Kata Te Hakko-dori.*

— **Mae Ryo-te-dori** *Aikido.* When *Uke* seizes both *Shite*'s wrists using both hands, Shite brings both hands together, drawing back and turning to the left, and delivers an *Atemi* blow with both hands crossed to Uke's face. He or she ends with an Atemi using the elbow. See *Te-dori.*

— **Mae Ryo-te Shime-age** *Aikido.* Uke seizes *Shite* by both lapels with both hands as if to strangle him or her. Shite pulls the lapels down away from his or her throat and passes under Uke's arms, using a turning action. Then Shite rises quickly and ends with an *Atemi* blow to Uke's face. See *Eri-tori.*

— **Mae Ryo-te Sode Tori** *Aikido.* Uke seizes *Shite* from the front by both sleeves. Shite brings both hands together, steps to the left and describes a big circle with arms stretched out, turning his or her body from right to left on the right foot. He or she ends with an *Atemi* blow. See *Sode Tori.*

— **Mae Shitate Kumi-tsuki** *Aikido.* *Uke* encircles *Shite* with his or her arms to lift him or her, from the front. Shite in reply digs his or her thumbs under Uke's ears and performs *Rofuse*, drawing back the left foot. See *Kumi-tsuki.*

— **Mae Tate Mitsu** *Sumo.* A type of loin-cloth (*Fundoshi*) made of silk, very closely woven and held by a knot under the belt (*Mawashi*). In combat it is forbidden to take hold of it.

— **Mae-te** *Karate.* A blow to the face with the palm of the hand.

— **Mae Tobi-geri** *Karate.* A forward, leaping kick, generally to the head.

— **Mae U-ate Kumi-tsuki** *Aikido.* Uke encircles *Shite* from the front, pinning down both arms. Shite strikes Uke by bringing his or her knee up into Uke's stomach, then steps back with the left foot at the same time raising the arms, turning to the left and applying a lock to Uke's left arm. The lock is applied at the same time as Shite steps back

Mae Tobi-geri

with the left foot a second time.

— **Mae Ude De-ai Osae** *Karate.* A blocking technique using pressure from the forearm.

— **Mae Ude Hineri Uke** *Karate.* A blocking technique using a turning action of the forearm.

— **Mae-zumo** see *Sumotori.*

Ma-itta 'I give up'. This is said when one of two contestants admits that he or she is defeated. See Rules of Competition *Judo,* 21.

Make (Maketa) 'Defeat'. See *Make-kata, Mansoku-make.*

Maketa see *Make, Make-kata.*

Maki 'Winding, wrapping'.

— **Maki-tomoe** *Judo.* Winding in a circle.

— **Maki-komi** *Judo.* A throw preceded by a blocking action when an opponent shows strong resistance, ending with a *Sutemi* (sacrifice: throwing oneself to the ground in order also to throw the opponent).

— **Maki-kote** 'Change.'

— **Maki-otoshi** *Sumo.* A powerful throwing technique in which the opponent is gripped by the arms, under the shoulders.

— **Maki-otosu** *Aikido.* Controlling an opponent's arm when he or she is on the ground.

Makimono see *Menkyo.*

Makino Toru. An expert in swordsmanship of the *Hokushin Itto-ryu* school, author

Maki-otoshi

Makura Kesa-gatame *Judo*. A groundwork technique (*Ne-waza*) in which pressure is brought on the side of the ribcage. *Tori* spreads his or her legs forward and backward to apply the pressure, aided by the arms gripping the neck and shoulder. Sometimes called a 'pillow' (*Makura*) grip.

Makura Kesa-gatame

of a famous work on *Kendo*, *Kendo Shugyo-no-Shiori* (Kendo Training) around 1930. In the book, he emphasized the concept of *Seishi-o Choetsu* and advocated that one should follow the virtues of loyalty and filial piety.

Makiwara *Karate*. A straw pad fixed to a wall or pole, or held in the hands of a partner, and used for training in punching and kicking techniques. The straw is usually closely woven and fixed to a short wooden plank. In Japan, the older type of *Makiwara* was often made of woven raffia, fastened to a post or round stake. Korean: *Dalyeun-ju*.
Kyudo. For archery training, the *Makiwara* is made of a round truss of rice straw. The stalks are parallel and very tightly held together to give a barrel shape about 0.60 m in diameter. It is placed horizontally on a trestle about 1.50 m from the ground. The archer stands about two metres from the Makiwara when training at perfecting his or her movements, as distinct from training at perfecting aim.

Makki 'Blocking'. See *Bang-o*

Makoto. A feeling of absolute sincerity and total frankness, which requires a pure mind, free from the pressure of events. This ethical concept, which is purely Japanese, includes a sense of moral purity and physical hygiene which is particularly relevant to those who participate in the martial arts. It is symbolized by the cherry blossom (impermanence of everything, fragility of life) and by snow (absolute purity). See *Heiko*.

Maku-shita see *Salt, Sumotori, Dohyo*.

Maku-uchi see *Sumotori, Dohyo, Salt*.

Mallavidja see *Vajramushti*.

Mamori-gatana see *Katana, Swords*.

Manabu 'Learning by imitating'. A method of studying movement and technique by following and imitating the instructor.

Maniwa-nen-ryu. An ancient school of martial arts, founded in the sixteenth century and transformed in the seventeenth century into a school advocating an art of 'peaceful' combat 'to preserve life rather than to take it'. This school still exists, and teaches most of the forms of *Budo* which use weapons. However, it specializes in *Ju-jutsu*, *Ken-jutsu* and the use of the *Kusari-gama*. One of the more spectacular methods of training is to cut a muffled arrow in two with a sword before it can reach the swordsman.

Manriki-gusari 'Ten-thousand-power chain'. This is an iron chain, almost 4 metres long, ending with a metal ball, invented in the seventeenth century by *Masaki Toshimitsu*, a guard at one of the gates of Edo. Since the gate was considered to be a holy place, the spilling of blood was forbid-

Exercise with the Manriki-gusari by Master Shimizu Takagi.

den and the killing of human beings would have defiled it, and was likewise forbidden. Masaki devised the ball and chain, which could be used like a bolas to bring down assailants. It could be easily hidden in the clothing, and when held in both hands could repel sword attacks. Thus, for those who guarded the gate, it replaced the sword. Also called *Kusari*.

Mao Bo see *Bo*.

Marman. In the martial arts of India, these are the vital points of the body which may be struck to incapacitate or kill an enemy. They are analogous to the *Kyusho* of Japanese martial arts. The same points are used in Ayurvedic medicine, indigenous to the subcontinent, for massage and percussion techniques, to relieve pain and illness. Knowledge of the *Marman* is necessary in the practice of *Kalaripayat* (also known as *Kalari*) and in the techniques of wrestling (*Mallayuddha*), which are both peculiar to India.

Marume Kurando see *Taisha-ryu, Kage-ryu.*

Masaki-ryu. A school of *Naginata*, created at the beginning of the twentieth century, embodying an approach somewhat similar to that of *Toda-ryu*. See *Chujo-ryu*.

Masaki Toshimitsu see *Manriki-gusari*.

Ma-sutemi Waza Judo. A *Sutemi* (sacrifice throw) 'on the back' technique comprising three movements: *Tomoe-nage, Ura-nage, Sumi-gaeshi*. See also *Sutemi-waza, Nage-no-kata*.

Mata. Internal part of the thigh. See *Uchi-mata, Body, Legs*.
— **'Start again'.** See *Sonomama*.

Ma-tan see *Tan Phap*.

Match Drawn see *Ikiwake*.

Mato 'Target'. See *Kyudo*.

Matsukaza 'Left carotid artery'. See *Hiza-gatame, Head, Murasame*.

Matsumura Sokon (1809–99). A martial arts master from a noble family of *Kyushu*. He was a guard in the palace of the princes of *Shuri* in Okinawa. After being initiated into the *Jigen-ryu* school of swordsmanship, he was sent to China to study the martial arts of that country. On his return to Shuri he created a style of *Karate* called *Shuri-te*, which he passed on to his disciple *Itosu Anko*. This famous *Karateka*, who lived from 1830 to 1915, adapted the techniques of the art into a physical training system which was used in the schools of Shuri, and developed the art itself even further. It was also known by its Chinese name, *Bucho*.

Matsuura Seizan. A *Daimyo* (chief of clan or province) of the Matsuura family of Hizen province (Nagasaki, *Kyushu*). He was born in 1760 and was famous as a martial arts expert. He created a school of swordsmanship, *Shinkeito-ryu*, or 'School of the technique and mind of the sword', which lasted until 1908.

Matsuyama Mondo see *Chujo-ryu* (*Nikai-do-ryu*).

Matte 'Wait!' (from the verb '*Matsu*', to wait). A word often used by the referee in a contest while awaiting a decision. See Competition Rules of *Judo*, 8, 12, 18, 29.

Ma-ukemi see *Ukemi*.

Mawashi *Sumo*. 'Belt' made of a long piece of silk (11 m by 0.61 m) folded six times and wound round the waist of a *Sumotori*. It can weigh up to 15 kg. This belt is decorated with rigid silk cords and hardened with bird-line. The cords, called *Sagari*, hang from the belt and have no practical function. Sometimes they come loose during a contest, but this has no bearing on the contest itself. Sumotori are allowed to grip the belt in order to bring off a throwing technique. It is usually black. See *Obi, Kesho-mawashi, Tae Tate Mitsu*.
— 'in a circle'. See *Space*.
— **Mawashi-geri** *Karate*, *Aikido*. A roundhouse kick, often delivered with a whiplike action. See *Yoko-geri, Cuoc Phap*.

Mawashi-geri

— **Mawashi-tsuki** *Karate*. A roundhouse or hook punch. Also *Mawashi-zuki*.
— **Mawashi-uki** *Karate*. A roundhouse block. Also the name given to a stretching exercise involving the raised, bent arm which benefits the muscles which cover the sides of the body.

Mawashi-tsuki

Meijin *Wa-jutsu*. 'Higher master'. An honorific title given to those who hold the highest grades in a martial arts system. Such martial artists wear a black or brown *Hakama*, and a white belt. See *Kyudan*.

Meikyo *Karate*. *Kata* of the 'Clear Mirror', in which the mind of one contestant is supposed to reflect the consciousness of his or her opponent.

Men 'Face'. *Kendo*. A piece of the armour used in *Kendo*; it protects the head and face. The *Men* is made of thickly padded cotton to which is attached a steel grill. A 'hood' covers the top and the sides of the head and gives way to flaps which protect the shoulders. A narrow fillet protects the throat. The grill is known as *Men-gane*, and the head and shoulder protectors *Men-dare*. The cords which hold the Men in place are called *Men-himo*. The word Men is also used to describe a blow to the head delivered by the *Shinai*, from the front: Men, direct; *Hidari-men*, left side; *Migi-men*, right side. See *Dogu, Kendo, Armour*.

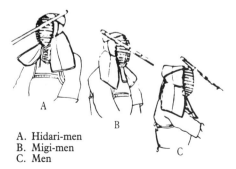

A. Hidari-men
B. Migi-men
C. Men

Menkyo. The ancient system of rankings or grades in the *Bugei* of byegone days. Ranks were conferred by granting a type of 'licence' or certificate (*Makimono*). These Makimono, numbering from three to five, were given by the master of a *Ryu* to his disciples, according to their teaching ability. See *Budo, Bugei, Kyudan.*

Mi-ateru 'Hand-to-hand combat'. This name is often given to the disciplines of *Ju-jutsu* and *Judo.*

Michi 'Path', 'Way'. See *Do, Kyuba-no-Michi.*

Mienai *Karate*. 'I could not see'. This term is used in refereeing a contest to indicate that a referee or judge has not seen what has taken place, for one reason or another.

Mifune Kyuzo *Judo*. A master of Judo (1883–1965) who entered the *Kodokan* in 1903 and became a pupil of *Kano Jigoro*. He was a small man and invented a technique specifically suited to small *Judoka*, called *Kukinage*. He reached the grade of *Judan* (10th *Dan*) in 1945 and wrote his memoirs, *Judo Kaikoroku*, in 1953.

Migi 'Right, on the right, right hand side'. Korean: **Orenchok**. See *Space, Hidari*. Also: *U*.

Migi-do

— **Migi-do *Kendo*.** A blow delivered with the *Shinai* to the right side of an opponent's chest.

— **Migi-men *Kendo*.** A blow delivered with the *Shinai* to the right side of an opponent's head.

Mijikai-mono see *Nagai-mono.*

Mikazuki see *Kyusho.*

Mikazuki-geri

— **Mikazuki-geri *Karate*.** A crescent kick, in which the foot describes an arc of a circle. The blocking movement used against this type of kick is called *Mikazuki-geri Uke*.

Mikazuki-geri Uke

Miku-daki see *Ura.*

Mikomi see *Ariake.*

Mimi 'Ear'. See *Head.*

Minamoto A famous warrior clan which opposed the rival *Taira* (*Heike*) clan in 118 and conquered it. The clan chief, *Minamoto no Yoritomo*, established the first Shogunate (a type of military government) in 1192, with the help of his half-brother *Minamoto no Yoshitsune*. The latter lived on in Japanese history and legend as the most famous general of his age (see *Yoshitsune*). The *Minamoto* family produced very many famous men of state and celebrated warriors in the ensuing centuries, some of whom created schools (*Ryu*) of martial arts (*Genji-no-Heiho*). The family is generally known by the name of *Genji* rather than *Minamoto*.

— **Minamoto no Hidetsuna** see *Araki-ryu*.

— **Minamoto no Masayoshi** see *Takeda Sokaku, Daito-ryu*.

— **Minamoto no Sonechika** see *Yawara*.

— **Minamoto no Yanagi** see *Tenjin Shin-yo-ryu*.

— **Minamoto no Yoshimitsu** see *Aikido*.

— **Minamoto no Yoritomo** see *Yoritomo, Kamakura*.

— **Minamoto no Yoshitsune** see *Yoshitsune*.

Mind see *Kokoro*.

Ming Quan see *Quan*.

Miru no Kokoro 'Mind of vision'. A global vision which takes in the opponent and his or her surroundings, while evaluating his or her position in space and the time interval which might be needed to close with him or her. See *Ma-ai*.

Mitokoro-zeme *Sumo*. A method of gripping an opponent by putting the hand under his thigh, close to the knee, and hooking the opposite leg around his other leg so that the top of the foot rests on the opponent's calf. The hooking leg is inserted between the opponent's legs.

Mura-ryu see *Yoshin-ryu*.

Mura Yoshin see *Yoshin-ryu*.

Miyabi 'Courtesy', 'Refinement'. This term was used to describe the lifestyle of the nobles of the imperial court at Kyoto during the Heian period (794–1185). It was

Mitokoro-zeme

taken up once more by the noble warriors (*Buke*) of the Kamakura period (1185–1333) to describe the ideal behaviour of the *Samurai*, the elegance of their thought and their ability to handle the 'noble' weapons, sword and bow.

Miyagi Chojun see *Goju-ryu*.

Mirahira Katsuya see *Jigen-ryu*.

Miyamoto Musashi (1584–1645). The most famous *Samurai* of Japan, pupil of his father Minisai Shinmen. The latter defeated in combat an expert with the large sword (*O-dachi*) from the Mori clan, *Sasaki Ganryu*, who then murdered him. *Miyamoto Musashi* went on to perfect himself in the art of swordsmanship, sought out his father's murderer and slew him in a duel which was as short as it is famous. Legend took possession of his adventurous life and his exploits are the subject matter of innumerable stories, novels and plays. The most famous work is the one which Yoshikawa Eiji dedicated to him, *Musashi, the Stone and the Sword*, followed by *The Perfect Light*, (Balland, Paris, 1983). Miyamoto created a school of sword-fighting called 'The Two-Sword School' (*Niten Ichi-ryu*) in which he taught a method of fighting with two swords, a long *Daito* or *Katana* and a short *Shoto* or *Wakizashi*. In 1643 he withdrew to a cave so that he could meditate and write the chief work of his life, the *Gorin-no-Sho* (Book of Five Rings), with the help of his disciple *Terao Katsunobu*. Miyamoto is also credited with the creation of another school of swordsmanship, *Emmei-ryu*, and is the author of another book called *Dokukodo*, which deals with the spirit of *Bushido*.

Mizougyi. A style of Chinese martial art (*Wushu*) akin to the external method (*Weijia*) of the *Shaolin-si* tradition, created during the Qing period (1644–1911).

Mizu 'Water'.
— **Mizu-guruma** see *Omote*.
— **Mizu-iri** see *Ura*.

Mizu-no-Kokoro 'A mind (spirit) like water'. This expression refers to the perfect calm which the mind or spirit can find, producing a non-aggressive state and a feeling of 'passive' resistance. Whoever possesses *Mizu-no-Kokoro* is thus sensitive to all impressions, just as water is sensitive to the slightest breath of wind, and his or her *Ki* is in harmony with all beings. See *Aiki*, *Kokoro*, *Miru-no-Kokoro*.

Mizu-nagare see *Omote*.

Mizuno Shinto-ryu. A school of *Iai-jutsu* founded by *Kobayashi Koemon Toshinari*, who died at the beginning of the seventeenth century. The techniques of the school consisted of an amalgam of swordplay and unarmed combat (*Ju-jutsu*) conceived by the weapons masters of Aizu province.

Moc Can see *Tonfa*.

Mochi 'To grip with the hands', 'To seize'. Also *Kensui*.
— **Mochi-age-otoshi *Judo***. To seize *Uke* by using both the hands and the arms.

Mochizuki Minoru see *Yoseikan*.

Mo-gar see *Shaolin-si*.

Mokuju see *Juken-jutsu*.

Mokuso. A recuperative and meditative posture, sometimes assumed at the end of martial arts training or contest. The position of the legs varies: kneeling down in the Japanese fashion with the tops of the feet resting on the floor, cross-legged, half lotus position or full lotus position. The back is straight, without strain, 'like a column of smoke rising on a calm day'. The hands can be placed palm down on the thighs or brought together, palms up, with thumbs touching. Each *Dojo* or *Ryu* has its own variation. The source of this practice almost certainly lies in *Zazen*, but it is possible that there is also some *Shinto* influence behind it too. In this posture one relaxes, breathes calmly and tries to maintain an 'empty' mind, thus freeing oneself from habitual tensions.

Momono-i Shunzo (1826–86). A *Samurai* of the *Kyoshin Meichi-ryu*, an expert in a variety of weapons. He opened a martial arts training hall in Edo (Tokyo), the *Shigakukan Dojo*, where he taught a number of Samurai who were hostile to the *Bakufu* (shogunate) of Edo. In this way he took part in the replacement of the Shogun-style government of the Tokugawa by the direct rule of the emperor.

Mondo. A formal meeting between a martial arts master and his pupils or disciples (*Monjin*) in the *Dojo*. At such a meeting the conversation centres on the subject of *Budo*. In the *Zen* discipline, *Mondo* is a form of simple dialogue between the master and one of his disciples, in the course of which the master gives the disciple a *Koan* on which to focus his attention. A Koan is a very short sentence or phrase which has no logical meaning but hides some truth which the disciple must struggle to discover. The aim of the Koan and the conversation between master and disciple is to go beyond the usual, conventional forms of thinking and see directly into the heart of things with the faculty of intuitive understanding.

Monjin see *Mondo*, *Montei*.

Mon-nyu see *Oku-iai*.

Monoji see *Shobu-shimpan*.

Monomi see *Ariake*, *Kyudo*, *Yami*.

Montei 'Disciple', 'Pupil', of a *Ryu* or of a martial arts master. Also *Monjin*.

Morikawa Kozan see *Yamato-ryu*.

Morote 'With two hands'.

— **Morote-jime** *Judo*. When *Uke* is on top of *Tori* in *Ne-waza* (groundwork), Tori strangles Uke with both hands under the jaw; the hands are not crossed.

Morote-jime

— **Morote Seoi-nage** *Judo*. A shoulder throw using both hands. *Tori* holds *Uke* in the standard grip, turns to make contact with Uke with the back of his or her body, lowers his or her stance, and by pulling with both hands throws Uke round and over his or her left side.

Morote Seoi-nage

— **Morote Sukui Uke** *Karate*. A scooping block using both hands.
— **Morote Tsukami Uke** *Karate*. A block by gripping both hands.
— **Morote-tsuki** *Karate*. An attack made by striking with both hands.
— **Morote-uchi** *Karate*. A blow delivered with both hands. Also *Morote-tsuki*. Blocking with both hands at once, or with one hand resting on and assisting the other, is called *Morote-Uke*.

Morote-tsuki

— **Morote-uke** see *Morote-uchi*.

Mo-sukoshi 'A little more'. This expression is used by a referee to ask for extra time when the normal period of time allotted to a contest has come to an end.

Morote-uke

Mot-Diem see *Ippon*.

Mu. The concept of the total negation of everything which seems to exist, analogous to that of *Shunya* (emptiness) of Buddhist philosophy, according to which the unity and totality of everything in existence is united in a single entity which cannot be known by the senses.

Muay Thai The Thai name given to Thai Boxing. See *Kick-boxing*.

Mudansha A pupil of a martial art who has only *Kyu* level grades. Korean: *Yukeup-ja*. See *Kyu, Kyudan, Yudansha*.

Mudra. An Indian word (Japanese: *In*) meaning gestures and positions of the fingers and hands which symbolize a Buddhist divinity or virtue and the power associated with them. In esoteric Buddhism the *Mudra* not only symbolize powers but actually play a part in the awakening of them. In such cases the Mudra performed are accompanied by a form of meditation and the chanting of mystic formulae or mantra. The practice is in its entirety a creative one. Because Mudra demand a high level of concentration, they were adopted by certain schools of martial arts as a help to self-knowledge, and to root out from the personality all feelings of fear and distress. In fact they serve primarily to control the emotions. The use and understanding of Mudra have been almost entirely lost in the field of martial arts but in certain schools of *Budo*, such as the *Katori Shinto-ryu*, some revitalization

has taken place. A number of martial arts masters have been initiated into the science of Mudra by Japanese monks, adepts of the Buddhist doctrine of Vajrayana, who mainly belong to the *Yamabushi* sects. Their effectiveness is regarded as purely subjective. See *Kuji-kiri*.

Mufudakake. A vertical wooden plaque bearing the names of deceased masters or founders of schools of martial arts which are placed in some *Dojo* at the side of the *Kamiza*. Before and after their training sessions, *Budoka* make a gesture of reverence towards the *Mufudakake*.

Muga. A state of mind which is of such intense concentrative power that no thought can disturb the execution of an action by the man or woman in that state. It has been described as the intuitive consciousness of the Whole, an identification with 'the Other' which enables one to act upon him or her.

Mugai-ryu. A school of *Ken-jutsu* founded

The Mudra called Chicken-in, demonstrated by Master Otake.

in 1695 by a peasant, *Tsuji Getten Sakemochi* (1650–1729). In his school he taught *Hyodo*. a method of fighting based on the Chinese philosophy of the interaction of the principles of *Yin* and *Yang*. In his view, these latter represented the civil and military powers respectively. He preached an alliance of the arts of literature and warfare, *Zen* meditation and the spirit of justice, which must lead to unification of being and non-being. see *Hyodo*, *Yamaguchi-ryu*, *Yin-Yang*.

Muka-mae *Aikido*. A posture similar to the one called *Shizen-hontai*.

Muken see *Yuken*.

Mune 'Chest'. See *Body*.
— **The back of a sword blade.** See *Katana*.
— **Mune-ate** *Kendo*. Lacquered bamboo armour invented in the eighteenth century by *Nakanishi Chuta*, a follower of the *Ono-ha Itto-ryu* and the *Nakanishi-ha Itto-ryu*. Also called *Do*. See *Dogu*, *Kendo*.
— **Mune-dori** *Aikido*. A grip on *Shite's* lapel by *Uke's* right hand.
— **Mune-garami** *Judo*. A groundwork (*Ne-waza*) technique of bending the arm on the chest.
— **Mune-gatame** *Judo*. A groundwork (*Ne-waza*) technique of controlling an opponent at the side of the chest.
— **Mune-gyaku** *Judo*. A groundwork (*Ne-waza*) technique of control and immobilization against the chest.
— **Mune-oshi** see *Ju-no-Kata*.

Munen-mushin see *Mushin*.

Murakami Tetsuji *Karate*. A Japanese *Karate* expert who died in 1987. He was invited to France by Henri Plée, who played a large part in introducing Karate to Europe. *Murakami* contributed a great deal to the development of Karate in Europe and in particular to the growth and spread of the *Shotokan* style.

Murasame 'Right carotid artery'. See *Hizagatame*, *Head*.

Mura-ryu see *Yoshin-ryu*.

Mura Yoshin see *Yoshin-ryu*.

Muromachi see *Ashikaga*.

Musha-shugyo. This is the practice of 'Wandering or roaming of the *Samurai*' in which members of the *Bushi* class travelled to different masters and different *Ryu* to widen their knowledge of martial arts as much as possible. This was an undertaking mainly followed by the *Ronin* or 'masterless' Samurai, since it was frowned upon (except in the Ryu following *Zen*) because every student was expected to stay attached to his master and school for life.

Mushin 'No mind', 'Original mind'; a mind not fixed upon anything and open to everything, reflecting everything like a mirror. It is the opposite of *Ushin*, a mind temporarily fixed and consequently superficial. *Munen-mushin* (*Muso*) is the state of emptiness (*Shunya*), of a total availability of the mind which is not fixed (*Mushin*) and is consequently never troubled by the appearance of things. This is the *Wu-wei*, the 'No action' of the Chinese Taoists. *Suisei-mushin* implies that life as we ordinarily conceive it is a kind of waking dream; an idea which is opposed to those of *Mushin* and *Satori*. See references to the above words and to *Kokoro*.

Mushotoku. This expression denotes nondesire to achieve an aim and non-desire for profit or reward for performing an action. It is a feeling which must guide anyone who acts, both in *Zen* and in the practice of martial arts. Only a person with a pure mind can reach this state, the ultimate state in life. It is non-consciousness, non-meditation (*Zazen*), which renders the mind perfectly open.

Muso Gonnosuke see *Jo-jutsu*.

Muso Jikiden-ryu A school of *Iai-jutsu*, founded in the sixteenth century by *Hojo Hayashizaki Jinsuke Shigenobu*, who was born in the province of Sagami. His school has endured to the present day as the principle one in the art of drawing the sword. However, members of the school do not train at *Tameshigiri* (cutting bamboo or straw targets). The teachings of the school were perfected in the eighteenth century by *Eishin* and then took the name *Muso Jikiden Eishin-ryu*. The style was modidied again at the beginning of the twentieth century by *Nakayama Hakudo* and assumed the definitive name of *Muso Shinden-ryu*. This school integrated the teachings of *Shoden Omoriryu*, created by *Omori Soemon Masamitsu*, which advocated the technique of *Iai* from a sitting position (in *Sei-za*). There are numerous *Kata* in this school: eleven in *Sei-za*, ten in *Tate-hiza*, eight in *Oku-iai* sitting down, thirteen in *Oku-iai* standing up, etc. This *Ryu* gave birth to numerous branches (*Ha*), of a more or less ephemeral nature, which elaborated in turn numerous Kata. The main ones were *Shimomura-ha* and *Tanimura-ha*. The principl masters of *Muso Shinden-ryu* were:

> Hayashizaki Jinsuke Shigenobu, the founder.
> Tamiya Taira no Hyoe Narimasa.
> Nagano Murakusai Kinro.
> Numo Gombei Matsushige.
> Arikawa Shozaemon Munetsugu.
> Manno Dan'emon Nobusode.
> Eishin.
> Arai Seitatsu.
> Hayashi Rokudayu Narimasa.
> Hosokawa, Yoshimasa.
> Nakayama Hakudo (Shimomura-ha).
> Morimoto Tokumi, of the *Tanimura-ha* branch, who gave the school the name *Muso Shinden-ryu Batto-jutsu* in 1933.

Muso Shinden-ryu Batto-jutsu see *Muso Jikiden-ryu, Eishin*.

Musoken *Kendo*. An attacking or defensive movement carried out without thinking about it, anticipating the movements of the opponent and determined by a kind of sixth sense.

Musubi-dachi *Karate*. A waiting position with the heels together and toes pointing outwards.

Mutekatsu. A principle of *Zen* attributed to Takuan (1573–1645) in which it is proposed that it is possible to conquer a foe without resorting to hands or weapons: 'To strike is not to strike, just as to kill is not to kill.' In fact this principle would lead one to avoid combat as far as possible by producing a situation in which an opponent would not be able to make an attack. This philosophical principle of 'evasion through the mind' was followed in part by the disciples of *Katori Shinto-ryu* and later put into practice by followers of *Shinkage-ryu*. See also *Kashima Shinto-ryu, Muto*.

Muteki-ryu. A school of *Ju-jutsu* advocating a blend of force (*Go*) and initiative (*Sen*), or *Yawara-riki*, created towards the middle of the Edo period in the seventeenth century.

Muto 'Without a sword'. A spiritual doctrine of combat, established by *Yagyu Tajima no Kami* (1527–1606), in which it was said that it is not necessary to use a sword to win a contest if the spirit is pure and one is sincerely desirous of avoiding a confrontation. This principle is in accordance with the principles of *Takuan* (see *Mutekatsu*) and that of *Ken-no-Shinzui* (or *Nukazu ni Sumu*), the art of resolving problems without drawing the sword. The school of *Muto-ryu* was founded according to these principles by *Yamaoka Tesshu* (1837–88), an expert in *Ken-jutsu* who was made secretary to the Emperor Meiji. Muto-ryu is also known as *Itto Shoden Muto-ryu*.
— **Muto-ryu** see *Chujo-ryu*.

Myojo see *Kyusho*.

N

aban see *Thaing*.

Naga-ashi *Karate, Kendo.* A throw brought about by sweeping the opponent's leg away.

Nagai-mono 'Long things'. A category of 'long' weapons such as swords, lances, halberds, etc., as distinct from *Mijikai-mono* or 'short weapons' such as daggers, sticks, chains, etc.

Nagakami see *Naginata*.

Nagao Kenmotsu see *Nagao-ryu*.

Nagao-ryu. A school of *Tai-jutsu* founded in the seventeenth century by *Nagao Kenmotsu*, a *Samurai* of the *Itto-ryu* and *Yagyu Shinkage-ryu* schools. He used a variety of weapons in real combat, including *Kakushi*. The school was mainly attended by the common people, since Kakushi were not considered 'noble' weapons. See *Bankoku-choki*.
Nagashi-tsuki *Karate.* A 'sweeping' type of punch delivered by a rotation of the body.
— **Nagashi-uke** *Karate.* Using the action of *Nagashi-tsuki* as a block.

Nagashi-uke

Nage. The name given to the person who performs the throw in a contest. The person who is thrown is called *Uke*. *Nage* is the equivalent of *Tori* in Judo, and of *Shite* in *Aikido*. In fact in many schools of Aikido, *Tori* is used instead of *Shite*. Vietnamese: *Vat*.
— **Nage no Kata.** These are the *Kata* or forms of throwing *Uke*. The *Kodokan* style of *Judo* includes, in the techniques of *Nage no Kata*, forms of throwing from a standing position (*Tachi-waza*) as well as throwing oneself to the ground in order to bring off an effective throw (*Sutemi-waza*). These *Kata* include five techniques: three for Tachi-waza (*Te-waza, Koshi-waza, Ashi-waza*) and two for Sutemi-waza (*Ma-Sutemi-waza, Yoko-Sutemi-waza*). See entries under the above names. Vietnamese: *Vat*.
Aikido. The *Nage-no-Kata* or *Nage-waza* consist of ten movements:

> *Shiho-nage*, four-quarters throw
> *Irimi-nage*, entering throw
> *Kote-gaeshi*, outward twisting of the wrist
> *Kaiten-nage*, turning throw
> *Tenshi-nage*, 'heaven and earth' throw (also spelt *Tenchi*)
> *Kokyu-nage*, 'breathing' throw
> *Koshi-nage*, loin throw
> *Tenbin-nage*, defence throw
> *Irimi-tsuki*, entering thrusting throw
> *Juji-garami*, cross control technique.

Nage-waza see *Nage no Kata*.

Naginata. A type of halberd with a long wooden handle (2 to 3 m). The metal blade is curved and has a single cutting edge on the convex side. This can be from 0.60 to 1 metre long. This weapon was used by the foot soldiers (*Zusa*) against horsemen or to cut the tendons of horses or to disembowel them. *Naginata* were also the favourite weapon of the wives of *Samurai* and of warrior monks. Some men sometimes

Naginata. Maniwa-nen-ryu school.

used a similar weapon, with a shorter handle and a longer blade, the *Nagakami*. This weapon was the subject of extensive technical examination and study, mainly by the warrior monks who used it from the beginning of the fifteenth century. The Naginata is part of the *Kobudo* armoury. For training purposes a Naginata with a bamboo blade is used. When they fight, contestants wear protective armour similar to that used in *Kendo*. There are no grades (*Kyudan*) in this martial art, which combines the movements of Kendo with those of *Bo-jutsu*. In Japan, competitions using the Naginata against a *Shinai* are held. The contestant using the *Shinai* is called *Uchi-dachi* and the contestant using the Naginata is called *Shi-dachi*. In Japan the art of using the Naginata is very popular among young women and there are at least four styles in existence. These are the major ones: *Jikishin Kage-ryu, Toda-ha-ryu, Tendo-ryu* and *Katori Shinto-ryu*. The whole art of using the Naginata is called *Naginata-do*. Vietnamese: **Dai Dao**. See *Ishizuki, Bisen-to*.

Naha-te see *Okinawa, Kenshikan, Karate, Higaonna Kanryo*.

Naike see *Kyusho*.

Nai-wan 'Inside of the arm'. See *Body, Arm, Wan*.

Nakadate (Nakadaka) Ippon-ken *Karate*. A blow delivered with the clenched fist but with the second knuckle of one finger, usually the middle finger, protruding beyond the rest, in order to produce a more penetrating effect. Also called *Nakayubi Ippon-ken*. See *Weapons*.

Nakamura Batto-jutsu see *Nakamura-ryu*.

Nakamura-ryu. A school of *Iai-jutsu* founded by *Nakamura Taisaburo* (1911–) of the *Toyama-ryu*. In this school the *Iai* techniques are performed only in a standing position. There are eight basic postures (*Kamae*) and eight cutting techniques (*Happo-giri*; see Tameshi-ryu). Also called *Nakamura Batto-jutsu*.

Blades and point of Naginata.

Young women training at the Budokan.

Nakamura Taisaburo see *Nakamura-ryu*, *Toyama-ryu*.

Nakanishi Chuta. A *Samurai*, pupil of *Ono Tadaaki* (1565–1628), who created a school of *Ken-jutsu*, *Nakanishi-ha Itto-ryu*. For training purposes an imitation sword was used, the *Fukuro-shinai*. Students wear protective gloves (*Kote*) and light bamboo armour (*Do*). See *Mune-ate*.

Nakanishi-ha Itto-ryu see *Nakanishi Chuta*.

Nakano Michiomi see *Shorinji Kempo*.

Nakasuji *Kyudo*. An imaginary line going from the target to the shoulder of the archer, passing through the wrist of the hand holding the bent bow.

Nakayama Hakudo see *Muso Jikiden-ryu*.

Nakayama Masatoshi *Karate*. A Japanese martial arts expert (1913–87) born in

Tokyo, the son of a military doctor. He met *Funakoshi Gichin* in 1922 and studied *Karate* with him. He was sent to China and returned in 1946. He then organized the *Shotokan* style of Karate with Nishiyama and the two men formed the Japan Karate Association (JKA), made up of numerous experts. The latter were sent to many countries to spread the teaching of Karate. After the death of Funakoshi Gichin in 1957, Nakayama organized the first Karate championships in Japan. Such events had been opposed by Funakoshi Gichin during his life, but they were a great success. Much is owed to Nakayama for the worldwide popularity of the sport.

Nakayubi Ippon-ken see *Nakadate Ippon-ken*, *Ippon-ken*, *Weapons*.

Nakayuwai *Kendo*. That part of the *Shinai* with which the blows are delivered; this generally means the upper third, i.e. nearest the tip.

Nambu-do (Nambu Budo). A modern form of *Karate* created by Nambu Yoshinao in 1984 and based not on competition but on harmony with nature. *Nambu-do* is mainly concerned with breathing movements called *Nambu Taiso*, consisting of ten series of exercises corresponding to movements in nature and carried out by controlling abdominal respiration. According to its author, it is the crowning result of *Sanku-kai*.

Names. Japanese names are always written with the family name first, followed by the first name. In former times the complete name was composed (for the nobility) of the clan name, followed by the function of the person, then the family name, and finally the surname. In general the Japanese have only one first name. Formerly they were given names which varied according to their occupation. Today the suffixes *San* or *Sama* are used after the family or first names, whether the person concerned is a man, a woman or a young girl, without distinction, as a sign of politeness.

The *Sumotori* sometimes have 'warrior' names, peculiar to their art, which end with such expressions as *-yama* (mountain), *-umi* (sea), *-kaze* (wind), etc., or names which indicate their grade (*Seki*, *-zeki*). See *Shikona*.

Nami-gaeshi *Karate.* Defence 'as in waves', implying several successive and connected movements, rapidly performed.
— **Nami-gaeshi Uke** *Karate.* A method

Nami-gaeshi Uke

of blocking a kick to the lower abdomen by bending the leg up to the groin and preventing the attacking foot from reaching its target.
— **Nami Juji-jime** *Judo.* In groundwork (*Ne-waza*), a strangulation technique from the front, wrists crossing and hands gripping the lapels of *Uke*'s *Judogi*.

Nami Juji-jime

Naname 'Obliquely'. See *Space.*
— **Naname-uchi** see *Ju-no-kata.*

Nanquan Beitui *Wushu.* 'Fists' in the South, Feet in the North' is a Chinese saying which means that fist techniques are more commonly found in the south of the country and foot techniques in the north. But since in fact all martial arts techniques have become widespread throughout China, this saying has no more than anecdotal value today. Schools in the north and south use both hand and foot techniques.

Narabi 'Side by side'.
— **Narabi Juji-jime** *Judo.* A strangulation technique with the arms crossed.

Narani Seug-gi see *Seug-gi.*

Nayashi *Kendo.* A technique of pressing down an opponent's *Shinai* towards the ground with one's own Shinai when the opponent makes a thrusting attack at the throat. See *Tsuki.*

Neck see *Kubi.*

Needles see *Kanzashi.*

Negative see *Ura, Yin (Yin-Yang).*

Negation see *Mu* . . .

Neijia see *Shaolin-si.*

Neko Ashi-dachi *Karate.* 'Cat stance'. The rear leg is bent, the front leg is raised so that only the ball of the foot rests on the ground, the knees spread a little, resembling to some extent a cat poised to rush forward. When this posture is taken in a more open way, with the legs at a wider angle, it is called *Hanmi-no-neko-dachi.*

Neko Ashi-dachi

Ne-waza *Judo.* The range of techniques carried out on the floor (*Ne*). These consist of immobilizations (*Osae-waza*, often called hold-downs), locking or bending the joints (*Kansetsu-waza*), and strangulation and choking techniques (*Shime-waza*). Such techniques are allowed only if *Tori* has not scored an *Ippon* when he or she throws *Uke*. See Competition Rules of *Judo.*

Nga Mi Phai see *E-mei-shan.*

Nganh Phap see *Hishigi, Shiwari.*

Nhao Lan *Qwan-ki-do.* Technique of falling (see *Ukemi*): falling forward techniques (*Te Truoc*), falling sideways techniques and falling backward techniques (*Te Sao*).

Nhi Tan see *Bo Phap.*

Nhu see *Ju.*

Nicho-nage *Sumo.* A hip throw using a blocking action against the thigh to break an opponent's balance, resembling the *Judo* technique of *Harai-goshi.*

Nicho-nage

Nidan 'Second level'. See *Kyudan, Space.*
— **Nidan-geri** *Karate.* An attack in the form of kicks delivered at two different levels of an opponent's body.
— **Nidan Ko-soto-gake** *Judo.* A counter-move against *Ko-soto-gake.*

Nihon Katana 'Technique of two swords', one in each hand, generally a *Katana* (*Daito*) in the right hand and a *Wakizashi* (*Shoto*) in the left. The origin of this fighting method seems to date back to *Miyamoto Musashi.* Also called *Nito.*

Nihon-me. In any martial arts competition this refers to the deciding encounter when each of the two contestants has obtained a victory.

Nihon-nukite *Karate.* A stabbing attack delivered by two 'forked' fingers to an opponent's eyes. Vietnamese: *Song Chi.* See *Hands, Atemi.*

Nihon-shobu. A contest which lasts until two points are scored.

Nijushi-ho *Karate.* A *Kata* referred to as 'the twenty-four steps'. With every step a different aspect of technique is demonstrated.

Nikaido-ryu see *Chujo-ryu.*

Nikyo Aikido. 'Second principle' (*Kyo*) of *Katame-waza*, consisting of three techniques of twisting the opponent's wrist inwards (*Kote-mawashi*), which can be performed in response to three attacks using *Mune-dori* (grip on the lapel(s)), *Shomen-uchi* (a descending blow) and *Shomen-tsuki* (blow to the face). See *Kote-mawashi*.

Nikyu see *Kyu*.

Nimai-geri *Sumo.* Breaking an opponent's balance by blocking his or her supporting leg and pulling on his or her belt.

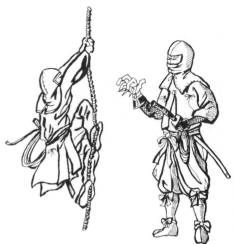

Ninja costume

Nimai-geri

Ninja. A group of men and women specially trained for espionage and assassination. It is said that they sprang up during the Heian period (794–1185) in the mountains around Kyoto, where they mingled with the *Yamabushi*. The members of *Ninja* groups were generally drawn from the lower classes and used by the *Daimyo* (chiefs of a clan or province) to assassinate enemies and penetrate enemy fortresses. They were particularly active at the beginning of the fifteenth century. Legend has taken hold of them and given them extraordinary powers such as the ability to become invisible, to walk on the ceiling, etc. This is all fiction, obviously, but need not detract from the genuinely unusual prowess of the Ninja. They were capable of the most amazing feats of acrobatic skill, developed from infancy (they usually belonged to one of a few families who specialized in the Ninja 'art'). Experts at scaling walls, swimming silently, concealment and disguise, they used specialized tools for their trade: gloves (*Shuko*) armed with metal hooks, collapsible boats, wooden buoys, 'not noble' weapons such as the dagger (*Ko-ugi, Kyotetsu-koge*), throwing weapons such as the *Shuriken* and *Shaken*, chains, ropes, etc. For nighttime missions they wore a completely black outfit with a black hood to hide the face. The Ninja resorted to any and every means to achieve their goals, and carried the idea of disguise to such an extent that they would disfigure their own faces to prevent identification. Among the names given to them in the course of their history are: the stealers in, the shadows of darkness, the shadow warriors, the men of stealth.

There was a hierarchy in the Ninja orders. The leader or commander of an undertaking was called *Jonin*. The men who organized an undertaking were called *Chunin* and the lowest order, who carried it out, were known as *Genin*. Ninja had to be able to use any type of weapon, have a knowledge of poisons and also chemistry (so that a smokescreen could be produced for instance). It is certain that they understood psychological techniques, had extremely well-developed senses and possessed various special means of communicating with one another. The common people were fearful of them; this fear was purposely cultivated by the Ninja. Consequently, if a Ninja were captured – a rare event – he was put to terrible torture

A Ninja attacking an enemy; a Ninja throwing Shuriken (pointed weapons); a Ninja climbing a rope. Drawing by Hokusai.

by the people so that they could extract his secrets from him. During the Edo period, when the country was relatively peaceful, numbers of Ninja turned to a form of licensed crime: they became brigands and assassins. One thing is certain: their aims were never noble, and they were indeed the living antithesis, therefore, of *Bushido*.

Despite their anonymity, certain Ninja families became famous at the end of the sixteenth century when they were swept up by the hostilities between the Daimyo. Most came from the provinces of *Iga* and *Koga*, to the east of Lake Biwa. *Oda Nobunaga*, who wanted to unite all the clans, sent an army of 46,000 men against 4,000 Ninja in 1581. Most of the Ninja were killed, captured and tortured. Those who managed to escape the carnage took refuge in the mountains or mingled with the country people. Their art continued to be passed down from father to son. Certain Ninja, in the course of particular missions, used a short bow and poisoned arrows. Others used weapons which they had invented themselves . . .

It is no small wonder that when the stories of these 'miracle men' reached the West some years after the Second World War, in the wake of the rise in the popularity of *Karate* and *Kung-fu*, they fired the youthful imagination of occidental martial artists. Some older Westerners travelled to Japan to find out more. In terms of popularity, the leading teacher in Japan whom most of them met is Dr Hatsumi Masaaki. Among those who studied with him and returned to their own countries to spread the modern Ninja training methods are Daron Navron of Israel, Stephen Hayes of the USA and Bo Munthe of Sweden. Several British instructors have also been trained in Japan. The modern approach to *Ninjutsu* does not focus on the fatal methods of the ancient Ninja but teaches a mixture of philosophy, unarmed combat, swordplay and various survival methods, sometimes borrowed from the schools of outdoor survival which are very popular in the USA. As always when a commercial advantage offers itself, confidence tricksters are at hand to exploit the gullible. The latter were those young people who had seen some of the sensational Ninja films and wanted to learn the techniques they had seen on the screen. In the early 1980s a number of bogus Ninja 'schools' and 'teachers' appeared, but with the gradual fall in the popularity of Ninjutsu they have now mostly disappeared. Korean: *Sulsa.*

— **Ninjutsu** 'Art' of the *Ninja*. Also called *Ninpo, Shinobi*. Korean: *Shin-bop*.

— **Ninjutsu-ka.** A *Ninjutsu* student.

— **Ninpo** see *Ninjutsu*.

Ninyo see *Bushido*.

Nippon Shorinji-Kempo see *Shorinji-kempo*.

Nissoku Itto no Ma-ai *Kendo*. The ideal distance between two opponents – two paces apart, with the points of their *Shinai* about ten centimetres from one another. See *Ma, Ma-ai*.

Niten Ichi-ryu. The surname sometimes given to *Miyamoto Musashi* (*Niten*) and to his 'school of two swords', *Nito*.

Nito 'Two swords'. See *Miyamoto Musashi, Nihon-katana, Niten, Shinai*.

Nitobe Inazo see *Bushido*.

Niwa Jurozaemon see *Itusai Chozan-shi*.

Nobushi see *Yamabushi*.

Nodawa-zeme see *Kimarite*.

Nogare. Technique of rapid breathing used in blocking actions. Breathing in is done through the nose, as in *Ibuki*, but breathing out is done through the half-opened mouth to make a guttural sound, as if proceeding directly from the *Hara*. When this expiration is violent and sudden it is akin to the *Ki-ai*. *Nogare* breathing is mainly used in the *Kyokushinkai* school of *Karate*. See *Ibuki*.

— **Nogare-kata** *Judo*. Techniques of evasion.

Nogi Maresuke (Kiten) (1849–1912). A Japanese general. After he had taken part in the Sino-Japanese war of 1894–5 he was made governor of Taiwan. During the Russo-Japanese war (1904–5) he beat the

Russian general Stoessel at Port Arthur and at Mukden. On the death of the Emperor Meiji, both he and his wife committed suicide rather than survive their emperor. He is cited as a great hero and a model of courage and fidelity.

Nojo-jutsu see *Takenouchi-ryu*.

Nokotta *Sumo*. An exclamation sometimes uttered by a referee (*Gyoji*) to call the wrestlers (*Sumotori*) to order when they are on the point of infringing a rule.

No-tachi see *Ba-jutsu, Swords*.

Noto *Iai-do*. The action of replacing the sword in its scabbard (*Saya*), having shaken the blood (*Chiburi*) from the blade. See *Omori-ryu*.

Nua-diem see *Yuko*.

Nukazu ni Sumu see *Muto*.

Nukido *Kendo*. An evasion of a frontal attack followed by a counter-attack to the side.

Nukide no Tsukasa see *Sechie-zumo*.

Nuki-gake see *Tachi-ai*.

Nukite *Karate*. A stabbing blow using the extended fingers of the hand. Also called Yonhon-nukite 'stab of four fingers'. Vietnamese: *Xia*. See *Atemi, Hands*.

Nukisuke *Iai-do*. The art of drawing the sword from its scabbard and cutting the opponent (*Kiri-tsuki*) all in one movement, before he has time to unsheath his sword completely. See *Omori-ryu*.

Nuki-uchi *Karate, Kendo*. A blow which is a combination of block, strike and cut, all in one action. It is delivered at a narrow angle so that there is no break; no marked change of direction.

Nuki-waza *Kendo*. Feinting techniques.

Numbers. Numbers are widely used in martial arts terminology. This is true of Japanese, Chinese, Korean and Vietnamese styles. Some of them are listed below as an aid to memory:

Korean:
Il (1), I (2), Sam (3), Sa (4), O (5), Yuk (6), Chil (7), Pal (8), Ku (9), Chib (10); or: Han (1), Dul (2), Set (3), Net (4), Dasot (5), Yosot (6), Ilgop (7), Yodol (8), Ahop (9), Yol (10).

Chinese:
Yi (1), Er (2), San (3), Si (4), Wu (5), Liu (6), Qi (7), Ba (8), Jiu (9), Shi (10).

Vietnamese:
Mot (1), Hai (2), Ba (3), Bon (4), Nam (5), Sau (6), Bay (7), Tam (8), Chin (9), Mu'o'i (10).

Japanese:
There are several ways of counting in Japanese, Sino-Japanese, and particular terms for counting long objects (*Hon*) people (*Nin*), etc.
— *Sino-Japanese*: Ichi (1), Ni (2), San (3), Yon or Shi (4), Go (5), Roku (6), Shichi or Nana (7), Hachi (8), Kyu or Ku (9), Ju (10).
— *Japanese*: Hitotsu (1), Futatsu (2), Mittsu (3), Yotsu (4), Itsutsu (5), Muttsu (6), Nanatsu (7), Yattsu (8), Kokonotsu (9), To (10) . . .
— *Long objects*: Ippon (1), Nihon (2), Sambon (3), Yonhon (4), Gohon (5), Roppon (6), Nanahon (7), Hichihon (8), Kyu-hon (9), Jippon (10) . . .
— *People*: Hitori (1), Futari (2), Sannin (3), Yonnin (4), Gonin (5), Rokunin (6), Shichinin (7), Hachinin (8), Kyunin (9), Junin (10) . . .

Nunchaku. This is a small flail consisting usually of two pieces of wood connected by a double cord or chain, used to beat rice straw; also called *So-setsu-kon*. The peasants of Okinawa used this farming implement as a formidable weapon, and developed numerous techniques for this purpose. The Bruce Lee films popularized the weapon in the West. It is one of the weapons of *Kobudo*, and as such it is often taught as part of martial arts training. Today the type of *Nunchaku* in use also consists of two cylindrical or octagonal pieces of wood joined by a cord or chain; in the latter the chain is often mounted on a swivel or ball-bearing device which give enormous freedom and flexibility

Nunchaku held in both hands.

of movement. The type joined by a cord can be lengthened or shortened by manipulating the cord's attachment to the handles. This regulation in length varies from 10 to 20 cm. The handles or 'grips' of the weapon are usually between 26 and 35 cm long. For safety purposes, Nunchaku of soft rubber or even hollow plastic have been produced, but the latter scarcely merit the name weapon and are little more than toys. Others, designed to be used in real fighting, have steel handles. *Viet Vo Dao* uses Nunchaku which are relatively long (40 cm). Certain variants of the weapon used in Chinese and Vietnamese martial arts are very short, also joined by cords or chains. Vietnamese: **Long gian**. See *Bleeder*.

Nu Taidu see *Taidu*.

Nyunan Shin 'Suppleness of mind'. This is a quality required in martial artists so that they humbly accept the teachings of a master whom they have chosen, and submerge their own egos. Also *Junan-shin*.

O

O 'Great'. Also *Dai*, *Oki*. See *O-dachi*, O-soto-gari, *O-guruma*, etc.

Obata Isao see *Kyudo*.

Obi 'Belt'. Belts distinguish the different grades in the martial arts. For the *Kyu* grades they are of different colours, indicating the technical skill which 'beginners' have reached. Though obviously the standard of skill varies enormously in the *Kyu* grades, it is not until a student has reached black belt grade (*Dan-sha*) that he or she is regarded as being truly established in the martial art concerned. Vietnamese: *Dai*. See *Kyu*, *Kyudan*. *Judo*. There are ten degrees of black belt (*Kuro-obi*):

> First *Dan* (*Shodan*): plain black belt
> Second *Dan* (*Nidan*): plain black belt
> Third *Dan* (*Sandan*): plain black belt
> Fourth *Dan* (*Yondan*): plain black belt
> Fifth *Dan* (*Godan*): plain black belt
> Sixth *Dan* (*Rokudan*): red and white belt
> Seventh *Dan* (*Shichidan*): red and white belt
> Eighth *Dan* (*Hachidan*): red and white belt
> Ninth *Dan* (*Kudan*): red and black belt
> Tenth *Dan* (*Judan*): red belt

The last grade is almost never conferred on anyone, being reserved for the founder of a style.

The belt of the *Judogi* is about two metres long and is wrapped twice round the jacket. It is five centimetres wide, and made of several layers of cotton stitched closely together to make it strong and solid in appearance. It is knotted at the front of the abdomen with a knot which lies flat, leaving the ends (about fifteen centimetres long) hanging down freely. Fastened in this way, it keeps the jacket firmly in place.

Colours of the *Mudansha* belts: see *Kyu*.
Aikido. In Europe, holders of black belt grade wear belts the same colour as those worn in *Judo*, but in addition they wear a *Hakama*. There are seven 'learning' grades (see *Kyu*).
Karate. In Europe the colours mainly correspond to those of *Judo*, with some variations depending on the style.

Wa-jutsu. The belts correspond to those of *Judo*, except that they have a white or violet band.
Tae-kwon-do. The belts of *Do Bok* are white, red, blue or black. See *Kyu* (*Keup*).
Qwan-ki-do. The belts of this art are white (first level, *Bach Dai*), black (second level, *Hyyen Dai*), and red and white (third level, *Hong Bach Dai*). The founder of the style alone wears a belt in which are mingled white, yellow, red and blue colours (*Chuong Mon Dai*). See also *Kyu*, *Kyudan*. The 'black belts' are called *Dai Den*.
Other martial arts, Wushu. The belts are more like sashes, usually made of satin, about ten centimetres wide, of varying colours such as white, red, royal blue, violet, black.
Sumo. The belts worn by the *Sumo* wrestlers (*Sumotori*) are called *Mawashi*, and made of silk. Colours are always dark, usually black. See *Mawashi*, *Keshomawashi*, *Sagari*, *Tsuna*.
— Obi-goshi *Judo*. A hip throw performed with the aid of the belt.
— Obi-otoshi *Judo*. A throw performed by gripping the top of the belt.
— Obi-tori see *Ju-no-Kata*.

O-dachi see *Katana*, *Swords*, *O-dachi-jutsu*.

O-dachi-jutsu. An ancient technique of fighting with a very long sword (about 1.5 m), mainly used by mounted *Samurai*. The sword was wielded with big circular movements. *Sasaki Ganryu*, the enemy of *Miyamoto Musashi*, was an expert in the use of this weapon. This style of fighting is no longer practised.

Oda Nobunaga (1534–82). A famous military dictator who did not have the title of *Shogun*. In 1573 he overthrew the last of the *Ashikaga* Shoguns and tried to unify the country, but he was obliged to commit suicide and it was one of his generals, *Toyotomi Hideyoshi*, who succeeded to his position as military dictator.

Odome see *Oshiki-uchi*.

Oenchok see *Hidari*.

Ogasawara-ryu. An ancient school of *Yabusame*, created in the Kamakura period (1185–1333) and still active today. Its participants have retained the ancient hunting costume dating from that period. See *Yabusame*.

— The name was taken by one of the great schools of *Kyudo*, directed by a descendant of Ogasawara. In our times, it is the only Japanese school which scrupulously observes all the ancient rules of etiquette. These require a code of behaviour which affects all aspects of its adherents' lives (marriage, sending gifts, invitations, homage to the emperor, etc.). The school currently has thousands of pupils.

Ogi see *Tessen*.

O-goshi *Judo.* 'Major hip throw'. A throwing technique (Nage-waza) similar to *Uki-goshi*. *Tori* lowers his or her body to help him or her to raise *Uke* more easily and bends forward through a vertical plane, throwing Uke forward.

O-goshi

Oguri Niemon see *Oguri-ryu*.

Oguri-ryu. An ancient school of *Ju-jitsu*, founded in 1616 by Oguri Niemon, who adapted methods of fighting in armour for the use of people wearing ordinary clothes. This school advocated *Wa-jutsu* or 'art of peace'.

O-guruma *Judo.* 'Big wheel'. *Tori* performs a hip movement, turning into *Uke* to make him or her bend forward in the horizontal plane, then brings him or her off

O-guruma

balance towards the front by pulling on his or her sleeve.

O-icho-mage *Sumo.* Hairstyle of the wrestlers (*Sumotori*) in the high grades, which consists of a fanlike chignon reminiscent of the leaf of the tree Ginkgo biloba (*Icho*). Lower-grade wrestlers wear their hair knotted in *Chon-mage*, the locks twisted together with strips of paper. These hairstyles date from the seventeenth and eighteenth centuries. The *O-icho-mage* is usually worn by the wrestlers in the top six grades, and the Chon-mage by all the rest.

Oi-tsuki *Karate.* 'Pursuit attack'. A punching attack immediately following another technique, accompanied by shifting the body forward, sometimes with a leaping action.

Oi-tsuki

O-irimi see *Irimi*.

Oishi Shinkage-ryu. A school of *Kendo* founded in Kyushu by *Oishi Susumu* (1798–1865) of the *Shinkage-ryu*. Students of the school used a very long *Shinai* held in one hand and wore a *Men* (face protector) to guard against blows. This school advocated force rather than suppleness of action.

Oishi Susumu see *Oishi Shinkage-ryu.*

Ojigi *Kendo.* A big ceremonial bow, part of the etiquette of the art.

Oji Kaeshi *Kendo, Karate.* The act of parrying a blow, immediately followed by a counter-attack.

— Oji-waza *Kendo.* A defensive technique accompanied by a simultaneous counter-attack.

Okada Morihiro (1893–1984). A master of *Kendo*, *Iai-do* and *Judo* who was also skilled in *Karate* and well known for his calligraphy. He played an important part in the martial arts of Japan and was decorated by the emperor for services rendered to traditional *Budo*. He held the grade of 8th *Dan* in Kendo and Iai-do.

Okinawa. The largest island of the Ryukyu archipelago south of Japan, between the latter and the island of Taiwan (Formosa). It is famous for the deadly fighting which took place there in 1945 between the Americans and the Japanese forces. This island was first conquered by the Chinese in the sixteenth century, then by the Japanese Satsuma (Kyusho) clan in the seventeenth century, and is now part of the Japanese Empire. Both the Chinese and Japanese invaders were worried by the obstinate resistance of the inhabitants and forbade them to possess weapons of any kind. It is said that an entire village was allowed only one knife, and this was chained to a post guarded by an armed soldier. Some of the peasants of Okinawa had been to China and brought back with them some of the techniques of *Kempo*. They transformed their farming implements into weapons and invented techniques suited to these weapons. The weapons were *Nunchaku*, *Tonfa*, *Sai*, *Kusari-gama*, etc. In addition to weapons they developed unarmed-combat techniques. Each village or region had its own style (*Naha-te*, 'Naha hand'; *Shuri-te*, 'Shuri hand'; *Tomari-*

te, 'Tomari hand'; etc.). (Shuri was the ancient royal capital of Okinawa.) All these styles came to be known collectively as *Okinawa-te* or *Tode* (Chinese hand). Some of the techniques were adopted by the *Samurai* and were the origins of the greater part of the martial arts, notably the art of *Karate*. See *Kempo*, *Karate*, *Kenshikan*, *Shorin-ryu*.

— Okinawa Karate-do. This title is used to describe the *Karate* techniques which came directly from *Okinawa-te*.

— Okinawa-te. The general name given to all the martial arts techniques coming from Okinawa. Also *Tode*.

Okuden 'Hidden teaching'. This was the secret teaching given by a martial arts master to certain chosen disciples who were sworn not to divulge them to anyone except specially selected *Budoka*. There was a very practical reason for this, analogous perhaps to not divulging modern weapons secrets. If the enemy did not know what techniques or tactics to expect, he remained at a certain disadvantage. See *Omote*, *Oku-iai*, *Hiden*, *Densho*.

Oku-iai *Iai-do.* *Kata* which includes two series of movements; one group performed in a sitting position (*Suwari*) and one in a standing position (*Tachi*). They are:

— in *Suwari* (eight movements):
Kasumi
Sune-gakoi
Tozume
Towaki
Shino-giri
Tanashita
Ryozume
Tora-bashiri

— in *Tachi* (thirteen movements):
Yuki-zure
Tsure-dachi
Somakuri
Sodome
Shinobu
Yuki Chigai
Sodesuri-gaeshi
Mon-nyu
Kabezoe
Uke-nagashi
Itomagoi (three movements).

This *Kata* also comes under the heading of *Okuden* or 'hidden teaching'.

Okuri 'The two'.
— **Okuri-ashi.** A sliding step in the opponent's direction.
— **Okuri-ashi-barai** *Judo.* 'Two feet sweep'. *Tori* sweeps both *Uke*'s feet when the latter brings them close together during the course of the contest. He or she assists the sweeping action by raising Uke with his or her hands, producing a forward loss of balance.

Okuri Eri-jime

Okuyama-ryu see *Kage-ryu.*

Okuyama Tadenobu see *Kage-ryu.*

Okuyama Yoshiji see *Hakko-ryu.*

Okuri ashi-barai

— **Okuri-dashi** *Sumo.* A powerful push on the opponent's back with both hands. See *Kimarite.*

Okuri-taoshi

O-mata *Sumo.* A throw brought about by seizing the inside of the opponent's thigh (*Mata*) and throwing him or her back over the attacker's thigh by disturbing the opponent's supporting leg.

Okuri-dashi

— **Okuri-Eri-jime** *Judo.* Strangulation technique by sliding the hand up the lapel from the rear, used in groundwork (*Ne-waza*).
— **Okuri-taoshi** *Sumo.* An action of 'leaning' down with force on the back of the opponent, with both hands, to crush him or her down to the ground. See *Kimarite.*

Okuyama Magojiro see *Kage-ryu.*

O-mata

Omori-ryu *Iai-do.* A *Kata* consisting of twelve movements which are fundamental to the art and enable one to assimilate the principles (*Jo*) of *Iai*. They are practised beginning from a sitting position (*Seiza* or *Suwari*). These are:

Shohatto
Sato (sword on the left)
Uto (sword on the right)
Atari-to
In-yo Shintai
Ryu-to
Jun-to (*Kaishaku-to*)
Gyaku-to
Seichu-to
Koran-to
Gyaku-te (*In-yo Shintai*)
Batto.

All these movements consist of four phases:
Nuki-tsuke (drawing the sword)
Kiri-tsuke (cutting)
Chiburi (shaking the sword clean of blood)
Noto (replacing the sword in the scabbard).

These techniques constitute the basic teaching (*Shoden*) of *Iai-do*. See *Hasegawa Eishin-ryu Oku-tai*.

Omori Soemon Masamitsu see *Muso Jikiden-ryu*.

Omote 'Positive', 'Above', 'Surface'. See *Irimi*.
— This is the teaching given to students who have not yet been granted access to the 'hidden' or 'profound' techniques (*Okuden*). See Space, *Koshi-kino-kata, Yin-Yang*.
Judo. One of the *Kata* of *Koshiki-no-Kata*, consisting of fourteen movements which must be broken down and performed slowly, so that one may assimilate them thoroughly. They are:

Tai: Body
Yume-no-uchi: As if in a dream
Ryoku-heki: Control of force and energy
Mizu-guruma: Waterwheel
Mizu-nagare: Flowing water
Hiki-otoshi: To throw by pulling
Ko-daore: To pretend to fall
Uchi-kudaki: To hit in order to break
Tani-otoshi: Valley drop
Kuruma-daori: Wheel drop
Shikoro-dori: To seize the helmet
Shikoro-gaeshi: To force back the helmet

Yu-dachi: Evening rain
Taki-otoshi: Falling like a waterfall.

Oni-kode see *Kote*.

Ono see *Shinden Fudo-ryu*.

Ono-ha Itto-ryu *Kendo*. A branch (*Ha*) of the *Itto-ryu* school, created by *Ono Tadaaki* (1565–1628), a disciple of *Ito Ittosai* and the teacher of *Nakanishi Chuta*. This school enjoyed considerable prestige and was followed by the *Shogun*. Its fundamental approach was to be able to produce one single and very powerful cut with the sword (which would settle a contest). See *Mune-ate*.

Ono Tadaaki see *Nakanishi Chuta*.

Orenai-te *Aikido*. 'Unbendable arm'. The arm which cannot be bent is sometimes demonstrated by *Aikido-ka* and is based on a mental attitude which calls upon the power of *Ki* to make it impossible for the outstretched arm to be bent. Muscular force alone is insufficient, and a form of muscle relaxation is used.

Osae 'Pressure' (from *Osaeru*, 'to hold'), 'Immobilization'.
— **Osae-komi** *Judo*. A groundwork (*Newaza*) technique in which *Uke* is immobilized. *Uke* can escape from such a technique only by using a movement of disengagement called *Toketa*. There are five *Osae-komi* movements: *Kesa* (*Gesa*)-*gatame, Kata-gatame, Kami-shiho-gatame, Yoko-shiho-gatame, Kuzure Kami-shiho-gatame*.
— **Osae-komi-toketa** *Judo*. Escape from an immobilization.
— **Osae-uke** *Karate*. A block employing a pressing action.

Osae-uke

— **Osae-waza** *Judo*. A technique of immobilizing *Uke* on the ground. See *Katame-no-kata*.

O-sensei see *Sensei*.

Oshi-dashi *Sumo*. A push applied with both hands to the chest or under the arms of an opponent, causing him or her to fall backwards or to the side. See *Kimarite*.

Oshi-dashi

Oshiki-uchi. Techniques of combat, with or without weapons, developed by the *Takeda* clan according to the system of *Aiki-in-yo-ho* and formerly reserved for high-ranking *Samurai*. The most famous master of these techniques was *Saigo Tanomo (Hoshina) Chikamasa* (1829–1905), a minister of the Aizu clan and priest of the *Shogun's Shinto* sanctuary at Nikko. Also called *Odome*.

Oshi-taoshi *Aikido*. Armlock (*Ude-hishigi*) performed by pushing on *Uke's* elbow. Also *Kansetsu-waza*.
Sumo see *Kimarite*.

O-soto 'Major outer'.
— **O-soto-gari** *Judo*. 'Major outer reaping throw'. *Tori* grips *Uke* in the standard manner, right side, and steps forward and left with the left foot, turning in towards Uke. He or she brings the right thigh into contact with the side or back of Uke's right thigh and 'reaps' (swings) Uke's leg away, throwing him or her backwards.
— **O-soto-guruma** *Judo*. 'Major outer wheel throw'. *Tori* takes his or her right leg behind both *Uke's* legs, from the right,

O-soto gari

blocking Uke's movement, and hooks the legs away, throwing him or her backwards.
— **O-soto-otoshi** *Judo*. Major outer throw.

O-soto-otoshi

Otani Shimosa no Kami Seiichiro (1789–1844). An expert in the art of swordsmanship of the *Jikishin-kage-ryu*, and the master of *Chiba Shusaku*. He directed the *Shogun's* school of martial arts, called *Kobusho*. He received the title *Cho-ichi-ryu*. See *Sakakibara Kenkichi*.

Oten 'To turn on to the side'.
— **Oten-gatame** *Judo*. A groundwork (*Ne-waza*) technique of bending the arm by twisting the body on to the side.
— **Oten-jime** *Judo*. A groundwork (*Ne-waza*) technique of strangulation by turning the body on to the side.

Otokodate. An expression used to describe a virile man, with the spirit of a knight errant, who defends the weak and the oppressed. He is a man of strong character who has gained mastery of his desires through the practice of martial arts. He is the equivalent of the European knight. Also *Kyokaku*.

Otoshi 'To cause to fall'.
Kendo. The action of strongly pushing an opponent's *Shinai* down towards the ground with one's own Shinai.
Judo. To cause one's partner to fall.
— **Otoshi Empi Uchi** *Karate*. A descending elbow blow. Also *Otoshi, Hiji-ate*.
— **Otoshi Hiji-ate** see *Otoshi Empi Uchi*.
— **Otoshi Uke** *Karate*. Blocking a blow by means of a straight push or thrust.

Otsubo-ryu. An ancient school of horsemanship for armed men (*Ba-jutsu*), created in the fifteenth century, the most famous of all the schools which taught this art to the *Bushi*. See *Ba-jutsu*.

O-tsuchi see *Shinden Fudo-ryu*.

Otsuka (Ohtsuka) Hidenori *Karate*. Founder (1892–) of the *Wado-ryu* style of *Karate* in 1939. Having studied *Ju-jutsu* of the *Shindo Yoshin-ryu*, he became a disciple of *Funakoshi Gichin* in 1922. He invented the technique of 'relaxed striking' followed by a swift withdrawal, and advocated the use of suppleness rather than force. He turned his back on the traditional *Makiwara* training designed to harden certain parts of the body. According to him, Karate must be essentially a spiritual discipline. See *Wado-ryu*.

O-uchi 'Major inner'.
— **O-uchi-gari** *Judo* 'Major inner reaping throw'. *Tori* makes a turning movement (*Tai-sabaki*), engages *Uke*'s leg by inserting his or her left leg between both Uke's legs, and hooks Uke's right leg backwards; at the same time pushing with both hands to send Uke to the ground.

O-uchi-gari

Oyama Masutatsu see *Kyokushinkai-kan*.

Oyayubi Nukite *Karate*. A blow to the eyes using the thumb, with the fingers lightly folded.

Ozeki (O-seki) *Sumo*. 'Great barrier', the second rank in the hierarchy, after that *Yokozuna*. It is the rank of 'Champion'. The best-known current *Ozeki* are:

Asashio Taro (1956–)
Wakashimazu Mutsuo (1957–)
Hokutenyu Katsuhiko (1961–)

P

ak Hok Bo 'White Crane stance'. See *Bo*.

Pa-kua see *Bagua Quan*.

Pal-Gwe (Palgue) see *Happo*, *Poom-se*.

Pal-mok 'Forearm'. See *Kote*, *Ude*.

Pandea *Tae Kwon Do*. A 'round' kick delivered by pivoting on the supporting leg and turning the body through 180 degrees.

Pai *Wushu*. Traditional schools (Japanese: *Ryu*) of Chinese martial arts, sometimes associated with secret societies such as the 'White Lotus'. Their favourite weapon is the sword *Jiang*. These schools also existed in Vietnam and were called *Phai*.

Pang Jiao see *Jiao*.

Pao. A sort of rectangular or trapezoidal shield, about 60 by 30 cm, rigid and padded. It is used in training as a target for kicks and punches. It is either fixed to a wall or held by a partner. Sometimes kicking and punching bags, suspended from a beam, are used instead. See *Makiwara*.

Peace see *Wa*, *Heian*.

Penchak-silat **(Pentjak-silat)** 'Lightning combat'. Styles of Indonesian and Malayan martial arts with roots in ancient times, perhaps influenced by Indian techniques of *Kalaripayat* and *Vajramushti*. Traces of Chinese *Wushu* are also believed to exist in these arts. As in *Karate*, the natural weapons of the body are used (*Juru*) and the vital points of the body (see *Kyusho*). The weapons are specifically Indonesian and Malayan. In addition to the Kris, they include a weapon comparable to the *Sai* of Okinawa, the *Tjabang*. The teachers of martial arts are called *Pendekar*; they have their own particular philosophy and make use of methods of self-hypnosis such as can still be seen in Bali during the 'dance of the Kris'. Over the centuries, Pentjak-silat assumed hundreds of forms and many schools appeared. All the terms used are Indonesian or Malayan.

A conservative estimate puts the number of styles at over 400; no one knows the exact number. See *Bersilat*, *Kundao*, *Pokulan*.

Pendekar see *Penchak-silat*.

Phai see *Pai*.

Pham Xuan Tong see *Chau Quan Khi*, *Qwan-ki-do*.

Phap see *Waza*.

Phat see *Chui*.

Phat Moc see *Cuong Dao*.

Phi Bang Sat Cuoc, Phi Hoanh Sat Cuoc, Phi Tieu Cuoc see *Cuoc Phap*.

Phoenix see *Fen Taidu*, *Taidu*.

Phuong Duc *Qwan Ki Do*. Elbow techniques:

a descending blow: *An Long*
a backward blow: *Bat Ho*
a curving horizontal blow: *Hoanh Wa*
a rising blow to the front: *Than Xa*
a curving backward blow: *Hoanh Phong*
a lateral blow using both elbows, to the side or the rear: *Thiet Giac*.

Ping-jing Taidu see *Taidu*.

Pi-gua-quan *Wushu*. Successive attacking blows, with the limbs stretched out, used in certain Chinese martial arts schools.

Pihag-gi 'Evasion'. See *Bang-o*.

Pinan *Karate*. In those styles of *Karate* which do not belong to the *Shotokan* school, this is the name given to the *Heian-no-kata*. In the *Pinan Kata* there are variations in movement and stance, but they serve, as in the *Heian*, to introduce beginners and relative beginners to the preliminary combination movements of the style.

Pokulan Indonesian style of martial arts with roots in Chinese *Wushu*. See *Penchak-silat*, *Bersilat*, *Kundao*.

Points see *Ippon*, *Waza-ari*, *Koka*, *Yuko*.

Poomse *Tae Kwon Do*. 'Forms', *Kata*, consisting of successive movements (usually twenty-four) which demonstrate kicks, punches, attacks to an opponent's vital points, attacking positions, evasions and counter-attacks. They are performed alone and provide practitioners with an opportunity to 'fight' against an imaginary opponent and at the same time perfect their technique. The most frequently used Poomse at present are: *Palgwe* (eight different ones), *Koryo*, *Kungang*, *Taebaek*, *Pyongwon*, *Shipjin*, *Jitae*, *Cheunkwon*, *Hansoo* and *Ilyeo*. Also written *Poom-se*, *Pumse*, *Pum-se*. Also called *Hyong* (*Hyung*).

Positive see *Yang*, *Omote*.

Postures. A great deal of emphasis is placed on posture in the martial arts because they play a very important part in the delivery of blows, defensive moves, intermediate moves and changes of position in the fighting area. Postures (*Kamae*) may be standing (*Tachi*) or sitting (*Sei-za*, *Suwari*).
General see *Shizen-tai*, *Shizen Hontai*, *Ai-gamae*, *Kamae*, *Jigotai*, *Mu-kamae*.
Aikido see *Kamae* (*-gamae*), *Waki-gamae* . . .
Judo see *Tachi-ai* . . .
Viet Vo Dao see *Tan Phap*, *Thu Phap* (guards), *Bophap*.

Kung-fu see *Taidu*, *Bo*.
Tae-kwon-do see *Seug-gi*.
Karate see *Heisoku-dachi*, *Hachiji-dachi*, *Kiba-dachi*, *Kokutsu-dachi*, *Neko-ashi-dachi*, *Sochin-dachi*, *Sanchin-dachi*, *Hangetsu-dachi*, *Zenkutsu-dachi* . . .

Praying Mantis see *Tang Lang Quan Pai*.

Principles see *Jo*, *Kyo*, *Gokyo*.

Prolongation see *Mo Sukoshi*.

Pu-fa see *Shaolin-si*.

Pum-se (Pumse) see *Poomse*.

Punchbag. For the training purposes of certain martial arts such as *Karate*, as in boxing, a heavy canvas or leather bag filled with sand or other materials is hung from an overhead support by chains or tough ropes. It is used for striking to improve technique and to toughen those parts of the body which come into contact with it. Its weight, which can vary from 25 to 50 kg, ensures a relatively inert target which is considerably harder to move than a live opponent. The length of the bag varies enormously in modern times, from 1 to 2 $\frac{1}{2}$ metres. See *Makiwara*, *Pao*.

Pyong-won see *Poomse*.

Q

Qi see *Ki, Taiji Quan*.

Qixing see *Tang Lang Quan Pai*.

Quan *Wushu*. 'Fist'. The main attacking techniques using the fist are:

Ming Quan, straight punch using hip power
Hang Quan, lateral punch
Yuan Quan, circular punch
Qua Shang Quan, forward reverse punch
Xiong Quan, 'bear punch', fingers held like claws, delivered low
Chui-zi Quan, a vertically or curving descending punch, like a hammer blow
Shang Quan, a rising punch
Dui Quan, double fist punch to the front
Yan-zi-guo Quan, 'swallow punch': from a position with both wrists crossed in front of the neck, the arms are swung back horizontally to the sides.

See *Ken, Kwon*.

Quan-bian Jiao see *Jiao*.

Quan Khi see *Quyen*.

Qua Shang Quan see *Quan*.

Quyen *Viet Vo Dao*. 'Forms', *Kata*. Successive movements. Some *Quyen* are performed alone; others are done with a partner and are called *Song Luyen*.

The three main solo Quyen are the 'Dragon-tiger' (*Long-ho*), the Harmonious (*Trung-hao*) and the Ten Characters (*Thap Tu*), but each school or style has its own Quyen which can be learned only in the school concerned.

Qwan Ki Do. Among the basic Quyen are found the *Bo Phap*, *Than Phap* and *Thu Phap*, as well as the ones called *Bo Linh Mot*, *Bo Linh Hai* and *Dang Mon*. According to the styles in question, the more advanced Quyen are the *Qwan-khi*, which belong to the *Nga Mi Phai* (or Chinese *E-mei*) or to various other current Chinese styles.

Quy Tan see *Bo Phap, Tan Phap*.

Qwan-ki-do (Quan-khi-do) 'Way of the

Qua Quan

Yuan Quan

Shang Quan

Yangzi Guo Quan

Dui Quan

Ming Quan

Yuan Quan

Quan

Xiong Quan

Quan Shang Quan

Chuizi Quan   Bang Quan

fist and the energy'. A Vietnamese martial art, slightly similar to *Karate* but more acrobatic and spectacular, founded after the Second World War by the Vietnamese *Pham Xuan Tong* (see *Chau Quan Khi*). This particular style uses conventional empty-hand methods but also includes the art of the Vietnamese sword, *Viet Long Guom*, which originated during the revolt of the *Tay-son* in the seventeenth century. The influence of the Chinese philosophy of the *Dao* was very strong in the development of this art, which tries to unite purely physical energy with the universal energy (*Khi, Ki*). The 'law of changes' (*Kin Dich*), as presented in the *Yijing* (*I-ching*), can be perceived in this attempted union. Training is made up of exercises, freestyle fighting (*Thao Quyen*) and traditional forms, or *Dan Tu Do*. During fighting one or both hands are gloved, and other types of protective equipment are worn. Techniques also include gripping movements and exercises with swords, halberds and other weapons. France has the most Qwan-ki-do students of all the European countries: in 1987 there were over 3,000 licensed members of clubs, and about one hundred clubs. See *Cuong Nhu Tuong Thai*.

In *Qwan Ki Do* there are numerous basic techniques:

Postures: *Bo Phap*
Displacements: *Than Phap*
Hand techniques: *Thu Phap*
Leg techniques: *Cuoc Phap*
Blocks: *Cung Thu*
Sweeps: *Tao Phong Cuoc*
Defensive techniques: *Tu Ve*
Throwing techniques: *Vat*
Armlocks: *Khao Go*
Falling techniques: *Nhao Lan*
'Breaking' techniques: *Nghanh Phap*, etc.

Qwan Ki Do is a complete discipline which also advocates meditation (*Tinh Phap*), breathing methods (*Khi Phap*) and of course the numerous *Quyen* or *Kata*. There are several kinds of bow (*Bai To*), as well as various techniques using 'sword-hand' (*Cuong Dao*), elbow blows (*Phuong Duc*), etc.

R

Rakuten-kai see *Shintaido*.

Randori *Judo, Aikido.* Free-fighting training which includes one or several techniques. In some clubs this is followed by analysis and study of some of the techniques used, with *Uchi-komi* to drive home various technical points. Korean: *Jayu-dae Ryeun*, *Kuryeung Opsi*. See *Suburi*.

Red *Aka*.

Referees and judges. Every fight or contest must take place under the control of a referee and judges or assistant referees. The number of these officials varies with the nature of the competition; also, the rules of competition can vary with different disciplines. When a referee makes a gesture to signal to the judges or the public some observation or decision, he must also announce it in a high, clear voice, using the words which are recognized by tradition. Referees or judges may equally well signal their decisions precisely by using flags (or signalling discs) of different colours. The gestures are described for *Judo* in Article 8 of the Rules (see *Judo*). As far as *Karate* is concerned, certain gestures can differ from those used in Judo:

> *Ippon*. Right arm raised to the side, 60 degrees.
> *Waza-ari*. Right arm lowered to the side at an angle of 45 degrees.
> *Tsukete Hajime*. Arms stretched forward, palms upwards.
> *Jikan*. Right arm raised vertically.
> *Fukushen-shugo*. Both arms raised to form a V-shape.
> *Hansoku*. Arm raised to the side, index finger pointing, at an angle of 60 degrees.
> *Ai-uchi*. Both arms folded on the chest, fists touching.
> *Chui*. Circling the arms above the head.
> *Hikiwake*. Arms crossed above the head.
> *Mienai*. The referee hides his or her face with both hands.
> *Fujubun*. The referee waves both hands horizontally in front of him or her.

See *Gyoji*, *Shobu-shimpan*, Competition Rules of *Judo*, 5, 7, 8; *Karate*, 13–16, 19, 20, *Uchiwa*.

Ippon   Waza-ari   Yuko

Koka   Chui, Hansoku   Yoshi

Matte   Annulation

Examples of the referee's hand signals

Rei 'Veneration', 'Respect'. Before and after every contest or training session, *Budoka* must bow to one another and to their teacher. This bow is part of the *Dojo* etiquette and should be observed wherever martial arts training is taking place. This particular bow is one which is made according to the rules, as distinct from any form of bow prescribed by a particular school or style. It is called '*Ritsu-rei*'. Different disciplines may use different expressions for this bow. It may be performed standing (*Tachi-rei*), kneeling with the fists placed on the ground and the forehead touching the ground (*Za-rei*) or sitting on the heels, the body inclined forward and the head straight (*Hai-rei*). Vietnamese: **Chao**. Also called *Reigi-sa-ho*. See *Rei-shiki*.

Rei no Ji-dachi *Karate*. Posture (*Kamae*) taken standing up with the feet making an L-shape.
Reisha *Kyudo*. Ceremonial drawing of the bow. The archer, dressed in traditional costume (*Kimono* and *Eboshi*), bares his shoulder to allow free movement. This ceremonial

draw is a *Shinto* rite. Its aim is to celebrate the spirit of the arrow which is used to unite the target and the archer closely together. In so doing, it joins the visible to the invisible and takes part in the *Ai-ki*. During certain great ceremonial draws (*Dosha*), the archer is assisted by a sword-bearer, a bow-bearer and a kind of attendant, as seen in presentations of *Sumo*. The first arrow to be fired is a *Kabura-ya*, whose whistle should frighten off the evil spirits.

Rei-shiki 'Ceremonial', 'Etiquette', as observed by certain traditional schools, of which the *Ogasawara* school is an existing example; they observe rigorous etiquette. Others have transformed certain ancient rules or adapted them according to the needs of their particular discipline. However, it must be said that all martial arts observe rules of etiquette, before, during and after competitions and training. From the moment a student enters a *Dojo*, he or she is required to follow the current rules of good behaviour and etiquette, not only in respect of the Dojo but also of the master and the other students. Rules concerning bowing and other marks of deference (*Rei*) are of primary importance, but rules of courtesy and mutual assistance are important also. This means that the *Rei-shiki* covers not just the accepted physical movements or ritual gestures but such qualities as modesty, compassion, concern for others and generosity. It is inconceivable that a martial art worthy of the name would be without this 'etiquette of the heart'.

Renko-ho *Karate*. Technique of immobilizing an opponent by blocking or locking the arms.

Renraku *Judo*. Combination attack using several techniques in succession.

Rensa-Sankaku 'Technique of three sticks', invented by the Takagi-ryu, for defending oneself against an assailant armed with a sword.

Renshi 'A person who has mastered him(her)self'. This is the title given to an 'expert', of 4th to 6th *Dan* grade, and is

necessary for anyone who wants to become an instructor. See *Kyudan*.

Wa-jutsu. Someone of this grade wears a white jacket, a black *Hakama* and a purple belt with two red bands. See *Kyudan*.

Renshu. A period of training; the practice of training in a martial art.

Rensoku-waza *Ju-jutsu*. A series of movements consisting of an *Atemi* blow, an armlock a throwing technique and a final Atemi blow.

Judo. A simple series of various movements.

Rentai-ho see *Kogi-judo*, *Kyogi-judo*.

Ren-tsuki *Karate*. Alternate punches. Also *Renzuki*.

Renzoku-geri *Karate*. Continuous kicking attacks.
— **Renzoku-tsuki** *Karate*.

Renzuki see *Ren-tsuki*.

Respiration see *Ibuki*, *Kokyu*, *Nogare*, *Yo-ibuki*.

Rest see *Mokuso*, *Yasumi*.

Reunion see *Ai*, *Mondo*.

Reverse see *Gyaku*, *Ura*.

Ri 'Moral'. See *Aikido*, *Ri-gi-ittai*.

Ridatsu-ho see *Joshi Judo Goshinho*.

Ri-gi-ittai. The principle of uniting theory (*Ri*) and techniques (*Gi*).

Riken-uchi *Karate*. A 'back-fist' blow delivered outwards in a *Kiba-dachi* stance.

Rikishi. A general term used to describe the wrestlers (*Sumotori*) of *Sumo*.

Rinzai-shu see *Zen*.

Ritsu-rei *Aikido*. A bow (*Rei*) made as

Riken-uchi

part of the ritual, before and after a confrontation or training session. It is performed standing, feet together, with the body slightly inclined towards the person concerned.

Rofuse *Aikido, Ju-jutsu.* Techniques of locking or bending the arms, applied at the elbow joints, using either the hands or the arms.

Rokkyu see *Kyu.*

Rokushaku-bo see *Bo.*

Ronin Before the tenth century this name was given to peasants who, to avoid crushing taxes, abandoned their land and established themselves in regions not yet owned by Buddhist monasteries or nobles of the imperial court. During the Edo period the name was given to all the *Bushi* and *Samurai* who did not serve a particular master, either because the latter was dead or because his lands had been confiscated. A number of these *Ronin* became martial arts teachers or embraced some other calling which was compatible with their Samurai status: bodyguards, protectors of villages, etc. Others became brigands, and the *Shogun*'s troops were often obliged to deal severely with them.

Various schools (*Ryu*) of martial arts were created by the Ronin, the most famous was *Miyamoto Musashi*. Between 1701 and 1703

Print illustrating a Ronin in the Kabuki theatre.

the famous forty-seven Ronin of Ako waited for three years for an opportunity to avenge the death of their lord, dishonoured by a courtier from the Shogun's entourage. After slaying the culprit they committed suicide together on the orders of the Shogun. See *Ako-gishi.*

Roppo *Aikido.* A technique of advancing or retreating by sliding the feet across the floor without changing the guard (*Kamae*), as distinct from *Ayumi.*

Round (Roundhouse) Kick see *Mawashi-geri.*

Ryo 'The two', or 'Both'.
— **Ryo-ashi-dori** *Judo.* Gripping both legs.
— **Ryo Kata-oshi** see *Ju-no-Kata.*
— **Ryoku** see *Itto-ryu, Omote.*
— **Ryote** 'Both hands'.
— **Ryote-dori** see *Tachi-ai, Idori, Ju-no-kata.*
— **Ryote Eri-tori** *Aikido. Uke* seizes (*Shite*) *Tori* by both lapels. The latter steps back one stride with the left foot and passes his or her right arm down between Uke's arms. Shite then grips Uke with his or her left hand, at the right elbow, and pulls it downwards, delivering an *Atemi* blow to the face with the right hand. See *Eri Tori.*
— **Ryote-kata-dori** *Aikido. Uke* seizes *Shite*'s right wrist with both hands. Shite brings both hands together and steps forward half a pace with the right foot. With a sudden sharp action, Shite drives both hands downwards, to the left, arms extended, then jerks the arms back upwards to shake off the grip. He or she ends the movement with an *Atemi* blow to Uke's face. See *Te-dori.*
— **Ryozume** see *Oku-tai.*

Ryu 'Dragon', 'School'. Korean: *Kwan.* A 'school' or 'style' of martial arts. Each martial art contains a large number of *Ryu.* These in turn are sometimes divided into branches (*Ha*), as a result of the various masters composing new sequences of movement or technique. Before the Restoration of the Meiji era (1868) a very large number of Ryu existed; certain of them were secret and others had only a few adherents. Some prided themselves on having thousands of students.

There was reckoned to be about 1,000 Ryu, but although they differed from one another the majority of them taught techniques of sword-fighting. Most of the Ryu had been created by noble *Samurai*, others simply by *Ronin* or even common people (peasants). They recruited their students from the class to which they belonged. The seat of a Ryu was located where the founder lived, generally in the provinces where there was less surveillance than in Edo (Tokyo) or the big cities. Some Ryu were independent, but others belonged to one of the great families (*Daimyo*) who directed the affairs of a clan or province. Each professor-master had his own style (*Ryugi*) and transmitted the secrets (*Okuden*) of the style to his chosen disciples. The other students had access only to the purely superficial parts of the teaching (*Omote*). Certain masters taught only technique (*Jutsu, Waza*) but others added to this by investigating more or less esoteric aspects based either upon their own philosophy or that of *Zen*, Confucianism or *Shinto*. The results of these investigations and studies were included in the teaching. Sometimes they left behind their writings, which dealt with their discoveries and techniques. A fine example of this is the *Gorin-no-sho* of *Miyamoto Musashi*. Such writings served either as a guide to existing and future disciples of the Ryu, or as assistance in perpetuating the tradition within the confines of the family circle.

Most of the Ryu which still existed before the Second World War have now disappeared, for the old masters are dead and the pupils have deserted the *Dojo* for the sake of the more lucrative fields of the modern martial arts such as *Judo, Aikido, Karate-do, Kendo, Kyudo*, and so on. Even so, a recent census by the Japanese government revealed about 1,000 Ryu scattered throughout Japan. Some forty-six of these were chosen to take part in a great annual *Taikai* in the Tokyo *Budokan*. Thus this regular event brings together all the Ryu which the Japanese authorities deem 'true' Ryu. Among them one can cite the following, in alphabetical order:

Aio-ryu (created *c.* 1600)
Araki-ryu (chains, *Kusari-gama*)

Daito-ryu
Fudo-ryu
Hioki-ryu
Hokusai-ryu (founded *c*. 1700)
Hozo-in-ryu (lances, *Yari*)
Hyoho Itten Ichi-ryu (sword, founded *c*. 1620)
Isshin-ryu (chains)
Jikishin Kage-ryu (Sword, *Bokken*, *Naginata*, founded sixteenth century.)
Juki-ryu (founded *c*. 1600)
Kage-ryu (sword)
Kashima Shinto-ryu (sword, founded *c*. 1647)
Katori-ryu
Kankai-ryu (swimming techniques)
Kito-ryu
Kurama-ryu (*Kendo*, founded *c*. 1574)
Kyushin-ryu (lance, Yari)
Muso Shinden-ryu (*Iai*, founded *c*. 1565)
Mutekatsu-ryu
Ogasawara-ryu (*Kyudo*, sixteenth century)
Oto-ryu (*Karate* of Okinawa)
Sekiguchi-ryu (founded early seventeenth century)
Shibukawa-ryu (*Kusarigama*, *Bo-jutsu*)
Shindo Muso-ryu (*Jo-jutsu*, founded sixteenth century)
Shin no Shindo-ryu
Shinkage-ryu (sword, lance)
Shoshitsu-ryu (using the sword wearing armour, founded 1646)

Sosuichi-ryu (*Ju-jutsu*, founded sixteenth century)
Takagi-ryu (*Bo-jutsu*, founded 1656)
Takenouchi-ryu
Tamita-ryu (sword)
Tenshin Shin-yo-ryu (*Ju-jutsu*, sixteenth century)
Wado-ryu (*Karate*, founded 1929)
Yagyu Shinkan-ryu (sword, from early seventeenth century)
Yanagi-ryu
Yo-ryu (firearms, seventeenth century)
Yoshin-ryu

etc. See *Bu-jutsu*.

According to the *Bu-jutsu-ryu Soroku*, a work published in 1843, there were in Japan at that date some 150 important *Ryu*: 66 teaching *Ken-jutsu* and *Iai-jutsu*, 31 teaching *So-jutsu*, 20 teaching *Ju-jutsu*, 19 the use of firearms and 14 devoted to *Kyu-jutsu*.

— **Ryugi.** The 'Style' taught in a *Ryu*.

— **Ryusetsu** see *Ura*.

— **Ryusha.** A disciple of a teacher of a *Ryu*, following the discipline taught by him or her.

— **Ryu-to** see *Omori-ryu*.

S a 'Left'. See *Hidari*.

Sabaori *Sumo.* Driving the opponent down on to the ground using the force of his or her own weight. It is performed by seizing his or her belt with both hands, reaching over his or her arms to do so. See *Kimarite*.

Sabaori

Sabda Pendita see *Setia-hati Terate*.

Sa-beum-nim *Tae-kwon-do.* Title given to a teacher, equivalent to 'Master'.

Sacrifice see *Sutemi, Tomoe-nage*.

Sagari see Mawashi.

Sageo see *Swords*.

Sageta-empi *Karate.* Low elbow blow.

Sagi-ashi-tachi *Karate.* 'Crane (or Heron) stance', on one leg.

Sai. A type of 'dagger', frequently used as a club or stick but potentially for stabbing also. It is usually made completely of metal and the guards consist of two hooklike 'wings'. Similar weapons are found in other countries but the *Sai* itself was first used in the Japanese-dominated part of the globe by the peasants of Okinawa to defend themselves against the weapons of the *Samurai* and brigands. In the Edo period (1603–1868) the *Shogun*'s police force was armed with the Sai to deflect sword blades and to break the bladed weapons of the rebels. The main section of the Sai, the 'blade', can be sharpened

Sai training demonstrated by Master Shiokawa.

for thrusting techniques and must be an inch or two longer than the user's forearm so that when it is used in reverse to stop a blade, with the main section held flat against the forearm, the blade slides *off* the end, not *on to* the elbow. It belongs in the *Kobudo* armoury but is frequently a complement to *Karate* training. The art of the Sai is called *Sai-jutsu*. One of the benefits of Sai training is the strengthening of the wrist. Another type of Sai with only one hook-guard is called the *Jitte* (or *Jutte*). See *Tjabang*.

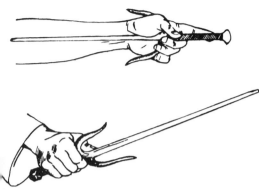

Basic Sai grips:
Blade reversed along the forearm (principally for blocking) with the index finger along the handle, one branch of the guard clasped in the fork formed by the thumb and index finger, the other three fingers wrapped around the second branch of the guard.

Blade pointing away from the user (principally for attacking):
the handle is held against the palm, the thumb is pressed against the junction of guard and blade.

— **Sai-jutsu.** Techniques of using the *Sai* or *Jitte* for warfare. The principal method was to catch a sword blade with the central section and cause it to slide down to lodge in between the guard and the middle, close to the handle. The wrist twisted the blade and either snapped it or perhaps dragged it from the swordsman's hands or simply pulled it aside so that the defender could attack with the other Sai. Sai were mainly used in pairs.

Saigo Shiro see *Shida Shiro*.

Saigo Takamori (1827–77). *Samurai* of the *Satsuma* clan, in the service of the *Daimyo* of the Shimazu family. He took an active role in the restoration of the Emperor Meiji in 1868 and was appointed commander of the imperial guard, but in 1873 he retired to Kagoshima, followed by several thousand young people. There, under cover of agricultural activities, they studied the science of weapons. In 1877 Saigo objected to the enforcement of universal conscription and rebelled. He was defeated after some months and committed suicide. Although he was a rebel, the people made him a hero: one who faced up to arbitrary authority. They attributed to him all the military virtues and saw in him a true fidelity to the Samurai ideal. His status was recognized once more by the authorities in 1891 and a bronze statue of him was erected in Ueno park in Tokyo, showing him accompanied by a dog, the symbol of fidelity. See *Satsuma*, *Jigen-ryu*.

Saigo Tanomo (Hoshina) Chikamasa see *Oshiki-uchi*.

Sakakibara Kenkichi (1830–94) *Kendo.* An expert in swordsmanship, disciple of *Otani Shimosa* who invented a Kendo technique using the *Shinai*. It is analagous to the cutting movements (*Tameshi-giri*) made with the *Katana*. He belonged to the *Jikishin-kage-ryu*, and was the master of *Takeda Sokaku*. In 1873 he gave demonstrations of his Kendo techniques throughout Japan (with the blessing of the government), in order to popularize this neglected art and bring it back to life as a sport devoid of warlike applications.

Saka-otoshi see *Ura*.

Saki see *Sen*.

Sakigawa *Kendo.* A small 'sheath' of tough leather which covers the point (*Kissaki*) of the *Shinai*.

Sakki. An instantaneous intuitive feeling which a *Budo* practitioner experiences, enabling him or her to perceive an aggressive intention of an adversary, making it possible for him or her to counter-attack even before the adversary has time to launch an effective attack. See *Haragei*.

Sakotsu 'Clavicle'. See *Body*.

Sakura see *Cherry*.

Salt *Sumo.* Salt is supposed to drive away evil spirits and combat pernicious influences. It is freely sprinkled on the floor of the *Dohyo* by wrestlers of the higher rank (*Maku-uchi, Juryo, Makushita*) before each contest. This salt is also supposed to protect them against injuries and, if these do occur, to heal them quickly.

Salutes see *Rei, Ritsurei, Le, Chao, Baito, Gassho, Zarei, Hormat.*

Sama see *San, Names.*

Sambo. A national sport of the USSR in which thousands of students compete annually. It is a type of wrestling inspired by Mongolian wrestling, performed on a carpet. The opponents wear lightweight shoes and socks, and a shot jacket similar to the one worn in *Judo*, held tight against the body by a red or blue belt. The referee is distinguishable by coloured cuffs. The aim of the contest is to immobilize the opponent with an armlock, which produces the maximum number of points, eight. A clean throw brings four points; dragging an opponent to the floor is worth one point. For a victory to be scored, one of the contestants must have at least four points more than his or her opponent at the end of the contest.

Samurai. A class of *Bushi* (warriors, *Shi*) attached to a lord at the imperial court. (The word comes from the older word, *Saburai*, from *Saburau*, meaning 'to keep to the side'.) These original *Samurai* were there for the protection of their lord and were specially trained in martial arts. Later the name was given to all Bushi of a certain rank belonging to warrior families (*Buke*). Only *Samurai* were allowed to carry two swords (*Daisho*). Warriors of a lower rank were more usually called *Bushi* or *Bujin*. In the Edo period (1603–1868) the Samurai constituted the dominant social class in Japan. See *Bushi, Ronin.*

San 'Three', in Sino-Japanese. See *Numbers.*
— An honorific suffix to a name, which means Mr, Madam or Miss, depending on the sex or marital status of the person to whom it is applied. Also *Sama.* See *Names.*

Sanbon Kumite *Kendo.* An attack to the front taking three steps or three successive attacks.

Karate. Three-step sparring in prearranged form.

Sanchin *Karate.* A slow-moving fundamental *Kata* of *Karate* training in which the breathing is synchronized with the movement and the muscles are maintained in an almost constant state of tension. See *Kokyu.*
— **Sanchin-dachi** *Karate.* A standing position, knees and feet turned in, with one leg in advance of the other.

Sanchin-dachi

Sandan 'Third level'. See *Kyudan, Dan.*
— **Sandanme** see *Sumotori.*

Sang-dang see *Jodan.*

Sango-ken *Shorinji.* Various techniques of defence and counter-attack used to parry kicks or punches to the chest.

Sankaku-jime *Judo.* *Tori* immobilizes *Uke* when the latter is kneeling on the floor. *Tori* kneels on one knee, 'sitting' on Uke's shoulders from the front, and grips his or her belt or *Judogi*.

Sankaku-tobi *Karate.* 'Triangle'. A leaping, triple kick to the head or chest.

Sankukai *Karate.* A modern style of acrobatic *Karate*, created by Nambu Yoshinao, which developed mainly in the United States

Sankaku-jime

and Japan in the 1970s. The name was also given to a series of animated drawings seen in Japan and the USA which depict the hero using his Karate skills.

Sankyo *Aikido.* 'Third principle' (*Kote-hineri*) of twisting the opponent's wrist in the following situations:

Hiji-dori, elbow grip
Shomen-uchi, descending blow
Ushiro Tekubi-kubi-dori, a grip on the wrist from the rear while the other arm is used to strangle the opponent
Ushiro-ryo-hiji-dori, grip on both elbows from the rear.

See *Kote-hineri*, *Katame-waza*.

Sankyu see *Kyu*.

San-nen Goroshi. In certain ancient *Bujutsu* schools, this was a 'secret' technique of striking an enemy in such a way that he did not die immediately but later (*San-nen* – three years). In Chinese martial arts a similar technique is sometimes called the 'Delayed Death Touch'. Nowadays this technique is regarded as the stuff of legend rather than reality. Even so, certain injuries resulting from an *Atemi* blow may lead to consequences which, in the long term, can shorten an individual's life.

Sanren-tsuki *Karate.* Three successive punching attacks.

Sansen-tachi *Karate.* 'Three battles posture'.

San-setsu-kon see *Nunchaku*.

San Shu *Wushu.* Training in the forms (*Dao*) of *Kung-fu* with a partner, in which each participant trains in the individual techniques of attack and defence. See *Randori*.

San-yaku see *Sumotori*.

Sasae-tsuri-kimo Ashi *Judo.* 'Propping-drawing ankle throw'. *Tori* blocks *Uke*'s ankle with his or her own foot, draws Uke on and lifts, causing him or her to fall to the side of the blocking foot. Loss of balance and fall takes place to the right or left front.

Sasae-tsuri-komi
Ashi

— Sasae-uke *Karate.* A blocking technique which is maintained rather than turning into an attack or different block.

Sasaki Kojiro see Chujo-ryu (*Gan-ryu*).

Sasaki Gan-ryu see *Miyamoto Musashi*.

Sashi-men *Kendo.* A direct attack to an opponent's head by thrusting with the point of the *Shinai*, the final target being the front of the neck (*Tsuki*).

Sa-soku 'Left foot', 'Left side'.

Sa Tan see *Tan Phap*.

Sa-to see *Omori-ryu*.

Satori. An opening of the mind and spirit, resulting either from the accumulation of

Calligraphy by Taisen Deshimaru expressing the realization of unity.

knowledge and its intuitive understanding or from a sudden experience which reveals the ultimate Reality of beings and things, as well as their total identity with the self and the universe. One may experience nu-

merous *Satori*, as the state itself is not a definitive one but valid for one given time and circumstance. It is not an experience of ecstasy but a transformation of the very essence of thought. The practice of one of the forms of *Budo* should be able to bring about this transformation in those who follow it sincerely. The experience of Satori is one of the major aims in *Zen* training, *Za-zen*. This is *Hishiryo*, the aspect of consciousness concerning the thinking processes. It is very close to the Hindus' *Moksha* and the Chinese *Zhengjue*. See *Zen, Mushin*.

Satsuma. A clan in the south of the island of Kyushu, Kagoshima, whose *Samurai* were known for their bravery. In 1866 the clan made an alliance with the clan of Choshu, a region now called Yamaguchi prefecture. The intention was to overthrow the Shogunate. After the restoration of the emperor in 1868, the lords of Shimazu occupied the important government posts. However, *Saigo Takamori*, then one of the chiefs of the

Warriors grouped around the head of the Satsuma clan.

Satsuma clan, revolted against the emperor in protest against the introduction of compulsory military service for all; a situation which deprived the Samurai of their rights. The revolt was quelled and Saigo Takamori committed suicide. See *Saigo Takamori*.

Sat Tich see *Cuong Dao*.

Sau Quay. 'Half-trunk', a type of displacement in the Vietnamese martial arts.

Saya. The scabbard of a sword. It was considered a grave affront for one *Samurai* to allow his scabbard to strike that of another (*Saya-ate*, 'scabbard-strike'). The person insulted in this way had the right to draw his own sword and attack the offender; thus the study of *Iai-jutsu* was indispensable in such situations.

Saya-undo Aikido. 'Left–right'. An exercise for balancing the body, performed from side to side, left–right–left, and so on, so that the muscles become supple.

Scissors see *Hasami*.

Sechie-zumo Sumo. Major Sumo tournaments which took place at the court of the emperor during the Nara period (645–794). Wrestlers from all parts of Japan came to take part. The events were staged within the confines of the *Shinto* sanctuaries, accompanied by music and sacred dances (*Kagura*); the aim was to invoke the goodwill of the *Kami* (superior forces) of fine harvests and social peace. The emperor was present at this time, watching the tournaments; hence their name, *Sechi-e*, 'seen by the emperor'. They began on 7 July, in the reign of Emperor Monmu (697–707). In 719 the Empress Gensho created an official post, *Nukide-no-tsukasa*; its holder was charged with recruiting wrestlers. One of these officials, *Shiga Seirin*, was given the title *Hote* (referee) in 740, and he codified the forty-eight 'grips' which were permitted in the art of Sumo. In 868 the Sechie ceremony was assimilated into the military arts, but another form of Sumo, *Shinji-sumo*, developed parallel to it; this was uniquely religious. From the blending of these two styles during the seventeenth century modern Sumo was born. See *Kanjin-sumo, Sumo, Gyoji*.

Seichu-to see *Omori-ryu*.

Seidon see *Kyusho*.

Seifuku-jutsu. A resuscitation technique following loss of consciousness. See *Kuatsu*.

Seigan Kendo. Middle guard (*Chu-dan*), a posture of readiness and preparation for an attack; a time of taking the measure of one's opponent. Also applied to fighting using the *Bokken*.

Seigo-ho see *Joshi Judo Goshin-ho*.

Seika no Itten see *Hara, Tanden*.
— **Seika-tanden** see *Tanden*.

Seiken Karate. The name given to a clenched fist and to a basic punching technique. see *Weapons*.
— **Seiken Choku-tsuki Karate.** A straight punch using *Seiken* fist. See *Hands*.

Seiken Choku-tsuki

Seiko see *Kito-ryu*.

Sequences see *Kata, Quyen, Song Luyen*.

Seiryoku-zen-yo. An essential principle of all the martial arts which consists of using the energy of *Wa* and *Ki* contained in the *Hara*, with the maximum efficiency. The same principle may be applied to all human activities. See *Ki, Hara, Wa, Jita-kyo-ei*.

— **Seiryoku Zen-yo Kokumin Tai-iku no Kata** 'Forms of national culture based on the principles of maximum efficiency'. This is a method of physical training in the martial arts, principally in *Judo*, divided into two groups of exercises:

Tandoku-renshu (twenty-eight movements) for exercising alone, as a preparation for attacking the vital points (see *Kyusho*) of an opponent.
Sotai-renshu (twenty 'soft' exercises requiring decisive and swift execution).

See *Kata*.

Seiryu-to *Karate*. 'Bull strike', delivered with the base of the 'knife-hand'.
— **Seiryu-to-uke** *Karate*. A blocking technique against a *Seiryu-to* attack.

Seishi-o Choetsu. A state of transcending life and death; one of the essential virtues of the *Samurai*, and in accordance with the tenets of *Bushido*. See *Makino Toru*.

Seishin Tanren. The process of forging the spiritual side of a man or woman, in which the mind, like a sword blade, is worked upon and purified to bring it to perfection.

Seitei-gata *Iai-do*. A standardized form of *Iai*, established by the *Nihon Kendo Renmei* of Japan and the Japanese Federation of *Iai-do*.

Sei-za. A position of rest or waiting used by practitioners of the martial arts, assumed before training or between training periods. One sits 'tailor-fashion' or in the traditional Japanese manner, on the knees, or even in the Lotus posture. In each case the spine should be erect and the head straight. The hands rest on the knees or thighs. Also *Za-ho*. See *Suwari, Za-zen*.

Seki (-zeki) *Sumo*. An honorific suffix used with the name of a *Sumotori*. See *Ozeki, Sekitori*.

Sekiguchi Jushin see *Sekiguchi-ryu*.

Sekiguchi-ryu. A school of unarmed combat (*Jujutsu*) created by Sekiguchi Jushin (1647–1711) of Suruga, who also developed the art of *Batto-jutsu*. See *Iai-do, Shibukawa-ryu, Yawara*.

Sekitori *Sumo*. In the classification (*Banzuke*) of the *Sumotori*, this particular class includes the *Maku-uchi* and the *Juryo*. The *Sumotori* cannot gain this rank until they have trained (*Keiko*) for at least two years.

Sekiwake *Sumo*. The third rank in the *Sumotori* hierarchy (*Banzuke*) after *Yokozuna* and *Ozeki*. The current best-known *Sekiwaki* in the *Sumo* world are:

Kotogaume Tsuyochi (1963–   )
Mitoizumi Masato (1962–   )

Seme *Kendo, Iai-do*. A menacing gesture made by the practitioner just after drawing the sword, and before lifting it to strike (*Furi-kaburi*).

Semeite *Kendo, Karate*. This is the name of the partner who carries out the attacks in the performance of a *Kata*. The one who submits to the attacks is called *Shi-tachi*.

Sempai. The master-at-arms in a *Dojo*. His students are often called *Kohai*.

Sen. 'Initiative' taken by someone who finds him- or herself in a given situation during combat. He or she performs a block against an attack and makes a strong counterattack (*Go-no-Sen*), prepares to meet an attack (*Saki, Sen-no-Sen*), or anticipates one (*Senken*). Also called *Sen-no-Saki*. See *Ken-no-sen, Tai-no-sen, Kyudan*.

Seni-ryu. Ancient school of *Naginata*.

Senken. A movement performed in anticipation of an opponent's movement. See *Sen, Sen-no-Sen*.

Senmai see *Dohyo*.

Sensei 'Teacher', 'Born before'. A title which expresses deference, used towards those who have accomplished something of note. In the martial arts this title is sometimes reserved for the chief or creator of a *Ryu* or style, in general a 10th *Dan*. Today, depending on the school, it may be reserved for the head teacher of a *Dojo* or used for referring to martial arts masters, or even simply for anyone who is instructing at the time. The title of *Dai-sensei* or *O-Sensei*, meaning 'Great Master', is used only for a few people such as *Kano Jigoro*, *Funakoshi Gichin* or *Ueshiba Morihei*. See *Waka-sensei*.

Sen no Sen see *Sen*, *Kyudan*.

Seoi 'On the back'.
— **Seoi-age *Judo*.** A throw performed by lifting and throwing *Uke* with the shoulder.
— **Seoi-nage *Judo*.** A *Judo* throw in which *Uke* is thrown by *Tori* by means of the action and use of the shoulder. In this case he or she is thrown over the shoulder. See *Ippon Seoi-nage*.
— **Seoi-otoshi *Judo*.** A throw in which *Uke* is turned over *Tori*'s shoulder.

Se-orang see *Setia-hate Terate*.

Seppuku. The act of ritual suicide performed by the *Samurai*. Seated on a platform covered with white cloth, and dressed in white himself, the Samurai pierces and cuts the lower abdomen (seat of the *Hara*) from left to right, rising slightly to the right, demonstrating by this wound to the body that he no longer wishes to continue his life. A companion then immediately cuts off his head with one stroke of the sword. The initial piercing of the abdomen is never deep, contrary to popular belief. The wives of Samurai committed suicide by severing the carotid artery with a dagger (*Kaiken*). The expression *Hara-kiri*, 'to cut the abdomen', more widely known in the West, is considered vulgar. Custom required that before he died, a Samurai should compose a farewell poem. For this purpose he always carried with him some paper and some means of writing.

Sesshin. A rigorous discipline enabling one to reach a state of intense concentration of thought.

Sete Iai *Iai-do*. The name given in 1968 to seven *Iai Kata* which are considered fundamental.

Setia-hati Terate *Penchak-silat*. Indonesian style of unarmed combat, 'waterlily of the faithful heart', at one time a secret art practised mainly by the peasants of Java, who were not at that time influenced by external sources. It was developed by ascetics called *Sabda Pendita* who emphasized 'inner force' in the individual (or force of the mind), which was known as *Tenagadalem*, and also the friendly relationships which should exist between the students themselves, the *Hormat* or salutation, and reciprocal respect (*Siap*). All the movements are based on a triangular balance (*Siku-tiga* or *Tritunga* 'trinity'). Training sessions take place to the rhythm of the Gamelan, an orchestra of percussion instruments typical of Indonesia. Training includes '*Kata*' which are called *Juru*. Breathing methods are based on the *Ilmu*, analogous to the Japanese *Ki*. The students are called *Se-orang*. This technique was recently imported into Europe by the Javanese master Turpijn. See *Penchak Silat*.

Seug-gi *Tae-kwon-do*. Standing techniques (see *Tachi*):

Narani Seug-gi, feet parallel, slightly spread
Cheung-ul Seug-gi, a position with the weight forward, one leg stretched to the rear and the other slightly bent
Fugul Seug-gi, weight on the back leg, which is bent
Kima Seug-gi, horse-riding posture, legs spread wide apart and slightly bent.

Shado see *Kyudo*.

'Shagakuseido'. the Japanese name of an ancient Chinese work from the Ming dynasty (1374–1644) dealing with archery techniques.

Shaken see *Shuriken*.

Shang Quan see *Quan*.

Shang Taidu see *Taidu*.

Shaolin-si 'Small forest temple'. A name given to a Chinese Buddhist temple founded in Henan, according to tradition, on Song-shan mountain in 496. The Indian monk *Bodhidharma* came there around 600 and introduced Indian principles of unarmed self-defence to the *Chan* monks (Chan is Chinese *Zen*). Some say his purpose was to enable them to defend themselves against brigands; others that it was to give them strength to withstand the rigours of meditation. There are two streams of combat within the *Shaolin* methods. One is usually referred to as 'hard style' or external (*Waijia*); the other as 'soft style' or internal (*Neijia*). The former relies on muscular strength as well as skill, while the latter relies on special methods of yielding to attack and making use of the opponent's momentum to bring him or her down.

In the eighteenth century five major schools of Shaolin emerged, with the Cantonese names of *Hong* (*Hung*)-gar, *Mo-gar, Choi-gar* and *Li-gar*. However, these schools elaborated styles from various monasteries. Among them were the E-mei-shan, Wutang, Fujian, Guangdong and Henan, from the names of the provinces or towns where they developed. The techniques of the schools (*Pai*) of Shaolin consisted of 108 (a magic number) movements, made up of postures (*Tui-fa*), displacements (*Pu-fa*), blocks (*Lan-fa*), punches (*Chuan-fa, Quan-fa*), hand techniques (*Shu-fa*) and leg techniques (*Tek-fa*), as well as various techniques of gripping (*Lu-fa*). The postures are often imitations of those of animals (crane, tiger, bear, monkey, etc. . . .). Vietnamese: *Thieu Lam*: Cantonese: *Siu Lam Ji*. See *Shorinji-kempo, Taiji Quan*.
— **Shaolin-pai**. A type of *Kung-fu* similar to *Shaolin-si*. Vietnamese: *Thieu Lam Nga Mi Phai* (*E-mei-shan*).
— **Shaolin-si** Quanfa see *Shorinji-kempo*.

Shashin. A type of deliberate opening made during a contest or fight to deceive an opponent.

She Bo see *Bo*.

Sheiho see *Heiho*.

Shen see *Taiji Quan, Wa*.

Shi 'Warrior'. See *Bushi, Bujin, Buke, Samurai*. 'Finger'. see *Shiatsu*.

Shiai 'Competition'. A contest during a competition or during training between two or several opponents. Korean: *Sihap*.
Kendo. This style has three forms of *Shiai*: *Ippon Shobu* (an attack giving one point), *Sambon Shobu* (an attack giving three points), and an attack limited by the duration which has been decided in advance, but without limitation of the number of points scored.

Shiai-jo *Karate*. A term equivalent to the word *Dojo*. The *Shiai-jo* has the same dimensions as a *Judo* Dojo – that is, in general, a square with sides between 8 and 10 metres long.

Shiatsu. From '*Shi*', finger, and '*Atsu*', to push. These are techniques of local massage and pressure on specific points of the body using the ends of the fingers in order to stimulate or disperse the energy circulating through the 'meridians' of acupuncture. Some of these characteristic points, when pressed, have a slowing down effect, while others have an invigorating action, caused by the reaction of the nervous system (reflexotherapy). It has sometimes been described as acupuncture without needles but is of course much less precise. See *Kuatsu*.

Shibori 'Strangulation'. See *Shime-waza*.

Shibukawa-ryu. A school (*Ryu*) of *Ju-jutsu* and *Bo-jutso*, founded by Sekiguchi Hachirozaemon, the son of *Sekiguchi Jushin*, in Hiroshima in the seventeenth century.

Shichidan Keri no Renshu-ho *Karate*. A method of successive combat training in the 'seven kicks'. These kicks are regarded as basic to Karate technique.

Shi-dachi see *Naginata*.

Shida Shiro. A disciple of *Kano Jigoro*, born in 1868, who came to the master's *Dojo* in 1881, having followed the teaching

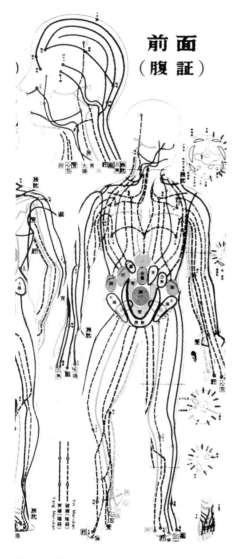

前 面
（腹 証）

Diagrams showing location of Shiatsu points.

of the *Tenjin Shin-yo-ryu*. He changed his name to *Saigo Shiro*. As a result of his talent and technical ability he made it possible for the newly established *Kodokan* to face up to the numerous other *Ryu* and win many competitions against them. He was appointed director of the *Kodokan* in 1888, but left a short time afterwards to devote himself to *Kyu-jutsu*. In this discipline he obtained the title of *Hanshi*.

Shido see *Chui*. Competition Rules of *Judo*, 28.

Shigaku-kan Dojo see *Momono-i Shunzo*.

Shiga Seirin see *Gyoji, Sechie-zumo*.

Shihan. A high rank in the martial arts. See *Kyudan*.
Wa-jutsu. Those who have attained this title wear a white jacket, a black *Hakama* and a purple belt with a red band in the middle.

Shiho 'Four quarters', 'Four limbs', 'Four directions'.
— **Shiho-gatame** *Judo*. 'Four quarters immobilization'. This is a groundwork (*Ne-waza*) technique in which *Tori* holds down *Uke* using the shoulders and hips to pin him or her. The elbows and knees may also be the 'targets' for pressure or gripping. There are six immobilizations of this type:

> *Yoko Shiho-gatame*, control from the side
> *Kami Shiho-gatame*, control from the rear, over the chest, using arms and belt
> *Kuzure Shiho-gatame*, a variation of control from the side
> *Kuzure Kami Shiho-gatame*, a variation of control over the chest using the belt
> *Kuzure Tate Shiho-gatame*, a variation of control over the chest sitting astride
> *Tate Shiho-gatame*, control sitting astride *Uke* face to face.

— **Shiho-giri** see *Oku-iai*.
— **Shiho-nage** *Aikido*. A series of four throws 'on four sides' or 'quarters', which are part of the *Nage-waza*. They are executed on: *Ryote-dori, Kata-dori, Yokomen-uchi, Shomen-tsuki* and *Ushiro-ryotekubi-dori*.
— **Shiho-wari** *Karate*. A 'break' of a wooden plank 'from four sides', performed with power.

Shijo see *Jo*.

Shiju-hatte see *Kimari-te*.

Shikaku see *Hansoku-make*.

Shikare-waza *Kendo*. An abrupt attack from an opponent who profits from a lowering of the guard.

Shiken *Judo*. A special examination of the *Kodokan*, reserved for certain categories of *Judoka*.

Shiki see *Bushido*.

Shikiri *Sumo*. This is the name of the ceremony performed on the *Dohyo* before fighting. The two wrestlers squat down face to face (*Chiri*) and stare at each other, then get up, throw salt by the handful about the Dohyo, take up the squatting position again and strike the ground with the soles of their feet (*Shiko*). This ceremony can last as long as four minutes (for the *Maku-uchi*) and may be repeated four times. For the *Juryo* it may only last three minutes. See *Sumo, Sumotori, Shiko Tachi*.

Shikko *Aikido*. Knee-walking, beginning from the *Seiza* position (*Za-ho*). Many *Aikido* techniques are performed from this kneeling–walking movement. See *Suzari-waza*.

Shikona *Sumo*. A poetic surname adopted by the high-ranking *Sumotori* and ending in **-yama** (mountain), **-umi** (sea), **-kawa** (river), **-shio** (tide), **-nobori** (rise), **-ryu** (dragon), **-hama** (beach), **-nishiki** (brocade), and others. Every Sumotori has at least three names: his own name, the name he chooses to fight under (*Shikona*) and finally the one he adopts when he retires from competition (*Toshiyori*). Usually an honorific suffix is added to the name of a Sumotori instead of the usual *-san*. This suffix is *Seki* (*-zeki*).

Shikoro-dori see *Omote*.

Shikoro-gaeshi see *Omote*.

Shiko-tachi *Sumo*. A posture with the legs wide apart and deeply bent, like a man riding a horse, (*Kiba*). When a *Sumotori* has assumed this posture he raises one foot high, then the other, very high, and lets his foot fall heavily back to the ground. See *Shikiri, Keiko, Kiba-dachi*.

Karate. Standing posture in *Kiba-dachi*.

Shikyu see *Kyu*.

Shimei *Karate*. An *Atemi* blow which, if it were delivered with full power, could be very dangerous or fatal. In competition it brings one point (*Ippon*) to the contestant who first delivers it. See *Yamato-ryu*.

Shimeru *Kendo*. A contracting movement of the hands around the handle of the *Shinai* or *Bokken*, performed when the *Kendoka* is standing, moving or sitting. It is done to strengthen the forearms. The action consists of delivering a downward blow (*Shomen-uchi*) and contracting the muscles of the hands, wrists and forearms only at the moment when the weapon reaches its target. One or two Shinai may be used for this exercise.

Shime (-jime) 'Strangulation'.
— Shime-garami *Judo*. The bending of an arm in strangulation technique used in groundwork (*Ne-waza*).
— Shime-waza *Judo*. Strangulation techniques (*Shibori*) used in groundwork (*Ne-waza*). They can be performed in the following ways:

Using the *Judogi*:
　Face to face (*Shime-ai* or *Juji-jime*), sitting astride *Uke*, strangulation using the forearm pressing down on the throat, the hand gripping the Judogi.
　From the rear (*Ushiro-Jime* or *Hadaka-jime*).

Without using the *Judogi*:
　From the rear, strangulation of the neck using the right forearm, helped by the left hand, drawing *Uke* back off balance.

Several methods of strangulation are described:
　Kata-ha-jime, to the right of the face
　Kata-juji-jime, crossing under the face
　Gyaku-juji-jime, strangulation beneath the face with one arm
　Morote-jime, strangulation beneath the face with the palms facing down
　Hadaka-jime, strangulation from the rear with the forearm
　Ashi-gatame-jime, strangulation using the arms and legs
　Okuri-eri-jime, strangulation using the lapels

Sode-guruma-jime, strangulation using the lapels of the *Judogi* rolled up.

Shimenawa see *Tsuna*.

Shimo Also *Shita*, 'Under'. See *Space*.

Shimoseki 'Lower side'. See *Space*, *Dojo*.

Shin 'Heart', 'Mind', 'Spirit', 'Feeling'. See *Kokoro*.

Shinai. A sword consisting of four small bamboo 'blades' joined together, with a handle (*Tsuka*), a guard (*Tsuba*) made of leather hide, and a small sheath at the tip (*Sakigawa*). The weapon is used in *Kendo*. It is said that the Shinai is invested with the spirit of the real sword and must be revered as such. The weights and lengths of the Shinai vary with the age (implying build) of the user. From thirteen to fifteen (size 37) the Shinai can measure 112 cm and weigh 375 to 450 gm. From sixteen to eighteen (size 38) it must be 115 cm long and weigh from 450 to 485 gm. Finally, above nineteen (size 39) it must be 118 cm and weigh about 500 gm. Where two Shinai are used, one in each hand, the longer of the two will be 110 cm and weigh 375 gm; and the shorter one 60 cm and weigh 265 gm. The Tsuba, usually of thick leather hide or tough plastic, is about 8 centimetres in diameter; its weight is not included in the overall weight of the Shinai. See *Fukuro Shinai*, *Kendo*.

The grand master of Kendo, Takano, surrounded by his pupils with their Shinai.

Shin-bop see *Ninjutsu*.

Shin-budo see *Budo*.

Shinden Fudo-ryu. A traditional school of *So-jutsu* or *Yari-jutsu*, founded in Edo (To-kyo) by *Izumo no Kanja Yoshiteru*, (1429–41) and his successor Yoshikane. According to tradition, the art of the *Yari* was taught to the founder by the *Tengu*. His techniques remained secret until the present day. The school employs several types of Yari or lance, war axes (*Ono*), 'war hammers' (*O-tsuchi*) and *Naginata*. It was mainly the *Yamabushi* who taught in this school.

Shindo Iten-ryu. A modern school of *Aikido*, created by the disciples of *Ueshiba Morihei*.

Shinden Munen-ryu. A school of *Kendo* created towards the end of the nineteenth century.

Shindo Muso-ryu see *Jo-jutsu*.

Shindon Rokugo-ryu *Aikido*. A style of protective combat, solely defensive, created by Noguchi Senryuken, a disciple of *Ueshiba Morihei*.

Shindo Shizen-ryu *Karate*. A school founded in 1934 by Konishi Yasuhiro, a disciple of *Funakoshi Gichin* and *Ueshiba Morihei*. It put the emphasis on the spiritual development of the *Karateka* and made great use of *Kata* training.

Shindo Yoshin-ryu. A school of *Ju-jutsu* founded in the nineteenth century. See *Otsuka Hidenori*.

Shingitai. In the martial arts this means the 'triple qualities' of those who reach black belt rank. These are: '*Shin*', moral worth, character; '*Gi*', technical skill; and '*Tai*', physical development. These three qualities (*Shin-gi-tai*) are inseparable and must go hand in hand with the two basic principles of the martial arts: *Seiryoku Zen-yo*, or effective use of energy, and *Jita-kyoei*, or mutual assistance and prosperity. These principles come from the code of *Bushido*.

The *Dansha* who possess Shingitai combine within themselves, by reason of the three human qualities, the presence of the Heavens (*Shin*), the earth (*Gi*) and Man (*Tai*). Such a person is thus a 'complete man' or 'complete woman'.

Shinji-sumo see *Sechie-zumo*.

Shinkage-ryu 'New *Kage-ryu*'. An ancient school of sword-fighting, using both the techniques of unarmed combat (*Ju-jutsu*) and those of the sword. It was founded by *Kami Izumi Ise no Kami, Fujiwara no Nobutsuna* (1508–78) from the *Katori* and *Kage-ryu*, in order to improve the techniques of *Kage-ryu*. *Yagyu Tajima no Kami* (1572–1606) added some philosophical principles drawn from *Zen*, such as the '*Munen*', 'no thought' and the *Muso*, a state of total emptiness which makes the mind instantly alert. See also *Aiki-ho*.

Shinkan-ryu see *Kage-ryu*.

Shinkeito-ryu see *Matsuura Seizan*.

Shinken-shobu see *Shobu*.

Shin Kime no Kata see *Goshin-jutsu*.

Shin-ki-ryoku see *Itto-ryu*.

Shinko-Kata *Karate*. Advanced *Kata*.

Shinkyu-shiai. A competition organized for the purposes of taking a grading examination in the martial arts.

Shinobi-shozoku see *Ninja, Ninjutsu*.

Shinobu see *Obu-iai*.

Shinpan (Shimpan). A judge or referee in a martial arts competition. See *Shiai*.

Shin no Shindo-ryu. An ancient school (*Ryu*) of *Ju-jutsu*, created in the sixteenth century, according to tradition. It taught 166 combat techniques.

Shin-shinto see *Swords*.

Shin no Tachi see *Swords*.

Shintai. A technique of displacing the body by gliding the feet across the ground, with the major part of the weight placed on the outer edges of the feet (*Tsuri-ashi*). When the displacement involves rapid stepping, one foot being placed in front of the other, it is called *Tsugi-ashi*. See *Ayumi*.

Shintai-do. A system of 'religious' physical culture whose aim is the harmonious development of body, will and mind. It is based on movements derived from martial arts movements. The founder of the system was Aoki Hiroyuki, a Japanese *Karate* expert who moved to California and made his system known there in 1966. He was a pupil of Egami Shigeru of Tokyo, another famous Karate man. Aoki adapted the principles of an association also founded in 1966 called the *Rakuten-kai*, which aimed at a rational study of the Bible. In the exact words of the founder himself, 'Shintai-do must have the same value as the works of Bach and Mozart in music, of Michelangelo, Cézanne or Picasso in art, and of the great works of literature'.

This cultural movement is more religious and artistic than scientific and tries chiefly to enable the individual to express him- or herself in his or her own particular way. All teaching is based on a practical aestheticism derived from the movements of *Bo-jutsu*, *Ju-jutsu* and *Kendo*, conceived as a kind of dance and adapted 'to the Western mind' – that is to say, the Christian outlook on life. Even so, veneration is shown to light and to nature. Aoki appeals to the ancient schools (*Ryu*) of the Japanese martial arts and has adopted a specifically Japanese terminology to describe the movements. He has based these movements on the *Kata*, but considers the gestures aesthetic expressions rather than combative art. This being so, it is difficult to place it alongside the various schools of *Budo*. The practitioners of Shintai-do wear a white *Keikogi* for their exercises and either have bare feet or wear *Tabi* (H. Aoki, *Shintaido, A New Art of Movement and Life Expression*, San Francisco, 1982).

Shin-to see *Swords*.

Shinto. This is the name of the ancestral religion of Japan, as distinct from the *Bukkyo* or Buddhist religion. *Shinto* is a form of Shamanism with no central, major divinity, in which each person venerates the gods belonging to his or her personal home and land. This probably explains why the followers of this religion have not attempted to proselytize or export their beliefs.

The divinities of Shinto, or *Kami*, meaning 'higher spirits', are innumerable. In effect, every tree, every stone, every mountain or river, and every dead person may become a Kami. The physical object itself is not worshipped, but its 'spirit' is worshipped in holy places which are consecrated to it. This is done so that it will look favourably on the wishes of the devotees. The clergy who look after these holy places are secular members of society, and the priests (*Kannushi*) are elected by the villagers. The emperor himself is the chief priest of Shinto. All the Japanese people, whoever they are, belong to Shinto, although they may follow other religions. Shinto is not exclusive. All the happy circumstances of the life of men are recognized by the Kami. Death alone is seen as a blemish on that life. Also, the Japanese leave the tending of the dead to the Buddhist monks.

Shinto has no philosophy, nor any moral teaching to propose, unless it is to avoid defilement (either of body or mind). If defilement occurs, the person must 'wash'; perform ablutions with water (*Misogi*). Shinto is a very simple religion of respect for the principles of nature. The female Kami of the sun (*Amaterasu*) holds an important place, but the Japanese also venerate the great ancestors who have become Kami and are charged with the protection of their descendants. Each family thus has its own particular Kami. The ceremonies are evocations based on mythology or on the life of the Kami. Life is celebrated in all its forms, with music and sacred drama (*Kagura*). And of course, the traditional sports, such as *Sumo* and the different martial arts, are themselves also dependent on the Kami.

Shinto-ryu. A school of sword-fighting (*Ken-jutsu*) which was founded, according to tradition, by *Iizasa Choisai* (1387–1488) and

Master Noda of the Shinto-ryu practising Iai.

called by its full name, *Tenshin Shoden Katori Shinto-ryu* (see *Katori Shinto-ryu, Kashima Shinto-ryu*). This school gave birth, in the course of several centuries, to numerous other *Ryu*, among which the most prominent were:

Kashima Shinto-ryu, founded by *Tsukahara Bokuden* (1490–1571)
Tendo-ryu, founded by Saito Denkibo
Jigen-ryu, founded by *Togo Shigekura*
Honma Shinto-ryu, founded by Honma Masayoshi
Arima Shinto-ryu, founded by Arima Motonobu
Shindo Muso-ryu, founded by *Muso Gonnosuke*
Mijin-ryu, founded by Negishi Tokaku
Hozo-in-ryu, founded by Hozo-in In-ei
Ippa-ryu, founded by Moroka Kagehisa
Tenshin Sho-ryu, founded by Icchu Baichu-ken

Shinden Munen-ryu, founded by Fukui Yoshihara, around 1750,

and so on

Shinwa Taido *Aikido*. A form of self-defence created by Inoue, a disciple of *Ueshiba Morihei*.

Shioda Gozo see *Yoshin Aikido*.

Shipjin see *Poomse*.

Shirai Toru (1783–1850). A master of the Japanese sword, of the *Kijin-ryu*, famous in his time, author of a work on the techniques of the sword entitled *Hyoho Michi Shirube*, 'Travelling the Way of the Sword'. He also followed the school of *Itto-ryu*, in which he trained with a heavy *Bokken*.

Shiranui *Sumo*. An 'offensive' or aggressive style adopted by certain *Sumotori* and created by the eighth *Yokozuna* of this name (1801–54). In this style, during *Shiko-tachi*, the Sumotori stretch out the arms horizontally on each side of the body. See *Unryu*.

Shirizaya-tachi see *Swords*.

Shiro 'White'.

Shirobo see *Araki-ryu, White staffs*.

Shisei. A position assumed by a fighter for defence or counter-attack. It can be 'natural' (*Shizen-tai*) or defensive (*Gigo-tai*). See *Postures, Uchi-komi*.

Shita 'Under'. See *Space*. Also *Shimo*.

Shi-tachi *Karate, Kendo*. When *Kata* is performed, this is the name given to the contestant who faces an attack from *Semeite* or counter-attacks this move.

Shitate Dashi-nage *Sumo*. A loss of balance by one of the contestants when his or her opponent pulls him or her by using a grip which goes under the arms and holds the belt. See *Uwate Dashi-nage, Kimarite*.
— **Shitate Hineri** *Sumo*. The same movement as *Uwate Hineri*, but holding the opponent's belt by passing one arm under his or

203

Shitate Dashi-nage

Shitate Yagura-nage

her arm. See *Kimarite*.

— **Shitate-nage** *Sumo*. The same movement as *Uwate-nage*, but taking hold of the opponent's belt by passing an arm under his or her arm. See *Kimarite*.

Shitate Hineri

— **Shitate Yagura-nage** *Sumo*. The same movement as *Uwate Yagura-nage*, but with the arm holding the opponent's belt by passing an arm under his or her arm. At the same time the attacker lifts the opponent's thigh with his or her own thigh. See *Kimarite*.

Shitate-nage

Shite *Aikido*. The one who throws *Uke*, equivalent to *Tori* in *Judo*. Also called *Nage*.

Shito-ryu *Karate*. A school of Okinawan Karate created in 1928 by *Mabuni Kenwa* (1889–1952). The school uses a large number of *Kata*, about fifty, and power plays a very important role in the performance of its techniques.

Shitotsu see *Juken-Jutsu*.

Shitsu 'Crossing the knees'. See *Legs*, *Kyusho*.

Shitsui *Karate*. 'Hammer-fist'. Also *Kentsui*. See *Hands*.

Shiwari *Karate*. Training and performing 'breaking' techniques, to toughen the striking surfaces of the body and to demonstrate the power and correct application of force. Pieces of wood, tiles, stone bricks, stone blocks and ice have all been used either in demonstrations or in *Dojo* training. All parts of the body which are used as 'weapons' are used in *Shiwari*, even the head in some styles. These very spectacular feats are not accepted by all schools of Karate. They do feature very prominently in the Korean art of *Tae-kwon-do*. Also *Tameshiwari*, *Hishigi*. Vietnamese: *Nghanh*; Korean: **Kyok-pa**.

Shizen Hontai (Shizen-tai). A natural, basic posture, also called *Mukamae*. See *Shisei*.

Shiwari at the Shotokan school.

Shizhou Taidu see *Taidu*.

Shobu. Formerly this meant a fight to the death (*Shinken-shobu*) between two martial arts experts.
Sumo, Karate. Official contest.
Aikido, Kendo. Standard competition.
— **Shobu-ari** 'End of contest'.
— **Shobu-hajime** *Karate, Kendo.* With these words, 'Begin the contest', the referee indicates to the contestants that they may begin.
— **Shobu-ho** see *Kogi-judo*.
— **Shobu no Kata** see *Kata*.
— **Shobu-shimpan** *Sumo.* These are the judges in a *Sumo* contest, usually chosen from among former *Sumotori* (*Toshiyori*). There are always five of them for each contest and they do not intervene except at the invitation of the referee (*Gyoji*). They may also intervene if some important difference of opinion arises. Their conference in such a case is known as *Monoji*. If there is a failure to reach a decision they may order a restart of a contest: *Tori-naoshi*. The *Shibo-shimpan* are dressed in a *Hakama* and a ceremonial *Kimono*. Also called *Kensa-yaku*.

Shochikubai Aikido. A term composed of *Sho*: a pine representing the *Makoto*; *Chiku*: bamboo, symbolizing force and suppleness; *Bai*: plum tree, a symbol of love. The complete word is used to describe a contest between opponents using swords, as taught by certain *Aikido* masters. It is a method of fighting which combines the movements of Aikido and *Kendo*. The art is one which develops speed of counter-attacking on the part of a person who is about to be attacked, but before the actual attack is launched. It depends on 'Yomi' of the opponent's 'Kimochi'; that is, 'reading' of the opponent's 'intention'.

Shochu-geiko see *Kangeiko*.

Shodai. The title given to one who founds a *Ryu* in the martial arts. Also called *Sokei*, *Shosei*.

Shodan see *Obi, Kyudan.*

Shoden see *Omori-ryu.*

Shoden Omori-ryu see *Muso Jikiden-ryu.*

Shoes see *Geta, Zori.*

Shogun. The name *Shogun* can be translated by the word *Generalissimo.* It was a name bestowed by the emperor on the *Daimyo* who showed himself to be the richest and the most powerful of all the lords. The Shoguns of Japan ruled in an authoritative manner in the name of the emperor, who, in terms of temporal power, was no more than a figurehead. The Shogun was in charge of all the Daimyo. There were three *Bakufu* (military governments) or Shogunates: in Kamakura (1185–1333), in Kyoto (the Ashikaga dynasty) from 1336 to 1574, and in Edo (Tokyo), from 1603 to 1868 (the Tokugawa dynasty). The 'Restoration' of the Meiji era in 1868 returned all power to the emperor.

Shohatto see *Omori-ryu.*

Shomen *Kendo*. A direct blow to the head using the *Shinai.*
— **Shomen-tsuki *Aikido*.** A descending blow from the front.
— **Shomen-uchi *Aikido*.** A rising blow from the front, generally applied with the palm of the hand. It is countered by *Tenbin-nage.* See *Nage-waza.*

Sho-mokuroka. The lower grades of black belt. See *Kyudan.*
Wa-jutsu. 'A confirmed student', wearing a white *Kimono*, black belt with purple band.

Shorinji Kempo *Karate*. This is the name used to describe a modern style of martial arts created by So Doshin (Nakano Michiomi, 1911–) after the Second World War. The expression is the Japanese translation of the Chinese word *Shaolin-si*, combined with the word *Quanfa (Kempo)* which gave *Shorinji Kempo – Shaolin-si Quanfa.* The Shaolin-si was a famous Chinese monastery where forms of 'boxing' were taught to strengthen the monks' physique

and enable them to defend themselves. So Doshin worked and studied in China, and when he returned to live in Japan established his own school based on the techniques he had learned there. In 1972 it was given the name *Nippon* (Japanese) *Shorinji Kempo.* Broadly speaking, it can be described as a mixture of *Karate, Aikido and Judo.* According to its creator,

'Shorinji Kempo teaches that the body and the mind are inseparable, and that the two entities should be trained by the practice of Kempo and *Zen* meditation, in a sitting (*Za-zen*) position. In this way the individual may be able to preserve his or her own integrity and so be useful to the world. The philosophy of Shorinji Kempo maintains that the power of love, based on the teachings of the Buddha and allied to the principle of *Yin* and *Yang* (negative and positive), can enable mankind to create on earth a veritable 'paradise'. It also supports and follows the teachings of Kongo-Zen or 'Diamond Zen'.

The physical techniques of the art number some 600 postures, displacements, body movements, blocks, attacks and *Atemi.* These place the main emphasis on defence and evasion. The terminology of Shorinji Kempo is exclusively Japanese and very similar to the terms used in other martial arts, with some exceptions and variations. The chief clothing for training purposes is a *Karate-gi* or *Judo-gi* with a Swastika embroidered on the jacket above the wearer's heart. This Swastika is a symbol of esoteric Buddhism and is the reverse of the Nazi emblem. It signifies the wheel of existence from which Buddhism aims to set its adherents free. Shorinji Kempo is registered in Japan as a religion, and as such it has temples rather than training halls. The main temple is in Tadatsu in Kagawa prefecture (island of Shikoku). See *Shaolin-si, Hakko-ryu.*

Shorin-ryu Karate-do *Karate*. A school of Karate created in 1830 in Okinawa by *Matsumura Sokon* (1809–99) and developed by his disciples and successors, *Itosu Anko* (1832–1916), *Chibana Choshin* (1885–1969) and *Katsuya Miyahira* (1916–). Until 1920, it was called *Shuri-te*, and it belongs to the

Karate training of the Shorinji Kempo school.

Karate-do of Okinawa, which is the name given to the entire range of Karate styles originating from that region. Shorin-ryu puts most emphasis on the study and performance of *Kata*. See *Goju-ryu*, *Chibana Choshin*.

Shorin-ryu school movement

Shosei see *Shodai*.

Shoshinsha *Kendo*. A beginner in the study of the *Shinai*.

Shotei see *Hands*.

Shoto see *Katana*, *Swords*.

Shotokai *Karate*. A school of Karate from the *Shotokan* style, created by *Funakoshi Yoshitaka*, the son of *Funakoshi Gichin*, around 1926 in Tokyo. It seeks above all to develop the spirit of its students, trying to make Karate into an art of living rather than a sport. To this end there is emphasis on *Kime* as a means of reaching the state of *Mushin*. This school was the basis of the '*Nippon Karate Kyokai*', the Japanese Karate Association, founded in 1937.

Shotokan *Karate*. The name of the principal *Dojo* of Karate, founded in Tokyo in 1938 by *Funakoshi Gichin*, for the spreading of *Karate-do*. In Japan it is the equivalent of the *Budokan* of *Judo* and *Aikido*. The building was destroyed in 1945 and reconstructed soon afterwards.

Shoulder see *Kata*.

Shout see *Ki-ai*.

Shuai Jiao *Wushu*. Chinese physical train-

Master Nakayama Masatoshi, 9th Dan, of the Shotokan school in his Dojo in Tokyo.

ing using apparatus such as weights, dumb-bells, 'wooden men' targets or 'straw men' targets (*Muk Yan Zhong*), stone jars, etc., to build up the muscles.

Shubaku see *Ju-jutsu*.

Shubo *Karate*. 'Arm stick', a movement in which the arm is used like a stick.

Shu-fa see *Shaolin-si*.

Shugeki *Kendo*. A name for attack.

Shugendo. A body of beliefs and practices of a highly individual nature, followed by the *Yamabushi* or 'Monks who have retired to the mountains'. The former come from the esoteric Buddhist sects of Shingon and Tendai. Although *Shugendo* lays claim to a founder, E no Otsunu (*En-no Gyoja*, 'En practising it'), who lived around the year 700, and also to several more or less mythical patriarchs, its doctrines were progressively created by amalgamation with others. Shugendo venerates all kinds of Buddhist divinities belonging to the esoteric pantheon and divinities from the *Kami* of *Shinto*. The veneration springs more from superstition than from knowledge, the majority of the Yamabushi being illiterate. The more religious of the followers more or less observed a doctrine which can be summed up in the words of an eleventh-centruy Buddhist monk, Renkaku:

> The three worlds of Heaven, Earth and Hell exist only in the mind. All the *Dharma* [observances] are simple Nota-tion. To know the equality of the three spirits is called the Great Awakening. There is the essential point of the Shugen; it is the great idea which reigns over its doctrine . . . The others and myself are equal and there is no difference over this subject in our thoughts . . . If this idea is held without reserve, then of themselves the ten 'absences of good' will disappear; what a man does, whether walking, stand-ing still, sitting or lying down, will be the work of the Buddha. If he has faith in the truth that our very body is the Buddha, without going to the trouble of reaching Buddha-hood by eliminating his passions, he will no longer think of life and death . . .

These concepts echo those of *Zen* to some degree, but they were 'thought about' only by very few of the Yamabushi. In 1872 the independent sect of Shugendo was officially suppressed and its monks obliged to join the Buddhist sects of *Shingon* and *Tendai*. After the Second World War some people in Japan tried to bring Shugendo back to life, but met with little success. See *Yamabushi*.

Shugyo 'Severe training'. Those who fol-low it are called *Shugyosha*.

Shuhaku see *Kempo*.

Shui Li Fu *China*. A school of Chinese *Wushu* (*Kung-fu*), also called **Choy Lee Fut** in Cantonese, deriving from the *Shaolin-si*. It consists of an 'external' method (*Weijia*) using the fists and various weapons, and an 'internal' method (*Neijia*) using knowledge of anatomy, medicine and philosophy. The external method studies various postures and successive movements called 'Five Fists' (hands and feet). The students practise this with the help of human-shaped dummies stuffed with cotton waste, in sandbags, or dummies which are articulated so that when struck the 'joints' cause an action on the part of the dummy itself which the student must avoid or block. When weapons training takes place the dummy used is a metal one. In addition to the classical weapons, there are also a number of others such as forks and flails, iron crutches and numerous other objects. See *Wushu, Kung-fu, Shaolin-si*.

Shuko. A type of leather glove reinforced with bands of iron with hooks on the inner side, used by the *Ninja* for climbing walls. They could also be used to deadly effect as human claws in hand-to-hand combat. Also called *Tekagi*. See *Ninja, Ninjutsu, Kyusho, Ashiko*.

Shukokai *Karate*. A school of Karate created in 1948 by Tani Chojiro (1921–   ), inspired by the techniques of *Goju-ryu* and *Shito-ryu*. Some people have described it as 'artistic' but this perhaps applies to the direction it took in France under *Nambu Yoshinao*, who imported it into that country in 1965. In the United Kingdom, under the inspiration of Thomas Morris and later with the help of other British instructors, Shukokai Karate became one of the chief sources of inspiration for a new approach to competition: direct, linear and based on observation rather than tradition. (To cite the direction into which Nambu Yoshinao led the original Shukokai style would be misleading for readers in the United Kingdom.) Morris produced a book of the *Kata* of Shukokai, *Shukokai Karate Kata*, which is now regarded as a chief reference work on the subject. Nambu developed his own style continuously and drew on material from the *Noh* and *Kabuki* theatrical forms of Japan. See *Nam-bu-do, Sankukai*.

Shukon-sho see *Sechie-zumo*.

Shuriken. A Japanese throwing weapon with many different shapes such as knife-shape, star-shape, diamond-shape, etc., used in bygone days by the *Ninja*. *Shuriken* were made of steel and their edges were sharpened. They measured from 5 to 10 cm in diameter and were thrown singly or in simultaneous volleys. If they struck a vital part of the body accurately, severe injury could result. Some Ninja put poison on them. The ones which took the form of a star were called *Shaken*, the dagger-shaped ones were called *Bo-shuriken* and the ones with a hole in the middle were called *Semban-shaken*. Some of the Ninja had some very fine, needle-shaped Shuriken (*Fukumi-bari*) which they held in their mouth and blew into the eyes of an enemy.

Projectiles or Shuriken

The art of throwing the Shuriken was called *Shuriken-jutsu*. See *Ninja, Ninjutsu*.

Shuri-te see *Okinawa, Kenshikan, Shorin-ryu, Karate*.

Shushin. The principal referee in a *Budo* competition. See *Shim(n)pan*.
— **Shushin-ho.** The cultivation of the mind and of the morality which should be observed, through the study of martial arts, leading to self-perfection. See *Kogi-judo*.

Shuto 'Sword-hand'. Korean: *Sudo, Son-nal*; Vietnamese: **Chem**. Also *Te-gatana*. See *Weapons, Hands*.
— **Shuto-uchi** *Kendo*. A direct attack with the *Shinai*.
Karate. A direct attack with the 'sword-hand' (*Shuto*).

Shuto-uchi

— **Shuto-uke** *Kendo*. A defensive movement made with the back of the *Shinai*.
Karate. A blocking technique with the hand in the 'sword-hand' formation (*Shuto*).

Shuto-uke

'Shuyo Shosei-ron' see *Yamada Jirokichi*.

Shuwan 'Palm of the hand'. See *Teisho, Shotei, Hands*.

Siap see *Setia-hati Terate*.

Side see *Yoko*.

Sihap. A *Tae-kwon-do* match.

Sijak see *Hajime*.

Siku-tiga see *Setia-hati Terate*.

Sila-buah see *Bersilat*.

Sila Pulat see *Bersilat*.

Silat see *Penchak Silat*.

Similar see *Ai-uchi*.

Sim-sa Tae-kwon-do. These are the tests which practitioners undergo with a view to gaining a *Keup* or a *Dan*. The tests for the rank of 1st *Dan* include obligatory *Hyong* (*Poomse*), a freestyle competition (*Kureung-opsi, Dai Ryeun*) and a 'destruction' test (*Kyok-pa*). The attitude of the person taking the test and his general behaviour are also taken into account.

Sincerity see *Makoto*.

Sittiing see *Za, Zazen*.

Small see *Ko, Sho*.

Sobi 'Bottom of the calf'. See *Legs*.

Sochin '*So*', violence; '*Chin*', calm.
Karate. A *Kata* used in branches of *Shito-ryu* and *Shotokai*, formerly called *Hakko*. The movements of this Kata vary according to the styles, but it is composed essentially of postures such as *Sochin-dachi*, and these allow one to prepare for the principal movements of attack and defence. It is one of the basic Kata of *Shotokan*.
— **Sochin-dachi** *Karate*. A posture similar to *Zen-kutsu-dachi*, but less extended and with the front foot turned. It is sometimes

called 'diagonal horse stance'. Also called *Fudo-dachi*. See *Kiba-dachi*.

Soda 'Seventh cervical vertebra'. See *Body*.

So-dang see *Kyu*.

Sochin-dachi

Sode 'Sleeve of the *Keikogi*'.
— **Sode-guruma** *Judo*. Rolling up of the sleeve to strangle *Uke*; a groundwork (*Newaza*) technique.

Sode-guruma

— **Sodesuri-gaeshi** see *Oku-iai*.
— **Sode-tori** *Aikido*. A series of five defences against grips on the sleeve by an opponent, such as: *Jun Kata Sode-tori, Dosoku Kata Sode-tori, Mae Ryo Kata Sode-tori, Ushiro Ryo Kata Sode-tori, Ushiro Eri Kata Sode-tori*. See *Te-dori, Te-hodoki, Tachi-ai*.

Sodome see *Oku-iai*.

So Doshin see *Shorinji-kempo*.

Softness see *Ju*.

Sogo-gachi *Judo*. 'A win by combination of a penalty and a *Waza-ari*'. See Competition Rules of *Judo*, 23.

So-in see *Kyusho, Feet*.

So-jutsu. Techniques of using the lance, and performed wearing the ancient armour of the *Samurai*. Part of the *Kobudo* armoury. See *Yari*.

Sokei see *Shodai*.

Sokumen Awase Uke *Karate*. Blocking of a blow delivered with both hands to the sides.

Sokutei Mawashi Uke *Karate*. A circular block using the sole of the foot.
— **Sokutei Osae Uke** *Karate*. Blocking technique using the sole of the foot to press down.

Sokuto 'Sword-foot'. *Karate*. A blow with the foot using the outside 'cutting' edge. See *Feet*.
— **Sokuto-geri** see *Yoko-geri*.
— **Sokuto-keage** *Karate*. A kicking blow using the foot 'like a sword', rising or delivered obliquely.
— **Sokuto Osae Uke** *Karate*. A blocking technique using pressure from the 'sword-foot'.

Somakuri see *Oku-iai*.

Son see *Zen, Te*.

Song Chi see *Nihon Nukite*.

Song Con see *Jo*.

Song Cuoc see *Cuoc Phap*.

Song Dao. Vietnamese cutlass, with one cutting edge and a guard which surrounds the hand, used in martial arts training.

Song Dau *Qwan Ki Do*. 'Exchange of techniques' or freestyle combat. There are several categories:

Espoirs (13–16 years): *Tieu Do*.
Grades (from 1st to 3rd *Cap*): *Vo Nanh*
Black belts (from 4th *Cap*): *Vo Si*
Women (from 15 years): *Tieu Lo*.

Song Doi *Qwan Ki Do*. Series of techniques combining punching, kicking, sweeping and various throws.

Song Luyen *Viet Vo Dao*. Successive series of movements (*Quyen*, *Kata*) performed with a partner. There are:

a punching series: *Don Song Luyen Dam*
a kicking series: *Don Song Luyen Chan*
a series of techniques using 'sword-hand'.

Sonkyo *Kendo*. Posture keeping a middle guard (*Chudan Kamae*), legs bent, taken before or after a technique during competition (*Shobu*); it places the competitor in a position of readiness for a further attack or counter-attack.

Sumo. A ritual salute to an opponent before a contest (*Torikumi*).

Son Lam. A Vietnamese school of martial arts, 'from the mountain and from the forest'.

Sonnal see *Shuto*, *Tegatana*.

Sono-mama *Judo*. The command given by the referee in a competition which brings the two contestants to a halt in a position which the referee wishes to examine. The referee can then order them back to the centre of the *Tatami* so that the contest can be resumed, by saying '*Mata*'. Korean: **Keuman**. See Competition Rules of *Judo*, 8, 12, 19, 27, 29.

Sorashi 'False attack', 'Feint'.

Soremade *Judo*. End of the contest, ordered by the referee when he wishes to stop it. See Competition Rules of *Judo*, 20.

So-setsu-ken see *Nunchaku*.

Sosuichi-ryu 'School of pure water'. An ancient school of *Ju-jutsu*, created in 1650

by the *Samurai Fugatami Misanori Han-no-Suke*, of the *Daito-ryu* school, and following the teachings of the *Takenouchi-ryu*.

Sotai Renshu The study and training in one or several movements of martial arts, performed with a partner. See *Seiryoku-zen-yo*.

Soto 'Exterior'. See *Space*.
— **Soto-gake *Judo*.** Hooking of the outside of the leg.
Sumo. A movement similar to O-*soto-gari* in *Judo*, but holding the opponent's belt under the arms and using the opposite leg to attack the opponent. See *Kimarite*.

Soto-gake

— **Soto-Komata *Sumo*.** A technique of O-*mata* seizing the opponent's thigh from underneath and from the outside. See *Kimarite*.

Soto-komata

— **Soto-maki-komi *Judo*.** 'Outer winding throw'. A sharp movement of the hips by *Tori*, who then falls to the ground on his or her side (*Yoko-sutemi*) to bring *Uke* down in

Soto-maki-komi

a forward direction. A counter-move against *O-soto-gari*.

— **Soto-muso** *Sumo*. A technique of blocking an opponent's thigh, using the opposite hand, from the outside, accompanied by a push from the shoulder to make the opponent fall to the side. See *Kimarite*.

Soto-muso

— **Soto-shakutaku** see *Kyusho*.
— **Soto-uke** *Karate*. An outward block using 'hammer-fist' (*Tetsui*) combined with the outer edge of the forearm. It can equally well describe a block performed with the top of the fist.

Soto-shu see *Zen*.

Space. In all the martial arts which involve two or more opposing persons the notion of space (*Ma*) is fundamental. Each contestant is in the centre of a sphere and the centre of the sphere is in fact the *Hara* of the contestant. All points in space should be related to this centre of gravity, and are named in the commonly used Japanese fashion:

Right: *Migi*

Left: *Hidari*
Front: *Mae*
Rear: *Ushiro*
Side (lateral): *Yoko, Hen*
Side (superior): *Joseki*
Side (inferior): *Shimoseki*
Big, great: *O, Oki*
Small: *Ko, Sho*
Level: *Dan*
Upper: *Jo*
Middle: *Chu*
Lower: *Ge, Shino*
Inner: *Uchi*
Outer: *Soto*
Angle: *Sumi*
Opposite: *Ura*
Floating: *Uki*
Above: *Omote, Ue (ni), Kami*
Below: *Shita, Ura*
Near, within, against: *Komi*
Distant: *To*
In a circle: *Kuruma (-guruma)*
In a semicircle: *Mawashi*
Hooking: *Kagi, Kake, (-gake)*
Flat: *Hira*
Obliquely: *Naname*
see also *Suki, Ma*.

Spikes see *Shuko, Ninja*.

Ssi-reum. Korean form of wrestling, inspired by Mongolian wrestling, which is still performed during certain festivals. Wearing only a pair of short trousers, the wrestlers fight in a circular arena some 9 metres in diameter. They kneel in the entre, shoulder to shoulder, and each grips the opponent's loin cloth. At the referee's whistle, both rise and begin the contest. The first person to touch the ground with any part of the body other than the feet is the loser of that round. Bouts consist of three to five rounds. There are four weight categories: *T'ae-baek* (less than 75 kg), *Keum-gang* (from 75 to 85 kg), *Han-ra* (from 85 to 95 kg) and *Paeg-du* (more than 95 kg). The winner is called *Chon-ha-chang-sa* (the strongest under the sun).

This type of wrestling is now considered as a separate sporting discipline. It is to be found in colleges and schools, following very simple rules. Inter-university competitions and tournaments take place regularly in South Korea. Formerly winners of tournaments were awarded prizes in the form of living bulls, the animal regarded as the strongest 'under the sun'.

Today, competitions take place four times a year and winners receive enormous sums of money as prizes instead of the bulls. To some extent one could claim that it is the Korean equivalent of Japanese *Sumo*.

Sticks see *Bo, Bo-jutsu, Jo, Jo-jutsu, Kendo, Bong, Lathi*.
— **(White) sticks** (*Shirobo*) see *araki-ryu*.

Stop see *Yame*.

Strangulation see *Shime*.

Strategy see *Hyoho, Shunzi*.

Straw see *Makiwara, Pao*.

Subak see Tae-kyon, *Tae-kwon-do*.

Suburi *Kendo*. Free exercise with the *Shinai* or the sword, or a repetition of blows. It corresponds to the *Randori* of *Judo*.

Sudo see *Shuto*.

'Sugata Sanshiro'. *The Legend of the Great Judo*. A film by Kurosawa Akira, produced in 1943, about the creation of Judo during the lifetime of *Kano Jigoro*. The film had a sequel, *Zoku Sugata Sanshiro* ('Sequel to the Legend of the Great Judo'), which Kurosawa produced in 1945.

Suginami-shiai *Judo*. A competition which takes place every month at the *Budokan* in Tokyo, for students who wish to take grading examinations for *Kyu* and *Dan*.

Master Takano of Kamakura (right) in a demonstration of Iai. Here, the participants' gaze and the Ma, or space, are the same.

See *Kyudan, Ko-haku Shiai, Shiai*.

Suicide see *Seppuku*.

Suigetsu 'Solar plexus'. See *Body, Kyusho*.

Suiot see *Yasumi*.

Suisei-mushin see *Mushin*.

Suki. A sense of 'empty space' (*Suki-ku*), typically Japanese, which lets the mind fill that space or leave it empty. It influences the placing of things and the movement and location of people in space (see *Ma, Ma-ai*). It can also mean, in the martial arts, an 'empty moment' in the mind: inattention, loss of concentration, mind-wandering, bringing inevitable defeat in the face of a concentrating opponent. See also *Sugita, Bonno*.
Karate, Kendo. 'Opening'.
— **Suki-o Mitsukeru** 'To wait and see coming'. The attitude of a contestant who observes his or her opponent, waiting for the right moment to attack or counter-attack.

Sukui-nage *Judo*. 'Backward throw'. *Tori* raises *Uke* by the thighs, leaning on his or her hips, and causes him or her to fall backwards. This is what is called 'backward spoon throw'.
Sumo. Throwing the opponent with a movement similar to the *Uchi-mata* of *Judo*. See *Kimarite*.

Sukui-nage

— **Sukui-uke** *Karate*. A 'spoon' block using one arm.

Sulsa see *Ninja*.

Sukui-uke

Sumi 'Coin', 'Angle'. See *Space*.
— **Sumi-gaeshi** *Judo*. 'Corner throw'. *Tori* lets him(her)self fall on to his (her) back, drawing *Uke* forward to the right or the left, raising him or her by pushing with the leg on the inside of the thigh.

Sumi-gaeshi

— **Sumi-otoshi** *Judo*. An arm technique in which *Tori* brings *Uke* off balance by pulling the sleeve down towards the ground and pushing on the opposite shoulder, producing a fall to the side.

Sumikiri. A concept of *Shinto* in which the mind is said to reach a crystal purity and the body a kind of state of grace. It is this particular state which the martial arts practitioner must try to attain.

Sumo. The origin of Japanese wrestling, according to legend, goes back to a contest between two *Kami* for the possession of the country. In fact, *Sumo* was more likely to have originated from a contest between two enemy chiefs; one Japanese, the other probably Korean. It dates from the dawn of Japanese history.

The first Sumo contests had a religious context, being part of the rites of *Shinto* to conciliate the Kami and obtain a good harvest. They took place in the presence of the emperor (see *Sechie-zumo*) and the rules of the contests are very different from those which are in force today. After the Nara period, which saw the unification of Japan under the rule of the emperor residing at Nara, then in Kyoto (called at that time Heian-Kyo), Sumo tournaments were organized each year. *Sumotori* faced one another, having flocked from all corners of Japan to take part in the event. Little by little, rules were established for these contests and during the period in which the military clans were in power, at the beginning of the twelfth century, Sumo became a military art (*Joran-zumo*). It changed into *Ju-jutsu*, but its religious aspect remained separate from affairs of war. It was mainly during the Edo period (1603–1868) that it extended and spread its influence, for at that time the country was relatively peaceful. The Sumo which was developed then is the Sumo we know today.

The rules are very simple. Matches or contests (*Torikumi*) take place in a special circular arena, the *Dohyo*, which is covered with a roof shaped like that of a Shinto sanctuary. To score a point, the wrestlers (*Sumotori* or *Rikishi*) must cause any part of the opponent's body to touch the floor, or push him outside the circle using one of the forty-eight techniques which are permitted (*Kimarite*). Blows, hair-pulling, strangulations, and kicks are all forbidden. The wrestlers can help their efforts by gripping the belt (*Mawashi*) of the opponent, but it is forbidden to grip that part of the belt which circles over the sexual organs (*Mae-tate-mitsu*). Wrestlers are often very heavy indeed, some weighting over 230 kg, as there is no weight category in Sumo and a light wrestler may be confronted with a giant opponent twice his own weight. Everything depends on suppleness, speed and skill.

Six tournaments are organized every year: three in Tokyo and the others in Osaka, Nagoya and Fukuoka. Each lasts fifteen days, during which every wrestler faces a different opponent each time. The winner of every tournament, the Rikishi who has

Drawings by Hokusai: Sumotori having his belt tightened (Mawashi); Sumotori in training.

gained the greatest number of victories, receives the Emperor's Cup. The other recognized prizes are the *Shukun-sho* for the wrestler who has thrown the most *Yokozuna* (Grand Champions) and *Ozeki* (Champions), the *Kanto-sho* awarded to the Sumotori who has displayed the most fighting spirit, and finally the *Gino-sho* awarded to the best technician. However, to receive a prize the Sumotori must have won at least eight out of his fifteen contests. Each day of the *Sumo* tournament follows a ritual course, under the supervision of a referee-in-chief (*Tate-gyoji*) and several referee-judges (*Gyogi*). At the beginning the *Dohyo-iri* takes place. This is the ceremony of presenting the participants in the tournament, clad in their ceremonial aprons (*Kesho-mawashi*). They are led in by the Yokozuna attended by a herald (*Tsuyuharai*) and a sword-bearer (*Tachimochi*). The Yokozuna wear a huge cord around the waist, made of hemp (*Tsuna*), bringing to mind the ones which decorate the entrances of Shinto sanctuaries (*Shimenawa*). The Yokozuna file on to the

Sumo competition.

Dohyo, then one by one the Sumotori divide into two camps, known as East and West. When the first pair has performed the small *Shikiri* ceremony and thrown salt around the arena to purify it, the first contest begins. At the end of the day, a low-ranking wrestler (*Maku-shita*) performs the dance of the bow (*Yumi-shiki*). Sumo tournaments are very popular in Japan and television never fails to show all the contests of the tournaments. The Japanese are fervent admirers of the Sumotori.

Sumotori *Sumo.* This is the general name used to describe Sumo wrestlers. (They are also called *Rikishi.*) The wrestlers are ranked according to a hierarchy based on the number of wins scored in tournaments. Newcomers are called *Uchi-deshi* and belong to the lowest rank (Mae-zumo). The wrestlers in the highest rank (*Maku-uchi*) include the Grand Champions (*Yokozuna*), the Champions (*Ozeki*), the *Sekiwake*, the *Komusubi*, and the *Mae-gashira*. Ranks 2, 3 and 4 are called collectively the 'three

217

Leg-strengthening exercises.

higher' (*Sanyaku*). After these champions come the *Juryo* (10 *Ryo*, of the 5th level), the *Maku-shita* (4th level), the *Sandanme* (3rd level), the *Jo-nidan* (2nd level), the *Jo-no-kuchi* (1st level) and finally the beginners or newcomers (*Mae-zumo*). An apprentice Sumotori may reach the rank of *Sekitori* (*Maku-uchi* and *Juryo*) only after at least two years of practice and training. All Sumotori belong to a 'school' or 'stable' (*Heya*) which is generally run by a former Yokozuna or *Toshiyori*. Before every tournament the names of the wrestlers who are to take part are written with special characters on notices called *Banzuke* (ratings) and published by the Japanese Sumo Association.

Sumotori fight barefoot and naked to the waist. They wear a loin covering (*Mae-tate-mitsu*) and a thick silk belt (*Mawashi*). Their hairstyle comes from ancient times and is called *O-icho-mage* or *Chon-mage*, according to the category to which a contestant belongs. Every Sumotori has a special name under which he fights his contests (*Shikona*). In 1986 there was only one Yokozuna in Japan; there were 37 Maku-uchi, 26 Juryo, 120 Makushita, 200 Sandanme, 316 Jo-nidan and 132 Jonokuchi. See *Sumo*, *Sechi-zumo* and the italicized words within these entries; *Ozeki*, *Yokozuna*.

Sune-gakoi see *Oku-iai*.

Sune Uke *Karate*. A defensive move performed with the leg placed obliquely.

Shunzi (Shun-tzu). A fourth-century BC Chinese military strategist from the state of Qi. According to tradition it was he who created the first techniques of combat and military strategy. He is also credited with the formation of a female army. But he is best known for his treatise on warfare, *Shunzi Bingfa*, in eighty-two chapters; only thirteen have reached our times. This is the oldest work on martial arts known to us. Japanese *Sonshi*.

Sun-tzu (-tze) see *Shunzi*.

Suo Taidu see *Taidu*.

Superior (Upper, High) see *Jo*, *Kami*, *Shang*.

Suriage-waza *Kendo*. A technique in which the attacker lifts the opponent's *Shinai* with his or her Shinai in order to make an opening for an attack. The lifting of the Shinai and the attack are made in one unbroken sequence.

Suri-konde *Karate*. Oblique attack.

Suso-harai *Sumo*. A movement of sweeping an opponent's foot with one's own foot, with similarities to the *De-ashi-barai* of *Judo*.

Suso-harai   Suso-tori

218

— **Suso-tori** *Sumo*. A technique of grasping and pulling an opponent's ankle, causing him to fall. See *Kimarite*.

Sute-geiko *Judo*. A kind of special training reserved for high-ranking *Judoka*.

Sutemi. 'Sacrifice', literally 'to risk one's life (in order to win)'. The sense of self-sacrifice has always been deeply rooted in the being of the Japanese people. Since the sixth century at least they have been fed on the Buddhist idea of the impermanence of all things. In particular the *Samurai* and *Bushi* were aware of this fact, due to the perilous nature of their calling, and they likened life to the cherry blossom: so fragile, so easily blown away by the wind. They did not put the same value on life as the peoples of the West. In effect, for them life had no meaning except in death – but not just any form of death; not a useless and pointless death, an involuntary or unexpected death. Death finds its meaning in sacrifice, which then gives its full significance to the act of living. And the Samurai who, with a light heart resulting from *Kokoro*, sacrifices his existence in the service of his lord or for the sake of a cause, had the feeling that by dying he created life. This is why the notion of sacrifice was always so important in Japan. The idea of death was of course present in the martial arts to the same extent as the idea of life. Ideally, its presence never left the warrior's awareness for an instant, for in the end he was truly living with death itself. See *Hagakure*.

— **Sutemi-waza** *Judo*. In the ancient techniques of hand-to-hand combat, as in modern Judo, the technique of sacrifice is placed at the service of victory; not the victory of the individual, who in the last analysis has little importance, but the victory of the whole. In present-day martial arts this is a technique of winning. Such techniques are called 'sacrifice techniques' and are mainly found in Judo and *Aikido*. They involve throwing oneself to the ground in order to bring down the opponent; a movement of 'self-abandon' in making an attack, or in responding to one. *Judo*. Sutemi are classed in two distinct categories: the *Ma-sutemi*, or 'sacrifice on the back', and the *Yoko-sutemi*,

or 'sacrifice on the side'. See *Nage-waza*.

— **Suwari-waza.** Techniques of studying movement, performed kneeling down. See *Za-ho*, *Shikko*.

Swords. The oldest swords found in Japan, the *Ken* or *Tsurugi*, were probably imported from the Korean peninsula. They were straight, double-edged weapons, used by mounted archers who came to Japan in the third century. Examples of these swords have been found in their megalithic sepulchres or *Kofun*. The blades were iron-forged and of poor quality. It was probably at the beginning of the ninth century that the Japanese smiths began to improve their methods, perhaps following those of the Chinese and Korean smiths whose eighth century blades are preserved in the Shoso-in museum in Nara. The Japanese smiths were also *Shinto* priests, because their role of making swords was regarded as sacred.

The smiths who were working at the end of the Heian period and during the Kamakura period (until 1333), as well as those of the Muromachi (1333–1530), reached a perfection of technique which has never been surpassed. The name *Koto* is given to these ancient blades of unequalled quality. During the period of the Ashikaga Shoguns (1336–1574) the decoration of blades and the fittings of swords enjoyed its greatest flowering. This continued during the Edo period, when a new type of blade known as the *Shin-to* (new sword), also of high quality, was produced. These blades were not, according to connoisseurs, equal to the swords of the 'ancient' period. After the restoration of the Meiji era (1868) very many swords were manufactured, not for the use of the *Samurai* but for army officers and members of the police force. These were the *Shin-shin-to* (recent blades) which, by reputation, were inferior. Curved swords appeared towards the eighth century, although no documentation is available to give us a precise date. Since that time, all sword blades of Japanese origin have been curved, with one cutting edge on the convex side. From then onwards, swords took on various dimensions and forms which, although very diverse, were classed as follows into two distinct types.

Short sword: Wakizashi; long sword: Katana, on the sword stand.

The *Tachi* were worn hanging from the belt, had a strong curve, and were quite long. They were used at first for fighting but increasingly became merely dress swords. The *Yefu-no-Tachi* were swords reserved for the imperial palace guards and for certain nobles (*Kuge*) of high rank. The *Shozoku-tachi* (or *Shin-no-tachi*) were part of the costume worn on ceremonial occasions by nobles at the imperial palace. Certain noble warriors wore the *Shirizaya-tachi* its scabbard covered with bearskin, fur on the outside. But all these weapons gave way very quickly to the second type of sword, with a smaller curve, the *To*, which was worn, probably from the beginning of the fourteenth century, slipped inside the belt, or *Obi*. The high-ranking *Bushi* (*Samurai*) were distinguished from others who could wear a sword by the fact that they were permitted to have two swords: a long one (*Daito*, also called *Katana*) and a shorter one (*Shoto* or *Wakizashi*). The pair of swords was called *Daisho*. Mounted warriors sometimes additionally used a very long sword, or *O-dachi*, for fighting on horseback (see *Ba-jutsu*). The sons of the Bushi also wore a sword, smaller than a normal sword, called *Mamori-gatana* (protective sword) which was regarded, perhaps with good reason, more as an amulet or lucky charm than as an effective weapon. See *Katana*.

Among the 'short' swords, which we would more readily describe as daggers, are included the *Tanto* (less than 31 cm) and the *Aikuchi*, similar to the Tanto but without a guard (*Tsuba*). The *Kaiken* were a type of knife, sometimes quite luxuriously decorated, carried by women who concealed them in the folds of their garments, especially in the pleats of the traditional *Kimono*. The weapon could be used for self-defence should the need arise, and for performing ritual suicide (*Seppuku*) by cutting the throat, when circumstances required it.

Swords and daggers always included a handle (*Tsuka*), sometimes a guard (*Tsuba*) and a scabbard with more or less decoration, the *Saya*. The Samurai always took great care of their swords, keeping them spotless and never allowing any blood to remain on the blade when it was replaced in the scabbard. (See *Chiburi*).

The old blades are very much sought after by collectors, and can sometimes fetch astronomical prices. They are rarely found on the market, but the Japanese smiths still make swords for tourists and martial artists. It goes without saying that these mass-produced swords, not made by specialists, have none of the traditional qualities associated with Japanese swords. During the Kamakura period large numbers of swords were exported throughout Asia, especially to China and Thailand, as they were one of the more highly prized Japanese products . . . Nowadays, since the valuable swords cannot be purchased, collectors concentrate on collecting the *Tsuba* or decorated guards. These are often very beautiful, covered with gold or silver, and are also highly prized.

A whole range of terms exists to describe the forms and decorations of these Tsuba, as well as the different parts of the sword blade and the accessories which accompany them, such as the *Kozuka* and *Kogai*, small knives fixed to the scabbards of the *Katana* or *Wakizashi*. The different parts of the handle and scabbard of a sword also have their own extensive terminology. The scabbards of swords, when not in use, were sometimes furnished with cotton or silk cords (*Sageo*) which were knotted in a complicated and attractive fashion. Finally, the sword stand, 'put to rest', was called a *Katana-kake*, and the box in which a sword was placed during a journey was known as a *Katana-zutsu*. The *Ninja* sometimes used a very short sword, with a straight blade, which included a small dagger (*Ko-ugi*) slipped into the scabbard. The handle of this sword often concealed a point dipped in poison. The scabbard of this same sword could sometimes be used as a blowpipe.

The terms used to describe the parts of the sword are as follows: *Saya*, meaning scabbard; guard or *Tsuba*; a small piece of wood thrust through the handle (*Tsuka*) to keep its covering in place, known as *Mekugi*; *Ha* or cutting edge; *Yakiba* or tempered part of the cutting edge; *Mune* or back of the blade; *Kissaki* or point of the blade; *Nakago* or tang of the blade; the holes for the Mekugi, generally two, or *Mekugi-ana*; the designs engraved on the blade or *Horimono* (when they were inscribed in Sanskrit they were known as *Bonji*); *Mei* or engraved name of the smith; *Same* or skin surrounding the handle; *Habaki* or copper piece enabling one to fix the *Tsuba* to the blade, etc.

The forging of blades fell to the artisans who were also *Shinto* priests. They passed on their craft from father to son, keeping their methods secret – so secret, in fact, that some have never reached the present day. In general the blade began life as an iron ingot. This was cut in two, and inside the two parts other pieces of metal of different degrees of hardness were placed. The whole was then hammered at suitable temperatures until the new pieces were absorbed, and finally forged to the desired shape. Then, once the blade had been filed down and correctly blanced, it was heated several times and plunged in salt water, the cutting edge being protected by a glaze so that it could be submitted to a different temperature. Finally the blade went to the polisher, who had to give it its final appearance and produce the necessary cutting edge. It often took several months to finish a blade, which then acquired a quasi-sacred role. There were several lines of famous smiths, who belonged to regional 'schools'. One of the most famous was *Goro Masamune* (1264–1343). See *Katana, Wakizashi, Bokken, Shinai.*

— 'Sword-arm' see *Wanto.*
— 'Sword-hand' see *Shuto, Tegatana, Cuong Dao.*
— 'Sword-foot' see *Sokuto.*
— Sword (Chinese): *Jiang.*
— Sword (Vietnamese): *Guom, Dao, Doan Guom, Viet Long Guom.*

T abi. A type of Japanese ankle sock, made in such a way that the big toe is separated from the others. They are worn to protect the feet inside the house. Certain Tabi are known as 'working Tabi'. Made of tough canvas, with a rubber sole, they are used by workers in factories and on gantries.

Tablier see *Kesho-mawashi.*

Tachi (-dachi) 'To stand or remain standing'. Korean: *Seuggi.* Also *Tatsu.* See *Postures, Swords.*
— **Tachi-ai** *Judo.* Defensive techniques (*Kime-no-kata*) performed in a standing position. These techniques are composed of twelve movements:

1. *Ryote-dori*: when seized by both wrists, *Tori* draws both arms towards his or her rear and strikes *Uke* in the groin with the knee. The technique continues with the application of an armlock on Uke (*Waki-gatame*).
2. *Sode-tori*: When seized by the sleeve by *Uke*, *Tori* delivers a heel kick to Uke's kneecap and continues with a throwing technique.
3. *Tsugake*: *Tori* evades a punch to the face by turning his or her body and causes *Uke* to lose balance by accentuating the movement. He or she continues with a strangulation from the rear (*Hadaka-jime*).
4. *Tsuki-age*: *Tori* avoids an uppercut by pushing *Uke*'s arm upwards and sending Uke backwards. The movement continues with an armlock (*Waki-gatame*).
5. *Tsuri-age*: *Tori* evades a punch to the face by raising *Uke*'s arm and countering with a strike to the solar plexus. The movement continues with a hip throw.
6. *Yoko-uchi*: *Tori* avoids a punch to the temple by stepping to the side and applying a rear strangulation technique.
7. *Ke-age*: *Tori* evades a kick to the groin by seizing *Uke*'s ankle and giving a kick to the same area.
8. *Ushiro-dori*: When *Tori* is gripped by both shoulders from the rear, he or she swiftly kneels down and throws *Uke* over his or her shoulder with *Seoi-otoshi* technique.
9. *Tsu-komi*: When *Uke* tries to stab *Tori* in the abdomen with a knife, Tori moves to

the side and responds with a punch between the eyes and an armlock.
10. *Kiri-komi*: A descending knife attaack aginst *Tori* is blocked by both hands. Tori then raises *Uke*'s knife-arm and applies an armlock taking the arm under his or her armpit.
11. *Nuki-gake*: As *Uke* tries to draw his or her sword, *Tori* stops the movement before the weapon can be drawn and continues with a strangulation technique.
12. *Kiri-otoshi*: *Tori* evades a sword blow by moving to one side and applies a lock with his or her arms on *Uke*'s leg, around the knee joint.
Sumo. The first attack in a contest.
— **Tachi-ate** *Wa-jutsu.* An identical technique to *Kao-ate*, but performed in a standing position.
— **Tachi-hiza-gatame** *Wa-jutsu.* An identical *Kata* to *Hiza-gatame*, but performed standing.
— **Tachimochi** see *Yokozuna.*
— **Tachi-oyogi** 'Standing swimming'. A technique which enabled a warrior clad in armour to move in a vertical posture through the water. He moved his legs like a frog and his arms in 'dog paddle' fashion.
— **Tachi-rei** see *Rei.*
— **Tachi Son** see *Thu Phap.*
— **Tachi-waza** *Judo.* Fighting techniques performed in a standing posture, which include hand techniques (*Te-waza*), hip techniques (*Koshi-waza*), and leg techniques (*Ashi-waza*). They are part of the *Nage-waza* and the *Nage-no-kata.*

Tae 'Foot'. See *Tae-kwon-do.*

Tae-kwon-do. '*Tae*', foot; '*Kwon*', fist; '*Do*', way. A Korean form of *Karate*, created in 1955 from the old training system of martial arts, *Tae-kyon* (or *Subak*), 'unarmed combat'. This system was originally the preserve of the *Hwa-rang*, young noblemen influenced by Confucianism who banded together to form a patriotic society during the unification of Korea in the Silla dynasty, around 600. Under the Japanese occupation from 1910 the teaching of Tae-kyon was forbidden and replaced the teaching of Karate and *Kempo* based on Chinese martial arts forms. The blending of these three styles gave birth to *Tae-kwon-do*. It is now a defensive sport whose credo is never to attack first.

Like all present-day martial arts, Tae-kwon-do aims for a perfect synthesis between body, mind and nature. Its combat techniques make great use of flying kicks and include, in addition to methods of training (*Hyong*), competitions and 'breaking' tests (*Kyok-pa*) on wooden boards. The teaching of striking the vital points (*Keupso*) of the body is also included. Tae-kwon-do does not teach hand-to-hand combat.

The uniform worn is very similar to a Karate uniform. The grading system is divided into ten *Keup* (*Kyu*) and ten *Dan* grades but the belts worn are different from those used in other martial arts, generally broader and thicker. Contests last for three rounds of three minutes with thirty-second breaks between rounds. Each contest is judged by two judges, a judge-referee and four line judges. Protective equipment (*Hogu*) is obligatory. There are ten weight categories: below 48 kg, from 48 to 52 kg, from 52 to 56 kg, from 56 to 60 kg, from 60 to 64 kg, from 64 to 68 kg, from 68 to 73 kg, from 73 to 78 kg, from 78 to 84 kg and over 84 kg.

Tae-kwon-do followers number some fifteen million worldwide (100 countries) and several thousand in Great Britain. Notable instructors include Rhee Ki Ha, David Oliver and Hee Il Cho (visiting from the USA). The sport was admitted as a demonstration element of the Korea national games in 1962 and was presented in the Olympic Games, also as a demonstration event, in Seoul in 1988.

Tae-kyon also *Subak*. See *Tae-kwon-do*.

Tae-rig-gi see *Kong Kyeuk*.

Tai 'Body'. Also *Mi*. 'Physical posture, or awaiting a contest in a perfect state of alertness'. See *Ken, Omote*.

Tai-chi Chuan see *Taiji Quan*.

Taidu *Kung-fu*. These are the on-guard positions (see *Kamae*) which are the bases of all the movements:

Shang Taidu, in a high stance with one hand in front

Suo Taidu, both arms crossed in front of the face, 'like a locked door'

Baozi Taidu, 'leopard stance', facing to the front but with the hands drawn back to make claws, at shoulder height.

Long-dong Taidu, 'eastern dragon posture', one hand in front of the forehead, palm facing outwards, the other level with the lower abdomen, palm down.

Nu Taidu, 'crossbow stance', one hand on top of the other in front of the abdomen.

Li Taidu, 'plough posture', one fist on the stomach and the other extended to the side.

Laohu Taidu, 'old tiger stance', weight thrust well forward with both hands in the shape of tiger claws, level with the shoulders.

Bai Hok Taidu, 'white crance stance', one knee raised high, palms facing outwards level with the eyes.

Yang-liu Taidu, 'willow leaf posture', feet crossed, one arm extended to the side, head turned to the side, the other arm bent across the chest, shoulder high, with the hands wide open, palms down.

Long-nan Taidu, 'southern dragon posture', *Ma-bo* stance, one hand in claw shape level with the throat, the other with fingers extended, palm facing the floor, level with the pubic bone.

Long-xi Taidu, 'western dragon posture', one arm extended downwards, the other bent across the upper part of the extended arm.

Bao-zi Taidu, 'high leopard stance', weight to the rear, one arm bent above the head and the other held forward; the forward palm forming leopard claws.

Hu-zi Taidu, 'monkey posture', weight forward, one hand in a claw shape palm down level with the eyes, the other hand held behind the body.

Tian-di Taidu, 'heaven and earth stance', *Ma-bo* leg position, one arm bent vertically with the palm in the 'sword-hand' position in front of the face, and the other in a similar position held in front of the groin.

Shi-zhou Taidu, 'four sides posture', *Ma-bo* stance, arms extended sideways.

Houzi   Longzi   Bao-zi   Shandian   Long Dong   Li Taidu

Feng   Shizhou   Lu Taidu   Binjing Chitang   Yingfu   Shang

Yueshi   Tiandi   Baozi   Nu Taidu   Bai-hou   Laohu

Suo   Yang-li   Long-nan

Lu Taidu, 'stag posture', both arms held in front at different heights.

Feng Taidu, 'phoenix stance', bending with the weight on one leg, in a type of half cross-legged position, sitting on the heel, the other leg extended to the front; one arm ahead and one bent on the chest.

Yue-shi Taidu, 'eclipse posture', with one foot ahead, fists crossed at the throat.

Pinjing-chitang Taidu, 'placid lake posture', one leg in front, arms bent back as if to give a back punch to the rear and to the side.

Ying-fu Taidu, 'ready stance', feet apart, hands in claw shape with palms up, level with the hips.

Taihen-jutsu see *Tai-jutsu*.

Tai no Henko *Aikido*. A turning movement of the body to avoid an attack, so that it can be neutralized. At the end of the movement the two opponents find themselves side by side, looking in the same direction. See *Tai-sabaki*.

Taiho-jutsu. A system of defence and attack created in 1947 by the Japanese police, incorporating diverse techniques which were judged to be effective, taken from *Ju-jutsu*, *Karate*, *Kendo*, *Bo-jutsu*, *Judo* and other recognized martial arts. This system was revised and improved up to 1968, but is still studied and examined in order to bring in refinements and adapt it to new conditions of street fighting. It makes great use of the *Keibo*, a short police baton, in a range of techniques called *Keibo-soho*, as well as the extending tubular baton (*Tokushu Keibo*) which was adopted by the Japanese police in 1966.

Taiji. 'Supreme ultimate', 'Great breath', the name given in China to that higher entity, identified in practice with the *Qi* (*Ki*) or Total Energy. Korean: *Taegeug*.
— **Taiji Quan** *China*. 'Supreme ultimate fist', a system of martial arts whose roots are lost in antiquity. A traditional founder is the elusive Taoist Chang Zhangfeng, but his life, dates and history are legendary rather than historical, according to reliable modern researchers. The art itself consists of slow, connected series of movements whose practice reduces tension, slows down the breath, clears the mind and produces long-term benefits to health which have been medically examined and proved. Training in *Taiji Quan* is divided into three: solo form done alone, pushing hands training with a partner and various weapons forms, also done alone or with a partner. There are several styles of *Taiji Quan*: Yang, Chen, Sun, Wu and in modern times various synthetic forms such as the Twenty-four Step Beijing Form, the Combined Form, and so on.

During training the student learns to move correctly, to sink his energy, *Qi*, to the lower abdomen, and how to let the Qi circulate freely through the body. This training includes a deepening understanding of the relationship between the *Yin* and the *Yang*. In training with a partner the student learns how to yield to a push, not resist it, so that the partner's energy is used to upset the

Exercises of Taiji Quan (T'ai-chi Chu'an).

partner's own balance. The partner in turn learns how to prevent this from happening. In studying the Taiji weapons, principally the classical double-edged straight sword, students learn how to apply the same principles that they have learnt in the 'unarmed' training. Taiji Quan was originally part of the Taoist *Dao* (Way), leading to harmony with nature and with one's fellow human beings, but in modern times this ideal has deteriorated in many cases and led to a much 'harder' combative approach to the art, even with competitions being held; something which is contrary to the fundamental Taoist principles.

Many teachers with a more traditional bent approach Taiji Quan by teaching ideas related to the 'three principles' of *Jing*, *Qi* and *Shen*. *Jing* is 'vital essence' which everyone receives at birth; *Qi* is the vital energy circulating through the body' and *Shen* is spirit. The aim is said to be to transform the *Jing* into *Qi* by 'nourishing the breath', and to transform the *Qi* into *Shen*, or spiritual power, in order to reach what is called the *Xu* or 'emptiness' (the *Shunyata* of the Buddhists). While one direction of Taiji Quan training is a spiritual one, the other benefits the muscles and bones by influencing the *Yi*, a principle governing those organs.

An important link in training is the effect

Movements of Taiji Quan. Drawings based on the movements of a Chinese master.

which the art has on the breath. By naturally influencing the depth and tempo of breathing the transformation of *Jing*, *Qi* and *Shen* is assisted. Breathing in (*Yin*), and breathing out (*Yang*) become harmonized and focus the *Qi* on the special point below the navel known as the *Dantian* or 'cinnabar field'. The theory is that this centralized energy can be released in a gradual or sudden, explosive release of energy, as well as forming part of the process of inner transformation. It must be said that much of the knowledge of Taiji Quan has been lost in its transmission from teacher to pupil, who in turn becomes a teacher, and so on. Most Chinese martial arts claim to make use of similar principles in their application to combat.

Taiju 'Weight'. The force of gravity which gives stability to a contestant and enables him or her, when this gravity is well rooted, to maintain good balance, centred in the *Hara*.

Tai-jutsu. A very ancient art of fighting, sometimes called *Koshi-no-mawari*, from which all the others, notably *Ju-jutsu*,

have emanated. It is not known precisely what form it originally took, but it was rediscovered and codified in the sixteenth century by a certain Nagao. It is now part of the *Kobudo* teachings. *Tai-jutsu* includes *Daken Tai-jutsu*, or the art of delivering *Atemi* blows, *Ju-tai-jutsu*, or the art of hand-to-hand combat, and *Taihen-jutsu*, the art of moving silently, falling and using *Sutemi*.

Taikai. 'Big meeting', or championship, tournament, training course. See *Ryu*.

Taiko. A face-to-face position taken by two combatants.

Taikyoku no Kata *Karate*. A collection of six *Kata* designed to achieve mastery of body movement.

Tai-otoshi *Judo*. 'Body drop'. *Tori* bends forward, stretching out his or her right leg and drawing *Uke* forward over the barrier provided by that leg, causing *Uke* to fall heavily forward.

Tai-sabaki. A rotation of the body brought

身勿太低、
太低勁斷

偏勁髙太

膝彎
重心
易下
坐

Tai-otoshi

about by the displacement of the feet with *Tsugi-ashi* steps. This produces a pivoting effect, forward or backward, and is used to avoid an attack or prepare for an attacking or defensive movement. See *Tai no Henko*.
Aikido. This is basic to Aikido movement, with *Te-hodoki*. It consists of three phases:

Koshi-sabaki, concentrating on the placing of the hips and pelvis
Ashi-sabaki, study of the displacement of the feet and legs
Te-sabaki, concentrating on the arms and the hand movements.

See *Tenkan-ho*.

Tai no Sen. When a defender takes the initiative at the moment when his or her opponent attacks. See *Ken-no-sen, Sen, Sen-no-sen, Go-no-sen*.

Taishi 'Great Master'. See *Wa-jutsu, Hi-gi*.

Taisha-ryu see *Kage-ryu*.

Taisho. The leader or captain or a competing team, whatever form the competition may take.

Tajima no Kami see *Yagyu-ryu*.

Takagi-ryu. A school of martial arts featuring a particular technique which was developed in the eighteenth century, called 'three sticks' (*Rensa Sankaku*), used as a defence against an opponent with a sword.

Taka-inu see *Inu-oi-mono*.

Takechi Zuizan *Kendo*. A sword master (*Ken-jutsu*) from the province of Tosa, born in 1829, died in 1865. He studied the art of the sword in Edo, then established his own school in Tosa. He returned to Edo in 1861, joined the emperor's partisans, and on his return to Tosa organized a group of *Samurai* determined to uphold the cause of the emperor against the *Shogun*. When he was defeated, Takechi Zuizan committed suicide.

Takeda. A *Samurai* family whose most famous member was Takeda Nobumitsu (1162–1248). He reorganized the techniques of warfare which were traditionally used by the *Minamoto* (*Genji*) family, called *Genji-no-Heiho*. Considered by some to be equally famous was Takeda Shingen (1521–73), author of *Shingen Hatto*, a code of provincial laws. His death inspired Kurosawa Akira to make the film *Kagemusha*. See *Genji-no-Heiho*, *Oshiki-uchi*.
— School of *Aikido*, a modern one.
— **Takeda-ryu.** A school of *Yabusame*, still active, sometimes called *Hosakawa-ryu*.
— **Takeda Taka Tadami no Kami Soemon** see *Araki In-yo-ho*.

Takeda Sokaku (Minamoto no Masayoshi). A martial arts master (1858/1860–1943), born in Aizu of a family of *Shinto* priests. From the age of thirteen he studied the art of the sword in the *Ono Itto-ryu* school and obtained his licence four years later. He then became the disciple of various masters among whom, perhaps, was *Sakakibara Kenkichi*. Rather than become a priest himself he led a wandering life after the style of the *Ronin*, cutting down his opponents indiscriminately until the authorities confiscated his sword. In 1888 he married and decided to open his own school of martial arts, the *Daito-ryu*. Even so, he continued his wanderings and met *Ueshiba Morihei* in Hokkaido around 1900–15, awarding him the title of 'master of *Ju-jutsu*'. He worked in Hokkaido for the police, spreading complete panic among all the numerous gangsters in the area. Many stories are told of his exploits at this time. He was reputed to be invincible with the sword, but his moral reputation was dubious. His son, Takeda Tokumine, born in 1916, succeeded him as head of the Daito-ryu, having also been an instructor to the police. See *Sakakibara Kenkichi*.

Takenouchi Hisamori see *Kogusoku-jutsu*, *Takenouchi-ryu*

Takenouchi-ryu. A school of self-defence using short weapons (*Mijikai-mono*), founded in 1532 by *Takenouchi Hisamori* (*Toichiro*). He called the school *Kogusoku* because it was designed to teach how to defend oneself against warriors clad in lightweight armour, and *Kogusoku* was the name given to that type of armour. Then the school adopted unarmed combat methods (*Ju-jutsu*) and added the art of immobilizing an enemy by using cords (*Hojo-jutsu*), the art of the *Naginata* and short sword. At one time it taught some 630 techniques, but only approximately 150 have survived. The school is also known by the name *Hisamori-ryu*.

Taki-otoshi see *Omote*.

Taki-shugyo. A series of exercises of a strongly ascetic nature consisting of remaining completely still under a waterfall (*Taki*), meditating at the same time. The purpose was to attain supernatural powers. *Yamabushi* and *Ninja*, as well as some other adherents of martial arts schools with an 'esoteric' aspect, performed these exercises whilst making specific *Mudra* which were supposed to confer particular moral powers upon them. These practices 'beneath the waterfall' are still ritually observed by certain religious people and martial artists.

Takuan Zenshi. A *Zen* Buddhist monk (Takuan Shuho), who lived from 1573 to 1645; a master of the Tea Ceremony (*Chanoyu*) and an artist. He founded the temple Tokai-ji at Shinagawa and was the Abbot of the Daitoku-ji temple in Kyoto. He was a great expert with the sword, and taught the art to *Miyamoto Musashi*. He made various 'secrets' (*Hiden*) of the martial arts known in two books, *Hontai* and *Seiko*, and developed the concept of *Mushin*.

Tambo (Tanbo) see *Bo*.

Tameshi-giri. A method of training with the sword by cutting green bamboo or clumps of straw clean through with one stroke. This action is meant to test whether the stroke is 'true', and is used in the training of *Ken-jutsu and Iai-jutsu* students. *Tameshi-giri* is no longer used in modern schools of *Iaido*. In the Edo period a swordsman was advised to test the edge of his sword and his cutting skill on human bodies; either those of criminals or corpses. Writings on sword techniques describe the way in which such cutting methods should be carried out so that they are done perfectly. The approach to this grim subject was coldly surgical. Later the use of bodies was brought to an end, on the one hand because it became more and more difficult to procure them, and on the other because it was easier to use green bamboo or clusters of straw. Certain schools of *Ken-jutsu* still practise the art on these latter objects, especially for demonstration purposes.

— **Tame-shiwari** *Karate*, *Tae-kwon-do*, *Qwan-ki-do*. Test of a student's capacity to break objects such as wooden boards, bricks, etc. See *Shiwari*.

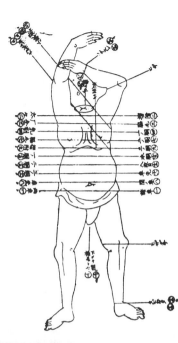

Above: Cuts to be practised on the bodies of condemned criminals. A custom used by the Samurai to test their new swords.

Opposite: Art of cutting green bamboo, demonstrated by Master Nakamura Taizaburo.

229

Tam The see *Kokyu*.

Tham Thiet Gian see *Nunchaku*.

Tanaka Goshin-jutsu. A style of *Ju-jutsu* created in 1952 in Tokyo by *Tanako Tatsu*, who eliminated all kicking techniques and taught a syllabus of some 150 fundamental movements. See *Goshin-jutsu*.

Tanaka Tatsu see *Tanaka Goshin-jutsu*.

Tanashita see *Oku-iai*.

Tanchu see *Kyusho*.

Tanden. A point located some two finger-widths below the navel, equivalent to the *Hara* of Buddhism. It is regarded as the spiritual centre of man, where all physical and psychic forces are centred. This is the spot which must be concentrated upon in order to cause the *Ki* to act. 'Any art of mastering the *Tanden*', says Sato Tsuji, 'consists in this: after one has set free all the energies spreading through the entire body, one must direct and concentrate them in the Tanden. This art was taught from time immemorial in all *Budo* schools, in *Geido* [arts] and in *Sado* [the art of sitting]'. The central point of the Tanden is called *Seika Tanden*, the Japanese translation of a Chinese expression (*Dantian*) meaning 'cinnabar field'. The substance cinnabar is coloured red, like blood, and symbolizes the vital force. It is also called *Kikai*, 'sea of Ki', *Seika-no-itten*. See *Hara, Haragei, Ki, Aiki*.

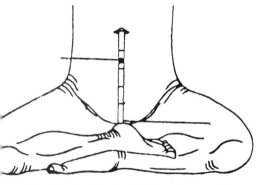

Drawing showing the Tanden point some 2 cm below the navel.

Tandoku Renshu *Judo*. Training in pure Judo, with no striking techniques. See *Seiryoku-zen-yo*.

Wa-jutsu. A method of training alone, going through one or several movements without the assistance of a partner.

Tang Lang Quan Pai (Tong Long Quan Pai) 'Praying Mantis Fist'. A style of *Wushu* belonging to the 'external style' (*Weijia*), created around 1650 by a *Shaolin* monk, Zhu Fudo, also known as Dongxing or Wang Lang. It divided into other branches such as 'Northern Style' or 'Seven Stars Praying Mantis' (*Qixing*) and the 'Southern Style' (*Zhugar*). Both these schools have their own specific movements, characteristic postures and favoured weapons: hook sword, flexible lance, iron rings, for *Qixing*; bracelets and iron belts, nine-section whip, iron staffs, etc., for the Southern Style. Vietnamese: *Duong Lang Phai*. See *Wushu*.

Tang Soo Do. A type of Korean *Tae-kwon-do*.

Tani Chojiro see *Shukokai*.

Taninzu-dori *Aikido*. An attack from several opponents in rapid succession.

Tani-otoshi *Judo*. 'Valley drop'. *Tori* lets him(her)self slip to the ground on his or her side, stretching out one leg along the ground, and pulls on *Uke*'s sleeve, causing him or her to lose balance backwards and fall on his or her side. See *Omote*.

Tan Phap *Viet Vo Dao*. Basic positions of *Vo Sinh* as follows:

> *Chuan-bi Tan*, feet spread apart, fists at the hips
> *Dinh Tan*, posture with weight forward, fists raised,
> *Ma Tan*, weight of the body on the rear leg
> *Ho Tan*, crouching down, legs very wide apart
> *Trung Bing Tan*, 'horse-riding' stance
> *Chao Ma Tan*, 'cat stance'; see *Neko-ashi*
> *Cung Tan*, archer posture, feet spread wide apart

Xa Tan, snake posture, left foot in front of right, in a straight line
Sa Tan, crouching to one side with weight on that side
Quy Tan, one knee on the ground
Hac Tan, crane stance, one leg raised, arms spread wide apart.

Tanren. A theory expressed by *Miyamoto Musashi*, according to which one must train continually along the lines of the theory if one wished to reach self-perfection.

Tanto. A sword-shaped dagger, less than 30 cm long, with a slightly curved blade. It resembles a small *Katana*, with all the same characteristics. It is worn in the belt. See *Katana*, Swords.
— **Tanto-jutsu.** The art of fighting with the *Tanto*. It is not practised as a sport.

Tao see *Dao, Do*.

'Tao Jeet Kune-do' see *Bruce Lee*.

Tao Phong Cuoc *Qwan Ki Do*. Techniques of sweeping an opponent off balance using one foot:

With the foot, inwards, a direct attack
Again inwards using a technique called 'double'
Backwards, with the outstretched leg, leaning on both hands
Backwards, calf against calf, with a turning movement
Directly backwards, tibia against calf.

See *Cuoc Phap*.

Tare (-dare) see *Kendo, Dogu, Men*.

Tasshi *Wa-jutsu*. Title given to a 'Higher Master'. He wears a white jacket, a brown or black *Hakama*, and a purple belt with four red bands.

Tatami. A type of mattress made of very tightly compressed, woven straw taken from the rice plant. The border is covered with stitched cloth. This matting has an average size of 188 × 94 cm, between 6 and 8 cm thick. It was used to cover the floorboards in noble houses and palaces from the seventeenth century onwards. Before this time the floors consisted of bare but highly polished wooden boards, and people sat on tightly

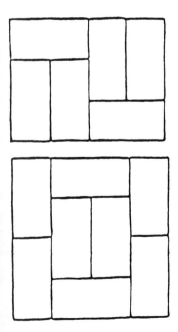

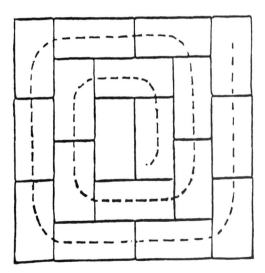

Arrangement of Tatami to form a spiral beginning in the centre.

compressed, woven cushions called *Zabuton*. Towards the end of the nineteenth century the use of Tatami spread into most houses in Japan. Shoes are not worn on Tatami, so that the surface is not soiled or damaged. As they are relatively soft compared with wood or concrete flooring, Tatami were adopted for use in martial arts training halls, *Dojo*, to soften the students' falls when they are thrown or lose their balance. Today they are covered with strong canvas, and often the straw has been replaced by modern synthetic materials which are compact but at the same time resilient, such as densely packed foam. The Tatami are laid to cover all the necessary space. In Japan, the size of a room is described in relation to the number of Tatami of the recognized, average size which will cover the floor. A surface which is equivalent to two Tatami placed side by side along the longer edge forms a square 188 × cm. This surface measurement is called *Tsubo*, and is used to indicate the size of a garden as well as that of a room.

Tate. From '*Tatsu*', to stand up straight; whence vertical, standing. See *Tachi*.
— **Tate-empi** *Karate*. An elbow blow delivered through a vertical plane, generally rising forward. Also *Tate-uchi*, *Tate-hiji*.
— **Tate-gyoji** see *Gyoji, Dohyo, Sumo*.
— **Tate-hiji** see *Tate-empi*.
— **Tate-hiza** *Kendo*. A defensive posture, sitting on one heel, the other leg bent at the knee with the sole of the foot on the floor.
— **Tate Sankaku-gatame** *Judo*. Control of *Uke* by *Tori* from the side, in a triangular formation used in groundwork (*Ne-waza*). See *Osae-waza*.
— **Tate Shiho-gatame** *Judo*. Control of the 'four corners' or 'four quarters' of *Uke* by *Tori*, in groundwork techniques (*Ne-waza*). See *Osae-waza*.

Tate-Shiho-gatame

— **Tate Shuto Uke** *Karate*. Blocking of a blow using 'sword-hand' (*Shuto*) in a vertical direction.
— **Tate-uchi** see *Tate-empi*.
— **Tate-zuki (Tate-tsuki)** *Karate*. A punch given with the fist, palm along a vertical plane.

Tate-tsuki

Tatsu see *Tachi, Tate*.
— **Tatsu-jin.** 'Vertical man', meaning 'the one who does not fall'; a title given to a *Kendo* expert or in sword-fighting.

Tay-son Nhan. A Vietnamese martial art, 'Mountain Phoenix'.

Tawara-gaeshi *Judo*. 'Rice bale throw'.

Tayu-jiai (-shiai). A competition between experts from different styles or belonging to different *Ryu*.

Te 'Hand'. Also *Shu*. See *Karate, Okinawa-te*, etc. Korean: **Son**: Vietnamese: **Chem**.
— **Te-dori** *Aikido*. 'Gripping by the hands or arms'. The term given to a series of counters to seven attacks:

1. *Jun Kata Te-dori*
2. *Gyaku Kata Te-dori*
3. *Dosoku Kata Te-dori*
4. *Ryote Kata Te-dori*
5. *Mae Ryote-dori*
6. *Ushiro Ryote-dori*
7. *Ushiro Oshiage Te-dori*.

See these names; *Te-hodoki*.
— **Te-gatana** *Aikido, Karate*. 'Sword-

hand'. Also *Shuto*. Vietnamese: **Chem**: Korean: **Sonnal**. See *Weapons*.
— **Te-guruma *Judo***. A throw executed with the hands, turning the body and twisting the hips.

Te-guruma

— **Te-hodoki *Aikido***. 'To untie the hands'. A series of fundamental movements used for defence, using *Tai-sabaki* or 'rotating displacement of the body'. The aim of the movements is to free oneself from an opponent by gripping the hands and by throwing. There are seven defences against grips to the wrist (*Te-dori*), five against grips to the sleeves (*Sode-tori*), nine against grips to the neck (*Eri-tori*), two against grips to the hair (*Kami-tori*) and four against grips to the belt (*Kumi-tsuki*). See also *Rofuse*, *Kote-gaeshi*.
Wa-jutsu see *Ate-waza*.
— **Temoto *Kendo***. The rigid part of the blade of a sword or *Shinai*. Can also mean the grip of the hand on the Shinai.
— **Te-nagashi Uke *Karate***. A blocking technique against a blow using a sweeping action of the hand.
— **Te-osae Uke *Karate***. A blocking technique using a pressing action of the hand.
— **Te no Uchi *Kyudo***. The gripping of the bow by the hand. See *Yugamae*. **Kendo**, *Iai-do*. The gripping of the *Shinai* or *Katana* by the hand.
— **Te-waza *Judo*, *Tae-kwon-do*** (*Suki*). 'Hand techniques'. In Judo, these techniques include three movements: *Uki-otoshi*, *Seoi-nage* and *Kata-guruma*.

Tea Ceremony see *Cha-no-Yu*.

Technique see *Jutsu*, *Waza*.

Teiji-dachi *Karate*. A standing posture with the feet in a 'T-shape'. See *Hidari Teiji-dachi*.

Teshin-ryu see *Kito-ryu*.

Teisho 'Base of the palm of the hand'. See *Shuwan*, *Hands*.
— **Teisho Awase Uke *Karate***. A block performed with the palm of the hand, sometimes combining with another block.
— **Teisho-tsuki *Karate***. A blow delivered with the base of the palm of the hand.
— **Teisho-uchi *Karate***. An attack made with the base of the palm of the hand (the 'heel' of the hand), usually at an opponent's face.

Teisho-uchi

— **Teisho-uke *Karate***. A block using the palm of the hand.

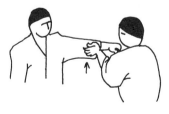

Teisho-uke

Teisoku 'Sole of the foot'. See *Feet*, *Sokuto*.

Tekagi see *Shuko*.

Tekkan-zu see *Bankoku-zu*

Tek-fa see *Shaolin-si*.

Tekki *Karate*. The general name given to three advanced *Kata*: *Tekki Shodan, Tekki Nidan, Tekki Sandan*. They are performed alone or with a partner, and have a certain similarity to the Kata of the Okinawan styles and the Northern Chinese styles (*Shaolin*). At one time they were done on horseback; hence the position of *Kiba-dachi*. See *Heian Kata*.

Tekubi 'Wrist'. See *Hands, Arms*.
— **Tekubi Kake Uke** *Karate*. Blocking by using a hooking action of the bent wrist.
— **Tekubi-osae** *Aikido*. The fourth principle (*Yonkyo*) of the *Katame-waza*, by twisting the wrist, used against *Shomen-uchi* and *Mune-dori* attacks.
— **Tekubi-undo** *Aikido*. Exercises for stretching and making the wrists supple.
— **Tekubi-waza** *Aikido*. Wrist techniques, including a strong pressure on the arm (*Kote-gaeshi*) or a twist of the wrist (*Kote-hineri*) of the opponent.

Tenaga-dalem see *Setia-hati Terate*.

Tenbin-nage *Aikido*. A movement of defence agianst *Shomen-uchi* and *Katate Ryote-dori* attacks. See *Nage-waza*.

Tenchiken see *Giwaken*.

Tendo see *Kyusho*.

Tengu. Mythical beings found in ancient Japanese folklore. Some have wings (*Ko-tengu* or 'small Tengu'), others take the form of crows (*Karasu-tengu*); sometimes they have very long noses (*Konsha-tengu*). The chief Tengu, known as Sojobo, has an insignia of a fan with seven plumes. Tengu inhabited the mountains and were reputed to be skilled in martial arts. It was they who taught the art of the sword to Minamoto no Yoshitsune. See *Yamabushi*.
— **Tengu Gei-jutsu-ron** see *Itsusai Cho-zanshi*.

Tenjin Shin-yo-ryu. A style of *Ju-jutsu* created in Osaka as a branch of *Yoshin-ryu* by *Iso Mataemon*, who died in Edo(Tokyo) in 1862. The style was based on 124 *Atemi* techniques which he amalgamated with the techniques of Yoshin-ryu and of *Shin-no-shindo-ryu*. Iso Mataemon had some 5,000 disciples and his school was famous for its Atemi techniques, immobilizations (*Osae*) and strangulations (*Shime*). See *Tenshin Shin-yo-ryu*.

Tenkan(-ho) *Aikido*. A movement of pivoting the body (*Tai-sabaki*) by sliding the feet over the ground in a circle. It is used at the same time as the technique of *Irimi*, or not resisting an opponent's pull or push. It is one of the fundamental movements of this discipline. When the defender makes a semi-circle around his or her axis, the movement is called *Zen-tenkan*. See *Irimi*.

Ten no Kata *Karate*. 'Kata of Heaven'.

Tenshi-nage *Aikido*. A series of 'breathing' throws, part of the *Nage-waza* series and used against attacks which use *Ryote-dori*, *Hiji-dori* and *Yokomen-uchi*.

Tenshin Shin-yo-ryu see *Tenjin Shin-yo-ryu*.

Tenshin Shoden Katori Shinto-ryu see *Katori Shinto-ryu*.

Tento see *Kyusho, Head*.

Tento-ryu. An ancient school of *Naginata* for women.

Tenugui. A small strip of lightweight cotton, long enough to circle the head and be tucked into place like a very small turban. It has several uses in Japan. *Budoka* use it to wipe the sweat from their bodies or as a bandage. When it is worn round the head it is called a *Hachimaki*. *Kendoka* wear it under the helmet (*Men*) to protect the head.

Ten-yo Kai see *Tenjin Shin-yo-ryu*.

Teppo see *Keiko* (Sumo).

Terada Ken-emon see *Jikishin-ryu, Kito-ryu*.

Demonstration in the style of the Shin-yo-ryu school.

Terama Heizaemon see *Kito-ryu*.

Terao Katsunobu see *Miyamoto Musashi*.

Te-sabaki see *Tai-sabaki*.

Te Sao see *Nhao Lan*.

Tessen. A flat fan, not folding (*Uchiwa*) or folding (*Ogi*), made of iron. It was used by officers in ancient times to indicate to their troops which manoeuvres to make in battle. When it was skilfully handled, this fan could be used as a defensive or offensive weapon. See *Uchiwa*.

A Kendo student (centre) placing a small rectangular piece of cloth around his head. This white cloth, Tenugui, fits under the helmet (Men). Kendo school, Shimonoseki.

Tessei no Yari. A lance made entirely of iron, including a handle, sometimes used in warfare.

Te Trouc see *Nhan Lam*.

Tetsubishi. This implement was a type of calthrop with four or six points, used by the *Ninja* to cover their retreat. At least one point protruded vertically from the ground and was intended to pierce the feet of the pursuing enemy.

Tetsui (Tettsui) 'Iron hammer'. See *Weapons*.
— **Tetsui-uchi** *Karate*. A fist blow, delivered with the little finger edge with a backward, reaping action.

Tetsui-uchi

235

— **Tetsui-uke** *Karate*. The technique of blocking a blow by delivering a 'hammer-fist' blow on the forearm of an opponent.

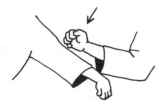

Tetsui-uke

Thai Boxing (*Muay Thai*) see *Kick-boxing*.

Thaing. A system of Burmese martial arts, mainly using techniques of self-defence, either unarmed (*Bando*) or armed (*Banshay*). Each ethnic group has its own style. There are also some styles of boxing (*Lethwei*) and wrestling (*Naban*) in Burma, but these cannot be counted as martial arts. The styles of Bando are very similar to *Muay Thai* or Thai Boxing (see *Kick-boxing*).

Tham Thiet Gian see *Nunchaku*.

Thanh Long. 'School of the Green Dragon' of Vietnamese martial arts.

Than Phap *Qwan Ki Do*. Techniques of displacement. There are several types:

With large steps sliding forward: *Xa Hanh*
With sliding steps: *Di Than*
With leaping steps: *Thiem Tu Qua Hai*
With sideways displacement in a U-shape: *Dao Than*
An evasive step, with one leg raised high: *Di Anh*
Legs bent, advancing as if to attack: *Chuyen Than*, etc.

Than Xa see *Phuong Duc, Thu Phap*.

Thap Thu see *Quyen*.

The Thu see Thu *Phap*.

Thiem Tu Qua Hai see *Than Phap*.

Thien see *Zen, Zazen*.

Thiet Giap see *Phong Duc*.

The doi Luyen *Qwan Ki Do*. 'Technique of five steps', including blocks and postures combined with displacements (*Dao Than*).
— 'Technique of three steps', simplified.

Thieu Lam see *Shaolin-si*.

Thoi see *Yame*.

Throws see *Nage, Vat*.

Thuong see *Yari*.

Thuong Dang see *Kyudan, Jodan*.

Thu Phap *Viet Vo Dao*. There are at least three main on-guard positions:

Slightly forward, as in Western boxing
The fist on the same side of the body as the leading leg is held low
One knee raised above the belt, fists level with the face.

These guards are also called *The Thu*. See *Kamae*.

Qwan Ki Do. Fist techniques:

Direct: *Thoi Son*
Direct-reversed (using the fist on the opposite side to the advancing foot): *Di Son*
'Circular': *Dao Son*
Vertical, in front: *Bat Phong Son*
Sweeping backwards: *Ta Chi Son*
Travelling forward, an uppercut: *Than Xa Son*
A horizontal swing: *Hoang Phong Son*
Vertical, using the back of the fist: *An Long Son*
Using both fists, bringing them together: *Long Tien*
Vertical, to the side: *Khoa Hau*.

Tien Bong see *Jo*.

Tieu Do see *Song Dau*.

Tieu Lo see *Song Dau*.

Tieu Tan see *Bo Phap*.

'Time' see *Jikan*.

Tian-di Taidu see *Taidu*.

Tjabang see *Penchak-silat*, *Sai*.

Time-keeping clock. This instrument (or chronometer) is used by referees in competitions to keep time during a contest and for judging immobilizations, as well as for any other time-check which the rules governing the type of competition require. In Japanese-based events the command *'Jikan'* is equivalent to the English word 'Time'. See Competition Rules of *Judo*, 2, 5.

To 'Swords'. See *Katana*, *Swords*, *Tegatana*, *Shuto* . . .
— **'Head'**. See *Head*.
— **'China'** (this comes from the Japanese name for the Tang dynasty).
— **'Far'**.

Tobi 'Leap', from Tobiageru, to leap. See *Keri*.
— **Tobi-geri** *Karate*. A leaping or jumping kick. See *Mae-tobi-geri*, *Yoko-tobi-geri*.
— **Tobi-komi-ashi** *Karate*. A technique of sweeping away an opponent's legs by leaping against them.
— **Tobi-komi Tsuki** *Karate*. A punch delivered while jumping (in the *Shotokan* style) or while taking a step forward (*Wado-ryu* style).
— **Tobi-konde** *Karate*. The action of leaping forward to meet an opponent.
— **Tobi-yoko-geri** *Karate*. A leaping side-kick.

Toda-ryu see *Chujo-ryu*.

To-de see *Okinawa-te*.

Togakure-ryu. A school of *Ninjutsu*, created in the twelfth century by Daisuke Nishina and still active in Iga. Also *Iga-ryu*.

Togasagake. An ancient exercise of firing a bow and arrow on horseback. Hats (*Kasa*) were used as targets, placed far (*To*) – that is, some 80 to 100 metres – away, on the top of stakes. The arrows were muffled (*Hikime*). See *Yabusame*, *Kasagake*.

Togo Bizen no Kami Shigekura (1563–1643). A *Samurai* from the province of Satsuma (Kyushu), who founded the *Jigen-ryu* school of swordsmanship.

Toho see *Weapons*.

Toho-sen. Combat on foot, as distinct from *Kiba-sen*, combat on horseback. See *Ken-jutsu*.

Toi 'Distant'. Used to describe an opponent who is out of range.

To-jin-ho *Karate*. Particular break-falls used for landing on a hard surface, not covered with *Tatami*. See *Ukemi*.

To-jutsu see *Ken-jutsu*.

Toketa *Judo*. Coming out of an immobilization in groundwork (*Ne-waza*). See *Osae-komi*, Competition Rules of *Judo*, 8, 15, 27.

Tokugawa. This *Daimyo* family provided Japan with fifteen *Shoguns* who made up the Edo Shogunate. The founder, *Tokugawa Ieyasu* (1542–1616), was a former general of *Toyotomi Hideyoshi* and the emperor named him as Shogun in 1603. He established himself in Edo and set to work to unify the country. After he had conquered the followers of Toyotomi's son in the Battle of Sekigahara (1600), he succeeded in taking their last castle, that of Osaka, in 1615 and 1616, but died from the effects of a wound. His son, Hidetada, succeeded him as Shogun, a post which had become hereditary. The last of the Tokugawa Shogun, belonging to a collateral branch of the family, Keiki, abdicated in favour of the emperor in 1868. This brought to an end the Edo *Bakufu*.

Tokui 'Particular', 'Favourite'.
— **Tokui-tsuki** *Karate*. Favourite punching technique.
— **Tokui-waza** *Judo*. Favourite technique of a *Judoka*.

Tokushu-keibo see *Taiho-jutsu*.

To-ma see *Ma, Keri.*

Tomari-te see *Okinawa-te, Kenshikan.*

Tomiki Aikido. A style of Aikido derived from the teachings of *Ueshiba Morihei,* with the distinction of freestyle competition (*Randori*) forming part of its training programme. Each contestant takes it in turn to attack his or her partner with a solid rubber knife. When a point is scored the defender takes over the use of the knife, and so forth, until the time allowed for the contest is over. One of the leading teachers in the United Kingdom is Dr Lee Ah Loi, who wrote two definitive books on the syllabus of the style: *Tomiki Aikido,* vols 1 and 2.

Tomita-ryu see *Chujo-ryu.*

Tomoe. A decorative comma-shaped motif, often used on the surfaces of drums and the tips of tiles, as well as in the adornment of weapons. There are two definite uses of the *Tomoe.* One, *Futatsu-tomoe,* consists of two 'commas' overlapping, head to tail, resembling the sign of the *Dao,* which represents the combination of *Yin* and *Yang* in Chinese philosophy. The other is the *Mitsu-tomoe,* a combination of three commas in a circle, somewhat analogous in their arrangement to the Ancient Egyptians' and Greeks' sign of Trismegistus, which was adopted by the alchemists of the Middle Ages. This latter symbol represents the intimate union of three rotating energies: the Trinity, the unceasing Creation and destruction of phenomena.
— 'Circle', 'Round', 'Curved line'. See *Space.*
— **Tomoe-jime *Judo.*** Strangulation 'in a circle' during groundwork (*Ne-waza*).
— **Tomoe-nage *Judo.*** 'Circle throw'. *Tori* lets him(her)self fall backwards to the ground (*Ma-sutemi*), with one leg bent up and placed in *Uke*'s groin. Tori pulls Uke forward as he or she falls backwards, and with the aid of the raised leg and hands sends Uke up and over to fall beyond Tori's head. See *Sutemi.*

Tonfa. A narrow piece of wood, usually hardwood, between 45 and 60 cm long.

Tomoe-nage

Three-quarters along its length is fixed a rounded handle, at right angles to the 'blade'. It was used by the peasants of Okinawa as a weapon against sword attacks. The 'blade' could be raised, protecting the forearm and body; then, by means of a swing or thrust, the attacker could be struck in return. The weapon is usually used in pairs. Like other Okinawan weapons taught in martial arts schools, the Tonfa was developed from a farming implement, in this case the handle of a rice-grinding mill. Its use as a weapon dates from the seventeenth century following the Japanese invasion. It weighs about one kilo. It is sometimes called *Tuifa* and is found as part of the *Kobudo* armoury. In addition to the basic attacking and defending techniques, it has its own *Kata.* In modern times it is most frequently found in *Karate* schools. Vietnamese: *Moc Can.*

Tong (Thong) see *Zori.*

Tong-bei Quan *Wushu.* A school of combat, popular in China, which uses very rapid, precise kicks and punches.

Tonki see *Shuriken.*

Tora-bashiri see *Oku-iai.*

Tori *Judo.* This is the name given in training and contests to 'the one who conquers' as distinct from *Uke,* who is 'the one who is conquered'. In *Aikido* Tori is called *Shite* or *Nage.*
— **Tori-kumi *Sumo.*** 'Encounter' or 'match' between two *Sumotori.* See *Sumo Sumotori, Dohyo.*
— **Tori-naoshi** see *Shobu-shimpan.*

Training with the Tonfa in an Okinawan Dojo.

— **Tori-te** An ancient form of *Ju-jutsu*.
— **Torite Kogusoku** see *Araki-ryu*.

Torimasen *Karate*. This is the word used to describe a situation in a contest when neither of the contestants has used a technique.

Toshiyori *Sumo*. The title given to a *Sumotori* of high rank (generally one of the *Yokozuna*) who has retired from competition. Such men usually direct one of the 'stables' (*Heya*) of Sumotori or become contest judges (*Gyoji*, Shobu-shimpan). See *Sumotori*.

Toshu-kakuto. A 'close-combat' method used in the Japanese army since 1954 and perfected by Major Chiba Sanshu. It resembles *Taiho-jutsu*.

Toshunobu. 'Attack with bare hands' as distinct from *Bukinobu*, 'attack with a weapon'. See *Goshin-jutsu*.

Tottari *Sumo*. A forward throw executed by locking an opponent's arm against one's chest and tipping him or her down. See *Kimarite*.

Tottari

Towaki see *Oku-iai*.

Toyama-ryu *Iai-do*. A school of *Iai* founded by *Nakamura Taisaburo*, (born 1911). All the techniques are performed in a standing position from eight fundamental postures (*Kamae*). There are eight cutting methods (*Happo-giri*, *Kiri-tsuke*, *Tameshi-giri*), whose principal aims are speed and effectiveness.

Toyotomi Hideyoshi (1536–98). A Japanese general who succeeded Oda Nobunaga and became a military dictator. He was named *Kampaku* (First Minister) by the emperor in 1586, and after the assassination of Oda Nobunaga he tried in his turn to unify the *Daimyo* in the provinces. He also tried to invade Korea, but his troops were repulsed, with heavy losses, by the Chinese in 1598. His own general *Tokugawa Ieyasu*, defeated the followers of Toyotomi's son at the Battle of *Sekigahara* (1600) and was then made *Shogun* by the emperor in 1603. He established the Tokugawa Shogunate in Edo.

Tozawa Tokusaburo see *Ueshiba Morihei*.

Tozume see *Oku-iai*.

Training see *Keiko*, *Thyong*.

Tram Tach, Tram Xa see *Cuong Dao*.

Tritunga see *Setia-hati Terate*.

Truc Cuoc see *Cuoc Phap*.

Trung Binh Tan see *Bo Phap*.

Trung Dang see *Chudan*.

Trung Hoa see *Quyen*.

Truong Dang see *Kyudan*.

Tsu 'Head'. Also *To, Atama, Kashira*.
— **Tsu-ate** *Aikido*. Blows to the head: front, side and back.

Tsuba. The guard of a sword or a *Shinai*. The *Tsuba* of the Shinai was formerly made of leather hide, but now is almost always made of tough plastic. The Tsuba of swords is always made of metal, though there are leather Tsuba for swords, lacquered and used in parades. The metal Tsuba are magnificently decorated, especially the ones made in the seventeenth and eighteenth centuries; they are very much sought after by collectors. They are usually in the shape of a flat disc, pierced in the centre with a roughly oblong opening to allow the blade to be inserted; the latter is held in place by a copper ring called a *Seppa*. Two oval openings in the sides are for the *Kogai* and the *Kozuka*. Two other small holes were sometimes worked into the Tsuba (in the older examples) to allow an attaching cord, the *Udenuki-ana*, to be passed through.
— **Tsubazeri-ai** *Kendo*. This is a term used to describe a situation in which two contestants are so close to each other that the *Tsuba* of their *Shinai* are touching.

Tsubame-gaeshi *Judo*. A counter-hold against *De-ashi-barai, Harai-tsuri-komi-ashi, Sasae-tsuri-komi-ashi, Okuri-ashi-barai*.

Tsubo see *Tatami*.

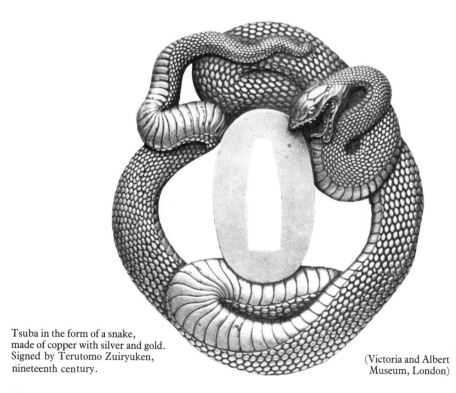

Tsuba in the form of a snake, made of copper with silver and gold. Signed by Terutomo Zuiryuken, nineteenth century.

(Victoria and Albert Museum, London)

Tsubu-neri see *Zubu-neri*.

Tsugake see *Tachi-ai*, *Idori*.

Tsugi 'One after the other'.
— **Tsugi-ashi** *Judo*. Steps taken by sliding the feet forward on the toes, one after the other. See *Ayumi-ashi*, *Shintai*.

Tsuji Getten Sakemochi see *Mugai-ryu*, *Hyodo*.

Tsuka. The handle of a sword, dagger or *Shinai*. Can also mean the way a handle is gripped. see *Katana*, *Sword*, *Shinai*.

Tsukahara Bokuden. A *Samurai* (Urabe Tomotaka, 1489–1571) who applied the concept of *Ken-no-Shinzui* (see *Mutekatsu*) and advocated an imperturbable spirit (*Fudo-no-seishin*) during combat.

Tsukami-uke *Karate*. A technique of blocking a blow by seizing an opponent's arm or leg.

Tsukami-uke

Tsuki (-zuki) 'Blow', 'Throat', 'Moon'.
See *Iri-tsuki*, *Keri-goho*.
Kendo. A direct thrusting attack at an opponent's throat; also the name given to the piece of cushioned material (*Tsuki-dare*) fixed beneath the grille of the helmet (*Men*) to protect the throat. See *Sashi-men*.
Karate. A direct attack with the fist.
— **Tsuki-age** see *Tachi-ai*, *Ju-no-kata*.
— **Tsuki-dare** *Kendo*. Throat protector (see *Tsuki*).
— **Tsuki-dashi** *Sumo*. A sharp push with both hands on the opponent's chest, sending him backwards. See *Kimarite*.
Judo see *Ju-no-Kata*.

Tsuki-dashi

— **Tsuki no Kokoro** 'Mind like the moon'. A state of concentrating the mind before starting a movement or beginning combat. It is a totally detached state which can see what is taking place in the environment, down to the smallest details; a global consciousness of the surroundings, just like the moon, seeing everything around it, but not affected by what it illuminates. See *Mizu-no-Kokoro*, *Kokoro*.
— **Tsuki-otoshi** *Sumo*. A twisting, powerful action which turns the opponent to the side so that he or she turns over the supporting leg. See *Kimarite*.

Tsuki-otoshi

— **Tsuki-taoshi** see *Kimarite*.
— **Tsuki-uke** *Karate*, *Kendo*. A stopping blow.
— **Tsuki-waza** *Karate*, *Kendo*. A direct blow. See *Jun-tsuki*, *Gyaku-tsuki*.
— **Tsuki-zue.** *Kata* using the medium-sized staff (*Jo*). See *Jo-jutsu*.

Tsukinami-shiai *Judo*. A competition specially organized for taking grading examinations. See *Kyudan*.

Tsukomi *Karate*. A punch delivered in

241

such a way that the chest inclines forward. Also called *Gyaku-tsuki*. See *Tachi-ai, Idori*.
— **Tsukomi-jime** *Judo*. Strangulation (*Shime*) carried out with application of weight during groundwork (*Ne-waza*).

Aikido. When *Uke* grips *Shite*'s left lapel and jacket to turn him or her, Shite draws slightly backwards, passes the right arm over and between Uke's arms, then leans on his or her own right elbow with the left hand and forces Uke to the ground. The technique ends with a blow at an *Atemi* point to Uke's face. See *Eri-tori*.

Tsukuri *Judo*. A counter-attack in which *Tori* upsets *Uke*'s balance by pushing or pulling on his or her arm or wrist. The effectiveness of the technique depends on its originating from the *Hara*, the body's centre of gravity. It is also a preparatory movement prior to making an attack or a counter-attack by a displacement of the body. See *Aite-no-tsukuri, Jibun-no-tsukuri*.

Tsuma 'Toes'. See *Feet*.
— **Tsumasaki** 'Tips of the toes'. See *Feet*.
— **Tsuma-tori** *Sumo*. A blocking action against the leg of an opponent who is trying to lift his or her rear leg. The attacker also pushes at the same time with his or her other hand on the opponent's buttocks to make him or her fall forward.

Tsuma-tori

Tsuna *Sumo*. A very thick cord made of hemp, bigger and thicker in the middle and twisted on the left side, similar to rice-straw ropes (*Shimenawa*). It is found at the entrance of *Shinto* sanctuaries and indicates the sacred nature of the place. It may weigh between 13 and 15 kg and is decorated at the front by pleated pieces of paper which make a zigzag formation (*Gohei*). These are symbolic of the offerings formerly made to the *Kami* in place of material. Only the 'Grand Champions' (*Yokozuna* and *Ozeki*) wear the Tsuna during the presentation (*Dohyo-iri*) which precedes the tournaments (*Tori-kumi*). See *Sumotori, Yokozuna*.

Tsuppari *Sumo*. A series of blows delivered with the palm of the hand to the opponent's chest in order to make him or her draw back or lose balance.

Tsure-dachi See *Oku-iai*.

Tsuri 'To fish', 'To raise'.
— **Tsuri-age** see *Tachi-ai, Idori*.
— **Tsuri-ai** *Kyudo*. A balance between the forces of tension and resistance between the hand holding the bow and the one pulling the bowstring.
— **Tsuri-ashi** see *Shintai*.
— **Tsuri-dashi** *Sumo*. A grip with both hands on an opponent's belt to raise and push him or her out of the *Dohyo*. See *Kimarite*.

Tsuri-dashi

— **Tsuri-goshi** *Judo*. 'To raise the hip'. With a turning movement, *Tori* places his or her hips against *Uke*'s lower abdomen, raises him or her and throws him or her by pulling on the sleeve, producing a forward fall.
— **Tsuri-komi-goshi** *Judo*. *Tori* throws *Uke* by using hips and hands, producing a forward fall. A variation of *Tai-otoshi* or *O-uchi-gari*.

TWO

Tsuri-komi-goshi

Tsurigane see *Kinteki, Kyusho*.

Tsuru-ashi-dachi *Karate*. A posture of standing on one leg (crane stance), the other knee raised.

Tsuru-garami *Kyudo*. A method of gripping the bowstring by lodging it inside the bent thumb. The latter is kept in place by the index finger, before the release of the arrow (*Hanare*). It is known as the 'Mongol

release'.

Tsurugi see *Swords*.

Tsuyoki. Someone with a strong personality, having powerful *Ki*. See *Ki*.

Tsuyuharai see *Yokozuna*.

Tsuzukete Hajime *Karate*. 'Carry on with the contest'. This is a command given by the referee after a contest has been stopped temporarily for one reason or another.

Tsuzuki (Tsu-tsuki) *Karate*. The top half of the forehead, which can be used as a weapon, often against an opponent's nose, popularly known as 'nutting' someone.

Tuifa see *Tonfa, Shaolin-si*.

Tul-khi see *Kong Kyeuk*.

Tu-ve *Qwan-ki-do*. Self-defence techniques.

Two see *Numbers, Okuri, Ryo, Morote*.

U

'Right' as distinct from 'left'. See *Migi*.

Uchi 'Interior, inner, inside'. An indirect form of attack.
— **Uchi-dachi** see *Naginata*.
— **Uchi-deshi** see *Sumo*.
— **Uchi-gake** *Sumo*. The same movement as *O-uchi-gari* in *Judo*, but one holds the opponent's belt under the arms. See *Kimarite*.

Uchi-mata

— **Uchi-majiri.** A contest between several opponents, indiscriminately (mêlée).
— **Uchi-make** *Kendo*. This describes a moment where one of the contestants 'touches' the other with his or her *Shinai* on a determined spot.
— **Uchi-muso** *Sumo*. A throw to the side by lifting the opponent by the inside of the thigh with the hand and turning him or her on to the back. See *Kimarite*.

Uchi-gake

— **Uchi Hachiji-dachi** *Karate*. A standing, ready posture, feet apart turned in.
— **Uchi-komi** *Judo*. During training periods, this is the study and repetition of a movement, using a partner who stands immobile. The completed movement which brings about the partner's fall is not carried out until the 'entry' into the movement is near perfect. This *Uchi-komi* must include: starting off from the correct posture of engagement (*Shisei*), body displacement (*Shintai*), gripping of *Uke*'s *Judogi* (known as *Kumi-kata*), loss of balance by Uke (*Kuzushi*), eventually a counter-attack (*Tsukuri*) and finally, after a number of repetitions, the throwing (*Kake*) of Uke, who must in turn fall correctly (*Ukemi*). This study and repetition of movements is sometimes called *Butsukari*.
— **Uchi-kote** see *Kote*.
— **Uchi-kudaki** see *Omote*.
— **Uchi-mata** *Judo*. 'Attacking the inside of the thigh'. *Tori* slips one leg between *Uke*'s legs and raises him or her by lifting his or her own leg against the inside of one of Uke's thighs. At the same time a pull is maintained on Uke's *Judogi*, and he or she falls around Tori's leg, losing balance in a forward direction. See *Uwate-nage*.

Uchi-muso

— **Uchi-okoshi** *Kyudo*. The fourth position of the archer, who lifts the bow above the head (arms at 45 degrees) without hunching the shoulders. He or she deliberately pauses for a short time to stabilize the position and, through using the breathing, brings all his or her force down into the *Hara*. Also called *Kikitori*.
— **Uchi-otoshi-waza** *Kendo*. A technique in which an attacker pushes down the opponent's *Shinai* and in the same movement delivers a blow. See *Ju-no-kata*.
— **Uchi-tachi** *Kendo*. The one who attacks.
— **Uchi-uke** *Karate*. 'Internal' defence.

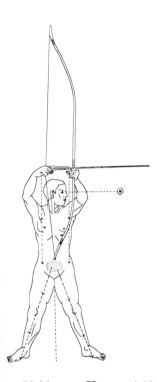

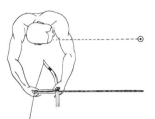

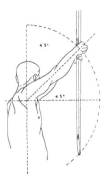

Uchi-okoshi

with Uke lying on his or her back. See *Kansetsu-waza*.

Aikido. Types of armlock including twisting techniques (*Ude-hineri*) and strong pressure (*Ude-gaeshi*). See *Kansetsu-waza*, *Hiji-waza*.

Ude-garami

— **Uchi-waza** *Karate*. A 'defensive' form of attack.

Uchiwa *Sumo*. A fan which does not fold, made of wood, leather or iron, generally decorated on one side by the moon and on the other by the sun. It is carried by the referees (*Gyoji*) to indicate their decisions to the contestants. The colour of the fan varies according to the rank of the Gyoji: black for a beginner, then blue, blue and white and finally purple for the *Tate-gyoji*. See *Tessen*.

Ude 'Forearm'. Korean: *Palmok*. See *Arms*, *Kote*.

— **Ude Furi-undo** *Aikido*. A stretching and softening exercise causing a wavelike motion throughout the body, performed on the spot, with the arms stretched out to maintain balance.

— **Ude-gaeshi** see *Ude-garami*.

— **Ude-garami** *Judo*. This is a ground-work (*Ne-waza*) technique in which *Uke*'s arm is bent and locked, with pressure exerted on the elbow joint. Usually performed

— **Ude-garami Henka-waza** *Judo*. Action which could produce dislocation, performed against a half-bent arm. See *Kansetsu-waza*.

— **Ude-gatame** *Judo*. A technique of pressure against an arm joint, in this case the elbow. *Uke*'s wrist is held against *Tori*'s neck and Tori presses against the elbow with both hands. A variation is to hold the wrist against Tori's shoulder.

Ude-gatame

245

— **Ude-hineri** *Aikido.* A twisting action against the arm. Groundwork (*Ne-waza*). See *Ude-garami.*
— **Ude-hishigi** *Judo.* A type of armlock used in groundwork (*Ne-waza*).
Aikido. One of the *Katame-waza* (armlocks held by the armpit), used against attacks such as *Shomen-tsuki* and *Ushiro-eri-dori.* Also called *Hiji-shime*, 'strangulation with the elbow'. See *Hiji-waza.*
— **Ude-hishigi Henka-waza** *Judo.* An armlock. See *Kansetsu-waza.*
— **Ude-hishigi Hiza-gatame** *Judo.* Control of the arm stretched across the knee. See *Kansetsu-waza.*
— **Ude-hishigi Juji-gatame** *Judo.* Armlock performed on arms forming a crosss shape. See *Kansetsu-waza.*
— **Ude-hishigi Ude-gatame** *Judo.* A locking technique performed against the outstretched arm. See *Kansetsu-waza.*

Ude-hishigi Juji-gatame

— **Ude-nobashi** *Aikido.* The fifth principle (*Gokyo*) of the *Katame-waza* (outstretched arm techniques), used against attacks such as *Shomen-uchi* and *Yokomen-uchi.*
— **Ude-osae** *Aikido.* The first principle (*Ikkyo*) of the *Katame-waza*, controlling *Uke*'s elbow, applied against attacks such as *Ryote-dori*, *Katate-ryote-dori*, *Shomen-uchi*, *Shomen-tsuki*, *Ushiro-Ryote-kubi-dori*, *Ushiro Tekubi-dori* and *Ushiro Eri-dori.*
— **Ude-uke** *Karate.* Technique of blocking a blow with the forearm.

Uechi-ryu. A school of *Karate* originating in Okinawa, founded in 1897 by Uechi Kambun, who had visited China and studied under master Zhu Shua of the Pangen-nu school of Wushu. Zhu Shua made him his successor, a conspicuous honour for a non-Chinese student. In his turn Uechi Kanei,

born in 1927, taught the art of Uechi-ryu from around 1940 onwards. The style has not found many followers in the United Kingdom. It contains eight combat *Kata.*

Ude-uke

Ueshiba Kishomaru see *Ueshiba Morihei.*

Ueshiba Morihei. Born on 14 December 1883 of a family of *Samurai*-peasants in the village of Tanabe in the Wakayama prefecture, he is known all over the world as the creator of *Aikido*. His life was very unusual and eventful. In childhood he was frail and suffered from frequent illnesses. Very early in his life he became interested in the Shingon esoteric Buddhist sect to which his parents belonged, and he assiduously venerated the *Shinto Kami* of the Kumano district in which he lived. At the same time he brought his body to a state of health and strength by performing regular physical exercises. After his secondary-school studies he had several small jobs and then went to Tokyo, where he opened a stationery shop in 1901. He was not cut out to be a businessman and soon returned to Tanabe, where he took up a martial arts course under *Tozawa Tokusaburo*, a master of the *Tenjin Shin-yo-ryu*. The following year saw him studying the principles of the *Yagyu Shinkage* school. He married in 1903 and was almost immediately conscripted into the army. He was considered too small for active service so was posted to the reserve in Osaka, and then sent to Manchurai in 1904. On his return he continued to study the teachings of *Yagyu-ryu* under the direction of master Nakai Masakatsu. He received his teacher's certificate, which gave him the right to teach martial arts, in 1908, and immediately opened a *Dojo* at Tanabe. His training continued unabated: he practised with devotion and unrelenting self-discipline.

In 1912 he went to the north of Hokkaído accompanied by eighty-four other people. There they founded a new village at Shirataki. Morihei worked hard as a woodcutter and farmer, putting himself to the roughest types of labour while still continuing his study of martial arts. Then in 1915 he met the celebrated swashbuckling swordsman *Takeda Sokaku*, the master of the *Daito-ryu Aiki-jutsu* school, who accepted him as a disciple and conferred a master's diploma in *Ju-jutsu* on him in 1916. [*Translator's note*: When one considers Morihei's earlier training, one year of study is not a short time in which to gain such a diploma. It is not unusual for an expert in one martial art to reach high levels of competence in another in a relatively short time.]

Morihei decided that he had not learned what he sought from Takeda, so he left Shirataki abruptly at the end of 1919 and went to Ayabe, near Tokyo, where he became the disciple of an enlightened man, Deguchi Onisaburo. The latter had founded a politically orientated religious sect, *Omoto-kyo*, and Morihei plunged into a deep study of the writings of the 'prophet' and gave himself over to mysticism. At Onisaburo's request, he started a Dojo to train the miracle-worker's disciples. In 1922 Takeda Sokaku rejoined him, but the two men did not see eye to eye. Ueshiba Morihei then followed Deguchi Onisaburo to Mongolia, where they both had a number of political adventures. Then Morihei returned to Ayabe, where – so the story goes – he had a vision in which he saw himself identified with the universe. He perfected his own individual techniques and in 1925 and 1926 gave demonstrations of his art in Tokyo to high military officials. He established himself in the capital and founded a Dojo where he taught the principles of the unarmed combat system which he had invented. It was basically a defensive system. He also taught at the naval academy of Toyama, the military police academy and the military college. In the meantime he studied *Kendo* at the *Kobukan*. However, his connections with

the Omoto-kyo sect, which the government saw as revolutionary, made his life difficult. He finally retired from public life in 1942, entrusting the direction of his Dojo to his son, Ueshiba Kishomaru, and retreated to the farm which he had bought in 1935 at Ayama, to the north of Tokyo. There he created a sanctuary devoted to *Aiki* and to the 'forty-two guardian divinities of the universe'. He continued to train at *Aikido*, the name which he had given to the system of techniques which he had developed. So although his art had been flourishing for many years, it was not until 1938 that it was officially given the name by which it is known worldwide today.

Only in 1949 did the Minister of Education allow him to reopen his Dojo in Tokyo. This was a period in which the martial arts had fallen into disrepute; probably to the lowest level in their history. His exemplary teaching brought him numerous disciples. In 1956 he gave a public demonstration of Aikido and then went to the Hawaiian islands in 1961. In 1964 the emperor decorated him. He opened a new Dojo in 1967. But then he developed cancer of the liver, retired to Ayabe for the last time, and died there on 26 April 1969, universally honoured and admired. His son succeeded him as head of the *Aiki-Kai*. See *Aikido, Tenjin Shin-yo-ryu, Yagyu Shinkage-ryu, Shotokan, Daito-ryu*.

Uke *Judo, Aikido.* This is the term for the partner who attacks and is then thrown by *Tori* (or *Shite, Nage*).
Karate. A defensive movement, generally in the form of a block against the opponent's attack. Korean: **Bang-o**.
— **Uke-nagashi** see *Oku-iai*.
— **Ukete** *Karate.* A block carried out with the hand. See *Ude-uke*.
— **Uke-waza.** Techniques of defence, evasion or counter-attack using an *Atemi* blow, a movement of unbalancing the attacker or a throwing technique, with or without *Sutemi*.

Ukemi. A method of falling to soften the impact of someone who is thrown to the ground (see *Uke, Tori, Nage, Shite*). The only way to dispel the hard impact experienced when the body strikes the floor (or the *Tatami*), is to use the 'break-falls' which produce a counter-impact and so nullify to a large extent the shock to the body. The chief technique is to strike the floor with the open palm of the hand and the forearm as one lands. Vietnamese: **Nhao Lan**.

There are three types of fall:

to the rear on the back (*Ma-ukemi, Ushiro-ukemi*): both forearms and palms strike the ground simultaneously on both sides of the body;

on the side (*Yoko-ukemi*): contact with the ground is made by the shoulder and hip, so that only one forearm and palm strikes the ground on the contact side.

forwards or forward-roll (*Mae-ukemi, Zempo- ukemi*): the right or left hand and arm is slightly curved and held in line with a dorsal diagonal coming from the right or left shoulder to the left or right hip respectively. *Uke* is then able to roll over his or her back and, with training, rise to standing position to complete the technique.

In all cases, the body must stay supple and relaxed with the chin drawn into the chest to protect the head and neck.

The same type of break-falls are used in all forms of *Budo*, with a few variations, notably in the case of *Karate*. (See *To-jin-ho*.) See *Nage-waza, Sutemi-waza, Tachi-waza, Nhao Lan*.

Uki 'Undulating like a wave'.

— **Uki-gatame** *Judo*. A type of 'floating' or mobile control of an opponent in ground-work (*Ne-waza*).

— **Uki-goshi** *Judo*. 'Floating hip throw.' A swift movement bringing *Tori*'s hip into contact with *Uke*'s lower abdomen or groin. Uke is raised from the floor and loses his or her balance forwards. It is the basis of all hip (*Koshi*) movements such as *Harai-goshi, Tsuri-komi-ashi, O-goshi, Uchi-mata*, etc.

— **Uki-otoshi** *Judo*. 'Floating throw'. *Tori* places one knee on the ground, at the same time pulling on *Uke*'s sleeve, causing him or her to pivot on the supporting leg and fall forward.

— **Uki-waza** *Judo*. 'Floating technique'.

Uki-goshi

A type of accentuated *Yoko-otoshi* technique, causing *Uke* to fall forward.

Uki-otoshi

Union see *Ai, Aiki*.

Unryu *Sumo*. A 'defensive' style adopted by certain *Sumotori*, created by the 10th *Yokozuna* (1823–91), who gave it his name. It is the opposite of the style called *Shiranui*. In this style, during *Shiko-tachi* the *Rikishi* extends only one arm to the side.

Uki-waza

Ura 'Opposite', 'Negative'. See *Omote, Yin (Yin-Yang)*. The edge of the sword which is not used for cutting.

Judo. The second part of *Koshiki-no-kata*, consisting of seven movements which must be carried out quickly:

Miku-daki, to bruise
Kuruma-gaeshi, to roll back like a wheel
Mizu-iri, to allow to flow like water
Ryu-setsu, to submit to the weight of the snow (to bend)
Saka-otoshi, to fall down a slope
Yuki-ore, to let the weight of the snow break the branch
Iwa-nami, the waves break against the rocks.

— **Ura-gatame *Judo.*** A groundwork (*Ne-waza*) technique involving the control of an opponent by his or her arms. See *Osae-waza.*

— **Ura-geri *Aikido.*** A backward kick. See *Keri-goho.*

— **Ura-ken *Karate.*** A reverse punch delivered with the back of the clenched fist, often as part of an evasion technique.

— **Ura-nage *Judo.*** 'Backward throw'. *Tori* wraps his or her arms around *Uke's* body, lowering his or her stance and then falling back, bringing Uke down at the same time.

Ura-nage

— **Ura Shiho-gatame *Judo.*** 'Rear four-quarters hold-down'. A groundwork (*Ne-waza*) technique from the immobilization section (*Osae-waza*) in which *Uke* is controlled by his or her hips and shoulders, from the rear.

— **Ura Tsuki *Karate.*** A blow from the fist held close to the body.

Ushin see *Mushin.*

Ura Tsuki

Ushiro 'Back', 'Rear'. See *Space.*

— **Ushiro Ashi-geri *Karate.*** A kick delivered to the rear.

— **Ushiro-denko** see *Kyusho.*

— **Ushiro-dori** see *Tachi-ai, Idori.*

— **Ushiro Empi-uchi *Karate.*** An elbow blow delivered to the rear.

— **Ushiro Eri Kata Sodetori *Aikido.*** *Shite* is attacked from the rear by *Uke*, who grips his or her collar and sleeve. Shite pivots on his or her right foot, taking a backward step and bending straight away under Uke's arms. Then Shite rises swiftly, lifting his or her right arm, and ends the movement by pressing hard on Uke's elbow with his or her free hand to throw him or her forward, finishing the opponent off with an *Atemi* blow from the foot. See *Sode-tori.*

— **Ushiro Eri Obi-tori *Aikido.*** *Uke* seizes *Shite* by the collar and belt from the rear. Shite takes a big step forward with the left foot, raising his or her right arm vertically as he or she turns to the right. Then he or she abruptly lowers it, taking a step back with the right foot, ending with an *Atemi* blow to Uke's sides. See *Eri-tori.*

— **Ushiro-geri *Karate, Aikido.*** A back kick (to the rear).

— **Ushiro Gesa-gatame *Judo.*** A groundwork (*Ne-waza*) technique in which *Tori* controls *Uke's* body by folding his or her arm around Uke's arm and pressing down on his or her ribs. The other hand grips Uke's belt.

— **Ushiro-goshi *Judo.*** 'Rear hip'. A counter-attack in which *Uke* is lifted by

Ushiro-geri

Tori's hips. Then Tori wraps one arm round the nape of Uke's neck to turn him or her and throw him or her backwards.

Ushiro Gesa-gatame

Ushiro-goshi

— **Ushiro Hiji-ate** *Karate*. An elbow blow delivered to the rear.
— **Ushiro-inazuma** see *Kyusho*.
— **Ushiro-jime** *Judo*. A groundwork (*Ne-*

Ushiro Hiji-ate

waza) technique of strangulation from the rear using the forearm.
— **Ushiro Gyaku Kata Te-dori** see *Mae Kata Te Hakko-dori*.
— **Ushiro Kami-dori** see *Kami-tori*.
— **Ushiro Kata Te-dori Erijime** *Aikido*. *Uke* grips *Shite* from the rear round the neck and also grips his or her left wrist. Shite stamps with the right heel on Uke's foot and raises the left arm, escaping on his or her right foot. Shite then lowers his or her shoulder and turns to the right to face Uke. The movement ends with an *Atemi* blow to the face. See *Eri-tori*.
— **Ushiro Kata Te Hakko-dori** see *Mae Kata To Hakko-dori*.
— **Ushiro Oshi-age Te-dori** *Aikido*. *Uke* grips *Shite* by the hands, from the rear. Shite takes a step forward and leans in the same direction, twisting his or her body to the left. Shite grips Uke by the elbow with one of his or her free hands, ending the movement with an *Atemi* blow. See *Te-dori*.
— **Ushiro Ryote-dori** *Aikido*. When *Uke* grips *Shite* by both wrists from the rear, the latter takes a big step to the right, and forwards, lifting the right hand and pivoting to the left on the right foot. He or she then grips Uke by the right elbow, stepping back half a pace, and delivers an *Atemi* blow to Uke's face. See *Te-dori*.
— **Ushiro Ryo Kata Sode-tori**. *Uke* grips *Shite* by the sleeves from the rear. Shite takes a step to the right, raising the bent elbows, and pivots on his or her right foot to pass under Uke's right arm. Shite then raises both arms vertically, ending with an Atemi blow to the face. See *Sode-tori*.
— **Ushiro Shitate Kumi-tsuki** *Aikido*. *Uke* seizes *Shite* under the arms from the

rear by gripping his or her belt. Shite widens his or her stance and delivers an *Atemi* blow with the heel to Uke's lower abdomen, then an *Atemi* to Uke's hand, simultaneously expanding his or her abdomen. He or she then turns around by pivoting on the left foot and executes a locking (*Rofuse*) technique on Uke's right elbow. See *Kumi-tsuki*.

— Ushiro U-ate Kumi-tsuki *Aikido.* Uke 'hugs' *Shite* from the rear, imprisoning his or her hands. Using the head, Shite strikes Uke backwards in the face, breaking free vigorously from the hug. Profiting from this blow to the face, Shite turns vigorously and steps back with the right foot, executing a strong locking technique (*Rofuse*) on Uke's left elbow. See *Kumi-tsuki*.

Uto see *Kyusho, Omori-ryu.*

Utsui. From *Utsuru*, to Displace: 'Displacement'.

Utsuri-goshi *Judo.* 'Against the hip'. A counter-hold against *Harai-goshi, Uchimata, Hane-goshi* and *O-soto-gari*, consisting of swinging *Uke* on the hip after lifting him or her to abdomen level, causing a loss of balance to the front.

Utsuri-goshi

Uttchari *Sumo.* Evasion from an attack by pivoting the body and simultaneously throwing the opponent by lifting him or her with the belt with a grip under the arms. See *Kimarite.*

Uwagi. The jacket of a *Keikogi* or *Judogi.*

Uttchari

Uwate 'Better hand'.
— Uwate-dashi-nage *Sumo.* A movement of the body disturbing the opponent's balance, gripping his or her belt over the top of his or her arms using only one hand. See *Shitate-dashi-nage, Kimarite.*

Uwate-dashi-nage

— Uwate-hineri *Sumo.* A clean throw using a pivoting action of the body, gripping the opponent's belt over the top of his or her arms. See *Kimarite.*

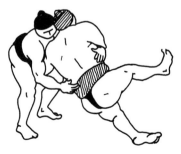

Uwate-hineri

— **Uwate-nage** *Sumo*. A hip throw using a sweeping action on the opponent's inner (*Mata*) thigh, holding his belt over the top of his arm: a movement somewhat similar to *Uchi-mata* in *Judo*. See *Kimarite*.

Uwate Yagura-nage

Uwate-nage

— **Uwate Yagura-nage** *Sumo*. A technique of throwing the opponent on his or her side by using the top of the thigh to lift the inside of his or her thigh (right leg against left or vice versa). The hand grip is on the belt, over the top of the arms. See *Kimarite*.

Uze-gaeshi *Judo*. The winner of a contest by superior technical skill. *Uze-gaeshi* is worth from three to five points, according to the referee's opinion. See *Ippon*, *Yuko*.

Vajramushti. An ancient type of wrestling and fighting originating in India (also called *Mallavidya*, 'science of combat'), developed by a Brahmin caste in the west of India, probably during the tenth century. This type of combat was undertaken mainly for religious reasons, in villages. The combatants wore a type of 'knuckleduster' on one hand and blows were permitted only to the face or chest. Rather than an art of combat it was a form of boxing, and often one of the contestants died from his injuries. This savage type of fighting is no longer popular today, but ritual contests are held annually, notably in Gujurat. Certain techniques of this art – for instance the 'diamond fist technique' – probably influenced the art of *Kalaripayat*.

Vat *Qwan-ki-do*. Throwing techniques. See *Nage-waza*.

Victory see *Kachi*, *Yusei-gachi*, *Sogo-gachi*, *Make*.

Viet Long Guom see *Swords*, *Qwan-ki-do*.

Vietnam (martial arts of). In Vietnam several techniques of unarmed and armed combat have developed, probably from Chinese influences; these qualify as martial arts. Most of the present-day schools come from techniques developed in Tonkin and are called **Vo Bach Ninh**. Others come from the Hue region (**Vo Quang Ninh**) and from Cochin-China under the name **Vo Binh Ninh**. The current schools are those of *Vovinam Viet Vo Dao*, *Qwan Ki Do* and *Viet Vo Dao*.

Viet Vo Dao see *Vovinam Viet Vo Dao*.

Vital energy see *Ki*.

Vital Points see *Kyusho*.

Vo see *Hajime*.

Vo 'Martial art' in Vietnamese.

Vo Dao Vietnam see *Vovinam Viet Vo Dao*.

Vo Nanh see *Song Dau*.

Vo Sinh An adept of *Vovinam Viet Vo Dao*.

Vo Su. A teacher of Vietnamese martial arts.

Vo Phuc. *Keikogi* of *Vovinam Viet Vo Dao*.

Vo Thuat see *Bu-jutsu*.

Vo Tu Do. 'Free martial art' of Vietnam, created in Saigon in 1954, in which contests take place in a boxing ring.

Vo Vat see *Vovinam Viet Vo Dao*.

Vovinam Viet Vo Dao (Vo Viet-nam, Vo Thuat Viet-nam, Vo Dao Viet-nam). Vietnamese styles of martial arts created in Hanoi in 1945 by Nguyen Loc (1912–60), who opened a school in Saigon in 1951. The style represents the quintessence of the Vietnamese martial arts schools. It uses the principles of *Vo Vat* or wrestling, of Force (*Cuong*) and Suppleness/Softness (*Nhu*), all combined with the techniques of *Judo*. Vovinam also uses basic techniques (*Don Can Ban*) and advanced techniques (*Don Trung Cap*):

> 16 flying kick techniques
> 7 fist techniques (*Dam*)
> 11 foot techniques (*Da*)
> 8 sword-hand techniques (*Chem*)
> 8 backfist techniques (*Dam Bat*)
> 4 elbow techniques (*Cho*)
> 4 knee techniques (*Goi*)
> 5 'scissors' techniques (*Don Chan*)
> 12 knife techniques (*Dao*).

As well as the Vo Vat techniques there are defences against armed attacks (*Song Luyen*) and various prearranged forms or *Quyen* (*Kata*). Techniques of blocking and guards (*Thu Phap*) complete the syllabus.

The motto of Vovinam is 'hand of steel and warm heart'. The training uniform (*Vo Phuc*) is completely black, with a white belt for beginners and a black belt with two red bands for graded students (*Vo Sinh*).

Vu Bai see *Bai To*.

W

W a 'Peace', 'Accord', 'Harmony'. This typically Japanese concept aims to unite in one whole serenity of mind and cosmic energy, to create a harmony between man and the rest of the universe. It is the equivalent of the principle of *Ju* (*Ju-no-ri*). In the *Ryuko no Maki*, 'Book of the Dragon and Tiger', it is written: 'If the enemy turns towards us, we meet him; if he goes away, we let him go.' It goes on: 'Face to face with the enemy, we are in accord with him. For 5 plus 5 equals 10, just as 9 plus 1 equals 10 also. All that is in accord (*Wa*).' Thus, Wa is the symbol of the unity of cosmic and human forces, of mind and body, of the interrelationship between beings. It is the fundamental identification of the Whole and the Self (see *Ai-ki*). In consequence, Wa conditions all the arts (*Gei*) and the sciences (*Jutsu*) and thus strives to reconcile the positive material aspects with the active states or energies. In fact, Wa is considered the essential principle of the universe, at one and the same time the creator and the destroyer; positive and negative, active and passive. It is in effect the same as the Chinese *Dao*, which unites in the same eternal principle the complementary forces of *Yin* and *Yang* found in the doctrines of Taoism. It is the Japanese *Do*, the 'supreme Way', which mankind must necessarily follow in order to achieve perfect union (as in Indian Yoga, 'union') of spiritual and material being with the Cosmos. Wa is the same essence which some call the Divine Principle (the *Shen* of the Chinese), God, Supreme Being, Cosmic Energy, and other names. See *Seiryoku-zen-yo*, *Jita Kyo-ei*, *Ju-no-ri*, *Ki*, *Dao*, *Taiji*, etc.

Wado-ryu *Karate*. 'School of the Way of Harmony'. A style of Karate based on natural movements, founded in 1939 by Otsuka Hidenori (born 1892), one of the disciples of Funakoshi Gichin. This particular style is less spectacular than the *Karate-do* of *Shotokan*, its stances are higher and its punches less extended. It combines the basic movements of *Ju-jutsu* with techniques of evasion, putting strong emphasis on 'softness' and 'the Way of Harmony' (*Wa-no-michi*).

Wait see *Matte*.

Wa-jutsu 'Science of Concord'. A synthesis of several martial arts (*Budo*) such as *Judo*, *Aikido* and *Karate* amongst others; it was created in 1983 by Jacques Quero. He added to it certain apposite aspects of an 'esoteric' and philosophical nature, taken from Zen, Taoism and Yoga. The teaching of Wa-jutsu harks back to the early spirit of Budo and has no time for competitions or spectacular display. It emphasizes instead the harmonious development of mind and body, with the intention of enabling its students to realize in themselves the universal harmony (*Wa*) and to participate in a movement of mutual assistance and understanding. In the words of its founder: 'Seen from this point of view, Wa-jutsu reflects very well the art of living; it is a principle of social life, in itself . . . There is only one person to be conquered in Wa-jutsu – oneself.' Practitioners of the art train on a *Tatami*-covered floor, with bare feet. They wear a standard type of *Keikogi*, a jacket (*Uwagi*) and a *Hakama*. The teaching consists basically of studying *Kata* and doing *Randori*. The terminology used is Japanese and corresponds to the vocabulary of Judo, Aikido and Karate. See *Oguri-ryu*. [J. Quero, '*Wa-jutsu, the art of accord and peace (the best use of energy)*', F.F.W.J., 34430 – Saint-Jean de Vedas, 1984].

Wakaru 'To understand', 'To divide', 'To cut in two'. This term signifies a man or woman who is separated from the Whole, in the sense that he or she has not realized that he or she *is* also the Whole.

Waka-Sensei 'Young master'. The title generally given to the son (or young successor) of the creator of a *Dojo* in the martial arts. See *Sensei*.

Waki 'Defence', 'On the side'. *Judo*. A position of face to face, a blow with the sword-hand (*Te-gatana*, *Shuto*) delivered to the side. See *Hasso*.
— Waki-gamae *Kendo*. A lateral type of guard holding the *Shinai* horizontally in order to deliver a blow with the point or to

make a sweeping blow. See *Postures*, *Kamae*.

— **Waki-gatame** *Aikido*, *Judo*. Armlocks effected on the side when both contestants are on the ground.

Waki-gatame

— **Wakizashi** 'Belt companion'. The short sword worn with the long sword (*Katana*) in a *Samurai*'s belt. See *Katana*, *Swords*, *Daisho*.

Wan 'Arm'. *Nai-wan* 'inside of the arm'; *Gai-wan* 'outside of the arm'.
— **Wanjun** see *Kyusho*.
— **Wanto** *Karate*. 'Sword-arm', a blow given with the outstretched arm as if it were a sword.

Warning see *Chui*, *Nokotta*.

Wasa Daiichiro *Kyudo*. A famous archer (1663–1713) from the province of Kii. In April 1686, at the Sanjusangendo temple in Kyoto, he shot 13,053 arrows, beginning at sunrise and ending at sunset. He fired at a target some 63 metres away, and 8,135 of his arrows hit the target. He dethroned the existing champion, Hoshino Kanzaemon. Wasa Daiichiro's performance has never been equalled, although a gathering of Kyudo enthusiasts takes place every year at the same date, in similar conditions.

Water see *Mizu*.

Washide see *Weapons*, *Hands*.

Watashi-komi *Sumo*. A push delivered to an opponent's chest, the other hand gripping him or her from the outside of the thigh, reaching over the extended arm. See *Kimarite*.

Watashi-komi

Watchfulness see *Hontai*, *Sen-no-sen*.

Waterfall see *Taki-shugyo*.

Wa-tsuki *Karate*. A circular, horizontal, sweeping blow.

Way see *Dao*, *Do*, *Michi*.

Waza 'Technique'. In the martial arts it means the application in contest or training of a movement from the *Kata*; either defensive or offensive. Vietnamese: ***Phap***.
— **Waza-ari** see Competition Rules of *Judo*, 24.

Weak points see *Kyusho*.

Weapons. In the unarmed martial arts, all the parts of the body which are used to attack an opponent are known as 'weapons'. Such blows can stop, injure or even kill if used with full force and correct application against vital points. (See *Kyusho* and *Atemi*). In those martial arts in which blows are struck they are never delivered with full force. The parts of the body used include the clenched fist, the open hand, the fingers, the wrists, the forearm, the elbow, the knee, the foot and even the head. The 'weapons' used most to attack Atemi points are:
— Fists:
Seiken: a direct blow with the knuckles, mainly of the first and middle fingers.
Ura-ken: with the clenched fist but using the first phalanges and the back of the hand.
Tetsui: 'hammer-fist', striking with the little

finger edge of the clenched fist.

Ippon-ken: fist clenched with the middle finger knuckle protruding a little, supported by the thumb pressed against the phalange. Also called *Nakayubi Ippon-ken*.

Hira-ken: the fingers are half clenched, so that the first set of phalanges form an extension of the back of the hand.

— Hands:

Seiryuto: a 'sword' blow delivered with the little finger edge of the hand, fingers extended and in line with one another. Also called *Te-gatana*, *Shuto*.

Haishu: a blow with the top of the hand.

Kumade: 'bear claws hand', fingers half clenched to attack the ears.

Toho: delivered with the 'fork' formed by the open thumb and first finger to strike or seize the throat.

— Fingers:

Haito: delivered with the top edge of the palm and thumb lying beside it, hand extended.

Barate: blow with the backs of the fingers.

Ippon-nukite: a thrusting blow with the tip of the index finger.

Nihon-nukite: a thrusting blow with the tips of the first and middle fingers spread to make a 'fork'.

Yonhon-nukite: a thrusting blow with the tips

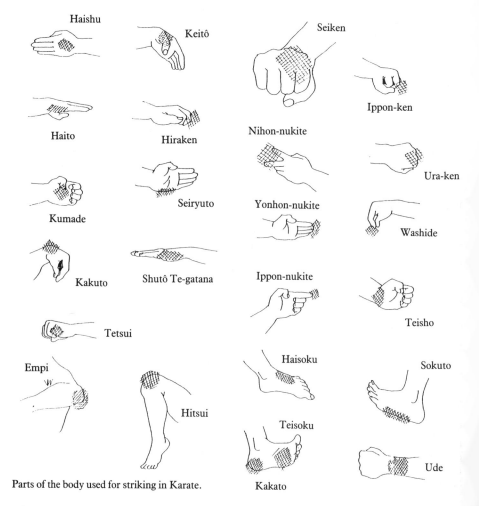

Parts of the body used for striking in Karate.

of all four extended fingers.
Keito: a blow with the back of the bent thumb.
Washide: a blow with the ends of the fingers and thumb joined, to make an 'eagle beak'. Also *Keiko*.
— Wrists:
Ude: a blow with the back of the wrist, hand extended.
Kakuto: a blow with the back of the wrist, hand clenched.
Teisho: with the inside of the wrist and the base of the palm.
Koken: a blow with the back of the bent wrist.
— Forearms: *Kote, Wanto, Hira-kote*.
— Elbows: *Empi, Hiji*.
— Knees: *Hitsui*.
— Feet:
Haisoku: using the top of the foot.
Sokuto: using the external edge of the foot, 'sword-foot'.
Kakato: a 'smashing' blow using the sole of the foot combined with the heel.
Koshi: using the front surface of the ball of the foot, toes turned up to avoid damage to them.
— Head:
Tsuzuki: a blow delivered with the top of the forehead.

Weapons (White) see *Swords, Katana*.

Weapons (Hidden) see *Kakushi*.

Weapons (Thrown) see *Shuriken*.

Weapons (Vietnamese) see *Co Vo Dao*.

Weijia 'External school'. See *Kung-fu, Wushu, Shaolin*.

White see *Shiro*.

Wing Chun Wushu. 'Radiant springtime' school of *Kung-fu*. It is best known for its rapid fist techniques and is said to have only three leg techniques, used to attack the lower (*Gedan*) parts of the body. It was one of *Bruce Lee*'s favourite styles and was invented in the fifteenth century by a Buddhist nun called Ngu Mai. In training, students make great use of a wooden dummy

called *Mok Yan Jing Fat* (in Cantonese). The name of the style is also transliterated as *Wing Shun* and *Wing Tsun*. It is the best-known style of Kung-fu outside China.

Winner see *Yusei-gachi, Make*.

Wrestlers see *Sumotori, Ssi-reum*.

Wudang Pai Wushu. The 'internal school' (*Neijia*) of martial arts belonging to the *Shaolin-si* tradition. It uses a sword (*Jiang*). One of the most famous masters of this style was the Chinese general Li Jinglin (1886–1932). Also *Wutang*.

Wushu 'Art of War'. (Japanese: *Bu-jutsu*.) The name given to the multitude of schools and styles (400 being a modern low estimate) of Chinese martial arts and 'gymnastic' exercises based largely on Taoist and Buddhist influences (see *Yijing* and *Shaolin-si*). In modern times in Western society the term *Kung-fu* is used indiscriminately for all these arts. It seems that Wushu has flourished in China at all periods of its history and in all parts of that immense country. Certain secret societies with political, religious or criminal aims taught or adapted certain styles and taught them to their members. In 1928 the Chinese government tried to unify all the styles of Wushu to make of them a 'national sport' called *Guoshu* or *Zhongguo Quan* (Chinese Fist), but without great success. Efforts in this direction were also made during the time of Mao Zedong. The diverse schools were classed as 'Northern styles' (*Shang Quan*) and 'Southern styles' (*Nan Quan*), but this did not stop the schools from multiplying and diversifying even further.

Even so, all Wushu schools have postures (*Bo*), guards (*Taidu*), fist attacks (*Quan*) and foot attacks (*Jiao*) as well as successive series of movements. Much of the training is done alone, such as in the 'Monkey Dance' or in *Taiji*.

Wushu is divided into two main approaches. One is called the 'internal method, style or system' (see *Neijia*); the other the 'external' (see *Weijia*). The former emphasizes inner force, the study of vital points and medicine, with a philosophical bias.

The latter regards the use of force and rapid movement as preferable. The schools (*Pai*) are divided into these two approaches, but some contain a mixture of both. Some schools perform almost exclusively unarmed techniques, while others use swords and other weapons. Uniforms vary from the simple Chinese modern national dress of jacket and trousers, usually in black, to much more elaborate and highly decorated costumes. Sashes made of satin or silk are frequently found but are not universal. The use of coloured sashes to distinguish degrees of skill is found, also after the fashion of the Japanese belt system (see *Kyudan*), but this too is not universal.

Competitions usually take place on a mat some 14 × 8 metres and take the form of displays of skill, boxing and fighting with and without weapons. There are three age groups: adults (over eighteen), juniors (between twelve and eighteen), children (under twelve). The score is evaluated out of 10 points. Four judges and one chief judge decide the score. There are also referees, varying in number.

The terminology for Wushu varies according to the region from which it comes. In addition to the Chinese Mandarin names, there are also those from the Cantonese dialect in the south, and those from Fujian (a maritime province inhabited by the Hakka). The translation and cross-referring from one dialect to another is often subject to variation and thus does not make for accuracy in identifying similar names in different dialects. In this book the authors have tried, as far as possible, to stick to the official Chinese versions known as *Pinyin*.

Wutang see *Wudang-pai.*

X

Xa Hanh see *Than Phap*.

Xa Tan see *Tan Phap, Bo Phap*.

Xia see *Nukite*.

Xia-lai Jiao see *Jiao*.

Xiang-xing Quan *Wushu*. A Chinese school of combat which includes a great number of styles which imitate the movements of animals.

Xingyi Quan (Hsing-I Chuan) *Wushu*. A school of Chinese boxing known as 'Mind-Body Boxing' in which all the movements imitate to some extent those of animals such as snake, monkey, cockerel, bear, etc. This school uses the 'internal' (*Neijia*) method.

Xiong Quan see *Quan*.

Xu see *Taiji Quan*.

Y

Ya *Kyudo* 'Arrow'. The arrows used with the large asymmetrical Japanese bow (*Yumi*) were very long (more than a metre). They were made from bamboo, tipped with eagle feathers, and their points were variously shaped; some being forked (*Karimata*). When the tips of the arrows were muffled for firing at animals (see *Inu Oi-mono*) or at training targets (see *Yabusame*), they were called *Hikime*. Notch: *Yahazu*. Feathers: *Ya-no-ha*. Shaft: *Ya-no-take*. Point: *Ya-no-ne*. Certain types of arrows produced a whistling sound which was intended to frighten away evil spirits. These whistling arrows were called *Kabura-ya*.

The iron points used by *Samurai* on their arrows were very varied in shape, and each clan had its preferences. The names given to them were also varied, conforming to the function foreseen by their 'inventor', to their shape or to the use to which they were put by the particular archers who used them. Such names ran into hundreds. These *Ya-no-ne* could be like the point of a sword, a willow leaf, triangular (*Sankaku*), flat (*Hira-ne*), very narrow (*Togari-ne*), like a needle (*Tsubeki-ne*), or even have a concave striking surface, with a cutting effect (*Ryokai*), etc. There were no hard and fast rules and archers simply chose the arrowheads which suited them. There were also iron arrows of different shapes. See *Yazuka, Yumi*.

Yaburi-dojo. The schools (*Ryu*) of martial arts were very numerous in all periods from at least the fifteenth century. It was not uncommon for the masters and pupils of one Ryu to visit the *Dojo* of another Ryu to challenge the members there. If a master of a Ryu was defeated as a result of accepting such a challenge, he lost face in the eyes of his disciples and they would leave him to enrol in the Dojo of the winner. Such challenges have continued into our times between Dojo of the same discipline; but they now take the form of relatively amicable competitions. Also called *Dojo-arashi*, 'Dojo Tempest' and *Dojo-yaburi*, 'Dojo Defeat' or 'Dojo Destruction'.

Yabusame *Kyudo*. A traditional art of military training in the 'Way of the bow

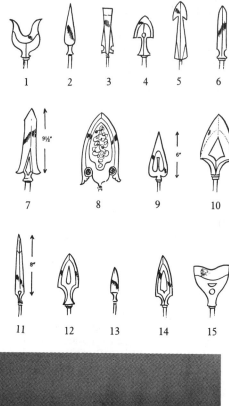

Arrowheads of Kyu-jutsu:

1. Kompaku gata, by Kompaku Hidetsuge
2. Sampaku, Maku-nuki (used for piercing screens)
3. Tsubeki-ne (in the form of an engraving tool)
4. Tsurugi-jiri (sword-shaped tip)
5. Tobu, Tobi-naoshi (in the shape of a kite)
6. Hoso-yanagiba (shaped like a willow leaf)
7. Watakushi (Satake clan)
8. Watakushi (for splitting open the skin)
9. Yanagi-ha (shaped like a willow leaf)
10. Togari-ya (pointed head)
11. Togari-ya
12. Kira-ha-hirane
13. Sankaku (triangular head)
14. Rinzetsu (a head in the form of a dragon's tongue)
15. Ryokai

and the horse' (*Kyuba-no-michi*). Mounted archers gallop past their targets, which are arranged parallel to the line of gallop. Yabusame began in the Heian period (794–1185) as a spectacle for the court, then the military men of the Kamakura (1185–1333) period adopted it as part of their training. In the Edo period (1603–1868) it became a rite at the court of the *Shogun*, instituted by Shogun *Tokugawa Yoshimune* (1684–1751), who was himself an excellent archer. For the purposes of this ceremony the Shogun himself created the 'Edo style', sometimes called *Kisha-hasami-mono*, which is celebrated every year at the *Shinto* sanctuary at Asakusa. The original ancient style had the archers dressed in hunting clothes. It was created by *Minamoto-no-Yoritomo*(1147–99), the first Shogun at Kamakura. This 'classical' style requires the participation of seven to thirty-six horsemen who follow one another down a slope some 220 metres long. It has three targets placed some three metres away. They are made of wood, square-shaped and fixed on stakes 1.5 metres high. Sometimes they are held above the heads of assistants.

At least two schools still exist in Japan: the Edo and the *Ogasawara*. They have only a religious, not a military purpose and take place in the presence of Shinto priests and *Gyoji* (referees) sitting close to each target. It is a sight which shows off the qualities of the participants: their skill in archery and their

Kaneko Yurin, master of Yabusame, in his youth, at Kamakura.

horsemanship. They use large bows (*Yumi*) and arrows with a wooden point (*Hikimi*). A variant of this art, called *Kasagake*, formerly performed at the court of the Shogun at Kamakura, required that the archers should fire, at the gallop, at hats (*Kasa*) or at straw or bamboo targets placed at a distance of 23 metres. See *Ba-jutsu, Togasagake, Kasagake, Ogasawara-ryu, Takeda-ryu, Inu-oi-mono.*

Yaghli-guresh see *Kirpinar*.

Yagyu Jubei (*c.* 1607–50). A famous swordsman who was blind in one eye. He was the son of *Yagyu Munenori*, belonging to the *Shinkage-ryu*, which was a style found at the root of some other schools of *Ken-jutsu*. See *Yagyu-ryu*.

Yagyu Munenori (1571–1646). A sword master who was an instructor in the art to the Tokugawa family. He became an adviser to the *Shogun Tokugawa Iemitsu*, who ruled from 1523 to 1651. The Shogun raised Yagyu to the nobility in 1636. Yagyu wrote some books on his art, notably *Heiho*

261

Kadensho (Family traditions concerning the art of the warrior) and *Gyokusei-shu*. He was the father of *Yagyu Jubei* and one of the founders of *Yagyu-ryu*.

Straw hat worn during Yabusame training and performances.

Master Yagyu (on the right), during a demonstration of stick techniques. The stick is red and is typical of this school.

Yagyu Muneyoshi see *Yagyu-ryu, Yagyu Tajima-no-Kami*.

Yagyu-ryu. A school of swordsmanship and *Ju-jutsu* founded by *Yagyu Muneyoshi Tajima-no-Kami* (1527–1606) and his son *Yagyu Munenori*. The latter gave the name of *Yagyu Shingan-ryu* to the style, in 1603. Yagyu is the name of a village close to Nara, where the family originated.

Yagyu Shingan-ryu see *Yagyu-ryu*.

Yagyu Shinkage-ryu see *Shinkage-ryu*.

Yagyu Tajima no Kami (1527–1606). An expert in the art of the sword (Yagyu Muneyoshi). He was an adept in the doctrine of *Muto* (without sword) and one of the founders of *Yagyu-ryu*. He was the father of *Yagyu Munenori*.

Yahazu see *Yugamae, Ya*.

Yako see *Kyusho*.

Yaku Soku-geiko *Judo*. Training in which repeated introductory movements to

a throw are made on a partner, but they are not carried through to completion until they are judged to be near-perfect. See *Randori, Uchi-komi*.

Wa-jutsu. A study of displacements of the body which may be used to defend oneself.

Yama-arashi *Judo*. 'Mountain storm.' A movement similar to *Harai-goshi*.

Yamabushi 'They who lie in the mountains'. Adepts of the esoteric Buddhist sects of Shingon and Tendai, who followed the rules and philosophy of *Shugendo* They were also called *Yamabushi-no-gyoja* or *Shugenja*, because they often retired to rustic hermitages in the mountains to observe forms of rigorous asceticism. Certain Yamabushi trained in the martial arts to strengthen their minds and bodies. The popular imagination lent them magical powers, such as the ability to fly, and this type of belief possibly lies at the root of the legends of the *Tengu*. These are mythological beings with a long nose who could transform themselves into birds. They were reputed to be unequalled masters in all the martial arts.

It seems that the first brotherhoods of Yamabushi were formed in the tenth cen-

A Yamabushi in a sacred Japanese sanctuary at Shingu. The costume is typical of the Yamabushi.

Japan. In 1872, when there was an official separation between *Shinto* and Buddhism, Shugendo was abolished. The number of Yamabushi at that time was estimated at 170,000. In modern times a few people have tried to revive the Yamabushi communities, but without much success. See *Shugendo*, *Mudra*, *Ninja*.

Yamada Heizaemon. An expert in swordsmanship who died in 1578, founder of *Jikishin Kage-ryu*. He was already using a type of wooden *Shinai* to train his disciples.

Yamada Jirokichi (1863–1931). A *Samurai*, fifteenth master of *Jikishin Kage-ryu*, who elevated the status of *Kendo* to a noble art in his writings on this form of *Budo*: *Kendo Ron* (Treatise on Kendo) and *Shuyo Shosei Ron* (Treatise on the education of mind and instruction on life). In them he expressed the idea that '*Zen* and the sword have the same goal: to kill the ego'. He emphasized individual and social morality and considered that Kendo was not so much a sport as a discipline for life, influencing both physique and spirit.

Yamaga-ryu see *Yamaga Soko*.

Yamage Soko (1622–85). A *Samurai* and philosopher from the Aizu clan, who was also a disciple of the Confucian philosopher Hayashi Razan (1583–1657). According to him, the Samurai, even in times when there was no armed conflict, should have absolute responsibility for the moral and intellectual aspects of society, and should follow certain Confucian ideals. In his work *Seikyo Yoroku* (where he critisized the conduct of the functionaries of the Shogunate in Edo, which caused him to be imprisoned for some twelve years) he posed the questions which seemed important to him about the philosophy of *Bushido*; and gave his own answers. He spoke out similarly in other works, notably in *Buke-jiki* and *Chucho Jujutsu*. To realize his aims he founded a school of martial arts, the *Yamaga-ryu* (also called *Sekitokudo*) in which he applied his theories. His tomb is situated in the Sosan-ji temple at Shinjuku (Tokyo) and is still a place of veneration.

tury. They are referred to in the writings of this period, where they are contrasted with the *Nobushi* or 'They who lie in the plain', who were ordinary Buddhist monks. When they made pilgrimages, the Yamabushi assembled in particular places; generally in Buddhist temples in the mountains such as Omine, Kimbusan and Kumano. Through their study and performance of asceticism, martial arts and magic they hoped to acquire magical powers and during their spiritual practices they performed *Mudra*. Down the course of the centuries, the Yamabushi were augmented by false monks, impostors, magicians and healers. The true Yamabushi grouped together in the fifteenth century in brotherhoods who brought some order to the diverse communities which swarmed over

Yamaguchi Gogen see *Karate-Shinto, Goju-ryu*.

Yamaguchi-ryu see *Hyodo, Goju-ryu*.

Yamamoto Tsunetomo see *Hagakure, Bushido*.

Yamaoka Tesshu (1837–88). A *Samurai* of the *Itto Shoden Muto-ryu*, who followed the teaching of the *Jikishin Kage-ryu*. He played an important political role in the rule of the last of the Tokugawa Shoguns, Keiki, and advised him to abdicate in favour of the emperor Mutsuhito (*Meiji*). See *Muto*.

Yamato-ryu. A traditional school of martial arts founded in the seventeenth century and reformed in 1664 by *Morikawa Kozan*, who created the non-military form of *Kyudo* and divided its study into six parts: logic of the bow (*Kyu-ri*), etiquette of the bow (*Kyu-rei*), technique of the bow (*Kyu-ho*), maintenance of the bow (*Kyu-ko*), analysis of the mechanism of the bow (*Kyu-ki*), and finally 'the four virtues of the development of the spirit of the bow' (*Shi-mei*).

Yama-zuki (Yama-tsuki) *Karate.* 'Mountain' fist or punch. A wide U-shaped double punch.

Yama-tsuki

Yame 'Stop!'. The shout uttered by a referee when he or she wishes to stop a contest for whatever reason. Vietnamese: **Thoi**. See Competition Rules of *Karate*, 22.

Yame no Uchi see *Omote*.

Yami *Kyudo*. A method of aiming (*Monomi*) at the target, the bow hiding it completely from view. See *Ariake*.

Yanagi-ryu see *Yoshin-ryu*.

Yang-liu Taidu see *Taidu*.

Yang Lushan (1799–1872). A master of Chinese martial arts (*Wushu*), who created the *Yang* style of *Taiji Quan*. He taught his art in Beijing (Peking) and opened a school to the public. He was considered unbeatable. His grandson *Yang Zhenfu* (Ch'eng-fu) (1883–1936) codified the style and taught it more as a health-giving exercise. See *Taiji Quan*.

Yang-ma Bo see *Bo*.

Yang Zhenfu see *Yang Lushan*.

Yan-zi-guo Quan see *Quan*.

Yara see *Chatan Yara*.

Yari. The general name given to all types of lance or halberd in Japanese martial arts. The most popular Yari had a handle some four metres long and an iron blade sharpened on both sides, sometimes in the form of a cross (*Jite*). During training sessions in the use of the Yari (*Sojutsu*) the blades are muffled (for *Yari-do*). See also *Naginata, Ishizuki, Tessei-no-yari*. Vietnamese: **Thuong**.

Yari-do. Training in the use of the *Yari*.

Yasumi 'Rest'. A term used for the periods between attacks during training or in contests when an air of calm prevails. Korean: **Suiot**.

Yawara. The ancient expression for unarmed combat arts (*Ju-jutsu*) during the Edo period (1603–1868). According to tradition, the word was invented by Sekiguchi Jushin Hachiroemon Minamoto no Sonechika (1647–1711), the founder of *Sekiguchi-ryu*. See *Ju-jutsu, Kumi-uchi*.

Defence against a Yari. Drawing by Hokusai.

Combat using a Jite against a Yari, featuring the two female Masters, Mitamura Takeko and Tokunaga Chiyoko. The Jite branches, in the shape of a cross, have cutting edges on all sides enabling cuts to be made to the arms, neck or tendons. Tento-ryu school.

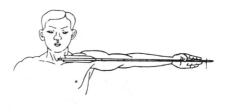

Training with the Yari (4 m long) against the Bo. Maniwa-nen school.

Yawara-riki see *Mutei-ryu*.

Yazuka *Kyudo*. The determining factor for the length of an arrow for a particular archer. Excluding the tip, it must be the same length as the distance from the top of the sternum to the tips of the fingers, when the archer has his or her arm stretched out horizontally sideways. See *Kyudo, Ya, Yumi*.

Yazuka

Yen Dao. A tapering Vietnamese dagger with a guard.

Yefu no Tachi see *Swords, Katana*.

Yi see *Taiji Quan*.

Yihe Quan *Wushu*. 'Harmonious and co-ordinated boxing' from the Northern schools, belonging to the *Shaolin-si* tradition.

'Yijing (I-ching)'. 'Book of Changes'. A Chinese book of divination and understanding of the world. It is at the root of numerous Taoist (see *Dao*) theories and Confucian ideas. In this treatise, all the possible aspects of life and behaviour of men and things are represented by sixty-four hexagrams composed of six lines each, one on top of the other. They are made up by combining the sign for *Yang* (—) and the sign for *Yin* (– –). Thus, each characteristic of the subject under consideration can be represented by a combination of Yin and Yang or by the symbol for complete Yin or complete Yang (see *Yin-Yang*). The *Yijing* is also a type of mathematical treatise based on the binary system (1 and/or 0). The original text of this work goes back to the Zhou dynasty (tenth – 4th centuries BC). Japanese: *Eki-kyo*; Korean: *I-gyeong, Ju-yeok*.

Yin-Yang. Two principles which are opposed to one another and as such are also complementary. One cannot exist without the other. In Chinese philosophy dealing with the *Dao*, these two principles are at the origin of creation and life. *Yang* (*Omote, Yo* in Japanese) symbolizes the positive, male, active aspects of things and their beginning. *Yin* (*Ura, In* in Japanese) symbolizes the negative, feminine, passive aspects of things and their ending. Yang is also light and dryness, while Yin is shade and humidity. All sciences of Chinese origin are based on the concept of the interaction of these two principles; it was understood that nothing could be totally Yang or totally Yin: everything must necessarily contain a small element of Yin in its Yang and of Yang in its Yin. The eternal interaction of the two is represented by the sign of the Dao, and sometimes by the eight trigrams which are regarded as fundamental, taken from the Taoist *Yijing* or 'Book of Changes'. The martial arts of Asia, especially those of the Far East, could not escape the concepts inherent in the principle of Yin and Yang. Certain martial arts masters whose teachings were written down provide us with evidence that from early times an attempt was made to classify diverse movements of their disciplines as Yin or Yang. Vietnamese: *An* (Yin) and *Duong* (Yang). See *Dao, Do, Taiji Quan, Yijing*.

Drawing of the Emperor Fuxi in front of the eight trigrams.

Ying-fu Taidu see *Taidu*.

Yo see *Yin-yang*.

Yobidashi *Sumo*. A kind of herald whose

Formation of the eight trigrams according to the Emperor Fuxi.

function is to address the *Sumotori* (*Rikishi*) on the *Dohyo*, to make sure that the latter is kept in good order, that its construction has been properly carried out, to distribute the purifying salt, which the Sumotori sprinkle on the Dohyo, and to make sure that water is available for them, and to give the signal for the beginning of the contests. During tournaments, the *Yobidashi* announces at the end of each day the contests which will take place the following day. See *Dohyo*.

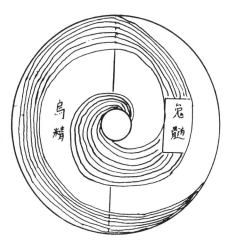

Symbol representing the movement of the two opposing and complementary principles.

Yofuku see *Kimono*.

'Yoi' 'Get ready!' This is the command uttered by the referee or other designated official at the beginning of a martial arts event to indicate to the contestant(s) that the moment has arrived when their performance is to start.

Yo-ibuki. Deep abdominal breathing designed to mobilize the energies of *Ki* in the *Hara*. See *Ibuki*.

Yoko 'Lateral', 'Side'. See *Space*.
— **Yoko-aruki** 'Sideways walking'. A crablike movement of the feet used by the *Ninja*.
— **Yoko Empi-uchi** *Karate*. An elbow blow delivered to the side.

— **Yoko-gake** *Judo*. 'Side body drop.' *Tori* draws *Uke* to him or her by gripping and pulling on the sleeve, places his or her foot to block Uke's ankle and then falls down backwards, bringing Uke down also, forwards and sideways. See *Sutemi*.

Yoko-gake

— **Yoko-geri** *Karate*. 'Side-kick'.
— **Yoko-geri Ke-age** *Karate*. A rising side-kick.
— **Yoko-geri Kekomi** *Karate*. A 'penetrating' side-kick. See *Kekomi*.

Yoko-geri

— **Yoko-guruma** *Judo*. 'Side-wheel'. *Tori* reaches under *Uke*'s shoulder, grips him or her by the belt and throws him(her)self to the ground in *Ma-sutemi* (on the back), bringing Uke down also, forwards and sideways.
— **Yoko Hiji-ate** *Karate*. A sideways blow with the elbow and forearm.

Yoko-guruma

Yoko-otoshi

— **Yoko Hiza-gatame** *Judo*. In ground-work (*Ne-waza*) this is a technique of bending an opponent's arm using the knee as a fulcrum.

Yoko Hiji-ate

— **Yoko Juji-gatame** *Judo*. A ground-work (*Ne-waza*) technique to strangle an opponent using a cross-shaped formation.
— **Yoko Kekomi** *Karate*. A 'penetrating' side-kick. See *Kekomi*.
— **Yoko Kata Te Hakko-dori** see *Mae Kata Te Hakko-dori*.
— **Yoko Mawashi Empi-uchi** *Karate*. A circular sideways elbow blow. Also called *Yoko Mawashi Hiji-ate*.
— **Yoko-otoshi** *Judo*. 'Side-drop'. *Tori* brings his or her weight forward, placing his or her thigh to block *Uke*'s path, and pulls on Uke's sleeve to pull him or her downwards. Then Tori rolls to the side, bringing Uke down at the same time and in the same direction.
— **Yoko Shiho-gatame** *Judo*. A ground-work (*Ne-waza*) technique which immobilizes an opponent by controlling the 'four

quarters' of the trunk, from the side. See *Osae-waza*.

Yoko-Shiho-gatame

— **Yoko Sutemi-waza** *Judo*. A *Sutemi* technique to the side which includes three principal separate throws: *Yoko-gake*, *Yoko-guruma* and *Uki-waza*. See *Sutemi-waza* and *Nage-no-kata*.
— **Yoko Tobi-geri** *Karate*. 'Side flying kick'.

Yoko-Tobi-geri

— **Yoko Tomoe** *Judo*. A throwing technique which sends *Uke* in a circle to the side.
— **Yoko-tsuki** see *Idori*.
— **Yoko-uchi** see *Tachi-ai*, *Idori*.
— **Yoko Ude-hishigi** *Judo*. A ground-work (*Ne-waza*) technique consisting of bending an opponent's arm to the side.
— **Yoko-ukemi** see *Ukemi*.

— **Yoko-wakare** *Judo*. 'Side separation'. *Tori* places both legs to bar *Uke*'s path and lets him(her)self slide to the floor, bringing Uke towards him or her by pulling on the sleeves. This causes Uke to fall diagonally forward right or left. This technique is sometimes used as a counter to *Koshi-guruma* and also against *Tai-otoshi*, to cite two possibilities. Also called *Yoko-otoshi*.

Yokozuna *Sumo*. 'Grand Champion'. In the *Dohyo-iri* ceremony, the *Yokozuna* plays the principal role and takes part in the opening contest. In the course of the Dohyo-iri he is accompanied by two other *Sumotori* of high rank, a herald (*Tsuyuharai*) and a sword-bearer (*Tachimochi*). When the Yokozuna takes part in a contest it must be conducted by a chief referee (*Tate-gyoji*). Only the Yokozuna may wear the sacred cord (*Tsuna*) during the Dohyo-iri; hence their title of *Yoko-tsuna* (Yokozuna). This title was bestowed from 1789 onwards, and was recognized in the general classification of Sumotori, the *Banzuke*, in 1890. Those who have attained to this rank and title never lose them, even if they are defeated. The Yokozuna follow two styles of presentation during the Dohyo-iri, *Unryu* and *Shiranui* (see the references to these two words). The official list of Yokozuna is as follows:

1. Akashi (seventeenth century)
2. Maruyama (1712–49)
3. Ayagawa (1700– ?)
4. Tanikaze (1750–95), Kajinosuke
5. Onogawa (1758–1805)
6. Ao-no-Matsu (1791–1851)
7. Inazuma (1795–1877)
8. Shiranui (I, 1801–54)
9. Hide-no-yama (1808–62)
10. Unryu (1823–91)
11. Shiranui (II, 1825–79)
12. Jinmaku (1829–1903)
13. Kimenzan (1826–71)
14. Sakaigawa (1843–89)
15. Ume-ga-tani (I, 1845–1928)
16. Nishi-ni-Umi (I, 1855–1908)
17. Konishiki (1867–1914)
18. Ozutsu (1870–1918)
19. Hitachiyama (1874–1922)
20. Ume-ga-tani (II, 1878–1927)
21. Wakashima (1876–1943)
22. Tachiyama (1877–1941)
23. Okido (1877–1916)
24. Otori (1887–1956)
25. Nishi-no-umi (II, 1880–1931)
26. Onishiki (I, 1855–1908), Kasugano
27. Tochigiyama (1892–1959)
28. Onishiki (II, 1892–1943)
29. Miyagiyama (1895–1943)
30. Nishi-no-umi (III, 1890–1933)
31. Tsune no Hana (1896–1960), Dewa-no-Umi
32. Tamanishiki (1903–38)
33. Musashiyama (1909–69)
34. Minanogawa (1903–71)
35. Futabayama (1912–68), Tokitsukaze
36. Haguroyama (1914–69), Tatsunami
37. Aki-no-umi (1914–   )
38. Terukuni (1919–77), Araiso
39. Maedayama (1914–71), Takasago
40. Azumafuji (1921–73)
41. Chiyo-no-yama (1926–77)
42. Kagamisato (1922–   )
43. Yoshibayama (1920–77)
44. Tochinishiki (1925–   )
45. Waka-no-Hana (1928–   )
46. Asashi-Ho (1929–   )
47. Kashiwado (1938–   )
48. Taiho (1940–   )
49. Tochi-no-Umi (1938–   )
50. Sadanoyama (1938–   )
51. Tama-no-Umi (1944–   )
52. Kitanofuji (1942–   )
53. Kitazakura (1940–   )
54. Wajima (1948–   )
55. Kita no Umi (1953–   )
56. Wakamisugi (Waka no Hana, 1953–   ) in 1978
57. Mie no Umi (   )
58. Chiyonofuji Mitsugu (1955–   )
59. Futahaguro Koji (1963–   ) in 1986. He was expelled in 1988 and does not have the title now.
60. Hokutsumi (1963–   ) in 1987.
61. Ono Kuni (1963–   ) in 1987.

Yomi 'Reading'. The art of reading the thoughts of a questioner or opponent before the latter has a chance to formulate them. In the martial arts it means the ability to foresee an attack. *Yomi* is also a function of the concept of *Ma-ai* and of *Hyoshi*. It is the equivalent of *Ishin-den Shin* (from one mind to the other). This attitude is characteristic of the Japanese in their personal relationships even today, when words so often seem inadequate to convey a feeling which cannot be formulated in a precise manner. Etiquette and social conventions too are considered to be a gross expression of this same attitude. It is a question of 'being with' someone, 'on the same wavelength', a form of true Compassion. See *Sakki, Ma-ai, Hyoshi, Ai, Genshin*.

Yon 'Four'. Also *Shi* (but the latter, being the same sound as the word for 'death', is rarely used). See *Numbers*.
— **Yonhon Nukite** *Karate*. A stabbing action using the extended fingers of the hand. Korean: *Kwansu*. See *Nukite, Hands, Weapons*.
— **Yonkyo** *Aikido*. The fourth principle (*Kyo*), consisting of applying painful pressure to *Uke*'s wrist (at the acupuncture point known as Shouzin Yin on the inner surface of the lower forearm, 'Heart Governor') when Uke has attacked with *Shomen-uchi* or *Mune-dori*. See *Tekubi-osae, Katame-waza*.

Yori-ashi *Karate*. Technique of approaching an opponent.
— **Yori-kiri** *Sumo*. A grip on the opponent's belt, underneath the arms, to lift him or her and push against the stomach. See *Kimarite*.

Yori-kiri

— **Yori-modoshi** see *Kimarite*.
— **Yori-taoshi** see *Kimarite*.

Yoroi. The complete suit of *Samurai* armour. Also *Kachu*. The lightweight armour is called *Kogusoku*. See *Armour*.

— **Yoroi-kumiuchi.** The minor techniques (*Kobudo*) of martial arts from the school of *Yagyu Shingan-ryu* (founded in 1603). It used all the combat arts of the sword and of unarmed combat (*Ju-jutsu*) in full *Samurai* armour. Also called *Kumiuchi*.

Yo-ryu see *Ho-jutsu*.

Yoseikan *Aikido*. An independent school founded by Mochizuki Minoru (1907–), one of the disciples of *Ueshiba Morihei*.
— **Yoseikan-budo.** A modern synthesis of the most 'effective' techniques of all the martial arts, created by Mochizuki Hiroo, the son of *Mochizuki Minoru*.

'Yoshi' 'Begin!'. The command given by a referee to start a contest. See Competition Rules of *Judo*, 8, 12, 19, 27.

Yoshin Aikido *Aikido*. An independent style founded by *Shioda Gozo*, one of the disciples of *Ueshiba Morihei*. It is orientated towards pure technique.

Yoshin-ryu 'Willow-heart school'. A school of *Ju-jutsu* and *Ken-jutsu* which was founded, according to tradition, in 1732 by *Akiyama Shinobu*, a doctor from Nagasaki. He had visited China and studied techniques of *Hakuda* and *Kappo* (see *Kuatsu*) there. On his return to Japan he put together 300 movements of Ju-jutsu, following the principle of non-resistance to force. Just as the branch of the willow bends beneath the weight of accumulating snow and so is not broken, so a student of *Yoshin-ryu* gives way to the force of his or her opponent. These movements were at the root of those used by *Kano Jigoro* in his compilation of the *Judo* syllabus. Another version of the beginnings of the style attributes it to another doctor from Nagasaki, Miura Yoshin. One of his disciples founded the *Yoshin-ryu* school and the other the *Miura-ryu*; so the alternative version states. But perhaps it is a case of both versions being about one and the same man. Also called *Yanagi-ryu*.

Yoshitsune (Minamoto no) (1159–89). A great warrior who made it possible for his brother *Minamoto no Yoritomo* to conquer

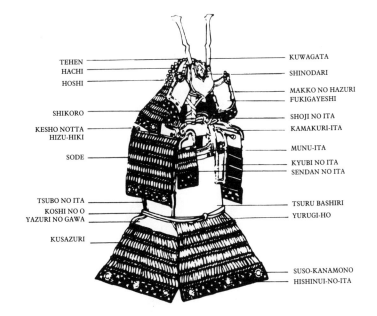

TEHEN
HACHI
HOSHI

SHIKORO

KESHO NOTTA
HIZU-HIKI

SODE

TSUBO NO ITA
KOSHI NO O
YAZURI NO GAWA

KUSAZURI

KUWAGATA

SHINODARI

MAKKO NO HAZURI
FUKIGAYESHI

SHOJI NO ITA
KAMAKURI-ITA

MUNU-ITA

KYUBI NO ITA
SENDAN NO ITA

TSURU BASHIRI
YURUGI-HO

SUSO-KANAMONO
HISHINUI-NO-ITA

Yoroi armour, end of the eleventh century.

the rival Taira clan and establish his *Bakafu* at *Kamakura* in 1185. Legend relates how he defeated a huge warrior-monk, *Benkei*, while still an adolescent. Benkei became his most faithful companion. Legend also tells how Yoshitsune was taught his martial skills by the *Tengu* (from the *Yamabushi* or the *Ninja*). His brother became jealous of his popularity and successes and attacked him. Yoshitsune committed suicide. He is considered to be one of the most herioc and famous men of Japan, the prototype of all the *Samurai*.

Yo-ten *Judo*. The key point in the execution of a movement or technique.

Yowaki. This word describes someone without much character or personality, with weak *Ki*. See *Ki*.

Yuan Jiao see *Jiao*.

Yuan Quan see *Quan*.

Yubi-hasami *Karate*. A 'scissor-fingers' blow. See *Weapons*.

Yudan-ja see *Yudansha*.

Yudansha. A Japanese title for someone who has passed one or more *Dan* grade examinations in a martial arts discipline. Korean: **Yudan-ja**. Also *Dansha*. See *Kyudan, Mudansha*.

Yu-dachi see *Omote*.

Yue-liang Jiao see *Jiao*.

Yue-shi Taidu see *Taidu*.

Yugake see *Yumi*.

Yuga-mae *Kyudo*. The third position of the archer, consisting of holding the bow in one hand (*Te-no-uchi*) and placing the arrow so that its notch rests against the string (*Yahazu*). The bow and arrow are held in front of the abdomen so that the part of the string below the arrow is in front of the *Hara*. The head is turned to the right, towards the target, so that the aim (*Monomi*) can take place.

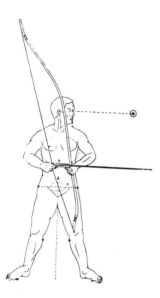

Yuga-mae

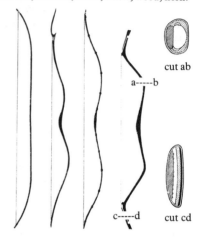

Left to right: old Japanese bows. The first two are taken from the Keisai Yesen Buryu Sakigake Zu-e; the third from Moko-shurai no E-kotoba (history of the Mongol conquest); the fourth is a Mongol bow belonging to the Museum of Mankind. The cuts *ab* and *cd* made into the latter bow show the different materials composing the body: leather, metal, sinew, wood, horn.

cut ab

a-----b

c-----d   cut cd

Yuken *Kendo*. This is the expression for the situation when the *Shinai* of the two contestants meet and cross, as distinct from *Muken*, in which they are not in contact.

Yukeup-ja see *Mudansha*.

Yuki-chigai see *Oku-iai*.

Yuki-ori see *Ura*.

Yuki-zure see *Oku-iai*.

Yuko. Technical points, worth five points or a half-*Ippon*. Vietnamese: **Nua-diem**. See also *Koka*, Competition Rules of *Judo*, 8, 14, 25.

Yumi 'Bow'. The asymmetrical Japanese bow, some 2.20 metres long, made of laminated bamboo (*Nakago* and *Sobagi*). The laminated effect is produced by glueing the bamboo, or sometimes boxwood, together. The initial glueing is strengthened by ligatures of rattan cane which are also stuck down with fish glue. The grip is located one-third from the base of the bow.

To hold the bowstring far back from the ear, the archer uses special gloves (*Yugake*)

and also a special 'Mongolian grip'. The Japanese bow is not very powerful, in contrast with the Mongolian bow with its double curvature and symmetrical shape. This is compensated for by the extreme extension which the bow affords, allowing one to use very long arrows (*Ya*). The *Ninja* sometimes used a Mongolian type of bow which was very powerful and effective, though very short (about 0.75 metres). See *Kyudo*, *Ya*, *Yabusame*.

— **Yumi-kobushi** *Karate*. A fist shape 'bent like a bow', used to deliver *Atemi* blows. See Weapons.

— **Yumi-uke** *Karate*. Using *Yumi-kobushi* defensively.

— **Yumitori-shiki** *Sumo*. The ceremonial dance using a bow (*Yumi*), performed at the end of the contests by a *Sumotori* of middle or low rank. This dance was introduced in 1575 by an archer called Miyai Ganzaemon, who won a tournament organized at the Azuchi castle by *Oda Nobunaga*, the military dictator. In honour of his success the archer was rewarded by the dictator with 500 *Koku* (one Koku = 180 litres) of rice and a bow. To display his joy Miyai performed a dance,

A form of dance using a bow, performed at the end of a Sumo tournament.

bow in hand, as a mark of respect for his lord. This ceremony has been performed ever since the day of Miyai's first performance, in memory of the event. See *Dohyo*.

Yup Cha Gi *Tae-kwon-do*. A side-kick, delivered with the heel and mainly used to stop an opponent's advance.

Yusei-gachi 'Winner by superiority'. When no scoring technique is made during a contest, the contestant who has shown the superior technique and power is awarded the victory on this alternative basis. See Competition Rules of *Karate*, 21, 27, 30.

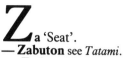
a 'Seat'.
— **Zabuton** see *Tatami*.
— **Za-ho.** The posture of sitting on the knees, Japanese style. See *Suwari*, *Shikko*, *Sei-za*.

Zanshin *Kyudo.* The eighth and final position of the archer, after the release of the arrow (*Hanare*). The archer should remain in the final position of having released the arrow at least until it has reached the target, without moving and without watching its flight. He or she waits, allowing the muscular and nervous tension to diminish, before returning to the starting position. In so doing he or she indicates that the act of firing never ends, thus emphasizing the idea of non-attachment to one's actions.
Karate, Kendo, Aikido. A state of vigilance and alertness of the contestant, before and after striking the opponent, so that he or she may be ready for any further offensive.

Zanshin

Zan-totsu 'To approach and strike'.

Za-rei. The traditional bow performed in a kneeling position. See *Bow*, *Rei*.

Zazen. A sitting position (*Sei-za*), either tailor fashion or lotus pose, the vertebral column straight, head straight, hands resting one on top of the other, palms up between the thighs, quite still. It is the position which the adepts of the Buddhist philosophy of *Zen* (Chinese *Chan*) assume for their exercises of stilling thought. During *Zazen*, which is not a form of mental exercise or meditation, the practitioner tries to have a completely thought-free mind, in an effort to remain totally receptive. It is seen as 'thought without thought', *Hishiryo*, a dimension of thought without the activity which modern psychology calls consciousness. It is experienced with the intention of returning to what is regarded as a normal human condition, free from the pressures and demands of daily life. Thus is the idea of *Mushotoku* included in it: a state free from any aims and any desires for gain.

The wish to reach any goal by performing Zazen prevents one from performing it. Only the posture, the breathing and the mental attitude count. All three should be peaceful, stable and natural. The pure state of Zazen is the equivalent of *Satori*, pure freedom of mind. It is through the practice of Zazen, or during a *Sesshin*, or period of training, that the *Bushi* arrived at the perfection of their art. This is why Zazen has sometimes been called 'the religion of the *Samurai*'. Internal Zazen, which is independent of posture or breathing, is an inexplicable state of being, the most profound condition of man, a state of complete inner freedom. Vietnamese: **Thien**. See *Zen*, *Mokuso*.

-zeki see *Seki*, *Ozeki*.

Zempo-ukemi see *Ukemi*.

Zen. A Japanese school of philosophy originating from the Chinese *Chan* school, which in turn came from the Buddhist *Dhyana* sect. It was modified in Japan by the influence of the *Shinto* feeling for and veneration of Nature. *Zen* was brought to Japan by the monk Eisai (1141–1215), who belonged to the Chinese school of thought known as Linji or Huang-long. He created the *Rinzai-shu* (Rinzai sect) in 1191. Then in 1227 the *Soto-shu* was created by the monk Dogen (1200–53) on his return from China. Zen puts forward four doctrinal points:

Direct transmission from master to disci-

ple of the doctrines of Dhyana (a form of transcendental meditation not to be confused with the modern teachings of Transcendental Meditation, or TM) without recourse to Buddhist writings.
Total independence of the mind from the Buddhist writings.
Direct communication of the individual with the Supreme Being.
Finally, the Realization of the nature of the Buddha (Buddha-deity) in each of us.

Zen puts the accent on intuitive knowledge (*Satori*), reached gradually or suddenly through the practice of *Zazen*, and refutes the Indian Buddhist theory of the transmigrations of 'essences' of beings. It displays total indifference towards all ritual aspects of religion such as statues, images, ceremonies, etc. For the Zen adept, it is not only a question of seeing the 'nature of the Buddha' in all things but of realizing it in one's own nature (*Kensho*), which is the equivalent of Satori. This realization of the state of the Buddha is known as *Daigo Tettei*. The spirit of Zen – detached from all things but at the same time present to all the realities, very often underlying that of the martial arts – found great favour among the *Bushi*. Korean: *Son*: Vietnamese: *Thien*. See *Zazen, Mushin, Kokoro*.

Zen 'All', 'Totality'.
— Zen-empi *Karate*. A powerful blow with the elbow, delivered with a rotation of the whole body against an *Atemi* point.

Zengo-undo *Aikido*. A training exercise which consists of pivoting the body on one spot.

Zenkan 'Forearm'. See *Arm*.

Zenkutsu-dachi *Karate, Kendo*. A position with the weight forward on the leading leg, which is bent, with the rear leg extended towards the back.

Zenpo-ukemi *Karate*. A fall forward to strike the ground with the palms of the hands and the forearms to disperse the shock wave. See *Ukemi, To-jin-ho*.

Zenkutsu-dachi

Zensho Masatsugu see *Hoki-ryu.*

Zen-tenkan see *Tenkan-ho.*

Zhongguo Quan 'Chinese fist'. A general term to describe all forms of Chinese martial arts using diverse movements to develop mind and body, but relatively few punches. Also called *Quanfa* (Fist Way) or *Quanshu* (Fist Method). The martial arts of China are more widely known as *Wushu* and even *Kung-fu*. The exact meanings of these words depends on usage rather than upon any universally agreed definition. See *Shaolin-si.*

Zhugar see *Tang Lang Quan Pai.*

Zori. Sandals made of woven straw held on to the foot by a thong passing between the big toe and the second toe. Nowadays such footwear comes in several different types of man-made materials. In the martial arts *Dojo* they are often worn between the changing room and the training area or *Tatami* so that the feet are clean and do not soil the floor or pick up any extraneous material.

Zour (Zur) Xaneh (Khane) 'House of Strength or Force'. This is a type of Iranian gymnasium or training hall where wrestlers train at wrestling, *Koshti*, or at exercises of skill or power, to the accompaniment of rhythmic instruments and frequently using wooden clubs of varying sizes to increase their strength. One of the chief exercises is to hold a club in each hand and turn it above the shoulder and over the top of the head. The exercises take place in a square or hexagonal pit. the *Gowd*, with a floor of hardened earth. The wrestlers wear only a pair of animal-skin trousers which are embroidered and tightly gathered at the knee. Their style of wrestling is similar to that of the Turks, the *Kirpinar*. The daily exercises in the Zour Xaneh follow numerous rules of courtesy and are always done in the name of Allah. Accessories to training for building up strength, but not for wrestling, include weights (*Seng*), wooden clubs (*Mil*) and a metal bow with a 'string' made of chain metal (*Kabadeh*). The wrestlers oil their bodies. The aim of the contests is to turn the opponent and throw him to the ground. Each round lasts ten minutes.

Zubon. The trousers of a *Keikogi*.

Zubu-neri Sumo. The pulling action exerted on an opponent's arm to the side and down to the ground, with the intention of increasing his or her loss of balance and throwing him or her to the side. Also *Tsubu-neri*.

-zuki see *Tsuki*.

Zusa. In ancient Japan, these were the foot

Zubu-neri

soldiers who were generally recruited from the people as distinct from the *Samurai* class. They served in this capacity by making use of very diverse types of weapons (see *Kakushi*) and wore either lightweight armour (*Kogusoku*) with a leather helmet which was sometimes lacquered (*Kasa*), or if their rank did not merit it they had no protection at all. They were the first to use firearms in battle.

Zuyanmen. A Chinese school of boxing (*Wushu*) belonging to the 'internal' school (*Neijia*) of the *Shaolin-si* tradition.